STICKS, STONES, AND SHADOWS

STICKS, STONES, AND SHADOWS

BUILDING THE EGYPTIAN PYRAMIDS

BY MARTIN ISLER
FOREWORD BY DIETER ARNOLD

UNIVERSITY OF OKLAHOMA PRESS : NORMAN

Library of Congress Cataloging-in-Publication Data

Isler, Martin, 1926–
    Sticks, stones, and shadows : building the Egyptian pyramids / by Martin Isler;
    foreword by Dieter Arnold.
        p.   cm.
    Includes bibliographical references and index.
    ISBN 0-8061-3342-2 (alk. paper)
    1. Pyramids—Egypt.   2. Pyramids—Design and construction.   I. Title.

DT63 .I85 2001
932—dc21

                                                                            20011027175

The paper in this book meets the guidelines for permanence and durability of the Committee on Production Guidelines for Book Longevity of the Council on Library Resources, Inc. ∞

1   2   3   4   5   6   7   8   9   10

CONTENTS

To Natalie, my wife, friend, and pillar of strength

FOREWORD

S hortly after I joined the Metropolitan Museum of Art in New York, Martin Isler informed me that T. G. H. James of the British Museum in London had suggested we get together because of our common interest in Egyptian architecture. Over the following years Martin and I became friends. We discussed problems of pharaonic building methods and other associated matters. Indeed, at one meeting at the excavation site of El-Lisht in Egypt, we even experimented with a method of leveling bedrock by sighting over several wooden poles erected with the help of a reconstructed builder's level.

As a result of his ongoing engagement with ancient Egypt, Martin now presents a volume devoted to understanding the methods used by the pyramid builders. His approach to questions of a technical nature and his presentation of solutions differ greatly from those in my *Building in Egypt* (1991). Rather than resenting what might have been considered an intrusion into this domain, however, I encouraged his challenge. Whereas my work focuses mainly on the archaeological evidence for pharaonic building methods, Martin's offers practical solutions for problems that cannot as yet be resolved by archaeological confirmation. He does not concentrate on the construction of Cheops pyramid, as so many other well-meant attempts do, but aims to place pyramid building in the wider context of early Near Eastern technology.

Martin Isler's theories are so professionally discussed and so effectively supported by his masterful illustrations that Egyptologists and lay readers alike will welcome the opportunity to share his views.

DIETER ARNOLD
Curator, Metropolitan Museum of Art

PREFACE

The human inhabitants of our planet are all governed by the same physical laws, observe the same natural events, and generally produce similar devices to cope with the world: a prosaic but interesting thought, considering the effect technology had on the ancient world. Its impact was so profound, at times, that the devices were themselves worshiped as gods.

Generations of archaeologists, their lives spent unearthing the past, seem to have hit a treasure chest in Egypt. No ancient society left more pictographic, epigraphic, and monumental evidence of humans contending with life. This occurred thanks to the Nile River, which flooded with an annual cycle ideal for the propagation of crops. The order and discipline to prepare for the flooding river—keeping the water channels free of silt and the locks in good repair—became a civilizing factor that welded the population under a central authority. Once ample food and water, the very basics of survival, were provided, artisans could devote more time to artistic and inventive endeavors.

The artifacts and monuments left behind by the ancient Egyptians have so intrigued scholars, adventurers, and archaeologists that almost every facet of their life has been studies, dissected, and recorded. Amazingly, we know more of what occurred in Egypt 4,500 years ago than we do of some aspects of medieval Europe. Of particular interest are the methods employed to build the great monuments dotting the land and the reason for their being. Although made of large blocks of stone, many pyramids have been sited with a precision that would challenge the architectural and engineering talents of today. Yet, while Egyptians seem to have left a chronicle of almost everything else, nothing exists on the procedures used to orient, level, and build the pyramids—much less on why a structure of this unusual size and shape was chosen for royal tombs. Though there has been much speculation on the possible construction method, many suggestions are not only unsupported by evidence but often suggest the use of devices beyond the capabilities of ancient people. Worse still, the builders are sometimes considered a superior race in control of mysterious forces.

This study shows how the ancient builders accomplished their most amazing feats by use of rudimentary tools, a keen understanding of natural laws, and superb organization under the guidance of a strong authoritative ruler. Indeed, they mastered subjects long since forgotten in the present age of machines and computers. Still, the skills and methods these artisans and architects used were not suddenly learned in the 3rd Dynasty, a time when the first pyramidal structure was raised; instead, they were based on preexisting technology that had been growing for all the years of human existence.

Like us, the prehistoric Egyptians formed groups, fashioned tools, and carefully observed the world around them. The crude devices they used (cracked rocks, digging sticks, and so forth) were probably discovered more by accident than by design, but once their usefulness was accepted, they were passed to succeeding generations and developed further, to become embedded in the collective memory. Through it all, humans beings, assisted by natural curiosity and competitiveness, were challenged by drastic changes in the climate and the river's flow. These changes tempered the will to survive and placed people in a continuing cycle of discovery and development. The knowledge acquired from these small beginnings has expanded exponentially, so that with each new find, the pace has quickened. Today the stream of information has become so overwhelming that if graduate students do not keep up with their chosen field, it will quickly pass them by. The technological road that started with sticks, stones, and shadows now has us reaching toward the stars.

My purpose in this book is to trace the start of monumental construction in Egypt and the means, once mastered, of building the pyramids of the Old Kingdom. In doing so I have covered, to the best of my ability, problems of construction virtually ignored for the last century. Brought to bear are my personal observations, those of countless others, and the experience gained during a lifetime of practical work as a draftsman, sculptor, and builder. Yet in this endeavor, it is not enough to offer some possible solutions. An explanation should also meet the existing evidence, however meager it may be; all science is built on the process of offering hypotheses and testing them against observations. However, being without the natural laws that govern science, archaeology is often forced to be interpretive and subjective and is hence unable to provide definitive solutions. Therefore, the work is leavened with a healthy dose of imagination, an ingredient without which a subject of this scope could not even be attempted.

I hope this book will persuade those who have held that pyramids could be built only by the use of major construction ramps to reconsider—realizing, of course, the difficulty of changing theories once they have become part of our lives. Accepted or not, if this work opens an avenue that others will explore more fully, my efforts will have been rewarded.

ACKNOWLEDGMENTS

For the first half of my life I knew no more of Egyptology than the fleeting curiosity about a great and ancient civilization. My real interest in the subject began with an invitation to the British Museum in 1975. I arrived a sculptor but came away intrigued by the possible methods and devices the ancient Egyptians used to accomplish their great building feats—my appetite whetted by a discussion with T. G. H. James, keeper of Egyptian antiquities.

Applying myself to the problem, and using the knowledge gained from moving 2- to 3-ton blocks of marble myself, I published my first paper under the guidance of Gerald E. Kadish, past editor of the *Journal of the American Research Center in Egypt* (*JARCE*). In what I thought was a curious request prior to publication, Kadish asked to spend a weekend at my home. This was later explained as an effort to protect the journal by not providing scholarly imprimatur to someone who might later turn out to be a pyramidiot. I hope he was correct in his judgment.

I am particularly grateful for the many fascinating hours of pyramid and stonework discussions with Dieter Arnold and for the counsel and insights given me by James P. Allen on other Egyptological matters. Both Allen and Arnold read my manuscript, offering criticism, important advice, and supporting evidence. Both gave willingly of their time—one could not hope for better mentors. Dorothea Arnold, always encouraging and supportive, honored me by exhibiting a drawing from this book in the Metropolitan Museum of Art. Indeed, the kindness and encouragement I received from these Egyptologists cannot be overemphasized. Despite the help and regardless of care, errors of fact and logic are bound to enter a work of this scope. These are entirely my own doing.

An early and most fortunate turning point in my endeavors came when, in Cairo, I received an invitation to the retirement party of Gerhard Haeny, director of the Swiss Institute. There I met Egyptologists Nabil M. A. Swelim, Joseph Dorner, and Rainer Stadelmann, who later gave me the benefit of their own work, thoughts, and experience. I am particularly indebted to Stadelmann and Zahi Hawass for making possible my research in the Dahshur necropolis during a difficult time.

My research and publications were aided by many people—in ways they may have thought insignificant—and the questions they answered and the directions of inquiry they suggested I pursue were of great importance: Edwin C. Krupp and LeRoy Doggett helped clarify my understanding of the heavens; I. E. S. Edwards led me to the study of Žába's works; Jean-Philippe Lauer showed me modern restoration techniques used at Saqqara; James A. Harrel lent advice and maps for researching quarries; Leonard Gorelick intrigued me with his research on old stone-cutting techniques; and John L. Foster published articles I submitted to *JARCE*. I also gained from the work of Dušan Magdolen, some of which is included in this book. Not to be forgotten is Badr Khattab, an Egyptian driver who could find a needle in a haystack.

Help also came from other quarters, especially from Diane Bergman and Mary Gow of the Wilbour Library, the resources of which I found invaluable. I doubt that my research could have been accomplished without Diane's help—and she never once snickered at my mispronunciation of names, a malady from which I still suffer. Others who helped in research were Faith M. Vis and Grace D. Levitt, whose abilities and thoughtfulness were nonpareil. I am indebted to Michael Barnes for allowing me to experiment with stone-moving ideas on the television show *Nova*. Not to be overlooked are John Suh and the people at InfoGraphics, who magically digitized my pen and ink drawings, making me a reluctant member of cyberspace. Still, all would have come to nought but for Jean Hurtado, acquisitions editor at the University of Oklahoma Press, who considered my manuscript worthy of publication, and managing editor Alice K. Stanton, who turned it into a book.

Above all, I had the help of my sons Edward and Jeffrey; Edward was tireless and uncomplaining with my continual demands for his time and effort. Fortunately for the success of this work, they insisted that my thoughts, though clear to me, be made understandable to others. They also tried to correct my recurring errors of punctuation and grammar but were finally overwhelmed by the effort and left it to the professional skills of copyeditor Sally Antrobus. Most important has been my wife Natalie, to whom this book is dedicated. The fount of all things good and true, this patient lady put up with a mentally absent husband as she lent advice, comfort, and encouragement throughout the long years of striving.

STICKS, STONES, AND SHADOWS

CHAPTER 1

MOUNTAINS OF THE SUN

The similarity of the monuments of Mexico to the earliest pyramid of Egypt, with its set-back levels, is startling. Here were two civilizations vastly remote from each other in time and distance, yet each had built pyramidal structures. This raises the question of whether the pyramids of Egypt represent more than just the tombs for dead kings. In one form or another, such brick, earth, or stone constructions, with no hint of being funerary depositories, are also found in Mesopotamia, North America, and China. Can it be an incredible coincidence, or is it possible that all ancient societies unknowingly shared some compelling need to raise mountain-like monuments? Is it also possible that such constructions played a role of great importance to the people of these far-flung cultures? What could have driven so many to so great an effort? Was it some common religious belief, or was it survival? Perhaps it was both. Yet what conceivable connection could there be between an elevated structure and the survival of a people?

Significantly, these constructions were not erected until a time when the propagation of crops played an important part in our societal development, a possible indication that some as yet unknown link exists between these tall structures and the development of agronomy. Considering this, I suggest that the Egyptian pyramid, with its four smooth sides meeting at a distant point in the sky, played a part in that link—perhaps being the ultimate example of that unique architectural category. Further, I suggest that Mesopotamia's need to prepare its vast system of artificial irrigation for the rainy season or overflowing rivers, and the means people used to track the sun for this purpose, played an important role in introducing to Egypt the art of monumental architecture. To discover the possible connection between the Egyptian pyramid and the growth of agriculture, it may be helpful to review some of the problems faced by others in their quest for sustenance and some of the solutions they devised for survival.

In the beginning, we obtained food as did much of the animal kingdom: by scavenging, hunting, fishing, and trapping. In times of drought or overpopulation, many starved, while others sought sustenance far afield. Eventually, we learned to cultivate plants, a process that probably came about by accident or by observing and imitating the growth of wild plants found along the banks of waterways. Only after long years of experimentation did people learn to irrigate and till the land in preparation for growing crops. Our distant ancestors took advantage of whatever circumstances nature provided in the areas where they lived. In Egypt, for example, pastoral nomads sowed some barley or millet after a rainstorm, pitched their tents until the ripened grain was gathered, and then moved on with their flocks. By sowing just enough for their immediate needs, without any attempt either to store for the future or to increase the available planting area, they suffered the consequences.

As groups of hunter-gatherers increasingly learned to care for wild crops and prepare the land, they brought its yield to a point where the storage of excess food enabled nomads to settle in small farming-pastoral communities. The earliest known of these cultures (8th millennium) seem to have come from three hubs in the Near East: the western slopes of the Zagros Mountains and their adjacent valley, the hill country of Turkish Mesopotamia, and the south Anatolian plateau.[1] With the development of the first wheat that could be separated from its husk by threshing, and the domestication of sheep and goats, the small settlements grew as the amount of arable land increased with the development of simple methods of irrigation. Not only did this enable people to store food for future needs; the excess food was supplied to artisans, who could now spend more time in specialties divorced from agriculture, thus starting a cycle that led to a further increase of discovery and invention.

After the mastery of fire, the greatest economic advances known to humankind came from the deliberate cultivation of cereal plants and the selection, taming, and breeding of animals. Once this road was taken there was no turning back. As more land is turned to crops, there are constant inroads on the feeding grounds of wildlife. In addition to preventing the growth of new plants on which wild herds depend, the changes reduce wild feeding grounds further by the grazing of domestic herds, which generally accompany the farming settlements. As the demands of a growing population involve an ever-increasing need for new fields to cultivate, the farmer becomes completely dependent on the very fields that were once only a supplemental source of food.

Successful farming, however, is dependent on water. Settlements distant from existing waterways therefore required the ability to predict with some degree of accuracy the patterns of local rainfall, seasonal patterns that occur at approximately the same time each year. After years of observing the heavenly bodies—the changes in their appearance, their height in the sky, the light and shadows they cast, and their rising or setting positions as related to fixed objects—various methods were devised to make these predictions. Indeed, there is strong evidence of monthly incisions made on bone that were based on the cycles of the moon from long before recorded history.[2]

The Moon

Of all the heavenly bodies, the moon was a logical choice to be the first seasonal indicator. The changes in its face seem to shout for attention as it moves through its monthly phases—transformations so easily understood and conveyed to others as to transcend language and geographical barriers. This is suggested by the calendars of early civilizations, all of which are lunar based, and by words that have since crept into our language: moon, measure, menstrual, and month, all stemming from the same root. With the ability to describe the flow of time by "suns" for days, "dark" for nights, and "moons" for months, hunters could relate distances traveled or periods to the next fertility rites. However, while monthly changes on the face of the moon are easily recognized, it is far more difficult to follow a complete cycle of the moon's path as it wanders across the sky—a task that requires dedicated observations over 18.62 years.

Even when discounting the length of the moon's cycles, observers soon discovered that no relationship exists between the phases of the moon and the seasons of the year, the interval between two consecutive full moons being only 29.53 days. Used without added days to make up the deficiency, for every 12 full-moon cycles of the year, 11.25 days would be lost. In fact, if planting time were based strictly on the lunar year, in a short time farmers would not only miss the seasonal rains but would find themselves sowing when they should be reaping.

Despite these problems, many societies came to rely on the moon as a basis for their official calendar. While adequate for society in general, the unreliability of the moon as an indicator forced those who worked the land to find other means of knowing when to plant. They came to rely instead on several indicators provided by nature and seemed to find signs of their presence everywhere. Often their discoveries were expressed by homilies; "the cry of the migrating cranes shows the time of plowing and sowing" or "if one sows too late, the crop may yet thrive if it rains within three days of the first hearing of the cuckoo."[3]

The Stars

When the uncertainty of relying on these signs became evident by their failings, other solutions were sought. Among these, Pliny suggested a connection between the seasons and the stars, claiming that if crops were sowed when the constellation Pleiades set, rain would shortly follow. Pliny was not alone in this observation. Many early agricultural societies considered the star groups Orion or the Pleiades important, both because they are among the brightest star groups in the sky and because they appear or disappear at significant times in the seasonal calendar.[4] Such knowledge, coming naturally to people dependent on nature for survival, seems to have been used to advantage all around the world: natives of New Guinea and of South Africa claim the position of Pleiades in the sky tells them when to plant; Brazilian Indians know the Pleiades as "Mother of those who are thirsty."[5] The Skidi Pawnee of the North American Plains adjusted the moon year by annually starting anew from the position of the Pleiades in the spring—a position found by viewing the constellation through a small hole in the lodge.[6]

The positions of constellations, the methods of locating them, and the proper time for planting differ in many parts of the world. Usually these positions are noted by their heliacal rising or setting; that is, their location relative to the sun at first or last moments of visibility. In some areas, such as the Indo-Malay region where the horizon is not visible

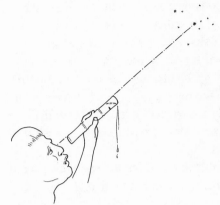

Figure 1.1. The Dyaks of the Indo-Malay area determined the proper time for planting with a short length of bamboo. Filled with water and aimed it at a selected star or constellation, it would spill some water. Planting began when the level of the water left matched a predetermined mark when the bamboo was once again held upright.

due to heavy forestation, other methods were substituted. For example, the Dyak tribe used a short length of bamboo as a diopter (angle-measuring device). Here a mark, the location of which was found empirically, was inscribed on the outside of the bamboo between the open end and its internal web near the top. Nightly, when the cuplike end was filled with water and aimed at a selected star, the angle caused some water to spill (**1.1**). When the bamboo was then held upright, the remaining water was gauged against the mark. Planting commenced when they coincided. A different method was used near Jogyakarta, in Central Java. At dusk the farmer raised his hand toward Orion with rice seeds in his flattened palm. The night the constellation reached an altitude that caused the seeds to roll down his arm was when these practitioners began their planting season (**1.2**). The nearby Maloh people used the hats they wore as an aid to judge the heliacal culmination of the Pleiades. For this tribe planting began when the ritual practitioner looked up to see the constellation Pleiades and his hat fell off.[7]

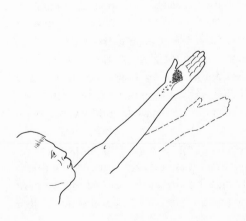

Figure 1.2. In Central Java the ritual practitioner raised his arm eastward toward the belt of stars in the constellation Orion. Planting began when the rice seeds in his flattened palm began to roll down his arm.

Solar Mountains

While spilled water, rolling rice, or falling hats may have been necessary in a heavily forested area, such exotic methods are not needed in open country where mountains are in view. Indeed, there has always been a unique association between mountains and the seasonal rains—a link so profound that since time immemorial, mountains have played an important role in the religion and culture of peoples throughout the world, often being viewed as mysterious and divine sources of life. Although formations like Olympus, Fuji, and Tai Shan are large and well-known, a mountain does not have to be high to be venerated; it need only form a contrast with the surrounding land. Mount Cynthus, on the Greek island of Delos, was considered sacred though only a granite outcrop 367 feet (112 m) high.[8]

People displayed belief in these geographical formations in many ways. Height and majesty encouraged them to view mountains as places to commune with the gods, as cosmic centers or as conduits of power to the earth below. For prosperity, health, and long life, people of many cultures made pilgrimages to the heights. According to Hindu belief, one night in late summer when the moon is full, the god Shiva appears inside a cave in Amarnath, 13,500 feet (4,115 m) up in the Himalayas, a sight which encouraged pilgrims to make the difficult three-day trek. Such devotion is not unique to Hindus. Irish Catholics walk barefoot up the path of Croagh Patrick in the hope that their pain and suffering will serve as penitence for their sins—both peoples feel that the more difficult the journey, the greater its worth.[9]

Since before the time of the Inca, Andeans have worshiped mountains as gods and had their ceremonial centers built on peaks reaching up to 22,000 feet (6,706 m). To date, archaeologists have found almost two dozen young Inca girls and boys, all apparently frozen sacrifices to the sacred mountains in Argentina, Chile, and Peru.[10] Even today, offerings are made in Bolivia, albeit in less drastic fashion, to Illimani, "king of the mountains," for rain to feed the crops and livestock.[11]

Another and probably more practical reason for venerating mountains is their relationship with the rising and setting sun. Much of ancient mythology stems from the sun rising or setting directly behind a mountain, a vision that could easily produce the thought that the mountain itself was responsible for swallowing or giving birth to the sun. Observing such events repeated year after year, even the most primitive mind could not fail to link the sun's "movement" to local weather patterns; people soon realized that the sun's position along the horizon as it rose and set was often a precursor to the coming rainy season. Indeed, by standing on the same spot an observer could judge by eye, or better yet with the use of a crude measuring stick held at arm's length, the extent in sun diameters from the rising or setting sun to the mountain (**1.3**). By this means they found that the more accurately this distance could be gauged, the more exactly the rainy season could be predicted.

I suggest that some such method was employed for viewing the sun long before recorded history. This simple procedure, presently to be explained, eventually led to the building of the Egyptian pyramids. While in time these structures became tombs for kings, they had their early beginnings as man-made mountains, the remains of which can still

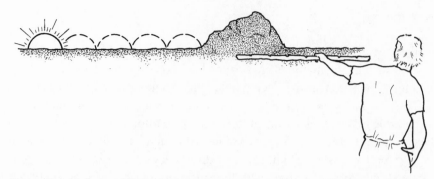

Figure 1.3. It is possible to measure the distance to a fixed geographical object by the number of solar diameters of the rising or setting sun. This can be done by eye, when standing in the same spot, or, for greater accuracy, with the use of a notched measuring stick.

be seen spaced along the length of Egypt. As step pyramids of the Early Dynasties, these distant markers enabled farmers to estimate the time remaining before the Nile began to overflow. Armed with this knowledge, they could prepare by removing silt from irrigation ditches that led to the more distant plots used to extend the amount of arable land.

Why There Are Seasons

The empirical knowledge likely gained by the Egyptian farmer is based on a natural event. The sun has both daily and annual cycles, which, if studied, can disclose the time of day or season of the year. This is caused by the earth rotating from west to east on an axis tilted relative to the plane in which the planet orbits (counterclockwise, viewed from above) around the sun. Unaware of these motions, an earthbound observer sees the sun rising in the east and setting in the west—much as someone seated on a moving train watches a stationary platform speed past. On a yearly basis, the apparent motion of the sun is not along the celestial equator, which would keep it on an even path around the earth, but along the ecliptic, a path which is at an angle of 23° 27' to the equator. The tilt of the earth's axis to its plane of orbit never varies and always points in the same direction. As a result, seasonal changes occur as each hemisphere points toward the sun for six months of each year and away from the sun for the next six months (**1.4**). Without the tilt, there would be a constant temperature for all the latitudes according to their distance from the equator, and the sun would seem to rise and set at the same point each day of the year.

The angle formed between the path of the celestial equator and the ecliptic is greatest at the equinoxes and smallest at the solstices, a time when they virtually run on a parallel course (**1.5**). This angular relationship changes regularly during the year and results in the sun apparently rising at slightly different points along the horizon each day, as it moves between its northern and southern limits (solstices).[12]

To an earthbound observer, the rising sun does not move at a uniform rate along the horizon as it seems to spiral back and forth around the earth (**1.6**). At the equinox, when day and night are equal, its daily movements are quite noticeable for about a week as it travels about one solar diameter each morning (30 arcminutes). However, on reaching

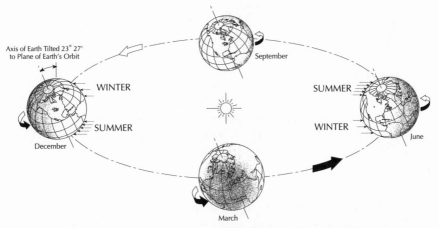

Figure 1.4. Seasons are caused by the tilt of the earth's axis as it orbits the sun. This tilt causes the northern and southern hemispheres to face toward or away from the sun every six months.

Figure 1.5. An earth-centered view of the stationary earth and rotating sun. The apparent motion of the sun is not along the celestial equator which would keep it on an even path around the earth, but along the ecliptic, which is at an angle of 23° 27' to the equator.

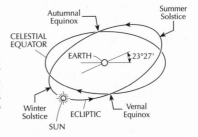

either solstice—a word that means "sun stand still"—the movement becomes almost imperceptible as it starts to reverse its course. At this time, it moves only about 0.1 of a solar diameter each day, or the equivalent of the diameter of a 50-cent piece at about half a mile (1 km) (**1.7**).[13]

Inspired by curiosity and imagination, diverse human cultures have often developed similar methods to track the path of the sun. While the earliest of these methods probably sought to predict the local rainy seasons by observing the sun's position relative to a mountain peak, at a later time man-made mountains were constructed to replicate and function as their natural counterparts. A wide range of devices, from passage tombs to gnomons,

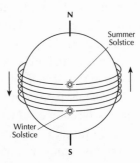

Figure 1.6. An earth-centered view of the sun as it seems to spiral around the earth from solstice to solstice.

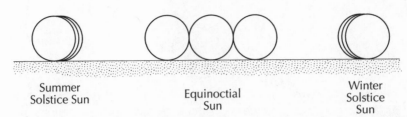

Summer
Solstice Sun

Equinoctial
Sun

Winter
Solstice
Sun

Figure 1.7. A comparison of the daily movements of the rising and setting solstitial and equinoctial sun. The sun moves one sun diameter each day at the
equinoxes but only about 0.1 of a sun diameter at the solstices.

were also devised to track or record the sun's movements. The people responsible for
recording these events were not precision-driven astronomers with extensive knowledge
of the heavens; in fact, to be useful, the means they employed needed only to provide a
benchmark that repeated at about the same time each year.[14] Yet the information gathered
by this priestly class was so important to survival that, as noted, the devices themselves
sometimes came to be worshiped as gods.

Mythology of the Sun

Fear that the sun would not return from the winter solstice—an event that would cause
the world to descend into perpetual cold and darkness—and efforts to encourage its return
have probably been the greatest central theme in human history and mythology. Signs of
this are seen in cultures from many parts of the world. The emperor of China, sole inter-
mediary with the heavens, offered sacrifice and would prostrate himself on an elevated
mound to implore the sun to return.[15] Giving thanks for its reappearance, cultures like the
Inca sacrificed to the sun the possessions they prized most—their children.

Besides the use of mountains or natural formations to gauge the movements of the
sun, the works of Mesopotamian, Egyptian, Chinese, Indian, and Meso-American cultures
are filled with examples of man-made structures designed to copy mountains. Interestingly, these structures were generally oriented in a somewhat solstitial or equinoctial direction to the sun. Chinese pyramids closely oriented to the cardinal points are seen near
Ch'ang, capital of the Western Han Dynasty (206 BCE–CE 220).[16] Mayans considered the
temples and pyramids they built to be sacred mountains and described them as such with
carvings of *witz* monsters that appear on their facades; *witz* is the Mayan word for mountain or hill. While Mayan cities were based on the cardinal directions, these people considered the principal axis to be the east-west path of the sun and used temples and pyramids
as man-made "Great Mountains" to track its course.[17]

An unusual architectural theme repeated at many Mayan sites can be seen at Uaxactún in Guatemala, where three equally spaced small buildings are placed on the east
side of a raised platform (**1.8**). At this location, the sun rises over the central building at the
time of the equinox and over the end buildings at the midsummer and midwinter solstices.
After viewing this event with Moctezuma, Cortés reported the Aztec king so upset by a
slight misalignment that he wished to pull the building down and have it properly posi-

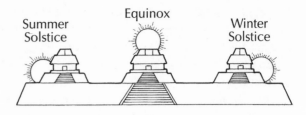

Figure 1.8. A view of the passage of the sun at Uaxactún from a temple station on the west side of the plaza. The sun rises over the central building at the equinox and over an end building at each solstice.

tioned. Cortés was sufficiently startled by this episode among a supposedly inferior people to report it to the king of Spain.[18]

Investigators in Meso-America found that the builders were not concerned with framing the equinoctial sun as it rose on the horizon but instead sought a point about 165 feet (50 m) above the ground—observations at this height have the advantage of reducing atmospheric refraction. Such refraction distorts the true position of the sun when it is viewed on the horizon, making it appear about half a degree higher than it actually is, the amount of distortion lessening as the sun's elevation increases.[19] While astronomical measurements may be accurate to 2 arcminutes with the naked eye, it is difficult to see anything but a very large object on a distant horizon. For example, a 50-foot-tall (15 m) standing stone has an angular size of only 2 arcminutes at 15.5 miles (25 km) and can easily be lost in the glare of the sun.[20] Although the sun is a large enough object to be seen, other problems exist when viewing the sunrise—should one look for the first or last gleam? Which part of the sun disc should be observed—its center or its edge?[21]

Sunlight

There are other ways of tracking the sun than by building an artificial mountain. Movements of the sun were sometimes found by observing the path taken by its light rays. At significant times of the year such diverse people as the inhabitants of Central and South America and the Dogon of Upper Volta waited at carefully selected positions for the sun to shine through a crevice or over a protrusion. The Zuni of North America had a more imaginative approach. They painted a likeness of the sun on the inside wall of their highest pueblo. Sunlight streaming through a porthole that faced the rising sun would signal particular times of the year by illuminating one end of the wall at planting time, the opposite end at the winter solstice, and the center of the wall, which held the likeness of the sun, at the equinox.[22]

Portholes used for the projection of light were common devices in the tropical zone of South America, a geographical area reaching 23° 30' north and south of the equator. In this region, rays of the zenith or midday sun were received in a darkened chamber from a hole in the ceiling.[23] Inhabitants throughout the tropical zone would treat the arrival of the zenith sun as an important occasion, often starting the New Year with its first sighting. Despite efforts in the 16th century by King Philip II of Spain to discourage any such signs of sun worship, the tradition persisted and is still celebrated in some areas of Guatemala during the rainy season and time of planting.[24]

Instead of using portholes, people of some cultures positioned the structures they built to find the sun on a special day of the year: Mayans built their temples to let light from the summer solstice illuminate an inner sanctuary. [25] The Skidi Pawnee laid their dome-shaped lodges on a circular plan to imitate the horizon and positioned the doorway of the lodge so that the rising equinoctial sun would illuminate an altar set at the rear.[26] In Egypt, a small chapel identified as a solar sanctuary in the temple of Hatshepsut has behind an altar in the northwest wall a niche that was illuminated on the winter solstice sunrise; the main entrance of the Egyptian Temple of Amun-Re, at Karnak, is axially aligned to the summer solstice sunset. It also has a small structure called a Counter Temple outside the southeast wall, sited to face the winter solstice sunrise (**1.9**). The likeness of a winged sun framed by two massive pylons is positioned on the portal of the northwest entrance to face the summer solstice sunset (**1.10**). This architectural design replicates the sun when positioned in an indent between two mountains—a position also noted in the Egyptian language by the hieroglyph *akhet,* which stands for "horizon" (**1.11**).[27] The portals' association with mountains is given by the name "Luminous Mountain Horizon of Heaven."[28] This solar position is also shown in Near Eastern iconography, where the sun-god Shamash is liberated at dawn from between two mountains (**1.12**).

Instead of positioning temples to face solstitial or equinoctial positions, some structures were planned to commemorate the day of a special event. For example, the 19th Dynasty rock-cut temple at Abu Simbel, actually an elaborate passage chamber, was oriented to allow rays of the sun to reach the terminus sanctuary deep inside. This event

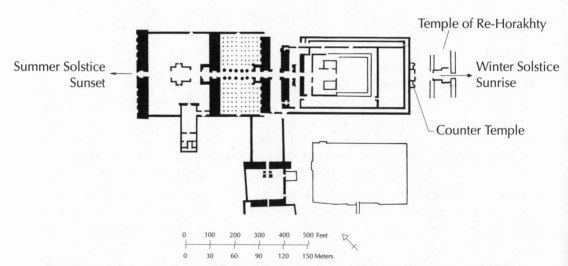

Figure 1.9. The main axis of the Great Temple of Amun-Re is aligned with the summer solstice sunset. The Counter Temple and Temple of Re-Horakhty link the main temple to the winter solstice sunrise.

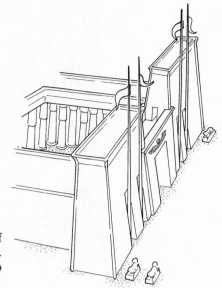

Figure 1.10. The northwest entrance of the Temple of Amun-Re shows its link to the sun by a winged likeness. It is depicted on a notch above a portal between two mountain peaks architecturally created by the pylons.

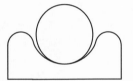

Figure 1.11. The *akhet* is an Egyptian hieroglyph that means "horizon." It repeats the theme of the temple entrance and also shows the strong interest of the Egyptians in the movements of the sun as it relates to the mountains.

Figure 1.12. A cylinder seal impression of the Akkadian period (2200 BCE) shows the sun god, Shamash, rising from between two mountains at dawn. The water god Ea is on his left and Ishtar, goddess of fertility, on his right.

occurred at the sunrise date of the 30th Jubilee celebration of Ramesses II, builder of the temple (**1.13**). It was so constructed that all the statues standing in an inner sanctum were illuminated but for the statue of Ptah, a god who supposedly dwells in the dark. The site also has a small open-air chapel built on the north end of the facade, sited to be exactly aligned with the winter solstice.[29]

Other passage chambers with solar orientations, such as Newgrange, a stone-built 5,000-year-old mound-tomb located in Ireland, and Maes Howe in the Scottish Orkney

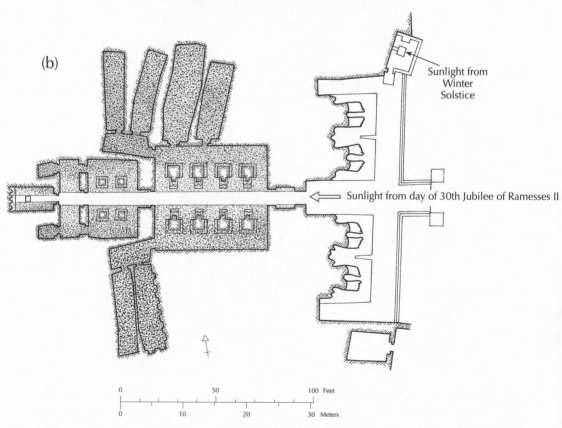

Figure 1.13. (a) The Great Temple at Abu Simbel. (b) The structure is oriented so that sunlight reaches a culminating niche on the day of the 30th Jubilee celebration of the builder, Ramesses II. The small chapel of Re-Horakhty is aligned to the winter solstice sunrise.

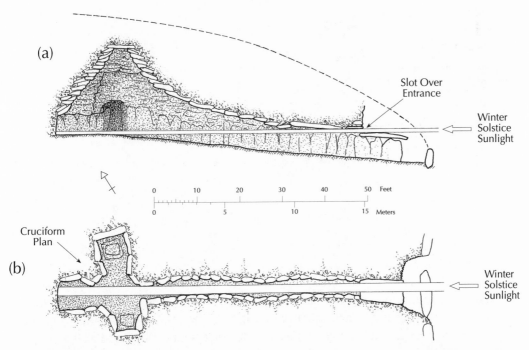

Figure 1.14. A passage chamber at Newgrange, Ireland. (a) A beam of sunlight enters a slot to illuminate the terminus vault for several days during the time of winter solstice. (b) The cruciform vault permits observers to view the event without interfering with the incoming sunlight.

Islands, began to appear in Europe some 2,000 years after the rise of agriculture in the Near East. The entrance at Newgrange leads to a corridor deep inside (62 feet [18 m]) that terminates in a cruciform vault of three chambers. The two side chambers of the vault contain stone basins, probably meant to hold sacred objects or human remains (**1.14**). Over a period of several days just before and after the midwinter solstice, an entering beam of light from the rising sun would illuminate the vault for about 20 minutes. This might be considered coincidental but for an intentionally formed slot located above the entrance that allowed sunlight to enter the passageway even with the entrance closed. The side chambers of the cruciform vault probably also allowed priestly observers to view the incoming sunbeams without blocking the passageway.[30]

The cruciform plan also appears in the great cathedrals in Europe, reflecting a belief that considered orientation to the east as being sacred. Although Pope Leo the Great (440–61 CE) issued a decree against worship of the rising sun, veneration of the sun was accepted if it were not viewed as a deity in itself but seen instead as a symbol of Christ entering the church. In time this substitutive identity became so entrenched that it generated a strong reaction. To prevent sunlight from streaming through the open doorway, Pope Vigilius (537–55 CE) decreed that all churches be oriented with the apse toward the east. At times, the church allowed the cathedral to be axially aligned to the rising sun of the winter solstice and the setting sun of the summer solstice (**1.15**), or to lie with its axis in the direction of the rising sun on a day of local importance, such as the birth date of a patron saint.[31]

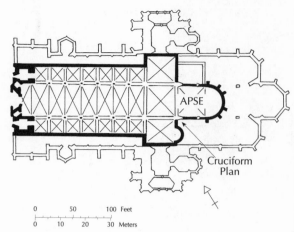

APSE

Cruciform
Plan

| 0 | 50 | 100 Feet |
| 0 | 10 | 20 | 30 Meters |

Figure 1.15. The cruciform plan of St. Stephen's Cathedral, in Vienna, has its axis oriented toward sunrise at the winter solstice and toward the setting sun at the summer solstice.

Sun Shadows

In lieu of mountains, passage chambers, or buildings to gauge the seasons, other cultures made use of shadow and its daily change in length. To measure shadows, they employed an ancient instrument called a gnomon—a device that is little more than a stick set perpendicular to the ground. Indian tribes, such as the Shawnees, Iroquois, and Miamis of North America, erected tall gnomons in the center of their villages to find the seasonal planting cycles.[32] The Chinese involvement with the gnomonic arts is shown by ancient ideograms and literary references from 654 BCE, describing the length of shadows at the equinoxes and solstices.[33] Indeed, the interest of Chinese astronomers in this was such that by 725 CE they had already placed a number of widely spaced 8-foot (2.4 m) gnomons along the 2,200 miles (3,500 km) of a single meridian in order to judge geographical distances by the changing length of the shadows the gnomons cast. The Chinese became so adept in this art that they devised a gnomon constructed so that its shadow touched the base on which it was mounted to announce the day of the summer solstice (**1.16**).[34]

The obelisk, an Egyptian gnomon, was considered to be sacred as far back as the 1st Dynasty (3100–2890 BCE). According to beliefs, the pyramidion on its apex represents the *benben* stone, an ancient object that was thought to receive the first rays of the rising sun. These tapered monoliths, up to 105 feet (32 m) tall, and up to 500 tons in weight, were

Figure 1.16. An 8-foot gnomon erected in a Confucian temple was designed to cast a shadow at the foot of its supporting base at high noon on the day of the summer solstice.

themselves looked upon as possessed by a god and entitled to veneration. In the case of the obelisks erected by Tuthmosis III in the Temple of Amun-Re at Karnak, the king decreed that 25 loaves of bread and a jar of beer be given as a daily offering to each of the four obelisks. When an obelisk was erected, scarabs were issued that showed the king kneeling before it in adoration: a vignette from the book of the dead shows a priest making offerings to two obelisks that embody Re-Horakhty (**1.17**).[35] Obelisks were usually erected in pairs. The eastern obelisk at the temple of Luxor (Thebes) is inscribed to Amun, the rising sun; the western monument, which now stands in Paris, is dedicated to Atum, the setting sun. Transported by the Romans from Heliopolis to Circus of Nero and used as a sundial, one such obelisk was later moved (1586 CE) by Italian architect Domenico Fontana to St. Peter's Square, where it stands to this day (**1.17**).

By incorporating the principle of the gnomon in a structure, Buddhists designed sacred buildings called stupas to be models of the cosmos. Like Egyptians, they considered the

(a)   (b)

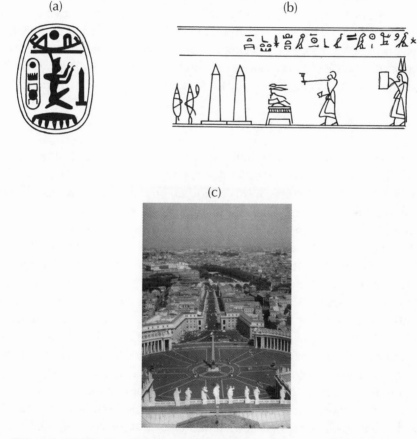

(c)

Figure 1.17. The Egyptian gnomon (obelisk) was so venerated that the device itself was considered to be a god. (a) When an obelisk was erected, scarabs were issued showing the king kneeling before it in adoration. (b) Priests making offerings to two obelisks that embody Re-Horakhty. (c) An Egyptian obelisk taken from Heliopolis to Circus of Nero and later moved by Domenico Fontana to St. Peter's Square.

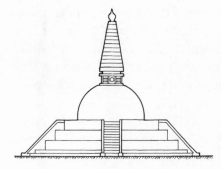

Figure 1.18. The stupa is a temple constructed around the central axis of a gnomon—a device considered by Buddhists to be a god. The sides of stupas were made to face the cardinal points, marked by pillars, niches, or statues of the Buddha if the stupa was circular.

gnomon to be a god and "a pillar of light extending downwards from the sun in the zenith to the rest of the earth," according to Adrian Snodgrass. Whatever the particular design of the building, whether domed, towered, or pyramidal, stupas were constructed around the central axis of a gnomon and were oriented with their sides to the cardinal points of the compass. If the structure was given a circular floor plan, the cardinal points were marked by gateways, pillars, niches, or statues of Buddha (**1.18**). Whatever its architectural style, the stupa was considered to be a "Mountain that Stands in the Center of the Universe," and its construction was based on a ritual geometric diagram of the solar cycle.[36] Another of the many links between temple structures and mountains is shown by the Hindus, whose temple spires are called *sikhara*, a Hindu word meaning mountain peak.[37]

Mesopotamia

Of all the structures that seem to be built in relation to the sun, the earliest occurred in Mesopotamia, the most unlikely place for this to happen, one would think. Devoid of all natural resources, including stone, it was a hard and unforgiving land situated between the Tigris and Euphrates rivers (**1.19**). Its summers, which lasted for five months, were almost unbearable, with temperatures that often ranged to 110–130° F (43–54° C) in the shade.[38] Yet, proving that difficulties are merely challenges to be overcome, it was in this place of scanty rainfall that people caused the wasteland to blossom and created one of the earliest of great civilizations.

The Tigris and Euphrates rivers, with their sources in the Taurus and Zagros mountains of Turkey and Iran, flow down to a vast bed of sedimentary rock that underlies the alluvial plain. The silt brought down with the water and deposited on the bedrock created one of the most fertile regions in the Near East. This occurred because a river having a low gradient deposits along its course the sediment it carries and can thus raise its own bed from the surrounding plains, the height of the bed depending on the gradient, the amount of sediment carried, and the flow rate of the water. By the time both rivers reached the area of Baghdad and Ramadi, the slower-flowing Euphrates was 29 feet (9 m) higher than the Tigris. This fortuitous difference allowed waters from the Euphrates to flow with the aid of sluices, canals, and reservoirs into the lower and faster-flowing Tigris and to fertilize the land between the two waterways.[39]

However, due to low runoff from the mountain areas and little rainfall in the lowlands, the twin rivers were barely more than trickles for eight months of the year. Yet even under

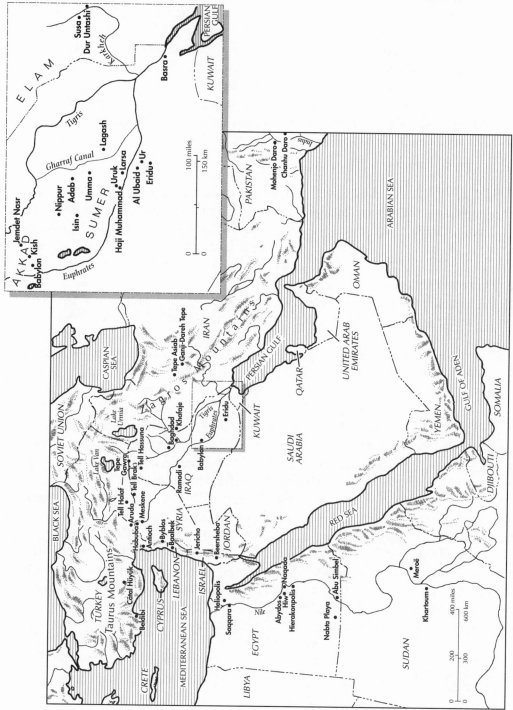

Figure 1.19. Map of the Near East. The offset area generally shows the Mesopotamian alluvium formed by confluence of Tigris and Euphrates rivers.

the best of conditions, perennial irrigation was required of both rivers because they flooded in the wrong season; in Mesopotamia, with the spring floods starting between April and June, the Tigris reached its peak flow first and the Euphrates about a month later—too late to help the main crop and too early for the winter crop.[40]

Faced with such adverse conditions, the benefits to be derived from an artificial system of irrigation were incalculable. Besides increased food production resulting from irrigation, sophistications are possible. Barley, for example, with two rows of grain in its uncultivated state, produces six-row mutants when well irrigated.[41] Due to intensive labor demands, however, such irrigation cannot continue effectively without the strong hand of a central authority and some early indication of the coming rainfall or river overflow. With such leadership an increased yield is only one of many beneficial aspects that arise from artificial irrigation. The cooperation necessary for the annual removal of silt built up in the water channels—in this case a result of rivers that carried five times the sediment of the Nile per gallon—welds the population into a cohesive social force.[42] The order and discipline brought by this force provides mutual protection against outside threats.[43] Artificial irrigation also causes settlements to form closer to each other than if they depend solely on rainfall. To avoid the natural friction brought by close living, rules for resolving conflicts must be enforced.

With its production of food and highly disciplined population, Mesopotamia was able to acquire through a vast system of trade the raw materials it lacked. No doubt Egypt, generally thought of as a country in isolation, was a recipient of that trade from a time before recorded history. With trade came people; and with people, ideas. Among the ideas brought to Egypt, I submit, was the concept of monumental building. However, putting this aside for the present, it may be of interest to note how dispersed the Mesopotamian trading network was and how far it extended into the past.

To identify the goods and the number of items being sent before writing was known, countable clay tokens of different representative shapes were included with the consignments—an idea so ancient that such tokens were used long before the invention of pottery (**1.20**). An indication of the vast trade distances covered by the tokens is their discovery at Beldibi in southwestern Turkey and Chanhu Daro in Pakistan. Their antiquity emerges in their being found at an 8th millennium site on the Nile, at Khartoum, and at two 9th millennium sites in the Zagros region of Iran, Tepe Asiab and Ganji-Dareh Tepe.[44]

At a later time, goods were safeguarded from unauthorized persons by molding clay over the covered mouth of a container and pressing the engraved stamp of the owner into the wet clay. In this way, impressions would be left of anything from animals to decorative designs. When dry, the clay sealings retained their impressions indefinitely—archaeologists still use them to identify the past occupants of newly uncovered sites (**1.21**). The

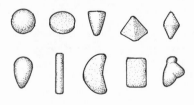

Figure 1.20. Tokens of different shapes may have been used to identify and give the number of goods in a consignment.

stamp seal was later replaced with a small cylinder carved of precious stone or metal, one of the many inventions of Mesopotamia (**1.22**). When the cylinder was rotated around an axle, or by the palm of the hand, it could be made to spread its signature over a larger area than the stamp seal. The scenes impressed in the clay are of a distinctive style and display a variety of subjects ranging from brocades to animals with entwined serpentine necks. Worn on a wristband or around the neck during life, these devices were often taken to the grave with the owner.

The cylinder seal was only one of the many innovations developed in Mesopotamia. Said to be devised by the people we now call Sumerians, this breadbasket of the Near East had a long history with many cultures before the Babylonians or the Sumerians brought it to eminence. To help classify its history, the northern and southern Mesopotamian alluvium was archaeologically divided into chronological order with names that generally referred to the sites at which objects of the period were found.

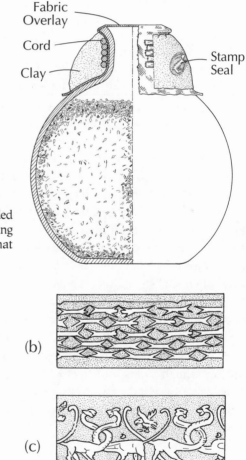

Fabric Overlay

Cord

Clay

Stamp Seal

Figure 1.21. To safeguard products, clay was molded over the covered mouth of a container. By pressing a stamp in the wet clay, impressions were left that served to identify the owner.

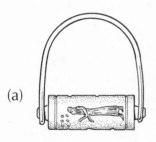

(a)

(b)

(c)

Figure 1.22. (a) Rotated in clay around an axle or by the palm of a hand, the cylinder seal could spread its unique signature over a much larger area than the stamp seal. (b, c) Samples of impressions left by the cylinder seals.

Table 1.1
CHRONOLOGY OF MESOPOTAMIA

Date (BCE)	North Mesopotamia	South Mesopotamia
2000–1500	Early Assyrian	Old Babylonian Akkado-Sumerian
2500–2000		Early Dynastic IIIb
3000–2500	Jemdet Nasr influence	Early Dynastic IIIa, II, I Jemdet Nasr Late Uruk
3500–3000	Uruk influence Ubaid influence	Early Sumerian Early Uruk
4000–3500		Late Ubaid
4500–4000	Late Halaf Early Ubaid	Ubaid
5000–4500	Early Halaf	Ubaid (Hajji Muhammad)
5500–5000	Late Hassuna	Early Ubaid (Eridu)

After Carrol L. Riley, *The Origins of Civilization*, 46, fig. 15.

At about 5400 BCE Eridu, the earliest settlement on the alluvium, was established, and by the end of the Ubaid period all the characteristics of cities in later periods were already in place. Although much of the earliest history of the area remains unknown, by 4500 BCE Ubaidians had so completely replaced the dominant Halaf culture that their settlements and towns dotted the northern and southern alluvial plains.[45] Besides the remains of ruined structures, our knowledge of Mesopotamia has been considerably increased by the written records left behind, in a style of writing involving wedge-shaped impressions made in clay with a reed stylus. When baked, clay can hold the records and thoughts of a culture for thousands of years. The Sumerians are credited with the introduction (about 3100 BCE), of cuneiform writing—Sumerian being a term that applies to the language and culture of a people known to have inhabited the southern plains from at least 3500 to 2350 BCE. There is much debate about Sumerians and the exact period at which they arrived on the Mesopotamian plains. Archaeologists suggest that they were among the original settlers. Philologists suggest they were latecomers since the names of many of the major towns they inhabited—Eridu, Larsa, Isin, Adab, Lagash, Nippur, and Kish—are derived from a language of which the origin is unknown.

Temple Structures

With the development of mud brick, first found at Halaf in the Ubaid period, the alluvial plain entered into what might be called "the Age of Architecture." This ideal building unit was small, easily handled, and could be used to build intricately formed structures on a scale previously unknown. The bricks were manufactured by the same simple method still used in the Near East—a dollop of mud is thrown on the ground into a wooden form open at the top and bottom. The mud consists of water and soil, preferably of a high clay content, into which chopped straw or dung is trodden—ingredients necessary to prevent warping or cracking during the drying process. After the excess is struck off the top and mud in the form is smoothed by hand, the form is removed and the brick faces are turned to dry in the sun. In use, the bricks are mortared in place and their outer faces are coated with a more fluid mixture of the same mud.

The Ubaid period not only saw isolated settlements develop into cities; it is distinguished by the earliest structure yet discovered that can unequivocally be called a temple. This was in Eridu, an ancient city south of the Euphrates. At Level XVII of the site was found the earliest (5000 BCE) of these buildings, a rectangular enclosure constructed of sun-dried mud brick. Just outside the enclosure were two circular ovens probably used for burnt offerings. The building had thin walls reinforced by inwardly projecting piers, called pilasters (**1.23**). Falling to ruin, this building was followed by a series of structures built on its remains and unique to the world.[46] Although close in design to the original, the next structure, on Level XVI (4900 BCE), had several important new features: the 11 × 15-foot (3.5 × 4.6 m) building was supplied with a centrally located offering table that faced a niche built into one wall. The niche held an altar that may have held a statue used in some form of religious service. Although some ground-level temples were constructed, buildings were typically given a token elevation above the ground, and their corners were generally oriented toward the cardinal points.[47]

The small room in Eridu that gave birth to the great ziggurats is the first evidence of a people who followed a religion conducted by priests in buildings dedicated to the worship of a deity. Indeed, the key features observed in this enclosure became characteristic of all

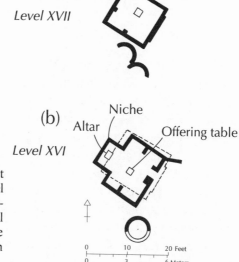

(a)

Level XVII

(b)   Altar   Niche   Offering table

Level XVI

Figure 1.23. (a) The earliest temple structure yet found is at Level XVII in Eridu (5000 BCE). (b) Level XVI (4900 BCE). All the features of future Mesopotamian temples—corners oriented to the cardinal points, cult niches, altars, and offering tables—are built directly over the structure of Level XVII (shown in dashed lines).

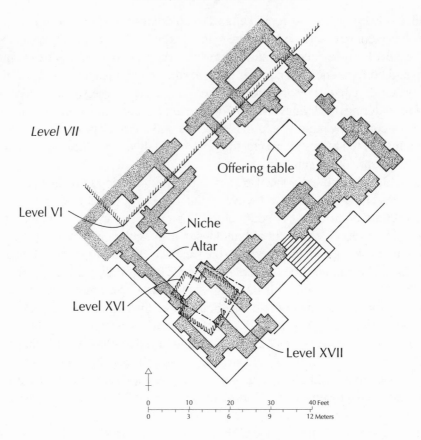

Level VII

Offering table

Level VI

Niche

Altar

Level XVI

Level XVII

0   10   20   30   40 Feet
0   3   6   9   12 Meters

Figure 1.24. The so-called tripartite plan of Level VII at Eridu (3800 BCE). The altar is placed in a wide niche defined by two inwardly projecting partitions. In addition to all the features of temples built 1,100 years earlier, Level VII has niches on the outside wall, which identify it as a religious structure.

future temples in Mesopotamia. Not only were subsequent temples built on the same hallowed ground as the original structure—they were placed directly upon the ruins of the old. This custom was followed even when stylistic changes were made, as in Level VII, where a temple was built directly over Level XVI some 1,100 years later (3800 BCE). Although the later temple was more elaborate, with a "tripartite" floor plan showing an elongated central sanctuary and entrances on both sides opening to small rooms, it continued to exhibit the earlier niche, altar, offering table, and corner orientation (**1.24**).

As these temples were built one upon the other for millennia, remains of the older ones were covered by platforms or terraces of solid mud brick (**1.25**). Their height increasing, the temples were reached by ramps, or stairways, which formed stepped towers of up to seven stages (**1.26**).[48] Though they varied considerably in style and height, Mesopotamian temples were always distinguished from secular buildings by a series of buttresses and

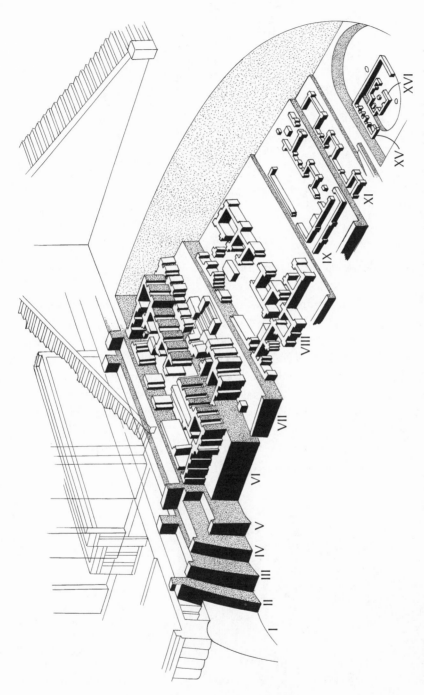

Figure 1.25. The sequence of temples uncovered at Eridu shows a continuity of tradition that lasted for thousands of years. Although each new temple is built directly upon ruins of the old, they are shown spaced apart for purposes of clarity.

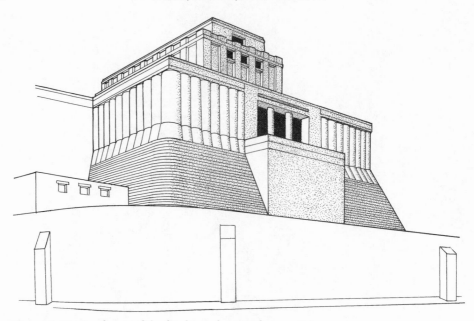

Figure 1.26. Rendering of the final temple at Eridu.

recesses on their outer walls.[49] In time, niches may also have lost their original solar purpose and become purely symbolic, as they were used as a decorative device placed in regular fashion around the inside of temple walls. Some scholars consider the temple buttresses to be imitations in brick of earlier piers still found on the reed-built shelters of the Marsh Arabs. These support the weight of the roof by reinforcing the thinly woven reed walls (**1.27**).[50] Supposedly, when later fashioned in brick, the niches became greatly exaggerated. At times, as in a precinct of Uruk, the alternating niche-and-buttress pattern of the temple of Eanna (3200 BCE) became so regularized in plan as to form what can best be described as a tooth pattern (**1.28**). Early constructions in Egypt also disclose the extensive use of niches on the outside of structures.

Figure 1.27. Reed houses, still used by Marsh Arabs, are thought to have remained unchanged since earliest times. Reed columns spaced along the walls help support the roof. These columns are thought to have been the origin of the niche when the settlers moved inland and used mud brick, instead of reeds, for construction.

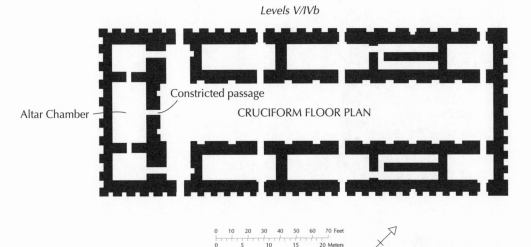

Levels V/IVb

Constricted passage

Altar Chamber

CRUCIFORM FLOOR PLAN

0 10 20 30 40 50 60 70 Feet
0   5   10   15   20 Meters

Figure 1.28. A temple in a precinct of Uruk Eanna, where Levels V–IVb (3200 BCE) disclose niches on the outside walls that are so regularized as to form a dental pattern. Instead of the usual niche in an end wall, it has a constricted passage that opens to an altar chamber. This tripartite temple has the same cruciform floor plan seen in Egypt, New grange, and the cathedrals of Europe.

Table 1.2

CHRONOLOGY FOR TEMPLES AT ERIDU

Date (BCE)	Period	Eridu
2750–2500	Early Dynastic IIIa–II	Palaces
3000–2750	Early Dynastic I	
	Jemdet Nasr	
		Temples I–II
3250–3000	Late Uruk	Temenos raised
		III–V
3500–3250	Early Uruk	Walled temenos
4000–3500	Ubaid	VI–VII
4500–4000		Temples VIII–XI
5000–4500	(Hajji Muhammad)	Levels XII–XIV
		Hajji Muhammad
5500–5000	Ubaid (Eridu)	Temples XV–XVIII

After S. Lloyd, *The Archaeology of Mesopotamia*, 36, table 3.

Once it was accepted as a facade for religious structures, attempts were made to accentuate the decorative aspect of the niche. At first, the indents were simply whitewashed. Later, the simple niche was set deeply into the wall and given a number of vertical facets, in an effort to make shadow patterns more interesting (**3.10**). They were also enriched with a geometric pattern of colored stones inserted into the soft clay, perhaps to reflect an earlier time when reed screens or stretched fabric wall panels had been used. The considerable effort to find stones with just the right color seems to have led to development of terra-cotta

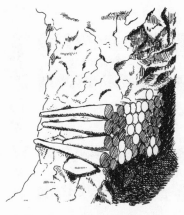

Figure 1.29. A portion of a temple wall at Uruk has terra-cotta cones, the outer faces of which were dipped into red, yellow, and black paint. The cones were inserted point first into wet clay to give the facade a decorative and hard protective crust.

Figure 1.30. The Pillar Hall of Enna IV, at Uruk, has two rows consisting of four large-diameter brick columns. The columns are coated with a thick layer of mud plaster and decorated with colored terra-cotta made to imitate basketry or reed matting.

inserts. Somewhat conical in shape, these fingerlike objects, which ranged in size from 3 to 12 inches long (8–30 cm), had their flat ends dipped in red, yellow, and black paint. Placed side by side with their points thrust into the soft clay (**1.29**), the stones not only formed a hard crust with their flat ends, which protected the mud-brick from erosion, but also formed an ornamental mosaic pattern of diamonds and triangles that resembled woven reeds of the earlier shelters (**1.30**). Experiments to decorate the ziggurat continued over time—first by hollowing the heads of the terra-cotta objects and later by adding a coloring agent to the indents.[51] Interestingly, cones of hard-baked Nile mud have also been found at Buto, an ancient site located in the northern delta.

The Sun and the Niche

The temples at Eridu probably had a function similar to those found elsewhere in the world; that is, they were oriented to allow the sun to illuminate the niche on the inside wall at some significant time of the year. Although little is left of the structures, later cylinder seals and carved reliefs indicate the existence of window openings high up between buttresses, no doubt to permit the entry of light (**1.35**).[52] The illuminated niche may have been used to signal any of several events: the solstices, time of the floods, or the rainy season. Although rain is not frequent in Mesopotamia, the more arid alluvial plains of south

Mesopotamia receive enough January rain to support a small crop of cereals.[53] With advanced knowledge of rainfall or the rising of rivers, the farming community could clear the heavily silted irrigation canals in advance of planting.

According to archaeologists, Mesopotamian temples in Ur, Uruk, and elsewhere have their axes oriented to the northeast to catch the prevailing winds or, perhaps, for some unknown religious reason.[54] The uncertain purpose of the niche is also reflected in the inconsistency of its direction—some face toward the southeast and others toward the northwest, opposite points of the compass. Indeed, an unusual directional change is seen at Eridu. For some reason, the first temple with a niche (Level XVI) was oriented to the southeast, while subsequent temples built at the same site have niches that face to the northeast. The niches face what may generally be described as solstitial directions, suggesting a search for the rising or setting sun on days six months apart. This would be puzzling but for the fact that the Near East offers two crops within a solar year. Periods of rainfall to help their growth were celebrated by New Year's festivals that could be held in the spring as well as in the fall, the choice of orientation probably being dictated by the local priesthood.[55]

The association between the New Year's festivals and the periods of rain is found in the Talmud. It shows the link in Jewish tradition between the creation of the world and the New Year's festivities in Tishri and Nisan, both months including the beginning of a new harvest. The treatise of Rosh Hashanah says the time of rainfall is in Tishri (7th month in the Jewish calendar) and Nisan (1st month in the Jewish calendar). The rebirth of the fields is linked in the Talmud not only with rainstorms and the New Year but also with the raising of the dead—an idea of death and resurrection that still survives in religions originating in the Near East.[56]

The Eanna Temple (Levels V–IVb), dated from 3200 BCE, displays a rather advanced cruciform floor plan. Instead of having the usual niche at the end of the temple axis, a constricted passageway (which in a sense may be considered a niche) leads to a terminus chamber. This construction serves a purpose similar to the small-diameter portholes used in the tropical zone used to find the zenith sun—it restricts the entry of light to a smaller segment of the year. Presumably, the privilege of watching the altar or a statue of the god being illuminated was an honor reserved for those high in the priesthood (**1.31**).

Mythology

The same solar interest structurally exhibited in the temples is also suggested by the cultural legends of Mesopotamia. Judging from our own time, beliefs held by a people tend to remain unchanged for millennia. If the basic characteristics of Mesopotamian temples were retained over the years, despite their increased size and more elaborate style, it seems reasonable to suppose that the myths encouraging their construction were also retained. An examination of scenes and texts concerning these myths may therefore reveal stories reflecting the techniques that helped the people to survive—perhaps by the described link between the temple niche and the sun.

Central to Mesopotamian thought was the need to serve the gods and to construct a place of residence for their worship. Toward this endeavor, each town had a special deity

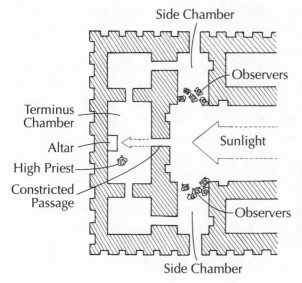

Figure 1.31. In an advanced design, a constricted passage takes the place of the usual niche. During a significant period of the year sunlight would enter the opening and illuminate the altar in the terminus chamber, permitting observers to view the event without interfering with the incoming sunlight.

to watch over its well-being and was dominated by one shrine or more. For example, Babylon, the capital of Mesopotamia under Hammurabi (1792–1750 BCE), was the cult center of the god Marduk, "he who created grain and plants and made green things to grow." Marduk was the supreme ruler who absorbed the duties and functions of all other gods and who organized the universe and fixed the course of the heavenly bodies. He was the son of a god variously called Ea, or Enki, a name meaning "House of the water." In the spring of each year Marduk's statue was solemnly carried to a temple called the Akitu, a word that means a new beginning in the annual cycle. The statue remained in place for an eleven-day ceremony, the theme of which was Marduk's death, resurrection, and marriage—a ritual ancient even for that time and representing the growing cycle. As a god of vegetation, Marduk was thought to live in a ziggurat as a temporary tomb. Each morning before sunrise during the holy season, the high priest would enter the inner sanctum, called the "Holy of Holies," to pray for his release. Following days of sacrifice, atonement, and purification, the god was liberated to bring the rainy season and another year of survival.[57]

Not only does the festival serve to encourage and celebrate the seasonal cycles; it signifies victory of the gods over chaos at the beginning of time and the renewal of natural life in the present. In a curious part of the ceremony, the king, who was always present on important occasions, was slapped by the priest. If tears were provoked, symbolizing rain, it was considered a good omen.[58] The foregoing seems to suggest that the mythology of Mesopotamia is based on efforts to track the seasons by the arrival of sunlight in the niche located in the Holy of Holies.

Ziggurats as Mountains

As elsewhere in the world, Mesopotamians considered mountains to be places where the potency of the earth was located and built structures to serve as their replicas. This is illustrated in the names given to ziggurats: at Eridu, the towering ziggurat of the storm god Enlil was called "House of the mountain," "Mountain of the storm," or the "Bond between heaven and earth."[59] The ziggurat supposedly stood for the mountain, as a symbol of the earth, the nether world, or the place of sunrise, a relationship also shown in an Akkadian relief from an earlier time in which Shamash, the sun-god, is liberated at dawn from between two mountains (1.12).[60] Akkadian is a Semitic tongue that can be traced back to its first appearance (3000 BCE) in Mesopotamia. Other Akkadian scenes seem to commemorate the New Year's festival as a new beginning, prevailing over the powers of evil with the resurrection of Tammuz, a god of vegetation from an earlier time.[61]

After centuries of adding new temples to old, the layered additions evolved into massive Sumerian ziggurats that dominated cities of the period. A ziggurat built for the moon god, Nanna (about 2000 BCE), measured 205 × 141 feet at its base and had a height of about 62 feet (62 × 43 × 19 m) (1.32).[62] Its several stages were distinguished by inward-leaning revetments of recesses and buttresses about 8 feet (2.4 m) thick. Made of mud brick, set in bitumen to make it waterproof, the entire mass was reinforced with a number of heavy twisted reed cables laid at right angles above every few courses. Layers of reeds or matting placed between every five or so courses also allowed the mass of mud brick to contract and expand with changes in temperature and humidity.[63] Similar layers of reeds were found in the Early Dynasties of Egypt, with their first use of mud brick in monumental architecture.

Besides the small room in Eridu giving evidence of a people building structures dedicated to the worship of a deity, the material culture of the Ubaid period also shows industrial skills and creative abilities with stone and clay implements—pottery, metalworking, carpentry, hoes, adzes, sickles, bricks, and figurines. This culture had itself developed from those of Hajji Muhammad and the Halaf period—the former probably from south Iran, the latter noted for building circular structures. Coming to flower with the help of improved irrigation techniques, the Ubaid culture spread over the whole of Mesopotamia by 4500 BCE, when it became the basis of the Uruk period, a time when great city-states began to form. Famous among these was Uruk (Erech in biblical times and today known as Warka), a city that reached an estimated population of 10,000 inhabitants by the end of the 4th

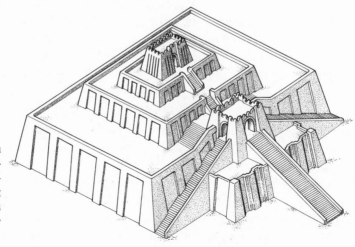

Figure 1.32. Reconstruction of the greatest Sumerian ziggurat. Begun by King Ur-Nammu, of Ur, the ziggurat of the moon god, Nanna, was finished about 2000 BCE by his son, Shulgi.

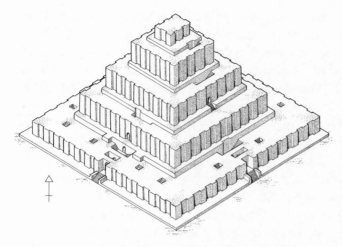

Figure 1.33. Reconstruction of the ziggurat of the Elamite king Untashgal. Preserved to a height of 82 feet (25 m), it was found to have several thousand glazed bricks and pegs at the foot of the structure.

millennium. The growth was probably brought about by the constant warfare and competition between Uruk and other cities, such as Ur and Umma. At Uruk, archaeologists found occupation levels with distinctive painted pottery and large buildings constructed of sun-dried and baked mud bricks. Much of the knowledge gleaned about the city of Uruk is based on information from their Elamite-speaking neighbors in Susa, a possible client state in southwestern Iran.

As with all societies that came into contact with the ideas that sprouted from the Mesopotamian alluvium, by the time of the Jemdet Nasr period (3200–3000 BCE), the Elamites were overwhelmed by its culture.[64] Founded by the Elamite king Untashgal, the city of Dur Untashi had a massive ziggurat about 140 feet high (43 m). Seen at the foot of the structure were thousands of glazed pegs and bricks that had probably fallen to the ground from the facade of the temple.[65] Departing from the usual Mesopotamian practice of using outside stairways, the staircases at this monument were built at a number of places within the ziggurat itself (1.33). Assuming that the renderings of the Sumerian and the Elamite ziggurats are correct, the set-back levels, particularly those of the Elamite ziggurat, exhibit a striking resemblance to the step pyramids of Egypt.

At Khafaje, a site east of Baghdad, where only the foundations of the temple platform and its oval enclosure walls have survived, the Oval Temple stands out as unique. Built in the Early Dynastic III period, it is a vast oval-shaped area composed of a double wall of bricks. Separating the religious from the secular is a *temenos* wall (the Greek term implies this separation) that once contained a large (maximum dimension 328 feet [100 m]) artificial platform holding a shrine. Amazingly, the platform area was sanctified prior to construction by excavating it to a depth of 15 feet (4.6 m) and replacing the soil with an enormous quantity of clean sand brought from outside the city (1.34).[66] The temenos wall and the oval structure built on a layer of clean white sand are contemporaneous with Hierakonpolis, an early site in Egypt.

Each of these massive ziggurats had at its apex a temple to receive the god when he was high in the air and at its foot a low temple to receive him when he came to earth. The topmost shrine of the ziggurat was called *shakhuru*, which means a "waiting room," or "room one passes through"—a room where the manifestation of the god was awaited.[67]

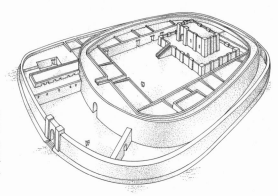

Figure 1.34. Rendering of the Oval Temple at Khafaje. Enclosed by a double-wall temenos, the entire area was sanctified before construction by excavating the soil and replacing it with clean sand brought from outside the city.

As with the mythology of Mesopotamia, this description indicates that the god who was expected was represented by a ray of sunlight that illuminated a niche in the upper temple at sunrise. It would also probably enter an opening in the lower temple at the base when the sun reached its zenith at noon.

Mesopotamia's Spreading Influence

The Jemdet Nasr and combined Late Uruk periods did not experience the great technological revolution wrought by the Ubaid and Early Uruk period; however, the dramatic use during this time of baked brick, terra-cotta, and fresco painting suggests an infusion of ideas from a foreign invasion.[68] The conflict may have inspired the Jemdet Nasr culture to extend their long reach, either directly or by intermediaries, to Oman, where Jemdet Nasr–type funeral vessels were found, and to Naqada and Hiw, in Egypt, where Mesopotamian-style cylinder seals were discovered from the Gerzean periods.[69] To ensure a constant supply of raw materials for their industries, the Jemdet Nasr rulers or intermediaries established a presence in places stretching from central Turkey to the southwest Arabian plateau, the northern highlands of Iran, and Syria.[70] Located in far-flung areas, these groups formed self-sufficient settled communities, evidence of which appears in the unique style of architecture, the iconography, and finds of mass-produced unpainted pottery made on a true potter's wheel (**1.35**).

Side by side with Sumer on the alluvial plain of southwest Iran, Susiana is a culture named after the city of Susa, founded at the end of the Uruk period. Excavations there have uncovered artifacts from the Late Uruk culture of Sumer.[71] Indeed, the successful Sumerian effort to dominate critical overland lines of trade and communication is shown by Uruk clusters at Habuba and Aruda on the border of Syria and Turkey, north of the modern town of Meskene.[72] In some cases the finds are dramatic and far-reaching—a horned temple in Susiana dedicated to worship of the bull (**1.35, F**) has its counterpart in Cätal Hüyük in southern Turkey, about a thousand miles away. As is suggested by these enclaves and temples, firm control of the Syro-Mesopotamian plains was important not only because of the great agricultural potential of the surrounding area but also because it provided a juncture for routes from the Iranian and Anatolian plateaus. Aided by the Tigris, the Euphrates, and their tributaries, superhighways of the day, Sumerians were

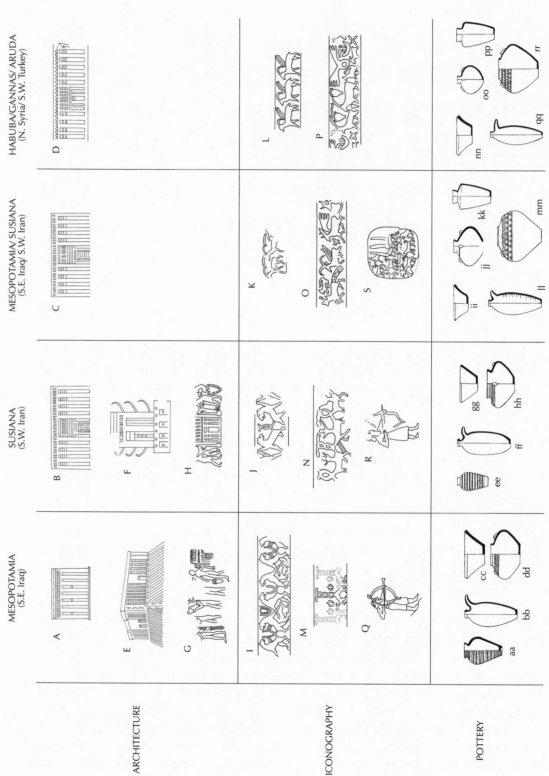

Figure 1.35. The similarity of architecture (A–H), iconography (L–S) and pottery (aa–rr) inspired by the culture of the Mesopotamian alluvium, and

provided with routes that extended from the Persian Gulf to the Mediterranean, Black, and Caspian seas.

Although life in southern Mesopotamia may have been difficult, the challenges presented and the solutions produced were the primary factors in the development of the culture, a civilization so advanced that it left its mark on all who came in contact with it. To reiterate these people's achievements: several millennia after settlement of Mesopotamia, writing began, and buildings worthy of being called great architecture were erected. These inventions, the basis of modern civilization, would not have been made without the stable communities brought about by artificial irrigation. The circumstances required to make irrigation work also brought people into close proximity and made small farms into the seeds of great cities by offering mutual protection, economic cooperation, and the dissemination of knowledge. The excess food produced enabled some people to add to invention by specializing in occupations separate from the production of food. For this to have occurred required that the fields be prepared and the canals be freed of silt—an effort best accomplished by knowing in advance the time of the rainy season or overflowing rivers. To help forecast these events, people made use of a niche, a device that helped locate the sun's position in the sky. When made in mud brick, the niche also seems to have been the genesis of monumental architecture in the Near East that later spread to the land of Egypt.

CHAPTER 2

EGYPT

If the Mesopotamians were an anxious people, fearful of what tomorrow might bring, the Egyptians could afford to be optimistic about life in general and about death in particular. These diametrically opposite attitudes were shaped by the rivers that flowed through their lands. While the twin rivers of Mesopotamia were wild, unpredictable, and completely out of phase with the growing season, the Egyptian river, although sometimes too high and sometimes too low, flooded with an annual cycle that made it ideal for the propagation of crops. With the overflowing Nile a mineral-rich silt brought down from the highlands of Ethiopia annually replenished the soil. To produce a bountiful crop in the Nile Delta or along the banks of the river, it was necessary only to trample some seeds into the soft mud left by the receding waters and wait for them to sprout. In time, to increase the amount of arable land, the country became a latticework of canals, ditches, sluices, and dikes. With this system of water retention and control, the narrow strip of land bordering the Nile became one of the richest and most stable food-producing areas in the ancient world (2.1).

Despite this advantage, it took longer for agriculture to succeed in Egypt and Nubia than in Mesopotamia. Although farming began in the Near East about 9000 BCE, the inhabitants of Egypt remained a hunting and gathering society, judging by the microlithic technology uncovered there. The few early indications of grain show a dramatic decline before an effective domestic crop was produced. This may have been due to a climatic change that brought dangerous floods to the bottomlands of the Nile valley—a change indicated by the tiny stone tools of the hunter-gatherer being replaced by the grinding stones and sickle blades of early farmers. The limited supply of game brought by the climatic change, and the competition provoked between rival bands of hunters, can be observed at grave sites, where over 40 percent of the human remains are the result of arrow wounds.[1]

The early failure to produce a domestic grain crop deprived the Egyptians of a basic form of sustenance. Not only can the mealy part of grain provide a stable food supply; a

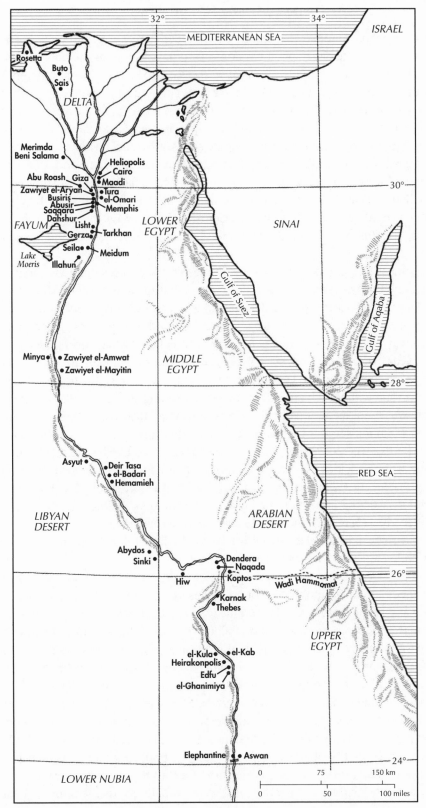

Figure 2.1. Map of Egypt from the Nile Delta to the First Cataract.

small portion set aside for sowing can be used to seed a new crop and provide an ongoing supply of food. The development of domestic grain also opens the door of the proto-
farmer to the concept of harvest. Because wild grasses put out seeds at different times,
there is a great advantage in planting a single strain of domestic cereal crop, row on row,
in a cultivated field. With the plants maturing at the same time, the harvester is free from
the interference of other plants, making the crop plants easier to gather. Additionally, if
the stems of the cereal plants are cut with ripe seeds still attached when harvested, they
can more easily be taken to a threshing ground where they are winnowed. Winnowing is
the process of separating grain by beating the husk with a flail and letting the wind blow
away the light grassy chaff. The seed, or mealy part inside of the hull, can then be separated from its hard protective cover by being crushed between two flattened stones. Freed
in this way, the fruit can be stored for future use and can be pulverized and baked at any
time.

The domestication of cereal crops was the result of a process that took thousands of
years before it brought about the genetic changes that make it economically beneficial.
When wild cereals ripen, they are self-propagating: their brittle heads burst and scatter the
sharp, spike-shaped seeds into crevices of the dry ground. This process, called shattering,
is nature's way of keeping seeds away from birds and allowing the growing cycle to repeat
year after year in the same area, but it makes grain extremely difficult to harvest. To facilitate the harvesting process, a standard method was to encourage the heads to shatter by
tapping the stem with a stick and collecting seeds in a bag as they fell. For millennia, this
procedure was employed for gathering seeds to sow the next crop. With this method of
collection, when the seeds were planted in distant areas, no genetic changes would have
occurred, for like wild seeds, they came from shattered heads. This changed with invention of the sickle. Originally a straight tool with a flint cutting edge embedded in bone or
wood, it was later curved to encompass a bundle of stalks more readily (**2.2**). When a stem
is cut with a sickle the impact on the head is reduced, making it less likely to burst and
scatter its seeds. As a result, when sickle-cut seeds are sown in areas distant from the self-
shattering variety, natural selection tends to favor the firmer nonshattering kind, a distin-
guishing characteristic of domestic cereals.[2]

At about 7000 BCE a wetter climatic phase brought dangerous floods that drove people from the Nile Valley into the surrounding desert. What would ordinarily have been
extremely arid terrain was favored for a time with more rainfall and a higher water table,
which caused the desert to bloom and enabled the farmer-herders to settle at sites distant from the Nile. While the amount of rain they enjoyed would be considered small by
most standards, only 2 inches (5 cm) of rainfall per year is needed to turn desert into ver-
dant pasturage almost overnight. The ability of plant life to survive under arid conditions
is shown by the wadis (dried river beds) around Cairo, where 22 different species of plants
live despite rainfall below even this small amount. With runoff from surrounding highlands factored in, plant and animal life is known to exist on as little as one inch (2.5 cm)
of rainfall annually.[3] Possibly it was during this wet phase that animals (sheep, goats,
and pigs) and major crops (wheat, barley, and flax) that had been domesticated successfully in the Near East at an earlier time were brought across the Sinai Peninsula to
Egypt.[4]

Predynastic Cultures

The Egyptian state is understood to have evolved from two main groups of people from the Predynastic period who came from opposite parts of the land, Upper Egypt in the south and Lower Egypt in the north, the terms referring to the upper reaches of the Nile and lower country near its delta. People in the north were separated from the southern group by an expanse of sand about 155 miles (249 km) wide. The northern group is represented in a geographical area between Cairo and Fayum and at a single site in the delta, Merimda Beni Salama. Due to large deposits of sediment brought down from the highlands of Ethiopia, many sites in the alluvial plain remain buried and undiscovered. However, recent excavations in the delta indicate it to be an area where settlement flourished in Predynastic and Early Dynastic times through trading with Near Eastern neighbors. Indeed, future findings in the delta may yet overturn current archaeological wisdom.

Today, most scholars consider the 2,500 or so years of the Predynastic period to show a steady progression in the Upper Egyptian culture from the Badarian to the Early Dynastic, instead of a sudden invasion or migration. While this may be so, strong evidence from the earliest time suggests a continuing influx of Near Eastern and Mediterranean people—migrations that came in spurts or in a slow but steady stream, according to the stimulus that drove them. The new arrivals changed the nature of the native populations of northern

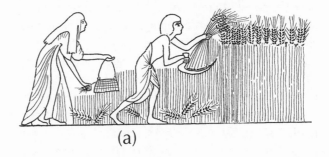

(a)

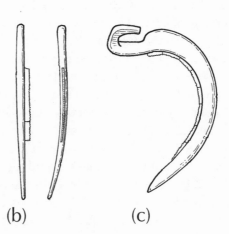

Figure 2.2. (a) Harvesting scene from a tomb at Deir el-Medina. (b) Straight sickle bone with flint teeth inserts from Fayum. (c) Curved wood sickle from Saqqara.

(b)   (c)

Africa. Even today, such population movements are a natural response to famine or strife. People make desperate land and sea journeys toward a more hopeful future, and although their arrival may be met with resentment and conflict, their genes and beliefs eventually blend in, changing both the native populations and themselves.

The early native cultures of Egypt did not themselves develop uniformly across the country, nor did they follow the course of the Nile. There are signs of hunter-gatherers living in the western desert from Abu Simbel, about 150 miles (241 km) south of Aswan, to the Fayum depression in the north, a spread of about 500 miles (800 km), Fayum A being the oldest known culture in the northern Predynastic sequence. These bands of hunter-gatherers left signs of extensive trade or travel: their marine shells from the Mediterranean and Red Sea and beads that may have come from the eastern desert or deep in the heart of the Sahara. Some sites have threshing implements, sickles, and communal granaries of mud-lined pits, which still show the remains of emmer, wheat, and barley.[5] Possessing tools not previously used in Egypt, such sites suggest that a new people had come into the area.

In the north of Egypt, Merimda Beni Salama was a delta site initially settled in 4880 BCE, near the Rosetta branch of the Nile. Merimda is the earliest evidence of fully sedentary village life in the Nile Valley. Contemporary with Fayum A, the site was occupied continually for about 650 years. Its strong foreign connections are shown by the mixing of herds (oxen, goats, and sheep) and by shelters of conically roofed wicker, wood, and mud houses—all of which are reminiscent of the farming areas of what is now southern Israel or of the coast of Libya. Approximately contemporary with the final occupation of Merimda is a group of settlements and cemeteries at el-Omari, located near the town of Helwan. According to their age, the Egyptologist M. Hoffman calls three of the sites Omari A, B, and C. The oldest, Omari A, shows signs of foreign ties with its ornamental objects such as pendants and beads from the Red Sea. Omari B was settled near two natural catchment basins at about the middle of the 4th millennium—a location that may indicate a desire to make use of every natural advantage or may have been an adaptation to diminishing rainfall. North of the el-Omari group is Maadi, a site spanning a period contemporary with the cultures of Naqada I and II of Upper Egypt. Its underground houses show it to have ties to Beersheba in southern Israel. Located near what is now a southern suburb of Cairo, the site was a trading post near the main road from Egypt to what would become Palestine and then Israel. This location made the Maadi site accessible to the Nile, the coast of the Mediterranean, and the eastern desert. Indeed, remains at the site suggest a foreign trade stretching from the western Mediterranean to the Indus Valley.[6]

In southern Egypt, the increased rainfall may have encouraged the sudden arrival in 5600 BCE of the Badarians at Hemamieh, only a few centuries after less advanced groups (el-Kabians) were hunting, fishing, and scavenging along the Nile. The site was occupied from the Badarian to the Gerzean period (5000–3500 BCE) by people who lived in tents and had objects and customs that contrasted sharply with those of other groups in the south (2.3).[7] The red-polished, blackened-top pottery they manufactured, seen in figure 2.3(p), was thinner than anything previously found. Both sexes wore jewelry, were clothed in linen, and used face paint of green malachite, a cosmetic ground on a slate palette and mixed to a paste with castor seed oil. Their desert cemeteries of shallow graves, located at a distance from the overflowing Nile, held bodies wrapped in goat skins or reed mats. By

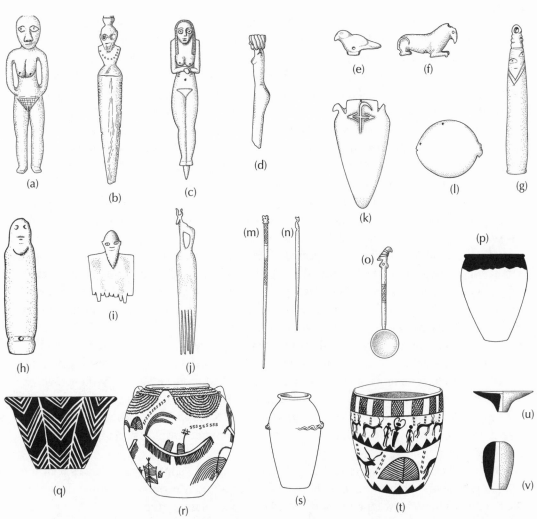

Figure 2.3. Artifacts typical of several Predynastic periods. (a) Ivory figure of a woman from Badari. (b) Woman with jar on head, carved from a hippopotamus incisor, from Naqada. (c) Bone figurine from Naqada. (d) Clay figure of woman from Abadiya. (e) Sandstone or faience figure of bird from Naqada. (f) Possible Seth animal from Naqada. (g) Tusk from Naqada with bearded face. (h) Tusk from Naqada shaped into head with beard. (i) Ivory comb from Naqada. (j) Comb with animal, from Naqada. (k) Slate palette with symbol of the god Min, opposing arrows overlying a bent staff. (l) Fish-shaped slate palette from Tell el-Amarna. (m) Decorated bone hairpin from Naqada. (n) Bone hairpin with bird, from Abadiya. (o) Bone spoon with falcon, from Naqada. (p) Red-polished pot with blackened top. (q) Red-polished pot with white line design. (r) Lug-handled jar decorated with boats, zigzag water lines, and strange s signs. (s) Wavy-handled vessel unprecedented in Egypt, but with a clear line of development from the Early Chalcolithic in Israel. (t) Jar with hills, gazelles, fan-like objects, ithyphallic men, and dancing women. (u) Disc-shaped diorite mace head from Abadiya. (v) Pear-shaped alabaster mace head from Naqada.

supplying the deceased with grave goods of pottery, cosmetics, slate palettes, ivory or bone combs, bone or faience figurines, and tools, they seem to have shown an early belief in the afterlife (**2.3**).[8] Faience is a nonclay ceramic that gets its color, usually a bright blue-green, from the use of copper.

Other sites in the south of Egypt suggest the blending of Mediterranean stock during Amratian times with the already blended African and Mediterranean people of the previous Badarian period. These Amratian or Naqada I period (4000–3500 BCE) sites extend from Deir Tasa to the Nubian border about 250 miles (402 km) to the south, with the most important sites located at Naqada and Hierakonpolis. The cemeteries show evidence of dismemberment and perhaps defleshing, which, among less pleasant thoughts, may have been an effort to avoid decay of the body. Grave goods consist of small, beautifully carved ivory combs, finely chipped flint tools, vessels of hard stone, disc-shaped maceheads, and hippopotamus tusks carved into the likeness of bearded men (**2.3**). Although their red-polished pottery with white cross-lined designs rarely depicts humans, by the Amratian period men are shown with penis sheaths and wearing feathers in their hair. Outerwear similar to this is known from the distant prehistoric Mediterranean culture of Crete and was worn in historic times by Libyans and Nubians.[9]

By the Gerzean or Naqada II period (3500 BCE), rapid changes occurred—changes indicating strong Near Eastern intrusion or influence. Human figures completely new to Egypt began to appear on pottery: lines of hills, females dancing with arms upraised, and ithyphallic male figures. The erect member of the latter in figure 2.3(**t**) evokes the fertility god Min of Koptos, discussed later in this chapter, a god of major importance in the Egyptian pantheon. The pottery also shows drawings of plants, sycamore trees, ostriches, gazelles, water, spirals, a strange recurring s sign, and boats with cabins displaying standards of various emblems, as seen in figure 2.3(**r**).[10] Without precedent in Egypt, wavy-handled vessels from this site, as in figure 2.3(**s**), show a clear line of development from the Early Chalcolithic period (4000–3600 BCE) in Israel. Copper, from a source in the Sinai Peninsula, appears in a wide variety of cast and hammered artifacts ranging from daggers to finger rings.[11]

In Naqada I, the replacement of native Egyptian disc-shaped mace heads with the larger pear-shaped mace heads imitative of Susiana and Mesopotamia show the speed with which a superior weapon is adopted when it proves its worth. Though the stone disc can impact with deadly cutting force, the clublike foreign mace head seen in figure 2.3(**v**), with its greater weight and larger strike-face, is a more effective weapon. Among the additional finds are numerous slate palettes, arrow heads, and necklaces; hairpins and ivory spoons shown in figure 2.3(**m–o**); baked clay figures, animal amulets, and throwing sticks. Ancient grave robbers plundered these graves selectively; their knowledge of the exact location of the grave goods suggests that they may have been in the burial party.[12] At Hierakonpolis the plunderers were able to tunnel directly to the neck of the deceased, make a small slit, and remove whatever object was located there.[13] The profession of grave robbing, which goes back at least to the Badarian period, probably began with the burial of the first object of value.[14]

Recent field work at the cemetery at Hierakonpolis has unearthed an unprecedented find: a Naqada I tomb shared by a man, his dogs, and a juvenile elephant. In a possible hunting ritual, the elephant was the first laid to rest, perhaps in an attempt to bring back the steadily disappearing game animals. The flourishing savanna fauna, including giraffes, ostriches, and elephants, seem to have changed drastically by Naqada II, when a decrease in rainfall led to their disappearance. In the same cemetery, pottery masks unique in the

Prehistoric repertoire were found in a so-called robber's tomb. One was a catlike mask fragment, the other a mask of a man's face. Both have eye and mouth openings and depressions for the nostrils. The mask of the man is bearded and Asian in appearance.[15]

Showing a steadily growing economy, no doubt stimulated by new foreign ideas, the increasingly large graves discovered seem to fill a requirement that the wealth of the deceased be reflected in the quality of the grave goods. Roofed with branches capped with low mounds of dirt, the new tomb-style burial sites show rectangular walls lined with brick and coated with mud plaster or wooden boards. Where previously a pit large enough for just one body had sufficed, this now expanded to a 12 × 8-foot (3.7 × 2.4 m) sepulcher. Possibly showing an early belief in the location of the "land of the dead," the heads were generally positioned at the south end of the tomb, the face turned to the west. Though embalming is not yet evident, the hot dry sands of the desert preserved the untreated bodies much better than the natron later used by official embalmers. Remains of the deceased show short, beardless people of mixed race with long hair, looking much like representations of the dynastic Egyptians shown in later drawings and sculpture and much as people of the region appear today.[16]

Table 2.1 gives a chronology based on evidence from the cemeteries in the north and south. The Mesopotamian periods of Uruk and Jemdet Nasr are contemporary with Naqada I and Naqada II in Egypt.

Early Building

Early Egyptians were protected from the elements by the flimsiest of structures. While no prehistoric buildings remain intact in Egypt, evidence of their past existence is seen in the postholes, steps, and ground plans left behind. Representations of the structures are seen in paintings, hieroglyphs, models found in contemporary graves, and in later stone buildings imitating the earlier ones of perishable materials. They all show early structures consisting of tents made of skins or reed matting supported by simple pole frameworks (**2.4**), perhaps even similar to the reed house in figure 1.27. At times, as shown by the hieroglyphic word for "booth," shelters were made of long bundles of reeds shaped as a roof and held up by a forked pole. Being readily available during the marshy Predynastic period,

Table 2.1

PREDYNASTIC CHRONOLOGY OF ANCIENT EGYPT,
BASED ON PRESENT ESTIMATES

DATE (BCE)	UPPER EGYPT	LOWER EGYPT
3100–3000	Protodynastic	Protodynastic
3300–3100	Late Gerzean (Naqada II)	Late Gerzean/Maadian
3500–3300	Early Gerzean (Naqada II)	Omari B?
4000–3500	Amratian (Naqada I)	Omari A?
5000–4000	Badarian	Merimda/Fayum A

After Michael Hoffman, *Egypt Before the Pharoahs*, 16, table 2.

Figure 2.4. Overview of Predynastic shelters taken from their remains on various sites, sealing impressions, hieroglyphs, scenes, and models. (a) Tentlike shelter from Narmer's mace head. (b) Hieroglyph for booth. (c) Seal from Abydos with lean-to shelter. (d) Hieroglyphs of shrine-huts. (e) Shrine-hut sealing of King Qa from Abydos. (f) Wooden label from King Aha. (g) Ivory of King Den with tower of possible fortification. (h) Ivory of early reed hut. (i) Two-story house with Khekher-style ornamentation on roof. (j) Predynastic pit shelter in Maadi. (k) Egyptianized shrine of Min with spiral extending to the horned standard. (l) Circular foundations of hut dwellings at Hemamieh. (m) Clay model of a mud hut. (n) Model house at El-Amrah with wood-framed doors and windows. (o) Ivory of King Djer with Mesopotamian-style facade. (p) Cylinder seal from Naqada, a structure of reeds and Mesopotamian-style facade. (q) Sealing of King Djer of structure shaped like an elephant, with Mesopotamian facade.

reeds were an adaptable building material. They could be woven into simple portable shelters that could be disassembled and transported to higher ground during the inundation. Some shrines are shown by hieroglyphs to have curvilinear roofs or bundles of lily or papyrus stalks projecting up from a flat roof. These were later transformed into curved roofs, buttresses, and cavetto cornices of stone.[17] Rising two stories, the so-called Khekher-style house in figure 2.4(**i**) shows stalks ornamentally bundled together and protruding through the roof at spaced intervals.[18]

Masonry, though rare at this time in Egypt, can be found in the more permanent pre-dynastic shelters of Maadi. Lined with posts to support a roof of woven mats, these shelters have slanted stepped entrances, seen in figure 2.4(**j**), dug into the subsoil and faced with stone.[19] In Hemamieh, the dome-roofed shelters of wattle-and-daub construction have low circular walls built of a mixture of mud, local limestone chips, and blocks.[20] Such layers of facing masonry were used to reinforce the low peripheral walls of above-ground shelters throughout Africa. Generally, these huts were constructed of reeds tied together on top and placed on sunken circular floors, reinforced by a rim of plaster or dry-laid stone to prevent erosion. When coated with mud, their conical shapes are reminiscent of the shrine of the god Min before the addition of Egyptian accouterments—the additions consisting of an entrance, a horned standard, and a spiral extending from the hut to tie all the elements together. This style of hut, its bulbous top enclosing the bundled and mud-encased reed ends, may have been the genesis for the white crown the king of Upper Egypt wears in figure 2.12(**a**); indeed, the spiral extending from the hut to the horned standard in figure 2.4(**k**) has been adapted in the king's crown as a symbol of the sun in figure 2.17. The symbols of Min and their unusual links to the sun are discussed later.

Although there was already a long history of building with mud brick in Mesopotamia, little evidence for its use is found in Egypt except as possibly indicated on one or two small clay models with thin walls. The model illustrated in figure 2.4(**a**) shows a rectangular house with doors and windows framed in wood. The first demonstration of use of mud brick on a practical scale occurs in the Late Predynastic period, when it was employed in Egypt to face the walls of underground tombs. Amazingly, just after these tentative beginnings, mud brick is found in a massive thick wall completely encircling the city of Hierakonpolis. The leap in technology from use of mud brick as a facing material to construction of a massive free-standing wall suggests a long period of building development as yet undiscovered—or its introduction by a people new to the area but long practiced in use of mud brick.

The closest prior use of mud-brick construction in Egypt, other than in the clay models, is suggested by two cylinder-seal impressions of the 1st Dynasty. The one from Naqada in figure 2.4(**p**) shows a building with brick or wood panels on the lower half supporting the bent hoops of a wattle roof. The other, a sealing of King Djer shown in figure 2.4(**q**), is an odd combination of native and foreign building styles in a structure imitative of an elephant with tusks and a tail. Suggesting the blending of two different building methods, both contain indications of the building facades seen in Mesopotamia or in areas under its influence (**1.35**). Such facades are also seen in drawings of the *serekh*, an early frame-like symbol of Egyptian kingship containing the king's Horus name (**2.18, 2.19**).

Another unusual device found in the 4th millennium city of Hierakonpolis is the temenos, separating the sacred sector from the secular, comparable to similar structures found in Uruk and elsewhere in Mesopotamia.[21]

Other Links to Mesopotamia

Naqada, about 17 miles (26 km) north of Thebes, and Hierakonpolis, about 50 miles (80 km) south of Thebes, are two cities in Upper Egypt strewn with evidence from the Predynastic period. The burial chambers at these locations suggest the presence of local kings. They exhibit craft work of new design in many media (metal, stone, ivory, etc.), have wheel-turned pottery, and display a large range of imported items.[22] Tomb 100 at Hierakonpolis is the earliest decorated tomb yet found in Egypt; unfortunately, its exact location is no longer known due to a poorly recorded excavation by its discoverers, J. E. Quibell and F. W. Green. This "Painted Tomb" has a mural on one wall of a complex scene—a procession of ships with both high and low prows and men shown in single combat or hunting and trapping wild animals. The lower left corner shows three bound captives being dispatched with blows from a mace, the first appearance of a theme later used throughout Egyptian history to show the king dominating his enemies (**2.5, 2.6**). It also shows a man subduing a pair of lions barehanded, a "master of animals" theme new to Egypt but shown

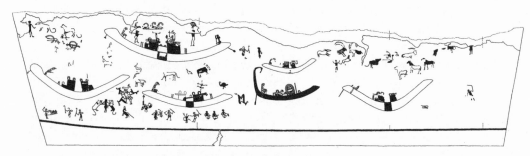

Figure 2.5. Scene from wall on Tomb 100 at Hierakonpolis.

Figure 2.6. Detail of three bound captives dispatched with a mace, and "master of animals" theme.

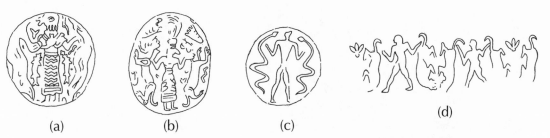

(a) (b) (c) (d)

Figure 2.7. Master of animals theme as it appears in Mesopotamia. (a) On a round button seal of Susa I, with snakes and fish. (b) With two lions. (c) With two snakes, from Iran. (d) On a cylinder seal with lions, from Susa.

earlier in seals from Sumer and Susa (**2.7**). At times, instead of a man as master, the same theme shows a lion as the dominant creature.[23] The master of animals theme also appears on the Gebel-el-Arak knife handle, an object found in Egypt, south of Abydos, decorated with the motifs of Mesopotamia: a frieze of animals and a lion attacking his prey. The obverse side of the handle shows men in combat and a battle between what may be identified as high-prow vessels of the Near East and low-profile vessels of Egypt (**2.8**).

Other objects found in Egypt show their foreign connections by means of a small flower with six to eight petals, a device often used in Mesopotamia as a decorative plaque in temples (**2.9**).[24] Elsewhere, it is found in Susan/Sumerian scenes portraying dominant or monstrous creatures or groups of hunted animals. In both kinds of scenes the small flower

Figure 2.8. Gebel-el-Arak knife handle with Mesopotamian themes. (a) Top register, master of animals theme; second register, opposing animals; third and fifth registers, frieze of animals; fourth register, lion attacking passive prey. (b) Obverse side: Top half, men in single combat; bottom half, battle scene with high-prow Mesopotamian boats and low-prow Egyptian boats.

(a) (b)

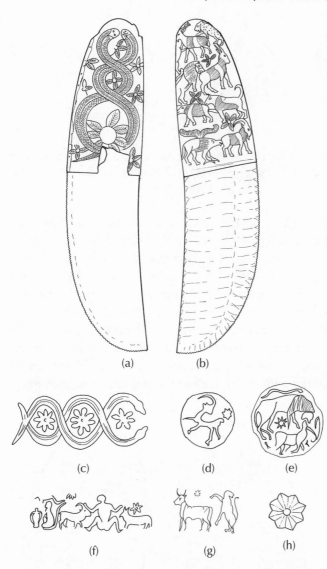

(a)   (b)

(c)   (d)   (e)

(f)   (g)   (h)

Figure 2.9. Florets on various objects. (a, b) A predynastic gold-foil knife, from Gebel-al-Tarif, Egypt, with entwined serpents, a lion attacking passive prey, and a winged griffin. (c) An archaic sealing with intertwined snakes from Susa. (d) With a cervine on a button seal from Iran. (e) Between two monstrous beasts. (f) With a master of animals theme. (g) With a lion attacking a bull, from predynastic Sumer. (h) As a decorative temple element, from the Uruk culture at Tell Brak.

seems to have represented something powerful or divine.[25] The same floret is seen on a gold-foil knife handle found in the Theban Hills at Gebel-el-Tarif, Egypt, which also exhibits other themes of pure Mesopotamian content: entwined serpents, and lions attacking passive prey. Although the knife handles of Gebel-el-Arak and Gebel-el-Tarif with their Mesopotamian themes may have arrived in Egypt by trade, the floret is also found on the Scorpion King mace head (**2.10**), an object with a decidedly Egyptian theme.

The mace head shows King Scorpion, considered to be an incarnation of the god Horus, attired in the garb of Upper Egyptian royalty as he uses a hoe in ritual opening of what may be the earliest irrigation canal yet recorded in Egypt.[26] In the Egyptian manner, the king is shown much larger in size than his attendants. Although he appears in the scene with a pictograph of the scorpion for which he is named, an Egyptian means of iden-

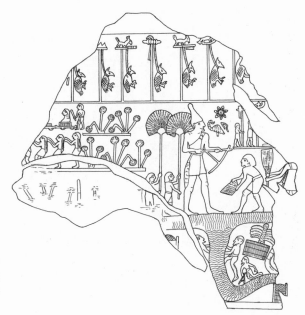

Figure 2.10. Mace head of the Scorpion King, showing opening of irrigation canal. The power of the king's station is indicated by a nearby floret ideogram.

tification, the power of his station is indicated in the Mesopotamia manner by a nearby floret ideogram. Egyptologists explain the floret as an early way of writing "Horus."[27] While it may be argued this object, like both knife handles, is small enough to have been fashioned in the Near East and brought to Egypt by trade, the mace head shows a scene devised and executed by an artisan with knowledge of both cultures.

Going well beyond the possibility of a trade item designed by a foreign craftsman is the city of Hierakonpolis, the very site in Egypt where the fragment of the Scorpion King mace head was uncovered. Once called Nekhen, Hierakonpolis flourished during the Late Predynastic and Early Dynastic periods (4000–2686 BCE). The location contains an oval mound in the temenos of the city, built sometime between the late Predynastic period (3000 BCE) and the 2nd or 3rd Dynasty (2700 BCE). This is an architectural device that could only have been built and used by a people strongly influenced by the Mesopotamian culture (**2.11**). Presumed originally to have supported a shrine, the Temple Oval is outlined by a revetment of unmortared courses of sandstone blocks, each set back from the one below to form a slope of about 45 degrees.[28] Astonishingly, this mound, 165 feet (50 m) wide and 8–10 foot (2–3 m) high, was built over a deliberately placed layer of white sand, as already noted. Used to sanctify the ground under the temple, the sand was completely free of the charcoal and potsherds found elsewhere in the area.[29] Although this strange architectural feature is unprecedented in Egypt, the oval mound and its clean sand underlayer are similar to those found at Al-Ubaid and Tepe Gawra[30] and are contemporary with the Oval Temple at Khafaje, Mesopotamia (**1.34**).[31] The concept of the oval structures dates back to the Ubaid people, who believed that certain areas of their cities were sacred for all time. When inherited by the Sumerians, this belief resulted in building one structure on the remains of another in the form of a ziggurat, the entire sacred site held within the confines of a wall.[32]

(a)

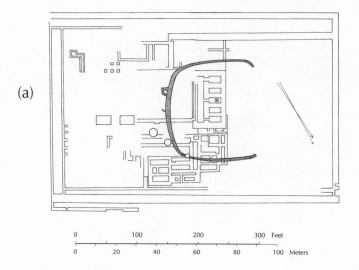

```
0            100          200          300  Feet
0    20      40      60      80      100  Meters
```

(b)

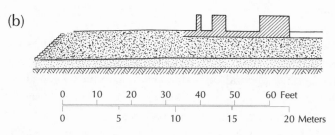

```
0    10    20    30    40    50    60  Feet
0         5         10        15        20 Meters
```

Figure 2.11. (a) Oval mound in Hierakonpolis built over a layer of clean white sand. (b) Section through the mound and revetment. Unprecedented in Egypt, the oval mound and base of clean sand are similar to and contemporary with the Temple Oval at Khafaje, Mesopotamia.

Narmer Palette

The south corner of Hierakonpolis contains a rectangular temple holding objects of great significance to Egypt's beginnings: the Two-Dog Head slate palette; a number of small, crudely made scorpions; some kneeling ibex; several carved mace heads; and most important, the Narmer Palette.[33] Showing the subjugation of the Nile Delta, the palette is an object stylistically dated to the Protodynastic period (3200–3100 BCE). An early ruler, Narmer is at times identified with Menes, founder of the Egyptian state and builder of the city of Memphis. One side of the large slate suggests a military campaign waged by the Egyptians against the Northerners, shown here as a bearded people (**2.12**). In Egyptian iconography, Northerners are identified as coming from Libya or the Near East; Libyans generally wear penis sheaths and have feathers in their hair.

The scene shows Narmer wearing the *hedjet*, or white crown of Upper Egypt, as he prepares to dispatch a kneeling Asian with a mace (a motif seen earlier at the Painted Tomb). A nearby floret signifies the power of the king. His victory over a defeated people of the delta (indicated by the papyrus grass) is shown by the king in the guise of Horus, the falcon, holding a cord tethered to the nose-ring of a defeated enemy. The bottom register shows the enemy fleeing from an indented rectangle, which represents a style of

(a)   (b)

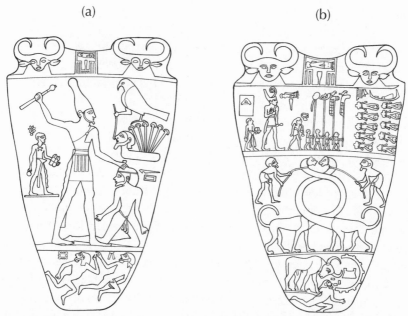

Figure 2.12. Headed by a symbol of paneled Mesopotamian architecture, the Narmer Palette shows the king in a military campaign against a bearded Asian enemy. (a) The king of Upper Egypt dispatches a kneeling captive with a mace. The king's power is signified by a floret near his upraised arm. The Horus-falcon leashes an enemy from the delta. The bottom register shows them fleeing from an indented structure styled after Mesopotamian temples. (b) The obverse side shows Narmer wearing the red crown of Upper Egypt in a victory procession with standards identifying participants as "Followers of Horus." The middle register has animals with the entwined serpent necks of Mesopotamia, leashed by their foreign handlers to signify surrender and compliance. The lower register shows the Egyptian king, in the guise of a bull, breaking into an oval structure similar to those of Hierakonpolis in Egypt and Khafaje in Mesopotamia.

brick architecture already shown to be associated with Mesopotamian temples. The serekh, or frame, at the head of both sides of the palette, holds a catfish, the Horus name of Narmer. It also displays the very style of facade earlier seen in drawings from the Near East.

The top register on the obverse side of the slate shows Narmer wearing the *deshert*, or red crown of Lower Egypt, in a victory procession (**2.12**). Preceded by bearers carrying standards identifying them as "Followers of Horus," the king is shown as he views the decapitated bodies of his enemies. The middle register contains two animals, with the iconographic entwined serpent necks of Mesopotamia, leashed by their foreign handlers to signify surrender and compliance. The lower register shows the Egyptian king, now in the guise of a bull, trampling the enemy as it breaks into an oval structure, scattering the brickwork of the revetment. Regardless of how this scene is interpreted—whether it involves a foreign people or a cult under the sway of some Near Eastern culture—it affirms that the oval structure on the Narmer Palette and found in Hierakonpolis, a city usually held to be the home of the Narmer Dynasty, was also used by the defeated enemies of the Egyptian king.[34]

Unification

By displaying the red crown of Lower Egypt together with the white crown of Upper Egypt, the Narmer Palette appears to be the earliest object yet discovered to commemorate unification of the north and south. It also suggests victory over an established and entrenched northern enemy in a conflict that may have contributed much to the continuing enmity toward Asians for the entire history of Egypt. Indeed, later scenes often portray vanquished Asian and African captives entwined in the tendrils of the combined papyrus plants of the north and lily of the south, a symbol of the two lands of Egypt united (**2.13**). Although it is natural for bordering cultures to be foes, such enmity would less likely exist with the more distant Asians unless they were a competing culture or had at one time intruded upon Egyptian soil. Possibly this hatred was reflected in the 26th Dynasty, when Cambyses, the Persian conquerer, whipped the mummy of the Egyptian King Amasis (526–520 BCE) and then burned him in his coffin.[35]

Further affirming the enemy portrayed in the Narmer Palette scenes as a people from the Near East is an ivory label commonly used to mark royal belongings (**2.14**). Commemorating "The first time of smiting the East," it shows King Den of the 1st Dynasty with a head cloth (*nemes*) that bears a cobra (*uraeus*), symbol of the north. By use of a mace, he is shown dispatching a bearded Asian who seems to have come from a mountainous land shown to his rear (many scenes alien to Egypt are pictured with mountains). The king is identified by the emblem of the Horus falcon that heads the serekh. A standard holds

Figure 2.13. African and Asian captives bound in the tendrils of a united Egypt, symbolized by the papyrus from the north on the right and lily or sedge of the south on the left.

Figure 2.14. Ivory label of King Den that shows the king dispatching an Asian, commemorating "The first time of smiting the East."

an emblem of Wepwawet, a jackal or wolf, similar in appearance to the Seth animal. Significantly, the standard is shown between the Asian and his avenue of escape to the mountains.[36] The name Wepwawet means "opener of the ways" and may have been connected to the idea of the king proceeding victoriously into battle.[37]

The wars between the north and south seem to be indicated by stone vases found in the south inscribed "Year of fighting of the northern enemy," and a schist statue, one of two of King Khasekhem found at Hierakonpolis. The slaughter of an astonishing 47,209 northern enemies can be seen crudely inscribed at the base of the statue. Khasekhem, last king of the second or Thinite Dynasty, having suppressed a revolt in Lower Egypt, changed his name from Horus Khasekhem ("the two powers have appeared") to Horus-Seth Khasekhemwy ("the two powerful ones appear"). Early opponents, Horus and the Seth animal later appear together on the 2nd Dynasty serekh of King Khasekhemwy, Figure 2.19(c), following a peace settlement between the two warring factions.[38]

Selim Hassan, excavator of the causeway leading to the pyramid of Unas, has also found scenes indicating a conflict with Near Eastern people. The reliefs clearly show a battle between Egyptians and Asians and the transport of the Asian captives aboard a ship.[39] The English archaeologist Walter Emery found possible evidence of the conflict in Saqqara. He discovered an ivory label (2.15) bearing the serekh of King Djet, fourth king of the 1st Dynasty, and containing signs that translate as "Year of taking the . . . (fortress ?) of the North."[40] The symbol used for the fortress is shown as a structure with an indented facade—possibly one of the many mastabas at Saqqara that so closely resemble the early temples in Mesopotamia (3.4).

Another site of early significance is Koptos, an ancient temple and town located 25 miles (40 km) northeast of Thebes, at the entrance of the Wadi Hammamat. On the west side of the Nile, opposite Koptos, is Naqada, a place known as "the Golden Town" because of the gold and other mineral wealth of the eastern desert that induced traders from southwest Asia to make the wadi an important route between the Nile Valley and the Red Sea.[41] Indeed, in the wadi about halfway to the sea, an enormous boulder can still be seen that has numerous drawings incised on its surface. Judging by the pictographs, which include

Figure 2.15. Ivory label that translates as "Year of taking the . . . [fortress ?] of the North."

high-prowed Mesopotamian boats and hunting scenes of game that no longer exists in Egypt, the boulder must have served the weary traveler as a rest stop for untold ages.

Min

Among the objects found in Koptos are the bodies, heads, and penis of three editions of a crudely hammer-carved colossal limestone statue of Min, an ithyphallic fertility god (**2.16**). The heavy beard and bald head of the fragmented statues are uncharacteristic of the indigenous people of Egypt. Also alien are the pictographs incised on its thigh showing stags, hyenas, bulls, elephants, and two items from the Red Sea: *Pteroceras* shells and bones from a saw fish. In addition, they show symbols associated with Min, the opposing barbed arrows superimposed on a staff with a bent top, seen in figure 2.3(**k**). The many pockmarks on the surface indicate the possible removal of stone as sacred relics by worshipers.[42] Certainly, the carving of three editions of the same statue suggest that it represent a god or some greatly venerated figure. Considering that when people worship a god with a human face, it is usually made in their own image, the facial characteristics of Min suggest that he was the god of a bearded people, such as the aforementioned Asians.

Sudden Advances in the Arts and Crafts

Beside these unusual finds, the Late Gerzean period (about 3300 BCE) was a time of great advancements in the arts and crafts. Copper implements were used as stone-working tools, ornate palettes and ivory knife handles began to appear, hieroglyphic writing developed, and great strides were made in monumental architecture. Devices such as cylinder seals from the Uruk–Jemdet Nasr period (about 3500–2900 BCE) are found in late Gerzean sites, as are motifs alien to the Egyptian imagination. These include the master of animals motif, winged griffins, carnivores attacking impassive prey, and figures wearing headdresses and long robes—all strange to Egypt but reminiscent of Mesopotamian or Susiana (Iran) cultures. Accompanying these new concepts, an increase in wealth and trade is reflected in burials, which contain grave goods of lead, obsidian, and lapis lazuli, none of these native to Egypt.[43] Dark blue in color and flecked with iron pyrites or gold, lapis lazuli was a substance the Egyptians thought imitated the heavens—no doubt the reason for its importation from northeastern Afghanistan as far back as the fourth millennium.[44] While it might be said these objects were small enough to have arrived indirectly by trade, other objects definitely were not. Indeed, the three Min statues—13.5 feet (4.1 m) tall and weighing 2 tons, when reconstructed—are as unlikely to have been trade objects as the sanctified oval mound at Hierakonpolis or the mural covered with foreign themes on the wall of the painted tomb.

Discoveries such as these indicate that an early, essentially African culture would have remained as static as those in Sudan and the sub-Saharan region but for the foreign ideas and wealth that infused the land for about five centuries prior to the 1st Dynasty (3100 BCE). During this period, contact between the Protoliterate cultures of the Near East and the indigenous population was responsible for more progress than in the entire subsequent history of Egypt. Yet, even as these ideas and techniques were seized upon and adapted

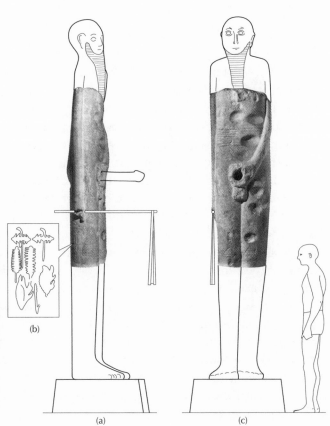

Figure 2.16. Reconstructions of one of the three statues of Min, an ithyphallic god from Koptos. (a) Incised on his upper thigh are the opposing barbed arrow emblem of Min and pictographs strange to Egypt. (b) Detail of pictographs. (c) Front view of statue. Other statues show an ostrich, harpoon, bird, elephant, and hyena and a bull standing on a range of mountains. (Photos courtesy Ashmolean Museum)

to Egyptian thought, some were short-lived, not outlasting the early dynasties. Others, however, were accepted into Egyptian iconography and used throughout her long history.

Whether foreign objects or people arrived in Egypt by trade or invasion, the routes taken must have been established in the dim reaches of the past. As the American archaeologist James Breasted noted:

> It was chiefly at the two northern corners of the Delta that outside influences and foreign elements, which were always sifting into the Nile valley, gained access to the country. Through the Eastern corner it was the prehistoric Semitic population of neighboring Asia, who forced their way across the dangerous intervening deserts; while the Libyan races, of possibly European origin, found entrance at the Western corner. The products of the South also, in spite of the cataracts, filtered in ever increasing volume into the regions of the lower river and the lower end of the first cataract became a trading post, ever after known as "Suan" (Assuan) or "market," where the Negro traders of the south met those of Egypt. The upper Nile thus gradually became a regular avenue of commerce with Sudan. The natural boundaries of Egypt, however, always presented sufficiently effective barriers to would-be invaders, to enable the natives slowly to assimilate the newcomers, without being displaced.[45]

Writing

The history of phonetic writing that is so evident in Sumer, and that appeared suddenly in Egypt at the very time contacts between Sumer, Elam, and Egypt were at their height, has suggested until recently that the idea of writing was of foreign origin. While Sumerian writing has a long history of known development, a similar evolution had not been found in Egypt. To account for this, some suggest that Egyptian writing may have been deliberately invented in a more or less finished form, its underlying principles fully in place from the outset. The Korean script, Han-gul, developed in 1444 CE by King Sejong, is cited as a parallel for this process.[46] This is questionable. Thousands of years before Han-gul was devised, the Koreans, using a different dialect, had a written language using Chinese characters.[47] This cannot be compared to the invention of a full-blown written Egyptian language, much less one with sounds, before the idea of writing was ever known. Instead, some scholars have suggested that early examples of Egyptian writing have not yet been discovered or were made on perishable materials, such as papyrus, and have long since disappeared.[48] Although it is not known when papyrus was first used, uninscribed sheets were discovered in the 1st Dynasty tomb 3035 of Hemaka, at Saqqara.[49]

Discoveries by Günter Dreyer of the German Archaeological Institute suggest that the origin of Egyptian writing needs to be reexamined, offering the possibility that the idea of writing was developed in Egypt several centuries before it occurred in the Near East. Inscriptions from hundreds of pots and labels found at the royal cemetery at Abydos show some hieroglyphic writing as far back as 3400 BCE, with most occurring about 3200 BCE.[50] Sumerian writing seems to have begun about 3100 BCE. The Egyptians formed and used writing in a different way than the Asians. The linguistic pictographs of Sumer were rudimentary and were primarily used for commerce. Those of Egypt were more representational of real objects and were primarily employed to identify kings, tombs, and the like.[51]

A remarkable find involving early experiments with alphabetic writing in Egypt has recently been made by John C. Darnell, an Egyptologist at Yale University, and his wife Deborah. Inscriptions discovered in the limestone cliffs on an ancient road between Thebes and Abydos, a route once heavily traveled by Asian traders and mercenaries in the Egyptian desert, are in a Semitic script with Egyptian influences. Dated between 1900 and 1800 BCE, they are two or three centuries older than previous evidence of an alphabet in the Semitic-speaking territory of the Sinai Peninsula or in the Syria-Palestine region occupied by the Canaanites. While there have always been indications that Semites were inventors of the alphabet, researchers had heretofore assumed that it was developed in their own lands by borrowing and simplifying Egyptian hieroglyphs. Instead, Darnell's discovery now suggests that, working with Semitic speakers in Egypt, native scribes simplified the formal pictographic Egyptian writing and modified the symbols into an early alphabet using a semicursive form commonly used in the Middle Kingdom.[52]

Genesis of Egyptian Politics

As foreign settlements became established in Egypt, a degree of resentment seems to have grown up between the native population and the more advanced Asian groups, the discontent growing stronger with the formation of Egypt's home-grown political factions in the Late Predynastic period. The probable stimulus was a gradually drying climate, which forced the desert inhabitants into settlements along the Nile. The rising population required a greater amount of food, necessitating that more land be won from the river by means of canals, dikes, and catch basins. Keeping the artificial waterways in good repair required specialists and organization. Organization required responsible oversight by people selected and controlled by a leader—one who could also attract skilled technicians and artisans to do his bidding.[53]

With the Nile extending the length of the country, and with the canals leading to all the crop-producing land, the people were thus in a position to be controlled more readily by government administrators using river craft. Closer living conditions also encouraged the local tribes, once separated into 42 nomes (districts), to coalesce into increasingly large political systems. This resulted in the establishment of two evenly divided competing kingdoms consisting of 20 nomes in the north and 22 in the south, each ruled by a royal house and aristocracy. The capitals were located at Hierakonpolis (Nekhen) in the south and at Buto (Pe) in the north. While the population of Egypt is estimated to have been as low as 100,000 to 200,000 inhabitants in late Predynastic times, by the Early Dynastic period a population of about 2,000,000 people is thought to have been dispersed in the villages and regional administrative centers along the Nile.[54]

A great deal of uncertainty still exists as to the political nature of Egypt before and after unification. According to Emery, the Egyptian state "was a dual monarchy and, so soon after the unification, the individuality of two states of the North and South was more marked than in later times. In fact there appear to have been two separate administrations united only under the throne. Even the elaborate ceremonies of the king's coronation, his 'Sed' festival or jubilee and ultimate burial, were twice repeated with different insignia, architecture, and customs of Upper and Lower Egypt." The *sed* festival was a jubilee in which the king's vigor was reaffirmed thirty years after his accession to the throne.[55]

Both the identity of the kings who ruled during these times and the times in which they ruled are uncertain. Even the dates given for the lengths of the early dynasties are at best scholarly estimates. According to Manetho, a native of Lower Egypt and priest of Heliopolis during the reign of Ptolomy II (285–246 CE), Menes was responsible for unifying the north and south and founding the Egyptian state. However, it is not clear whether he is to be identified with Narmer or with Aha, an early ruler of the 1st Dynasty. In addition to the writings of Manetho, much of what is known of this time is based on the Palermo Stone, a record of kings and events inscribed in stone 700 years after unification in the 5th Dynasty.[56]

In an effort to unite the land, Menes built Memphis, about 15 miles (24 km) south of modern Cairo, as a new capital near a natural frontier between the two kingdoms. In a great feat of engineering the course of the Nile was deflected, the land drained, and the city, which remained the center of culture for the next 3,000 years, was established.

The king permitted each nome to be ruled by a nomarch (governor) and started what was to become a provincial ruling class. Nomes were allowed to keep their long-established local gods, whose importance was indictated by the size of their following and the wealth of temples dedicated to them. Although the gods were usually restricted to the areas from

Table 2.2
CHRONOLOGY OF EARLY KINGS

Predynastic Period	1st Dynasty (3100–2890 BCE)	2nd Dynasty (2890–2686 BCE)
Scorpion (?)	Narmer (Menes?)	Hetepsekhemy
Ka (Sekhen)	Aha (Menes?)	Raneb
	Djer (Zer, Sekhty)	Nynetjer
	Djet (Zet, Uadji, Edjo)	Weneg
	Den (Udimu)	Sened
	Merneith (queen regent?)	Sekhemib/Peribsen (Horus/Seth)
	Anedjib (Andjyeb, Enezib)	Khasekhemwy
	Semerkhet	
	Qa-a (Ka'a)	

After Ian Shaw and Paul Nicholson, *The Dictionary of Ancient Egypt*, 310. A different estimate suggests 1st Dynasty 2920–2770 BCE and 2nd Dynasty 2770–2649 BCE (John Baines and Jaromír Málek, *Atlas of Ancient Egypt*, 36).

which they originated, those representing the elements of nature received the widest following. Taking animal, human, or anthropomorphic forms, all the gods were superseded by Horus, a sky god, symbolically shown as a falcon.[57] With an equally wide following, Seth was a god of chaos—appearing with a canine body and an erect forked tail or in various abhorred animal forms, such as the hippopotamus, pig, or donkey. The Horus cult, which stood for settled areas dominated by cattle breeding and agriculture, was in conflict with the Seth cult, which was linked to the remote desert and represented religious ideas deriving from before the introduction of agriculture and cattle breeding.[58] The struggle between the two deities is contained in myths relating to the triumph of order (Horus) over chaos (Seth).

Gods of Egypt

Osiris, an early fertility god overseeing the growth of crops, is usually seen in mummy wrappings, his projecting hands holding crook and flail. Reflecting the cycle of growth, he is a god of death and resurrection, with a role similar to that of Tammuz or Marduk, gods of fertility in Mesopotamia. Although the Osiris myth has many variations, its basic theme involves his murder by his brother, Seth, contending for the throne. To avenge his father's death, Horus struggles with Seth in an extended series of contests that are finally decided when a divine tribunal declares Osiris ruler of the underworld and Horus ruler of the living. While this is viewed as an allegorical struggle between order and chaos, the resurrection of Osiris seems to be regarded by the Egyptian people as a promise of their own immortality—an idea that caused them to devote much of their time and wealth toward its fulfillment.

On losing their primitive characteristics in the 2nd Dynasty, these tribal gods were assimilated into a new solar synthesis. Horus, for example, fused with Re, the sun-god, and became Re-Harakhte. Although many gods were similarly combined in the name of unification, Seth always remained the focus of a cult apart, as did several other local deities who retained their individual power throughout Egyptian history—Ptah at Memphis, Osiris at Busiris, and Min at Koptos.[59]

Blending the North and South

Much of the political blending of north and south was conducted in the person of the king, whose primary role was to keep the halves of Egypt united. This was symbolically accomplished in many ways. The red and white crowns of the north and south were joined to produce the "double crown" (*pschent*) of the two lands (**2.17**). Political blending is also seen in royal titles (**2.18**). In the Early Dynasties, the first and most important of the king's five titles, the Horus or *ka* name, shows a falcon representing kingship seated on the serekh. The Nebty, second title of the king, is represented by the vulture goddess Nekhbet and the cobra goddess Wadjet, of Upper and Lower Egypt respectively (**2.18b**). The Golden

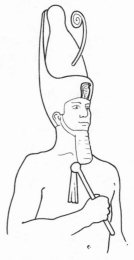

Figure 2.17. The crowns of Lower Egypt and Upper Egypt combined to form the double crown uniting the two lands. The similarity between the Min hut seen in figure 2.4(k) and the crown of Upper Egypt is striking. In addition, both objects also display a spiral representation of the sun, here extending from the crown's surface.

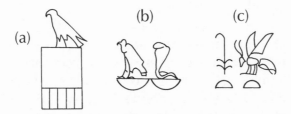

Figure 2.18. (a) The king's Horus name on a serekh with a framework suggesting the paneled architecture of Mesopotamia. (b) The king's Nebty title represented by the vulture goddess of the south and cobra of the north. (c) The king's Nesu-Bit name with the sedge of the south and bee of the north.

(a)

(b)

(c)

Figure 2.19. The early strife and later peace between north and south are indicated by the changing symbols heading the serekh. (a) King Sekhemib (2nd Dynasty) first used the Horus-falcon. (b) He later changed his name to Peribsen and adopted the Seth animal. (c) His successor, King Khasekhemwy, whose name means "The two gods are at peace in him," placed Horus and Seth together on the serekh.

Horus name, third in the king's titulary, shows the falcon seated on the Egyptian sign for gold. Of the two additional names given in the pyramid age, the Nesu-Bit, a name given at coronation, contains both the sedge (plant) symbol of the south and the bee of the north. This *prenomen* or cartouche name is the most identifiable and frequently used name. The last of his five titles, *nomen*, Son of Re, has his own birth name equated with the sun.[60]

Despite the blending of royal symbols and the help of a vast civil and priestly bureaucracy, attempts to bring north and south together were not completely successful. Their continued antagonism is reflected in Sekhemib, a 2nd Dynasty king, changing his name to Peribsen and abandoning the Horus falcon seated on his serekh in favor of the Seth animal (**2.19**). The accompanying religious or political wars that may have helped inspire this name change seem to be indicated by destructive fires in the tombs at Abydos, Naqada, and Saqqara. These underground chambers had outside walls of mud brick, which were baked as if in a kiln when the wood-lined interior walls of the chambers and their flammable contents were burned. According to Emery, the fires may have been deliberate sanctions in an effort to destroy the afterlife of dynastic opponents. The conflict may finally have been resolved at the end of the 2nd Dynasty when Khasekhemwy—one of whose names means "the two powers have appeared," as we have seen—next took the throne and placed the figures of Horus and Seth on equal footing above his serekh.[61] Later scenes portray the blending of Horus and Seth as they bind the papyrus and lily of their respective lands around the hieroglyph representing the word unification (**2.20**).

The Ba and the Ka

Central to Egyptian culture was the belief that each person, including the king, was made of five separate parts considered essential to the human being: name, shadow, *ba*, *ka*, and physical body. While it takes strong belief to equate one's name with one's body, signs of this tenet can still be seen all across Egypt where the names of some individuals were obliterated by enemies after death. Indeed, the removal of all personal or royal names from a statue or monument was considered equivalent to the complete destruction of that person's memory and existence. No less strange, Egyptians considered the shadow to be an essential adjunct to the body, presumably since it routinely accompanied the body.

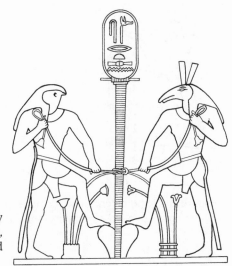

Figure 2.20. Upper and Lower Egypt symbolically united. Their respective chief gods, Horus and Seth, are shown joining the papyrus plant of the north and lily of the south.

More difficult to comprehend is the Egyptian belief in the ba and the ka. The ba was the spiritual part of a person, a part that lived on after the body died. It is symbolized as a bird with a human head and arms and represents everything that makes a person an individual except for the body. While it is similar to one's personality, it may also be thought of as the soul or vital principle of a human being. Possessing the gift of animation if supplied with a corpse or statue, the ba was thought to have the ability to move in and out of the tomb while assuming any shape it wished. Although the concept of ba is associated with people and gods, according to James Allen, the American Egyptologist, inanimate objects could also have a personality or ba.

The ka is different in the sense that while the ba is spirit, whatever else the ka represents, it is pure energy. Born with a person as his or her other self, the ka continued to live after the death of the individual, possibly returning someone to life if supplied with sustenance. Although it was known at the time that the ka did not physically eat or drink the offerings, it was thought magically to absorb their life-giving qualities. To "go to one's ka" was to return home to the land of one's ancestors—who in early dynasties were believed to dwell in the cemetery, a location identified with the geographical west. As a life force, the ka lingered like a double near whoever it represented. For the deceased to become an *akh*, one of the "blessed dead," it was necessary for the ba to join the ka in the underworld. Offerings to the ka were made at the portals of false doors—spiritual entrances to the underworld, styled after niches found outside the tombs at Saqqara and the temples of Mesopotamia.

The Egyptian ka symbol is supposedly unique to the Egyptian concept of human nature. When depicted with arms squared off at the elbow and extended so as to embrace, it is thought to represent the life force being passed to an individual by gods or the creator (**2.21**).[62] Whatever its true meaning, the Egyptian symbol for the ka bears a striking resemblance to that shown on a Mesopotamian seal from Uruk, carried in procession on a standard. Since Mesopotamians do not share the same belief in the ka as the Egyptians, perhaps the symbol had its genesis outside Egypt and had a different original meaning.

(a)   (b)

Figure 2.21. (a) Offerings being made to the ka on an Egyptian standard. (b) The ka-like symbol carried to a reed temple at an earlier time in Mesopotamia.

Faced up on the Mesopotamian standard to be seen more clearly, the symbol may represent, in plan, the early temple niche said to receive sunlight at a significant time of the year. Assuming this to be so, the Mesopotamian scene also suggests that the niche, as represented by the ka symbol, was not an accidental by-product of using mud brick. Indeed, shown as in figure 2.21(**b**) being carried to a flimsy temple structure, it was already considered a sacred symbol at a time when the Near Eastern temples were still made of reeds.[63]

In Mesopotamia, the single niche on an inside wall evolved into a patterned decoration used on the outside walls, the niches becoming more multifaceted with time. Interestingly, the first mud-brick structures found in Egypt are contemporary and show a remarkable resemblance to the later multifaceted temple niches of Mesopotamia. The ka symbol, seen in the Mesopotamian scene, is also found among the 1st Dynasty ruins in Saqqara, the very site in Egypt where the greatest number of these indented structures are located. However, because the 1st Dynasty tombs in Egypt have niches all around their outside walls and none on their inside walls, they do not support the contention suggested for Mesopotamia, that the niche was a receptor for sunlight at a particular time of the year.[64]

In due course, I show that the niched facades in the Saqqaran structures were reduced in number by the 2nd Dynasty until only two remained facing the eastern sky—domain of the rising sun and symbol of rebirth—the one near the burial chamber being the larger. By receiving sunlight at the solstices, equinoxes, date of the jubilee celebration of the deceased, or some such event, the niche may have served the same purpose in Egypt as that postulated for Mesopotamia. Indeed, in Egypt, not only could it serve to receive funerary offerings for the deceased; it could also link the deceased to the rising sun, reenergizing the ka with life-giving energy.

We may conclude that while an influx of people entered Egypt in a steady trickle for untold ages, the numbers from Asia increased greatly during the Gerzean period. The Mesopotamian-style evidence found in Egypt and the lack of reciprocal Egyptian influence in Asia suggest that in the Predynastic period, Egypt was considered a land of opportunity, where one might live and prosper. Although many of the ideas brought by immigrants were short-lived (such as entwined serpent necks, the master of animals motif, lions attacking passive prey, and oval structures with clean sand underlayments), their impact on the Predynastic period was profound enough to stimulate Egyptian society to a cycle of great advancement.

CHAPTER 3

EARLY MONUMENTS

The effects of Mesopotamian influence are best seen in the Early Dynastic architecture of Upper and Lower Egypt—two areas of the country that exhibit the sudden appearance of advanced monuments with a distinctive form of indented architecture. The decorative pattern on the tombs in the north and on the massive so-called palace-facade walls of the south was the result of a mud-brick building style that compares favorably with temples found in the Near East. Indeed, the very basis of these unusual facades stems from an elaboration of the single niche discovered in the first temple in Eridu, some 2,000 years older. In contrast to the short-lived nature of some imported Mesopotamian ideas, these mysterious niches coming from an earlier and more advanced culture had as lasting an effect when planted on Egyptian soil as they did in the Near East. From the first appearance of the niche, the device became so fixed in Egyptian iconography that it is later seen on sarcophagi, false doors, temenos walls, and the offering places of tomb chapels. The importance of this singular device to the canon and architecture of Egypt cannot be overestimated.

Abydos

The increase in wealth that accompanied the introduction of the niche can be seen in Upper Egypt at Abydos, a desert cemetery west of the limit of cultivation called Umm el Ga'ab, "Mother of pots" (**3.1**). The tombs at this site were found with greatly expanded underground chambers built to contain burial goods sufficient to last the dead king well into his afterlife. The additional storage rooms were made by constructing a number of brick-lined storerooms around a larger brick burial chamber lined with wood paneling and having a wooden floor (**3.1b**). Of the ten tombs found at Abydos, eight were occupied by kings and a possible queen regent from the 1st Dynasty and two by kings of the 2nd Dynasty. Royal ownership of the tombs is indicated by inscribed jar seals, wooden labels, and a pair

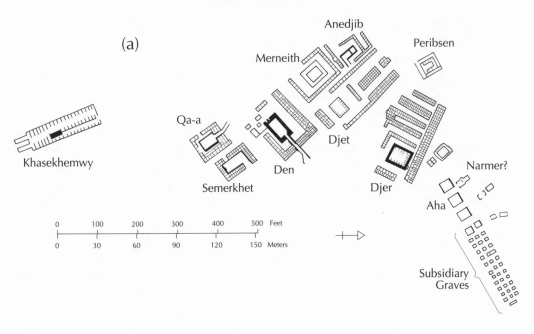

(a)

Anedjib

Merneith

Peribsen

Qa-a

Khasekhemwy

Djet

Den

Semerkhet

Djer

Narmer?

Aha

Subsidiary
Graves

| 0 | 100 | 200 | 300 | 400 | 500 | Feet |

| 0 | 30 | 60 | 90 | 120 | 150 | Meters |

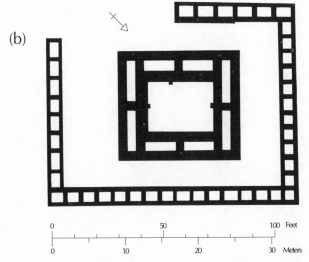

(b)

| 0 | | 50 | | 100 | Feet |

| 0 | 10 | 20 | 30 | Meters |

Figure 3.1. (a) Royal cemetery of Abydos. (b) Subterranean chambers of the tomb of Merneith, a possible queen regent.

of stone stelae outside the tomb bearing the Horus name of the king. Among the finds was a mummified arm that held beaded jewelry and a bracelet of gold, lapis lazuli, and turquoise plaques taking the form of a serekh with the name of King Djer, third king of the 1st Dynasty—a remarkable find, considering that, as noted, the closest source for lapis lazuli, a deep blue or violet metamorphosed limestone, is northern Afghanistan.

Günter Dreyer made an interesting discovery in the tomb of Scorpion, a king who may
have ruled in 3150 BCE. Of the tomb's seven subsidiary rooms, three were found stocked
with jars that may once have contained up to 1,200 gallons of wine. The unique style of
the jars is evidence of an overland trade route called the "Ways of Horus" existing between
Egypt, the lowlands of Israel, and the hill country of the Jordan Valley in the Early Bronze
Age I (3300–3000 BCE). Once wine making became an established enterprise in the Late
Uruk period (late 4th millennium), trade routes between the delta and Israel were extended
to Uruk, in Mesopotamia, and the Elamite capital of Susa, in Iran. According to chemical
tests, remnants of the same kind of wine found in the tomb of Scorpion in Egypt were discovered in a mud-brick building in northwestern Iran from 5400–5000 BCE.[1]

The coverings of the tombs of Abydos have long since disappeared, but judging by the
proximity of their underground works, these overhead constructions could not have been
large. Their disappearance was probably due to the means of support—remains suggest a
wooden plank floor probably overlaid with brick and mud and held up by large wooden
posts, materials bound to fail (**3.2**). The substance and shape of the coverings have been
matters of considerable conjecture. Tombs previously thought to be simple brick-encased
structures, low in profile, are now being reconsidered. Some may have been fragile wood
frame and reed structures; others may have had two moundlike formations, one a hidden
tumulus above the burial chamber but below the desert surface, and the second one covering the hidden tumulus and rising above the surface.[2] Outside the main tomb a number
of subsidiary graves held the bodies of servants, artisans, women, court dwarfs, and even
dogs. At Abydos, an analysis of the remains in the subsidiary graves shows them all to be
under the age of 25.[3] Just as in the Dynastic period of Mesopotamia, they show that early

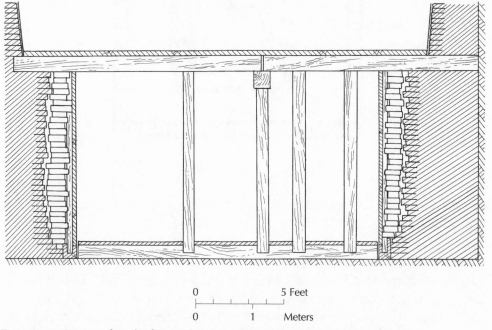

0   5 Feet

0   1   Meters

Figure 3.2. Section of tomb of Qa-a showing wood support posts and planking.

Egyptian kings were accompanied to the afterlife by a large retinue. The entire funerary complex—tomb, subsidiary graves, and open offering place, the last probably containing two round-top stelae identifying the interred king—were thought to be surrounded by a temenos wall. With the burial of 580 retainers during the reign of Djer, third king of the 1st Dynasty, the loss of skilled people became so great that the practice was as brief in Egypt as it had been in Mesopotamia, Shang China, and other cultures in their early formative years.[4]

With their shafts sloping to multichambered compartments, and their vaulted ceilings of stone or brick, the tombs of Mesopotamia differ markedly from those of Egypt. Yet there is one feature that the two have in common: the tombs in Abydos follow the Mesopotamian example of having their corners toward the cardinal points. Indeed, the remains of the wooden floor in the tomb of King Semerkhet, of the 1st Dynasty, still bear the hieroglyphic sign "north" at the northernmost corner.[5] This sign indicates a deliberate orientation to the cardinal points instead of an effort to align the tomb with the course of the Nile, a feature often claimed for Egyptian temples. Although the tomb of Semerkhet and other tombs of Abydos are not solstitially correct or even oriented in the same way, the directional sign indicates the quest for a symbolic orientation (3.3).

The effort to consider the cardinal points even in common graves was identified by Renee Friedman, an American Egyptologist. In an early Predynastic cemetery at Hierakonpolis, she found that the great majority of bodies were placed on the left side, head pointing upstream in accordance with most Predynastic burials. However, because the

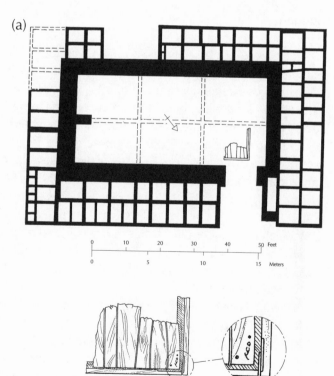

Figure 3.3. (a) The 1st Dynasty tomb of King Semerkhet. (b) A hieroglyph that indicates the direction north was found carved in one corner of the floor.

Nile does not run truly north-south at Hierakonpolis, a choice had to be made to face the body to the river or to true west, a difference of 23 degrees of arc. Of the excavated adult burials, regardless of sex or age, twice as many bodies were oriented to true west than to the river. Friedman noted: "The decision to face true west indicates a clear knowledge of the cardinal directions, which can only have been gleaned from a study of the circumpolar stars, as the river is not an accurate indicator, nor is the setting of the sun."[6] Overlooked is another possibility. As I show later, the cardinal directions seen here and at Nabta Playa, a yet earlier Predynastic site, may have been discovered not just by watching the setting of the sun but by tracking the sun's movements across the sky.

The concern for orientation at Semerkhet's tomb is also shown at the 1st Dynasty tomb of Djet, where Dreyer found evidence of a niche (reminiscent of niches found inside the temple walls of Mesopotamia) in the southwest corner of the large underground chamber.[7] The directions in which the niches in Mesopotamia and Egypt face are often not correctly oriented to the solstices, equinoxes, or cardinal points. At least in Egypt, this was not necessary. As seen in the royal tombs of the New Kingdom, strict adherence to some geographical or astronomical feature was not always a major concern. As was reported by Kent R. Weeks, the discoverer of KV 5, burial site of the sons of Ramesses II, "For the sake of laying out the decoration, the main axis of a tomb was simply considered to run from east to west, no matter what its actual orientation. Walking down its corridors, one was said to proceed from the horizon of the rising sun to that of the setting, from this life to the next, from the realm of the god Re to the realm of Osiris."[8]

Saqqara

Another series of Early Dynastic tombs was found along the western escarpment of Saqqara, about 300 miles (480 km) north of Abydos (**3.4**). The substructures of these tombs conform generally to those of the south.[9] However, the burial chambers, also of brick-lined rooms with floors of wooden planking, were for the first time excavated from rock.[10] Constructed as they were of mud brick and protected by a covering of sand, enough of the Saqqaran superstructures was preserved to ascertain their form. The low rectangular buildings, called mastabas because of their resemblance to a common Egyptian bench, range in size from 50–80 feet (15–25 m) to 130–200 feet (40–60 m). Larger than any aboveground structures that could have existed at Abydos, they are seen to enclose inner cross walls of brickwork reaching about 23 feet (7 m), the same height as the outside walls. Floored and roofed with timber, filled with sand, gravel, and rubbish, the compartments form additional storerooms above ground. Reminiscent of the great temples of Sumer due to the pattern of recesses on their outside walls, these are among the earliest examples of Egyptian monumental architecture.

Having no entrances to the burial chamber, the earliest tombs of Saqqara were either built after burial or provided with a passageway in the roof, which was later sealed. By the middle of the 1st Dynasty, however, tombs at both Abydos and Saqqara include an outside stairway blocked by heavy limestone portcullis slabs (**3.5**). These large rectangular stones were lowered by rope along vertical channels cut in the rock on each side of the passageway. A similar means of blocking can be seen in the 3rd Dynasty tombs at Meidum. The

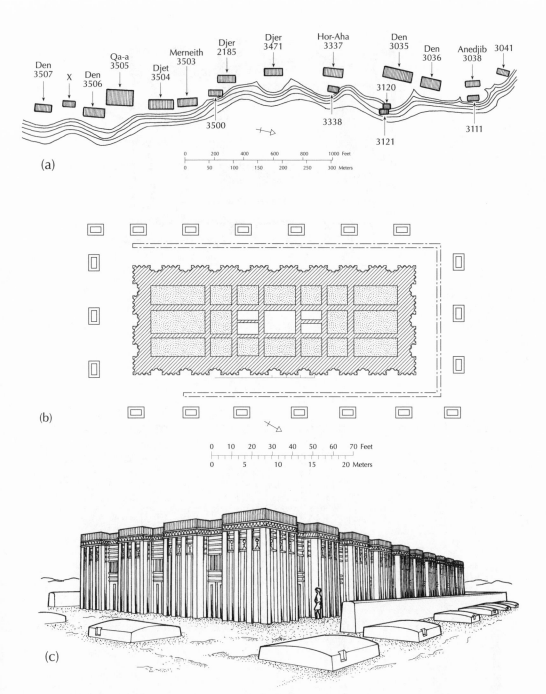

Figure 3.4. (a) Tomb field of Saqqara, with owners identified with rulers found at Abydos. (b) Subterranean chambers of mastaba from reign of Queen Merneith. (c) Its greater size and advanced styling appear in a possible reconstruction that shows by its niches a remarkable resemblance to the Mesopotamian architecture (1.35).

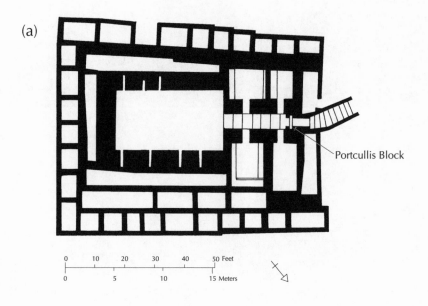

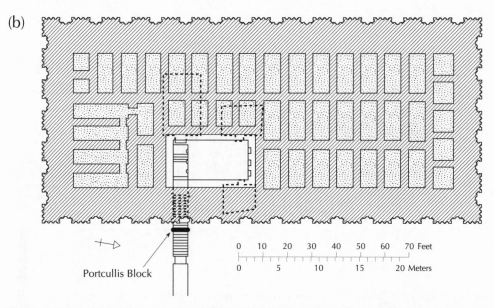

Figure 3.5. Tombs in Upper and Lower Egypt (1st Dynasty) showing outside entry stairways with stone portcullis blocks. (a) Tomb of Qa-a, at Abydos. (b) Mastaba from the reign of Den, at Saqqara.

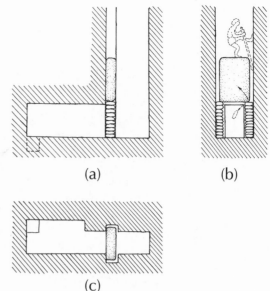

Figure 3.6. A deep underground tomb (3rd Dynasty) at Meidum: (a) side, (b) front, (c) and plan. An entrance is prepared for the deceased by holding the portcullis block over the chamber entrance with a cribbing of small stones under each side. The block can be lowered by one man with a lever if he alternately tilts each side of the block as a companion removes the small stones.

(a) (b)

(c)

deep vertical shafts, which lead to burial chambers, have 7-foot portcullis slabs held above the doorway by small piles of stones under each corner (**3.6**).[11]

During the period of the Early Dynastic tombs at Saqqara, mummification had not yet been developed. Instead, the body was wrapped in linen, placed in a wooden sarcophagus located in the central chamber, and supplied with enough food and drink within reach to sustain the ka until it was able to obtain the reserves stored in nearby rooms. These rooms also contained enough games, weapons, furniture, sleeping quarters, and latrines to ensure that the king would be equipped with all pleasures and necessities for the afterlife. The storage rooms above ground held goods of lesser value, being farther away from the body. Although no sign of roofing was found at the tombs of Saqqara, it is assumed that this was similar to that of coffins of the period, themselves considered houses for eternity—some being flat on top, as at Mycerinus, and some slightly rounded, perhaps with a flat parapet at each end (**3.7**).[12] To ensure that the soul of the deceased was brought safely to the afterlife, boats were placed in oblong pits near the tombs at both Saqqara and Abydos. The royal boat repositories at these sites were small compared to those next to the pyramid of Cheops (Khufu), one of which held the jumbled pieces of a boat 142 feet (43 m) long when assembled. David O'Connor recently found thirteen boats, buried in parallel, near mortuary monuments of Abydos. For each boat, a hole was dug in the sand and its flat bottom lined with bricks. The boat was placed in the hole and 2-foot-thick (0.6 m) walls were built around and on top of the boat before covering it with mud plaster to encase the boat completely. The shape of the side walls is noteworthy; although they follow the contour of the long narrow boat for its entire length, they depart to form opposing arrowheads at the bow and stern. In plan, this shape is reminiscent of the Min symbols seen in figure 6.18(**i, j, k**).[13] Remains indicate that the boats were associated with kings of the 1st Dynasty. One of the boats is about 75 feet long and about 8.5 feet wide (23 × 2.5 m). With narrow prow and stern and shallow draft, they seem to be direct ancestors of the Cheops boat.

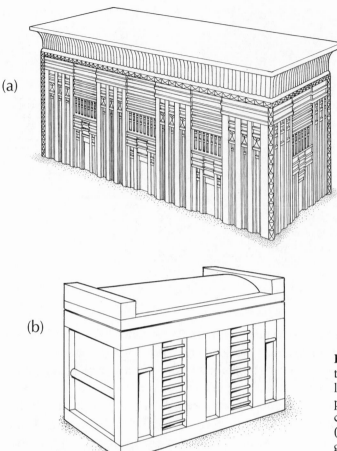

(a)

(b)

Figure 3.7. It is assumed that the roofs of mastabas were similar to those of coffins of the period, which were themselves considered houses for eternity. (a) The coffin of Mycerinus was given a flat roof. (b) The curved roof of a coffin from Tarkhan.

Similarities to Mesopotamia

Of all the finds in Egypt—the scenes in the Painted Tomb, the three statues of Min, and the sanctified oval mound at Hierakonpolis—none is more persuasively Mesopotamian than the mud brick structures of Saqqara. Generally oriented, with their corners toward the cardinal points, like the tombs of Abydos and Mesopotamia, the structures at Saqqara have outer walls formed of alternating panels and recesses impressively similar to the religious buildings of the Near East (**3.8**). Indeed, in some cases the recesses at Saqqara are so intricately formed, one within the other, as to suggest an almost baroque elaboration of an earlier and simpler form (**3.9**). Yet, despite the lack of mud-brick structures in Egypt prior to the 1st Dynasty—temples typically being simple wood or reed pavilions of the sed festival, as in figure 2.4(**a**)—the intricate designs at Saqqara seem to have been incorporated into Egyptian building practices without any earlier and simpler examples.[14]

Although no signs exist of a developmental period in Egypt for the indented facade, a good number of religious structures with recessed and alternating panels on their faces were produced in Mesopotamia over the centuries (**1.28**), some having almost the exact patterns seen in Egypt. Tomb 3504, a 1st Dynasty (3100 BCE) monument at Saqqara (**3.9**),

Figure 3.8. Remains of indented facade of Tomb 3507 from the 1st Dynasty reign of King Den.

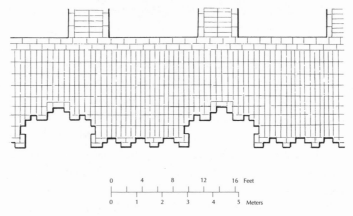

Figure 3.9. Detail of tomb 3504 from the 1st Dynasty reign of King Djet, showing the indented facade so distinctive of religious buildings of the Near East.

is closely comparable to the paneled walls of a structure at Level IVa (3100 BCE) from the Eanna Precinct of Warka (Uruk). Although this has been suggested to be a Mesopotamian temple, it seemed, unlike others, to be without a niche on the inside wall. However, careful study of the plan shows it to be a more advanced form of the original simple indent. Generally described as T-shaped, it instead has a narrow slot centrally located in the head of the T—a slot extending to a small room beyond, thus indicating that the true shape of the floor plan is cruciform (**3.10**). In this layout, when the sun is aligned to the slot, perhaps on the day of the summer solstice, light coming from a window in the opposite wall will enter the narrow opening and illuminate the terminus chamber beyond. The cruciform floor plan as shown in this temple was not restricted to south Mesopotamia; according to the English archaeologist S. Lloyd, examples of the same arrangement were found in northern Assyria from about the same period.[15]

While the earliest of these alternating niche-and-panel constructions were fairly simple, as their patterns grew more complicated, the methods by which they were made probably evolved to meet the challenge. Many possibilities exist for their construction, but the easiest means of laying brick for the more intricately formed recesses would entail the use of

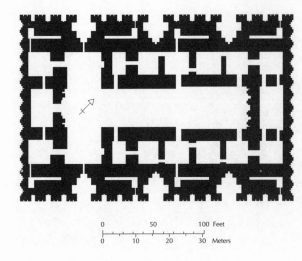

Figure 3.10. Temple from Eanna Precinct of Uruk (3100 BCE) with a cruciform floor plan inside and a pattern of cruciform niches on the facade. The niches on the facade may be favorably compared to those found at Saqqara from the same period.

a small wood pattern as a guide. Hand-held, or supported by bricks, the pattern could be aligned to a cord stretched against the face of the wall from the corners of a surrounding embankment, rising with each course (**3.11**).

Together with the corner orientation and the niched facade, the mastabas at Saqqara display another building practice long known in Mesopotamia but suddenly appearing in Egypt with these mud-brick constructions. The builders placed layers of reeds between every five or eight courses of brick—a step taken for several reasons. It helped to bind the structure together; it provided small passages to help dry the newly laid brick deep within the structure; and it provided a series of expansion joints to accommodate changes in temperature and humidity.[16] This sophisticated building technique could only have been discovered by people who had experienced many failures before arriving at a solution. It certainly would not be known to or used by Egyptians in their first effort at building a monumental mud-brick structure.

Henri Frankfort, who claimed that this form of architecture had been borrowed from Mesopotamia, states that "the first generation of Egyptians to use bricks on any scale at all was at the same time familiar with every refinement of which the material was capable. . . . It was not merely the use of bricks that appears to have been adopted under the First Dynasty but the use of bricks in a definite application to a very specific type of building, namely, to structures decorated all round with graduated recesses. And it is precisely this advanced and sophisticated type of brick building which is found in Mesopotamia during the period when contact with Egypt is known by a great deal of evidence to have taken place."[17]

Hybrid Structures

Although the tombs at Saqqara are similar to those at Mesopotamia, they seem to be a hybrid development. In Mesopotamia buildings with paneled facades and a niche on the inside wall were religious monuments. They did not contain burial chambers, as at Saqqara. Further, while tombs at Saqqara mimic Mesopotamian temples on the outside, they are

Figure 3.11. The employment of a movable wooden pattern aligned to a stretched cord, as a possible method of forming the multifaceted indents of the facade.

different on the inside. The niche on the inside corner of Djet's tomb, for example, is not on the axis of the structure and does not have the altar present in Mesopotamia. These are important changes, but perhaps what one might expect when a foreign structure is adapted in a new land for a different purpose.

This transition seems to be shown by the changing location of the burial chamber with each passing ruler. The earliest of the mastabas, Queen Nithotep's tomb at Naqada (**3.12**),

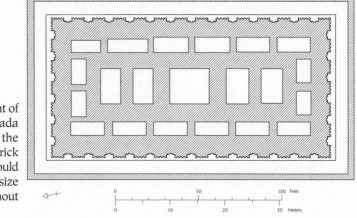

Figure 3.12. The monument of Queen Nithotep at Naqada raises the question of how the paneling on the earliest brick building yet found in Egypt could have achieved so great a size and so intricate a design without signs of prior development.

has its burial chamber constructed at ground level, a primitive location for interment compared to the elaborate underground burial chambers later found at Saqqara. Despite this, the sizable mastaba (175 × 86 feet [53 × 26 m]) of the queen already has a facade of niches so intricately formed that they are multifaceted.[18] A gradual development of the underground burial chamber can be seen by comparing the 1st Dynasty at Saqqara, where Tomb 3357 from the reign of Aha and Tomb 3503 from the reign of Djer penetrate the ground surface, the form becoming a fully subterranean chamber by the time of Tomb 3035 from the reign of Den (**3.13**).

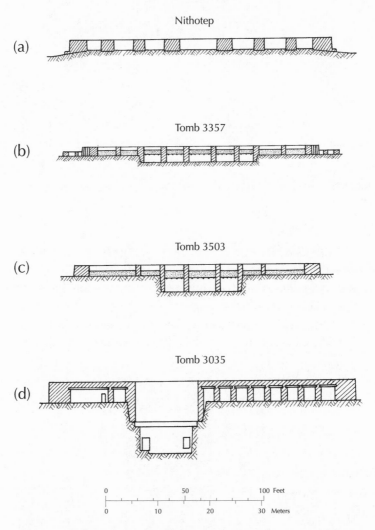

Figure 3.13. The rapid 1st Dynasty development of in-ground burial chambers, as shown by the chronological sequence of the tombs of (a) Queen Nithotep, at Naqada; (b) Tomb 3357 from the reign of Aha, at Saqqara; (c) Tomb 3503 from the reign of Djer, at Saqqara; and (d) Tomb 3035 from the reign of Den, at Saqqara.

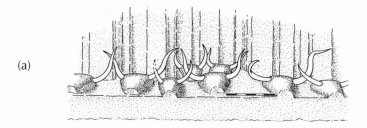

(a)

Figure 3.14. (a) The low terrace surrounding Tomb 3504,
from the reign of Djet, which
holds clay replicas of 350 cattle (b)
heads with inserts of real horns.
(b) Reconstruction of a shrine
in Cätal Hüyük, southern Turkey. Made of plaster, the animal heads have inserts of real
horns.

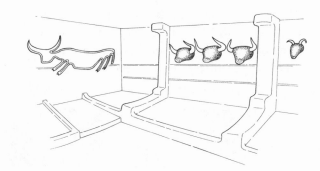

Bull Heads

Three other mastabas at Saqqara have features that seem to have a foreign origin. These
structures have low surrounding platforms holding clay heads of cattle with real horns
(**3.14**).[19] Mastaba 3504, from the reign of Djet (1st Dynasty), has over 300 cattle heads,
a feature somewhat reminiscent of the findings in Cätal Hüyük in Turkey seen in figure
3.14(**b**) and of the Horned Temple of Susa in southern Mesopotamia in figure 1.35(**f**).[20] In
Turkey, such heads are seen to cover walls and benches in a sign of bull worship that has
been observed in Near Eastern and Mediterranean areas for millennia. Although such
devices were omitted from later Egyptian monuments, the bull was venerated in the early
dynasties due to its strength, size, and fertility; it was thought to represent the royal might
in the person of the king. Bulls were also associated with the sun, the constellation of Ursa
Major, and the cult of Mnevis (worship of an unblemished totally black bull).[21] The solar
connection may stem from the appearance of the horns of a bull mounted outside the hut
of the god Min. Here a spiral symbol of the sun is seen to extend to the center of the
horns—a linkage important enough to be used later as a model for the crown of the king
of Upper Egypt (**2.17**). The unusual relationship of the sun and the horns of a bull is
explained later.

The Mounds

Some of the early tombs at Saqqara, such as 3507, 3471, and possibly 3506, disclose an
unusual construction that may have religious significance—they all have a superstructure

in the form of a low square or rectangular tumulus deep within the body of the mastaba.[22] Built directly over the timber roof of the central burial shafts, these mounds of sand and rubble, initially given a layer of brick, were later formed into sloping embankments of steps. When the mound and its thin brick covering were subsequently incorporated into the mastaba, the entire monument, including storage compartments, was built over and around the top of the mound (3.15).

Egyptologist David O'Connor found indications of a brick-encased sand and rubble mound in the Shunet el Zebib, at Abydos, that was strikingly similiar to those at Saqqara.[23] These puzzling internal mounds, perhaps an Egyptianized version of the oval mounds of the Near East, may also be symbolically connected to the Egyptian view of creation, in which the primeval mound was the first land to emerge from the floodwaters. As such, mounds were supposedly imbued with a mysterious power to aid in resurrecting the dead. Indeed, the importance of the mound was such that a tumulus-covered burial chamber became a feature used regularly for royal tombs. In addition to Khasekhemwy's tomb and those at

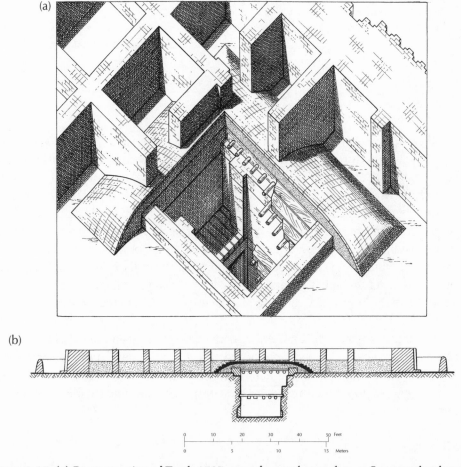

Figure 3.15. (a) Reconstruction of Tomb 3507, one of several mastabas at Saqqara that have an earlier superstructure in the form of a rectangular tumulus constructed over the burial shaft. (b) Section of Tomb 3507.

Saqqara, these mounds or "high sands" have been detected in the temples of Hierakon-polis, Heliopolis, and probably in the temple complex of Osiris at Abydos.[24]

Temple Stairways

Another perplexing feature is seen in monument 3038 at Saqqara, a building that seems to be more than just a tomb (**3.16**). Constructed in three phases, the structure was erected around a rectangular chamber flanked by two rooms at a higher level. Three sides of the structure were enclosed by a pyramid-like configuration of steps that led to the roof and the fourth side by a perpendicular wall pierced by two stairways, one leading to a timber roof and one to a room below ground (**3.17**). Although the structure was enlarged by a terrace in the second building phase and bounded by a wall in the third phase, the roof was always made accessible by some form of staircase. In the final building phase, stair-ways were even made to pierce the north and south sides of a palace-facade wall sur-rounding the entire construction.[25]

Structure 3038 is odd in relation to other tombs at Saqqara, especially in having stair-ways leading to the roof. Indeed, stairs are a utilitarian device meant more for the living than the dead. In the mastaba from the reign of Den, for example, the stairway was used to carry the body of the deceased to the burial chamber and was later sealed to prevent the entry of tomb robbers (**3.5**). When we consider that the ba of a dead Egyptian king was thought to move easily around the tomb by flying or passing through walls, stairways become an unnecessary feature. Clearly, the appearance of stairways at the Saqqaran monu-ment suggests that the structure was built more as a temple than a tomb—and not only a temple but one styled somewhat after those in Mesopotamia.

Priests needed stairways in Mesopotamian temples as a means of ascent for perform-ing sacrifices on a portable roof altar. The height would bring the priest closer to the gods and would allow the populace to view his actions better as he sacrificed an animal and recited an incantation over its welling blood.[26] Although known as a Mesopotamian feature, a sac-rificial temple has also been found in the Egyptian funerary complex of Raneferef (5th Dynasty), at Abusir. Discovered by the Czech Egyptologist Miroslav Verner, the site con-tained a mortuary temple that held statuettes of kneeling prisoners and a relief of a captured

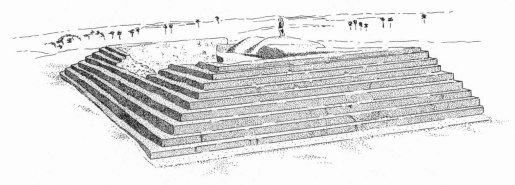

Figure 3.16. An early phase of Tomb 3038 at Saqqara showing steps on three sides.

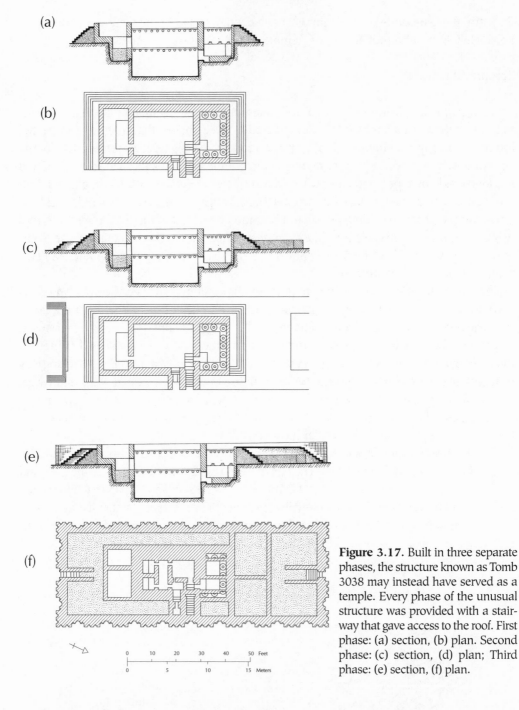

Figure 3.17. Built in three separate phases, the structure known as Tomb 3038 may instead have served as a temple. Every phase of the unusual structure was provided with a stairway that gave access to the roof. First phase: (a) section, (b) plan. Second phase: (c) section, (d) plan; Third phase: (e) section, (f) plan.

Asian chieftain with Libyan and Nubian prisoners. Southeast of the temple was Raneferef's slaughter house, "the Sanctuary of the Knife." Papyri disclose that during a ten-day religious festival a possible 130 bulls were slaughtered in the open courtyard of the structure.

The slaughterhouse of Raneferef and the monument 3038 at Saqqara have similar features; both have outside stairways to the roof, storage rooms, and a place for washing, anointing, and the burning of incense. According to Verner, "a staircase leading to the roof terrace suggests that this space too fulfilled a particular function in the context of the slaughterhouse; perhaps the meat would have been dried in the sun here."[27] It is also possible that sacrificial rites were held on the roof using the king's prisoners as the victims.

Besides the numerous flint knives at the Sanctuary of the Knife, Verner found written confirmation—potsherds of grease vessels showing the *nmt* sign, 𓌦, a hieroglyph meaning "that which is under the knife," or "slaughter." The symbol shows the pyramidal object *hr*, which means "under." Egyptian hieroglyphs, a written language that uses figures or objects to represent words or sounds, are a virtual gold mine of information. Coming from the most remote phases of Egyptian civilization, the writing is an offshoot of pictorial art formed by scribes who drew from representations used in the Predynastic period. Its earliest and most important function was to provide a visible record of facts and occurrences.

In time, things not easily represented by pictures (ideograms), were represented by things that chanced to have a similar sound (phonograms). Even considering the later introduction of phonetic elements, hieroglyphs remained a picture writing throughout their history and did not attempt to replace pictorial elements completely with sound elements.[28] Accordingly, while the pyramidal object *hr* is identified as a butcher's block, no one knows the true meaning of the original object depicted.[29] Instead of a butcher's block, I suggest that the pyramidal object may represent a temple having a stairway leading to the roof— the stairway shown by the lines centered in the structure.

Internal and external stairs are not uncommon in Egyptian temples. They can still be seen leading to roof chapels at the temple of Hathor at Dendera. At this location processions would climb a flight of stairs to unite the ba statue of Hathor with the sun on the roof chapel during the New Year.[30] Similar processions took place at Edfu, the site of the ancient city of Djeba and the place where the mythological battle was fought between Horus and Seth. The winged disc associated with Edfu was traditionally set up over temple entrances in commemoration of the victory of Horus over Seth (**1.10**). As at Dendera, scenes show priests carrying images of the gods in procession on stairs to the roof, where a "Chapel of the Disk" allowed the gods to be joined to the sun, at one time.[31]

Conflagration

Some of the tombs at Abydos and Saqqara had been burned, perhaps as a result of conflict brought by the wars of unification between the north and south. Generated by fires fed by the wood interior, the resulting heat baked much of the internal mud brick to a hard, red finish. Although the fired brick was reused by the ancient builders, making its benefits known, Egyptian builders ignored its superior qualities and continued throughout their history to build with sun-dried mud bricks. The alluvial mud that was formed into bricks was a surprisingly versatile material—it could also be used for the lintels of window panels and for other details, such as moldings. It was often shaped to imitate the earlier building material of vertical reeding. Light in weight, the mud was given extraordinary strength by embedding in it strips of flax linen and drying the mud under great pressure in some unknown manner. Remarkably, a broken portion of an ancient mud lintel has been found, measuring 24 × 7 × 4 inches (63 × 18 × 10 cm) in its broken state.[32]

The same indented walls seen at the mastabas of Saqqara can also be found in the massive enclosure walls of Upper Egypt—a design referred to as palace-facade paneling (**3.18**). At Abydos, King Khasekhemwy built a double wall at Shunet el Zebib around the perimeter of an enclosure of almost 54,000 square feet. The true purpose of this late 2nd Dynasty structure is unknown. Some scholars consider it to be a mortuary monument; others identify it as the location of religious or commemorative ceremonies. South of Abydos, at Hierakonpolis, a similar niched structure called the "Fort" was likewise built by Khasekhemwy (**3.18**). Although geographically distant from Mesopotamia, the Fort has a sacred temple area enclosed by a temenos wall standing amid randomly placed secular structures of the populace, a layout with similarities to the plan of the city of Uruk.[33]

Burial Site of the Kings

One of the ongoing puzzles in Egypt is the location of the true burial site of the Early Dynastic kings, who seem to have built tombs for themselves at two distant locations, north and south. Although all the rulers of the 1st Dynasty, and at least two from the 2nd Dynasty, are known to be interred at Abydos, ownership of the mastabas at Saqqara in the north is less certain. Suggesting that they involve high officials, the tombs also contain items identifying the occupants with kings of the period. However, if Abydos in the south is the true site of the Early Dynastic kings, it is difficult to believe that a ruler would knowingly permit his tomb to be dwarfed by a larger one at Saqqara, regardless of the importance of the northern owner.

Some scholars assume that the tombs at Abydos are cenotaphs (empty tombs or memorials), enabling the king, as ruler of the two lands, to be represented in both places—Saqqara taking precedence, being near Memphis, the city founded with the newly united Egypt; and Abydos, associated with Osiris, the god of death and resurrection, receiving the empty grave.[34] Others claim that when the area of a tomb is considered, it should also include all the subsidiary structures erected by the king. With this perspective, while some tombs from the same period may be larger at Saqqara, they would not exceed the total area at Abydos if the tombs were combined with the niched funerary palaces and the subsidiary burials attributed to the king.[35] Accordingly, this would make the southern cemetery, at Abydos, the true resting place of the early kings. Boat pits like those on the east side of Khasekhemwy's complex at Abydos and at Saqqara, for boats used symbolically to transport the king to the netherworld, are later seen at a number of pyramid sites.[36]

The complications brought by the possibility of two royal burial sites suggest the existence of two societies, a southern Horus group indigenous to Egypt, with some tenuous connections to the Near East, and a northern Seth group with strong Mesopotamian ties. Each area observed some architectural traditions of Mesopotamia: they placed the corners of their structures toward the cardinal points, they built ovals with an underlayment of clean sand, and they made prominent use of decorative niches. The niches used on enclosure walls in the south of Egypt were executed in a simple pattern of alternating panels and recesses; those on mastabas in the north have the compound niches of a more advanced style, suggesting stronger ties to Mesopotamia and therefore a more advanced technology. The northerners may initially have controlled the more numerous southern

Figure 3.18. Built by King Khasekhemwy, at Abydos, the Shunet el Zebib (a) is a great double-walled structure with a pattern of panels on the outside face of the inner wall. (b) A similar structure called the Fort was built by the same king at Hierakonpolis.

group until overcome by rebellion. After their defeat, those remaining in the north were probably forced to accept southern rule. Over time, as the vanquished northerners blended with the native population, their architecture became increasingly Egyptianized in the same way that the symbols of Upper and Lower Egypt were blended in the person of the king after unification.

Origination of the Niche

The blending of the northern group into Egyptian society may best be seen in the palace-facade, its iconographic appearance as a serekh, and its use on the 1st Dynasty mastaba of Nithotep, at Naqada. Frankfort feels that nothing in the early building practices could have led Egyptians to construct the mastabas of the 1st Dynasty. The claim is often made that the decorative paintings of wood frames and mats on the brick mastabas evolved from an earlier structure of the same type. However, when viewing the size of the compound panels, this could not be true. A wooden framework having mats lashed to horizontal poles would by necessity lead to wide, unbroken stretches of surface. Contrary to this, the facade holding the decorations consists of a series of indented vertical panels having widths of 4–8 inches (10–20 cm), a form ideally suited for brickwork. It is almost as though the paintings were fashioned by one building tradition upon a structure designed by a different building tradition (**3.19**).[37]

As always, there are differing scholarly opinions about the origin of the niche. W. M. Flinders Petrie argued that the niched facade on mastabas was a parallel and independent development of both countries—a supposition based on a protodynastic find at Tarkhan, where coffins were made with reused planks. He considered niches to be based on previously existing but undiscovered Egyptian palaces and houses made of wood. Walls of the structure, he claimed, gave the appearance of paneling in having the planks lashed together in vertical patterns—the style being copied and elaborated in mud brick when it later came into general use (**3.20**).[38]

(a) Elevation

(b) Plan

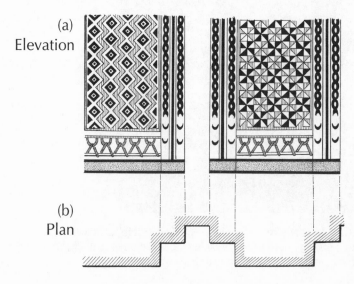

Figure 3.19. Painted to imitate mats of blue, yellow, red, white, and black designs on panels 4–8 inches (10–20 cm) wide, the niches of Tomb 3505 are of a size ideally suited for brickwork; (a) elevation, (b) plan. Yet the decoration seems to be by artisans from one building tradition upon a structure designed by a different building tradition.

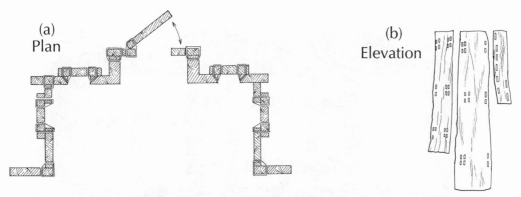

(a)
Plan

(b)
Elevation

Figure 3.20. (a) Petrie suggests that brick niches were developed independently in Egypt and used in a yet undiscovered wooden structure. (b) They were supposedly formed with planks, such as those found at a protodynastic site in Tarkhan.

According to Frankfort, the circumstances Petrie proposed are not substantiated by the evidence. The curved, irregular nature of the planks of Tarkhan indicates that they were reused from Nile river boats, and their shape is inconsistent with the vertical niches proposed (**3.20b**). In addition to the complete absence of the supposed structures, the use of wooden planking is also incompatible as an antecedent for paintings of mats lashed to wooden poles.[39]

George Reisner reasons differently when he discounts a connection of the serekhs to Mesopotamia. Instead of being the facade of a wall, he considers the drawings of the serekh to represent the false door or ka door in the superstructure of a yet undiscovered predynastic tomb. Used for communicating with the dead, the false door is thought to have been placed in a wooden or wattle frame containing the loose rubble of which the tumulus was made. When brick later replaced wood, Reisner claims, doors were decoratively spaced around the entire structure—some being part of the design and others acting as sacred entrances. Thus, he contends, the serekh is derived from an Egyptian structure instead of from the wall of a Mesopotamian temple.[40]

According to evidence, however, just the reverse happened. In Egypt, the niche became a ka door only by the 2nd Dynasty. Studies show no distinction between individual niches in mastabas until the middle of the 1st Dynasty during the reign of Den, when one among all the evenly spaced niches at Tarkhan was found to have a wooden back and floor (**3.21**). From that time forward, instead of continuing as a decorative device, the niche began to assume a different role, tomb facades being progressively simplified until only one or two niches are found in the surrounding wall. Of these, the principal niche always appears, as at Tarkhan, on the southeast wall opposite the burial chamber.[41] Indeed, the southeast assumed such importance that it became the location of choice for the primary false doors of the 2nd Dynasty mastabas, the main entrance for the enclosure of King Khasekhemwy at Abydos, and later the principal entrance of the 3rd Dynasty enclosure wall of Djoser's complex at Saqqara.

Since the Early Dynasties, niches found on various structures have ranged in design from simple to more elaborate forms. Some are shallow indents, while others are set

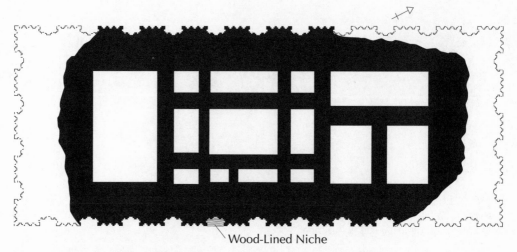

Wood-Lined Niche

Figure 3.21. Tomb 1060, at Tarkhan, the first example yet found in which one niche is distinguished from all others. Opposite the burial chamber on the southeast corner, this niche has a wooden back and floor.

deeply into the walls with the possible intent of bringing them close to the burial chamber **(3.22)**.[42] In later royal tombs, the passage into which the rays of the sun could penetrate farthest was called "The Passage of Re."[43] Also discovered among the tombs of Meidum, Dendera, Saqqara, and Abydos are niches of a cruciform style. Up until the late 2nd Dynasty, these were open to the sky, thereby permitting offerings to be made from the transept while still leaving a path for incoming rays of the sun.[44] As with other forms of niches, some of the cruciform niches are startlingly close imitations of those found in Mesopotamia. The group at Dendera has a cruciform niche in one tomb **(3.23)** very similar to that found in the temple of Eanna in Uruk **(3.10)**. Another close replica of the same Uruk niche is shown in the stone-lined cruciform chapel of Methen, a brick mastaba at Saqqara dated to the reign of Sneferu, first king of the 4th Dynasty **(3.24)**. The 4th

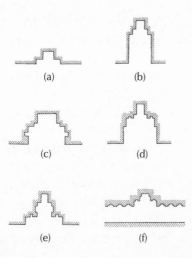

(a)   (b)

(c)   (d)

(e)   (f)

Figure 3.22. A sampling of the many niches Reisner found while investigating the development of the Egyptian tomb.

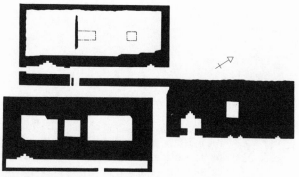

Figure 3.23. Group of mastabas from Dendera with niches (false doors) appearing only on the east face. At the tomb of Abu Suten (top), the small niche on the northeast is the usual location for the door of the owner's wife. The larger stone niche on the south end displays a figure of Abu Suten, owner of the tomb. A wall in front is to provide privacy. The cruciform niche on the right provides privacy yet allows the incoming sun to illuminate the niche. The shape of this cruciform niche is almost exactly the same as those found in the temple of Eanna at Uruk, as seen in figure 3.10.

Figure 3.24. The cruciform 4th Dynasty chapel of Methen, at Saqqara.

Dynasty tomb enlargement of Nefermaat and his wife Atet, at Meidum, shows side chambers added to an existing deeply set niche. When the tomb was again enlarged, the cruciform configuration was blocked, for some unknown reason, and once again replaced with a simple deep niche (3.25).[45]

The cruciform configurations found in Egypt, reminiscent of those in Mesopotamia, may have the same function as those in Newgrange, Ireland, and in the cathedrals of Europe—locations where the sun illuminated an altar placed in a sanctuary. Facing east, as they usually did in Egypt when above ground, a niche served in many ways. It linked the deceased to the center of the sun's travels on the horizon; it was used as a sacred chapel for offerings and communication; it acted as a false door, or as a ritual entry to allow the spirit to pass from the realm of the dead to the land of the living. This feature was often emphasized by the placement of a life-size figure in relief of the ka, or spiritual double, stepping out of the niche.[46]

One such likeness has a portrait bust of Idu in the false door of his underground tomb at Giza (3.26). Palms up, forearms extending from close to each side, Idu symbolically receives offerings of bread, beer, and cakes.[47] No doubt, it is a pose also meant to reproduce in human form the squared-off U shape of the niche in which he appears, perhaps

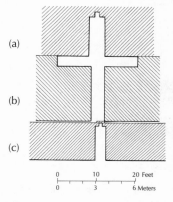

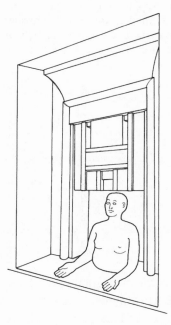

(a)

(b)

(c)

0   10   20 Feet
0   3   6 Meters

Figure 3.25. Changing niches are shown by the enlargement at the mastaba of Nefermaat and his wife Atet at Meidum. (a) A first niche was placed deep in the main body of the monument. (b) A surrounding wall was later provided with a cruciform niche. (c) A final enlargement reverted once again to the simple niche.

Figure 3.26. False door with portrait bust of Idu, his forearms extended to receive offerings of bread, beer, and cakes. In plan, he seems to imitate the ka sign seen elsewhere on the standards of Mesopotamia and Egypt.

confirming that its early purpose was to receive the life-giving rays of the sun. Viewing Idu in plan also supports the suggestion that the U-shaped ka sign of two extended forearms on the standards of Egypt and Mesopotamia is a symbolic representation common to the early niches and to the pose of Idu (**2.21**).

The ka signs of Mesopotamia and 1st Dynasty Egypt, in their simplest shape, appear long before they became the elaborately shaped false doors theologically defined in Egypt as portals for offerings and communication.[48] Although these false doors were originally made to provide a clear view of the east to energize the ka by the rays of the sun, once they were placed underground or blocked by later constructions, their practical function took second place to their theological aspect.[49] When located underground, many false doors, placed on the main axis of the tomb, were faced, if only symbolically, toward the land of the dead in the west.

(a)

(b)

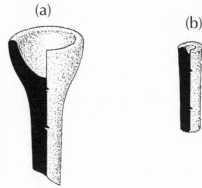

Figure 3.27. Two examples of a number of like objects found in the delta at Buto and similar to those used in Sumer during the period of Uruk VII/VI (3500 BCE). Made of Nile mud, these fired objects were not trade objects.

Terra-cotta Pegs

In Sumer as we have seen, temples were decorated with thousands of terra-cotta pegs inserted into the walls, their painted heads forming a protective and decorative crust for the mud brick. Already shown to have had a long history in Eridu, they were recently found in Buto, capital of Upper Egypt. This is an area covered by deep layers of alluvial mud brought down from the highlands of Ethiopia. Despite the difficulties, German Egyptologist Thomas von der Way has uncovered clay cones dating from Naqada II (3500–3300 BCE) that are similar to those used in Sumer during the period Uruk VII/VI (3500 BCE). These terra-cotta objects were of two types: small, with straight or tapered sides, and long, with conical stems (**3.27**). Both types show indents in their enlarged heads to receive a coloring agent, though none was present.[50] While no mastabas have been found nearby, it is likely the pegs were put to the same decorative use in Egypt as in Mesopotamia. Although exact imitations of those in Mesopotamia, the objects found in Buto were made of hard-baked Nile mud, by or under the supervision of someone familiar with Mesopotamian architecture from the middle Uruk period.

Pottery fragments discovered at the site date from the same period. They belong to small bowls having a glaze of horizontal whitish stripes, probably applied by a sophisticated technique. Unknown in Egypt, the decoration is characteristic of pottery in the plain of 'Amug near Antioch, northern Syria. The pottery was made when the settlements of 'Amug were closely related to the Uruk culture of Mesopotamia and was shipped directly to the Delta.[51]

Although the idea of monumental architecture was brought to Egypt by others, it did not retain its Mesopotamian style for long except in the form of the niches appearing on tombs and enclosure walls. Given the fresh outlook of Egyptian builders, governed by a ruler with supreme power and blessed with an unlimited source of stone, Egyptian architecture took its own unique direction and far surpassed that of those who laid the groundwork.

CHAPTER 4

STEP PYRAMIDS

Although the idea of monumental architecture brought to Egypt by the Mesopotamians eventually led to construction of the pyramids, the transition came in slow steps, the entire 3rd Dynasty being devoted to the very building experiments that made possible the unique Egyptian character and permanency of the 4th Dynasty structures. And permanent it was! Although the mud-brick structures of the Near East have long since collapsed into misshapen heaps, the stone monuments of Egypt have stood for almost 5,000 years, the greatest threat to their existence being the value of the outer layer of fine casing stone.

While Egyptians were able to fashion the hardest stone into bowls, vases, and the like before the 1st Dynasty, stone was sparingly used for early construction purposes. Soil in one form or another was the main building ingredient: mud plaster to line graves, foundations, and firepits or as a binder for branches or matting. Evidence for true mud-brick Predynastic building is rare, although it is found as a lining for burial chambers of the elite. When stone was employed, it was generally restricted to small items such as door jambs and false doors, the most ambitious projects being the granite paving used in the burial chambers of Den in the 1st Dynasty and Khasekhemwy in the 2nd Dynasty. However, when it was found that limestone could withstand large spans, that it would support considerable weight, and that a corbeled vault or high ceiling could be made by placing each succeeding course of stone inward, monumental architecture began to increase in scale. Yet, as shown by the pyramid complex of Djoser, second king of the 3rd Dynasty, even with this awareness, stone was still often shaped to imitate the reed bundles, wattles, and hanging mats used in the makeshift buildings of earlier times. This is not unusual—when a new material is introduced to a culture, it is often made to imitate the old tried and true substance.

In our own time this is illustrated in iron being cast in the Industrial Age to imitate ornately carved wood or stone and plastic being made to resemble the characteristics of the wood it replaces. In Egypt, when fragile materials such as reeds, lilies, and papyrus were translated into stone, they were generally employed as they had been in earlier flimsy pre-dynastic temples and shelters. This transition can be seen, for example, at Djoser's pyramid complex at Saqqara, where reed bundles replicated in stone were formed to support a ceiling or were used as pilasters for a wall (**4.1, 4.2**). These, however, were not the ornamental round columns of base, shaft, and capital, a hallmark of Egyptian architecture that took a number of generations to become a standard building form.

Although the stone supports of the 3rd Dynasty were imitative of bundled plant forms, they were not free standing; the still timid architects designed them as extended pilasters, fixing them along their full length to the end of a projecting wall. Only by the 4th Dynasty, with the need for more interior light and with the more confident use of stone that came with experience, were freestanding columns used as supports. As shown in the temples of Chephren (Khafre) and Mycerinus (Menkaure), these columns were square in section—functional but without a hint of vegetation. The mortuary temple of Sahure at Abusir shows that another change occurred in the 5th Dynasty. With renewed confidence, and a desire for still more interior light, the unadorned square supports were once again made into bundled plant forms, but now they stood as fully rounded free columns. This natural evolution of vegetable matter into ornate stone construction shows that the decorative mistakes made earlier on the mastabas, an architectural style foisted on the Egyptians, were not repeated on the stonework, an architectural style that they themselves had developed.

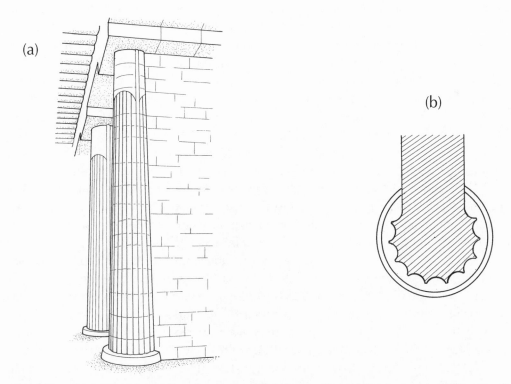

Figure 4.1. (a) Pavilion at Saqqara showing reed bundles used as attached columns. (b) Section of attached column.

(a)

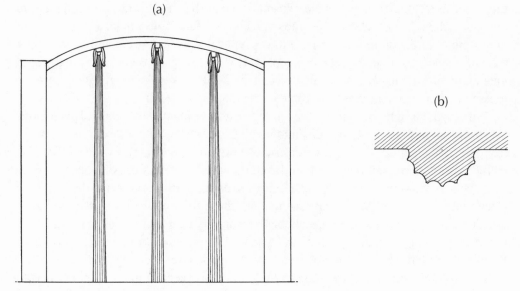

(b)

Figure 4.2. (a) Theoretical restoration of attached reedlike pilaster supporting the roof of the entrance colonnade. (b) Section of pilaster.

The Step Pyramid of Djoser

The Step Pyramid of Djoser at Saqqara, a 411 × 358-foot (125 × 109 m) structure that launched the Pyramid Age, was not originally planned as a pyramid (**4.3**). Rising to a final height of 204 feet (62 m), the six-step monument was built in several phases. It started as a smooth-faced mastaba of local stone in horizontal courses, 207 feet (63 m) square. The 26-foot (8 m) height of its initial phase was close in design to mastabas of the 2nd Dynasty. Due to later additions, it is not known if the original (M1) mastaba had the same false doors on the east face as did 2nd Dynasty counterparts. In a departure from earlier times and from Near Eastern antecedents, the mastaba of Djoser was not only made square instead of rectangular; it also had its sides instead of its corners oriented to the cardinal points. These two characteristics became a common feature of all later pyramids.

The perimeter of the square mastaba was first enlarged by a slight amount around its perimeter (M2) and then enlarged a second time (M3), but only on the east side (**4.4**). Neither addition was brought to the same height as the preceding mastaba, making the resultant structure asymmetrical and aesthetically unappealing—as good a reason as any to cover it up. A structure comprising several circumferential layers of masonry was then built to encompass the mastaba and its additions. The layers leaned inward upon each other at an angle of 75 degrees, and as they rose in height, they were interrupted by set-backs that formed four steps (P1) of a pyramid 131 feet (40 m) high. Still dissatisfied with its size, Imhotep, King Djoser's architect, once again enlarged the base by adding two additional steps on the north and west sides (P2). The result was a rectangular structure about 411 feet (125 m) from east to west and 358 feet (109 m) from north to south. Although the layers of stone forming the mass of the pyramid are of low quality and poor workmanship, the outside face of the four- and six-step building phases is a single layer of well-fitted Tura

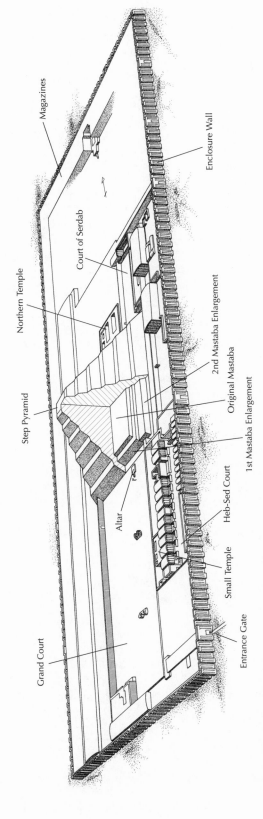

Figure 4.3. The Step Pyramid complex of King Djoser.

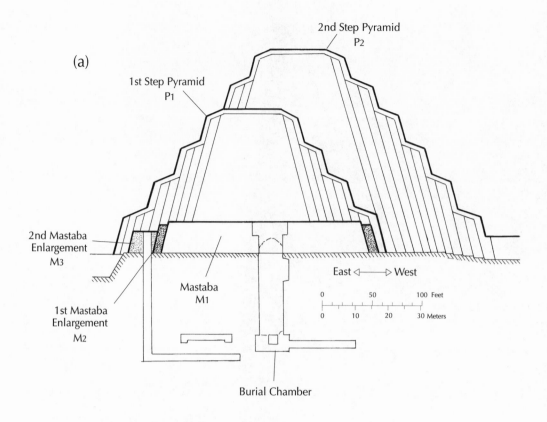

(a)

2nd Step Pyramid
P2

1st Step Pyramid
P1

2nd Mastaba
Enlargement
M3

1st Mastaba
Enlargement
M2

Mastaba
M1

East ◁——▷ West

0	50	100 Feet
0	10	20	30 Meters

Burial Chamber

(b)

Figure 4.4. (a) Section looking south through the Step Pyramid and burial chamber. (b) Detail of accretion layers.

limestone.[1] Overlooking the city of Memphis as a gigantic white stairway leading to the heavens, the pyramid of Djoser dramatically departed from its Near Eastern antecedents and became the most inspired architectural work yet conceived (**4.5**).

Although startling, it was not a complete architectural break from its Mesopotamian progenitors. Indeed, the entire pyramid complex is surrounded by a 33-foot-high (10 m) enclosure wall of alternating panels and recesses similar to those on the panel-facade enclosure walls of King Khasekhemwy at Hierakonpolis and Abydos (**4.6**). However, as noted,

Figure 4.5. The Step Pyramid from inside the enclosure wall.

Figure 4.6. Indented facade on the southeast corner entrance of the enclosure wall of King Djoser.

instead of having its corners oriented to the cardinal points like those structures, the sides of Djoser's pyramid face those points and the temenos walls are oriented to match.

This enormous wall—1,800 × 900 feet (550 × 275 m)—surrounds all the structures and dummy buildings necessary for the life of the deceased in the afterworld. Among the buildings are a mortuary temple and a *serdab*, a small structure where a sealed limestone likeness of Djoser looks to the east through two peepholes. This arrangement supposedly enabled the ka to leave the chamber, permitted offerings to pass through, and allowed the deceased to view the rising sun. The enclosure also holds a ceremonial court used by the king to celebrate the Heb-Sed festival, a reenactment of the coronation and a symbolic renewal of his physical and magical powers, held in his 30th reigning year and every three years thereafter. Although the underground tomb of the Step Pyramid was generally similar to those found in earlier dynasties, this location, hewn out of rock to a depth of about 92 feet (28 m), had an even more elaborate complex of storage rooms and burial areas.[2]

Djoser made the greatest contribution to the architecture of the 3rd Dynasty. Similar funerary structures were begun by other kings of the dynasty, but none was able to bring one to completion despite construction and orientation that were close copies of Djoser's pyramid and would not have required the several building phases used earlier by Imhotep. Judging by the remains, Sekhemket's seven-step pyramid (**4.7**) would have risen to 230 feet (70 m) from a square base of 395 feet (120 m). The Layer Pyramid (**4.8**), possibly built by Khaba at Zawiyet el-Aryan, was planned to rise in six or seven steps from a base of 276 feet (84 m) on each side. Only the lower courses of both monuments remain. These show that all the step pyramids of the 3rd Dynasty were built of "accretion layers," a term used in a now abandoned theory whereby the number of layers applied around the central core of a pyramid supposedly had a direct relation to the length of the king's reign—the more layers, the longer his reign.

Possible Genesis of the Step Pyramid

While there are few clues to the religious ideas behind early monuments, concepts of special importance may have been incorporated into the 3rd Dynasty funerary complexes in a continuing effort at symbolic unification of the country. According to Emery, the mounds

Table 4.1
CHRONOLOGY OF 3RD DYNASTY KINGS

KING	DATE (BCE)
Sanakht (= Nebka ?)	2686–2667
Djoser (Netjerykhet)	2667–2648
Sekhemkhet	2648–2640
Khaba	2640–2637
Huni (?)	2637–2613

After Ian Shaw and Paul Nicholson, *The Dictionary of Ancient Egypt*, 310. A different estimate suggests the 3rd Dynasty as 2649–2575 BCE (John Baines and Jaromír Málek, *Atlas of Ancient Egypt*, 36).

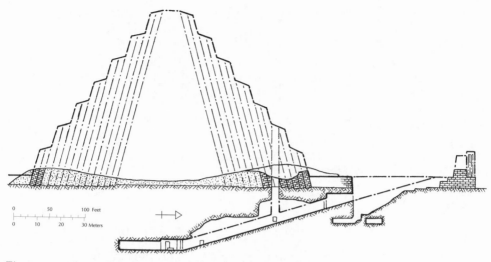

Figure 4.7. The unfinished pyramid of Sekhemkhet, looking west.

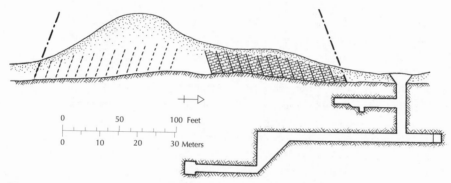

Figure 4.8. The layer pyramid of Zawiyet el-Aryan, looking west.

found inside the mastaba of Saqqara were an attempt by the Egyptians to blend the southern tumulus with the northern paneled mastaba. He postulates that the mound was used to cover the burial pit and the paneled temenos wall was used to encompass the entire site. When heightened in stages, Emery suggests, the mounds of Abydos developed into a stepped pyramid. When later combined with the paneled facades of the Saqqaran mastabas, he claims, they led directly to the Step Pyramid complex of King Djoser (**4.9**).[3]

This idea is palatable in that the main entrance through Djoser's temenos wall is near the southeast corner, the same location as the main ka door of the 2nd Dynasty pyramids. Still, the discovery of a hidden mound at the tomb of Djet at Abydos suggests that Emery's theory requires modification. This new find indicates that some tombs in both parts of the country were made of two elements: a low brick-encased mound over the burial pit and a second roof covering the whole area of the tomb. According to David O'Connor, this indicates that the original version of the Step Pyramid complex was modeled on the Abydos traditions instead of on a tradition developed at Saqqara.[4] Considering this, perhaps the mastaba in the Step Pyramid is not simply an early building phase. It may cover a yet

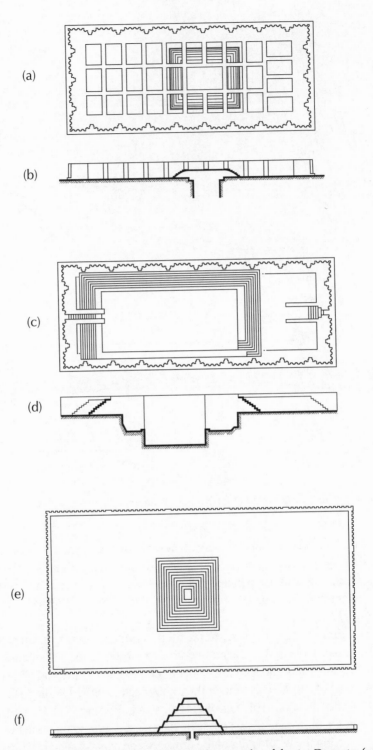

(a)

(b)

(c)

(d)

(e)

(f)

Figure 4.9. Possible development of a step pyramid from tombs of the 1st Dynasty. (a, b) Plan and section of paneled mastaba containing a mound covering the burial pit. (c, d) Plan and section of a stepped mound covering the burial pit of a paneled mastaba. (e, f) Heightening the steps of the mound and separating the paneled walls may have led to the Step Pyramid of Djoser.

Horizontal Layers
of Mastaba

Inclined Layer of
Step Pyramid

Figure 4.10. Djoser's Step Pyramid shows the accretion layers overlaying an internal mastaba built of horizontal courses.

undiscovered low brick-encased mound. Indeed, instead of being built on the mound, as Emery suggests, the Step Pyramid was actually built from the ground up as a completely independent structure.[5]

The inward-leaning accretion layers that surround the horizontal courses of the mastaba are an addition visible even today (**4.10**). Later step pyramids of the 3rd Dynasty do not seem to contain this inner structure, suggesting that the practice of covering the burial chamber with a hidden mound stopped with Djoser.

Puzzling Pyramids

Other pyramids generally attributed to the 3rd Dynasty consist of a series of six small step pyramids, Zawiyet el-Mayitin (**4.11**), Abydos (Sinki) (**4.12**), el-Kula (**4.13**), Naqada (Nubt) (**4.14**), el-Ghanimiya (Edfu), and Elephantine (**4.15**). The builder of these small

Figure 4.11. Small step pyramid of Zawiyet el-Mayitin.

Figure 4.12. Small step pyramid at Abydos.

Figure 4.13. Small step pyramid of el-Kula.

Figure 4.14. Small step pyramid at Naqada.

Figure 4.15. Small step pyramid of Elephantine.

pyramids is unknown, as is the purpose for their construction, since they lack burial chambers and cannot be considered tombs. Crudely built with layers of local fieldstone, they are held together with a mortar of desert clay. Sinki, el-Kula, Zawiyet el-Mayitin, and Nubt are approximately aligned by their corners to the cardinal points. Elephantine has an uncertain orientation somewhere between its corner and sides. Yet to be cleared, el-Ghanimiya has one partly exposed side oriented close to north.

Constructed in some undetermined sequence at locations generally along the Nile, these puzzling three- and four-step pyramids are on the west side of the river, except for Zawiyet el-Mayitin, which is on the east side, and Elephantine, located on an island in the Nile near Aswan. Plundered by treasure seekers and archaeologists alike, and used by local inhabitants as quarries, the small pyramids have been left in a ruinous state, standing now only 16–26 feet (5–8 m) high. Each has a core surrounded by three or four outer layers forming a base dimension of about 60 feet (18 m). Slightly larger, Zawiyet el-Mayitin is 74 feet square (23 m). The surrounding layers, which maintain an outer slope of about 75 degrees, are built of inwardly leaning stone, the greatest weight of a single block being between 500 and 1,000 pounds (226–453 kg).[6] This is the same angle given to all mastabas and, as far as we know, to the internal stepped cores of all true pyramids. Judging from remaining foundations, the same smooth facing layer at Zawiyet el-Mayitin, of which only a few courses remain, was probably used at some of the other minor pyramids.

The Unfinished Pyramid of Sinki

The unfinished pyramid at Abydos (Sinki), uncovered by Nabil Swelim and Günter Dreyer, typifies these early structures. With a height of 16 feet (5 m) and a core and two layers of inwardly inclined fieldstones, Sinki is surrounded by a foundation square intended to support a layer of casing stone. The layers of stone that comprise the nucleus are carelessly

(a)

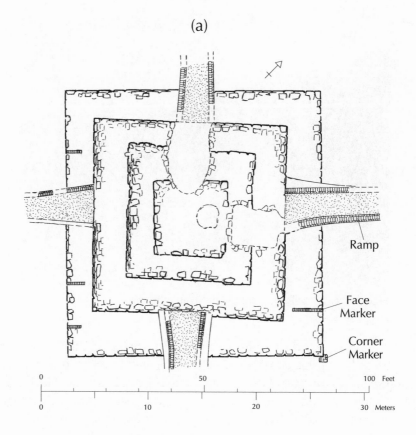

Ramp

Face
Marker

Corner
Marker

0   50   100   Feet

0   10   20   30   Meters

(b)

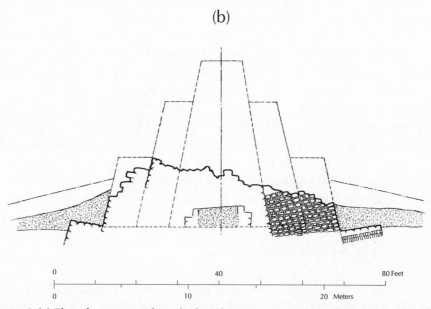

0   40   80 Feet

0   10   20   Meters

Figure 4.16. (a) Plan of step pyramid, at Abydos, showing ramps to raise the stone. Brick-wall markers were used to guide construction of corners, faces, core, and layers of the nucleus. (b) Side view showing estimated height of the completed accretion layers.

oriented, badly squared, uneven in the length of their sides, and unequal not only in thickness of layers but also within each layer. On the other hand, the foundation for the casing stone, defined by two courses of inclined fieldstone, is well oriented, squared, and has sides of almost identical length. When construction was stopped, the builders left in place four ramps, which extend at right angles from each side of the nucleus to beyond the square of the pyramid base (4.16).

According to Swelim, the manner in which the pyramid was built is suggested by the remains: having selected a site and cleared it of sand and rubble to a depth of about 20 inches (50 cm), the builders leveled the entire area and a layer of mortar was applied to the surface. After marking the approximate positions for the corners, faces, core, and layers of the nucleus, they built the core to a height of approximately 40 inches or one meter— the maximum distance people can readily lift stone. Following this, a first layer leaning inward onto the core was brought to the same height. With the upper level of this first layer used as a step, stone lifted from the ground allowed the core to be built up by one more meter. With a second inward-leaning layer used as a step, the height of both the first layer and the core were again increased by one meter. The core having reached its maximum height of 10 feet (3 m) without the need for a ramp, work on the nucleus seems to have stopped for a careful remeasurement, squaring, and reorientation of the casing stone. The survey completed, the second layer was heightened with the aid of ramps.[7]

Although its final shape can only be imagined, with a base length of 79 feet (24 m), Swelim claims its height would have been between 33 and 39 feet (10–12 m).[8] However, given the 12- to 15-degree angle of the ramp and its present 39-foot (12 m) length, the ramp could only have reached a maximum height of 20 feet (6 m).[9] Therefore, considering the small size of the pyramid, it is assumed that the height of the ramps was increased until the nucleus was completed. The ramps may then have been disassembled and reerected to apply the mantle of casing stone. A greater height could also have been achieved by increasing the number of layers surrounding the central core. This would have formed a somewhat regularized staircase of steps, each about one meter high, which would have allowed stone to be passed by hand or by gradually being chocked up from one step to another as before (4.17).[10]

The small four-step pyramid of Seila, known to have been built by Sneferu, first king of the 4th Dynasty, is often though incorrectly associated with this group, since it shares elements with them: it is without a burial chamber and is constructed of accretion layers of local stone (4.18).[11] However, at about 99 feet (30 m) square, Seila contains a volume of stone more than 50 percent greater. Of more significance, it follows the mastaba inside Djoser's Step Pyramid by having its sides oriented to the cardinal points.[12] Supposedly so planned to enable their sides to follow the course of the Nile, some small pyramids, such as Zawiyet el-Mayitin, do not adhere to this rule, and others that do, such as Seila and el-Ghanimiya, are too distant for any such linkage.

The puzzling series of small step pyramids, of unknown dates and ownership, opens the door to some interesting conjecture concerning their chronologies. All forms of technology have a natural progression that starts with small, tentative steps before a major work can be accomplished. This is particularly so in architecture, where each effort seems to challenge the imagination and daring of others to produce a yet greater work—especially when

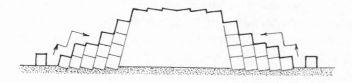

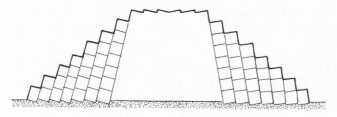

Figure 4.17. Schematic of a step pyramid constructed by raising stone one step at a time. The step pyramid can be erected without the use of ramps if it has enough circumferential layers.

Figure 4.18. Small step pyramid of Seila, built by Sneferu, first king of the 4th Dynasty.

the sponsor (in this case, a king) considers the structure to be a reflection of his power and is able to marshal the unlimited forces necessary for its successful completion. Therefore, while it is generally assumed that Djoser's pyramid was a new form of construction inspired by the mind of Imhotep, in reality it may have been a more ambitious effort in an earlier and already proven system of building—one that may have had its beginnings in the afore-mentioned smaller and less important step pyramids dotted around the country. Contin-uing the mysteries surrounding the 3rd Dynasty, an earlier king than Djoser may have invented the art of building in stone.[13]

Helping to support this hypothesis is an anonymous enclosure west of the Sekhemkhet complex, called Gisr el-Mudir. Although the walls seem to have been built with a rubble core, the structure has corners of solid masonry formed in two tiers with courses sloping inward. Pottery from the fill is provisionally dated to the 2nd or the beginning of the 3rd Dynasty. If the dates are accurate, this structure may represent an intermediate stage between the mud-brick enclosures of Abydos and the small stone step pyramids of the 3rd Dynasty.[14] This leads to the intriguing thought that these small pyramids, with their set-back stages, may have been a reflection in stone of the ziggurats of the Near East (**1.32, 1.33**). Although the examples cited come from a later time than the Egyptian step pyra-mids, the Near East structures are clearly descended from a long history of the same archi-tectural style.

I. E. S. Edwards, the English Egyptologist, considers that the small step pyramids belong to the same stage of technical achievement as those of Djoser and Sekhemkhet. Basing this claim on the squareness of their bases, he dates them after the unfinished pyra-mid of Sekhemkhet, builder of the first pyramid with a square base.[15] However, this view does not allow for the square mastaba built deep within Djoser's pyramid even before the rest of the structure was erected.

An earlier date for the small step pyramids than has previously been imagined also seems to be supported by their orientation. Although in height they are structurally more daring than anything built earlier, the corners of the small step pyramids are still generally made to favor the cardinal points—the same direction as in the early tombs at Abydos and Saqqara and the yet earlier structures of Mesopotamia. The first change in the orientation of a major tomb occurs with the mastaba in Djoser's pyramid, with its sides faced to the cardinal points—an orientation used from that time forward for all pyramidal structures. Considering this, the small step pyramids seem to have been built before the mastaba of Djoser's pyramid—either sometime in the 2nd Dynasty or by Sanakht or an earlier and yet unknown king of the 3rd Dynasty. Indeed, stepped structures, some of which appear to have a stela mounted on their apex, are found on pottery markings from the 1st Dynasty, at Abydos.[16]

The Step Pyramid as a Solar Mountain

Although the 4th Dynasty pyramid of Seila is not to be considered part of the series of small 3rd Dynasty step pyramids, it may have served the same purpose as that for which the others were built. Devoid of burial chambers and distant from contemporary ceme-teries, the small pyramids, appearing at the edge of cultivation, may have functioned as

man-made solar mountains for identifying the time of the inundation or some such periodic event. As elsewhere in the world, this could be done by estimating, from the same
standpoint, the distance of the rising or setting sun to the pyramid as the sun progressed
along the horizon from solstice to solstice (4.19). Not only would this be an easier method
to judge the time of year than the careful measurement of shadows cast by some gnomonic
device; it would also be seen by a wider audience of farmers than would any gnomon. The
small step pyramids spaced down the length of Egypt are possible structures for perform-
ing this function.

Over time, these small pyramids of Egypt seem to have departed from their Near Eastern, solstitially favored antecedents and become, as at Seila, oriented to the equinox. Presumably this change was encouraged by the increasing need of believers in the Heliopolitan cult to associate the life and death of the king to the rising and setting of the sun. The
connection between sun and pyramid finds its genesis in the Pyramid Texts (2375–2345
BCE), a funerary tract consisting of hundreds of spells or utterances, which include the oldest description yet found in Egypt of how the universe was formed. Portions of the text
were found in nine pyramids of the Old Kingdom. The archaic language and oft-repeated
nature of references to the sun-god suggest that they originate from a time long before, in
the city of Heliopolis. (At an earlier time, the city was called Iunu. In the Book of Genesis, Heliopolis, now referred to as On, was the place where the daughter of a priest was
given to Joseph in marriage as a reward for his services.)

Egyptian Genesis

According to the utterances found in the ancient Pyramid Texts, at the beginning all was
water, the basic ingredient of the universe and the source of all life. In the story Atum, who
is identified with the sun here and in the later Coffin Texts (2055–1795 BCE), was at first a
seed of undeveloped matter immersed in Nun, the Primeval Waters.[17] Finding himself
without a place to stand at the moment of creation, he formed the Primeval Mound in his

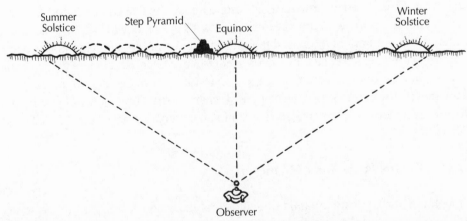

Figure 4.19. To approximate a time for the inundation, Egyptians may have viewed the rising or setting sun from the same point and estimated sun diameters to one of the many small
step pyramids located across the country.

first act as manifestation of the sun-god, Atum.[18] While seated on the mound, by sneezing, spitting, or masturbating, he produced from himself Shu, a son who represents space and sunlight, and Tefnut, a daughter who represented order and moisture.[19] Often pictured as lion and lioness, the twins Shu and Tefnut are called the eyes of Ra, a name given to Atum when he later combined names to form Ra-Atum.

The union between the two siblings brought forth a son, Geb, god of the earth, and a daughter, Nut, goddess of the sky. With Shu supporting the elongated body of Nut as she leans over to span the earth, they form a void in the infinite waters separating the earth from the sky. While so positioned, Nut is depicted as swallowing the evening sun and, after it has traveled through her body, giving birth to it at sunrise. Her brother-husband Geb has a dual personality: keeping the dead within his body he is seen as a malevolent force; reclined, with his erect penis pointing skyward, he is considered a benevolent god of fertility. Completing the pantheon of nine gods of Heliopolis, called the ennead, Geb and Nut have four offspring, Osiris, Isis, Set, and Nephthys.

Of the siblings, Osiris, the god of death, resurrection, and fertility, was the most important. As such, he is shown as a standing mummy, his hands projecting from beneath the wrappings and clutching the royal crook and flail, symbols of his rank, tightly to his chest. He is also the dead manifestation of the earthly king and has an important cult center at Abydos. Dismembered by his brother Seth, god of chaos and confusion, he was made whole by his sister-wife Isis, known to be great in magic, medicine, and cunning. Seth had cult centers in the delta and at Naqada, where he had been venerated since the predynastic period. Often portrayed as a mythical beast with the head of an anteater, Seth is sometimes shown with an erect forked tail and the body of a dog. His sister-wife Nephthys is one of the deities guarding the four cardinal points and the canopic jars of the dead, vessels used for burial of the viscera removed during the embalming process. Linked to the north, Nephthys protects the lungs; Isis, the liver (south); creator-goddess Neith, the stomach (east); and scorpion-goddess Selket, the intestines (west).

The Benben Stone

Into the absolute darkness of the primordial waters, the space created by Shu allowed light to enter with the first morning. The morning light and its daily occurrence are symbolized by the Benu or light-bird (phoenix) landing on the *benben*, a sacred object upon which the sun shines. In a strange association, typical of Egypt, the ancient word for heron or phoenix, *benu*, made the bird analogous in the Egyptian mind to the benben stone. While the derivation of the benben stone is unknown, it has both sexual and solar connotations, due among other reasons to the wordplay between its name and the verb *weben*, "to shine" or "to rise" (as of the sun).[20] Considered to have been the first piece of solid matter to exist in the universe, the stone is an important part of the creation myth. Supposedly made by a drop of semen from Atum falling into the primeval ocean, it is shown in its earliest and most primitive form as a standing stone having a rounded top (**4.20**). The similarity between the masculine benben form in figure 4.20(**c**) and the shrine of Min in figure 2.4(**k**), without the later Egyptian accouterments, and the white crown of Upper Egypt in figure 2.12 is especially noteworthy. When manifest in its feminine form as a square object with

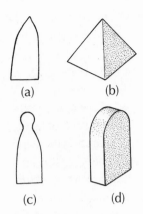

(a)   (b)

(c)   (d)

Figure 4.20. Two styles of benben used throughout the history of Egypt. (a, b) The feminine form known as benbent. (c, d) The masculine form.

a pointed top, it is more properly a *benbent*, but in common use it is called a benben. As stela or pyramidion, these two architectural forms, male and female, recur throughout the long history of Egypt. As an attribute of the sun-god, the pyramidion in its feminine form was either used for the capstone of pyramids or held aloft by the long shaft of an obelisk and covered with gold foil or electum (a mixture of gold and silver) to reflect the sunlight.[21]

Memphite Theology

The importance of the mound in Egyptian thought is shown by the Memphite Theology, a later and different creation doctrine. Copied from an older text during the reign of Shabaka, a 25th Dynasty pharaoh (715–701 BCE), the train of thought it contains goes back at least to the Coffin Texts. In this new cosmogony, instead of the hand of Atum playing the prominent role in formation of the world, all creation was preceded by a thought.[22] Indeed, everything that exists first finds its origin in the mind and the word of the creator, the ultimate spirit, Ptah being the link between the creator's thoughts and their physical realization.[23]

He created simply by naming things. Egyptians believed that the teeth and lips of the creator corresponded to the seed and hands of Atum. They imagined the tongue to be the organ of speech and believed that objects were made by having their names pronounced by the creator's tongue.[24] The creative power of the divine word has since become central to all Near East religious thought. In Sumerian cosmogony, when the people observed the power of the king to achieve his desire with a simple command, they concluded that their gods could accomplish much more, being more powerful.[25] The idea is reflected in the Old Testament, where God creates heaven and earth with a series of commands— "And God said let there be light. And there was light"—and is carried over to the New Testament with "In the beginning was the Word, and the word was with God, and the Word was God."

Ptah was a god who dwelt within the earth and was the source of everything that grows; he was Ptah-Ta-Tjenen, a Memphite name for god of the primeval mound.[26] It has been suggested that the Egyptians fashioned the concept of the mound by observing the high points of land teeming with vegetation and insect life as the floodwaters of the inundation receded. The "Mound of the First Time" is thought to be the site of Heliopolis, the dwelling place of the high god (the sun rising on the first morning), and the place where the king, in all his glory and finery, ascends the primeval mound to meet and be recognized by God in his form as the sun—the implication being that the mound symbolizes the world mountain.[27] The Ethiopian king Piankhi, who visited Heliopolis at a later time (about 730 BCE), reported that the city temple contained a man-made hill north of the town.[28] In Egypt, this hill, or "high sand," was symbolically used in religious rites reenacting the events of creation. For example, when a statue of the deceased king was presented with the crown of Lower Egypt during the final ceremony inside the pyramid, the statue was first placed on a heap of sand.[29]

Not only did a primeval mound exist in the temple at Heliopolis; every temple in Egypt was required to stand on a hill, just as they had in Mesopotamia. The road along this hill varied, being steep in the case of pyramid temples or rock temples and less noticeable in other cases—sometimes just a few steps or a ramp to mark the rise. From its lowest point at the entrance through successive courts to the highest point, it reached a small dark room called the holy of holies, the most potent sanctuary in Egypt. This place was conceived as the primeval hill, the first land to arise from the waters of creation.[30] At Karnak, for example, an inscription of Hatshepsut states: "I know that Karnak is the Light Mountain (horizon) upon earth, the venerable hill of primeval beginning, the healthy eye of the Lord of All—his favorite place which carries his beauty and encompasses his suite."[31] Probably a fetish of the sun-god, such as a niche or a benben, was kept in the darkened shrine to be illuminated at a time when the sun reached a significant position in the sky.

Although the primeval mound and benben were both manifest as having round tops in an early period, the mound was later shown as a platform with sloping or stepped sides. Imitative of the primeval mound, the platform holding the throne of the king is reached by what is sometimes shown as a double stairway (**4.21**).[32] Even the hieroglyph ⌂,

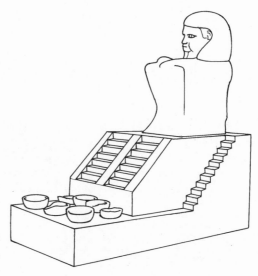

Figure 4.21. The platform that holds the king's throne, shown as an offering site for the deceased, is sometimes pictured as a mound with a stairway.

meaning "appear," has the sun depicted as rising from behind the primeval mound—as with the solar mountain, an event of mystical importance. Indeed, the benben and primeval mound retained their magical powers on the Egyptian mind throughout their long history. They also had a profound effect on the architecture used to link the deceased king to the sun.

CHAPTER 5

THE TRUE PYRAMID

Although the low mounds that covered burial pits in early tombs and the step pyramids both had solar connections, they served different purposes. As a primeval mound formed by the sun-god when he required a place to stand, the mound was symbolically thought to have the power to raise the dead. When the mound was formed into a step pyramid, it seems to have acquired a more practical function—that of helping to estimate yearly cycles of the rising and setting sun. The benben stone, a sacred object used to greet the rising sun, had not yet entered the funerary scene except possibly as round-topped stelae found outside the early tombs. This omission was remedied in the 4th Dynasty when, for the first time, benben and primeval mound were united in a single architectural configuration.[1] The resulting structure was a smooth-sided, equinoctially oriented pyramid that combined the concepts of creation and kingly rule with that of the sun, elements most central to Egyptian thought. With this blending, the dead king's link to the heavens was complete—in life, he was viewed as the reincarnation of Horus, the earthly son of Ra; in death, he actually became the heavenly sun-god Ra.

The linkage between the rising sun and a pyramid oriented by its sides to the cardinal points is straightforward. As the sun travels from winter to summer solstice, it moves along the horizon in an arc of about 50 degrees from north to south at the latitude of Giza. To equate the king's pyramid with the sun, a celestial object that moves continuously through the sky, required that the sides of the structure face due east and west. Due east is the midway point for the sun as it moves between the summer and winter solstice. It is also the only position in which a structure square in plan can have one side face the birth of the sun in the east, another face its death in the west, and still have its north side directed at the circumpolar stars (**5.1**). These stars, which never set as they circle the pole, were thought to "hold out their arms" to aid the king in his ascension to the sky. Their importance to the ancient Egyptian religion is shown in the 4th Dynasty—a time when

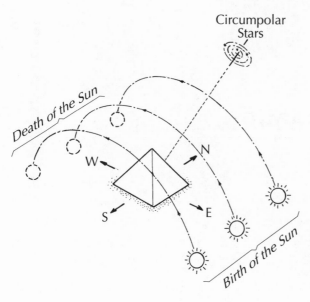

Figure 5.1. True pyramids were oriented with sides to the cardinal points to link the life and death of the entombed king to those of the sun.

pyramid entrances made to point in their direction became a feature helping to distinguish the pyramids from those of the 3rd Dynasty.[2]

It is interesting to note that placement of the entrance may also have been based on a belief that persisted for millennia in later times. Evidence exists of a medieval thought that stars were visible by day when excess light was excluded by observing the sky from the bottom of a deep well. Though much evidence exists for these wells, their effectiveness is uncertain. More certain is the greater visibility of faint stars at night when extraneous light is excluded by use of a sighting tube of metal or wood. The astronomers and surveyors of ancient Babylonia and China employed such tubes.[3] Possibly, it was thought that the king could more readily see the circumpolar stars, even during the day, from the deep well formed by the pyramid's entrance shaft.

Meidum Pyramid

The ruler responsible for successfully blending the primeval mound with the benben was Sneferu, first king of the 4th Dynasty. His efforts at pyramid building probably began with the aforementioned Seila pyramid. Located on a high bluff west of Meidum, the small step pyramid overlooks an agricultural area fed by the waters of a canal from Lake Moeris, in the Fayum. Also used to judge seasonal movements of the rising sun, this structure was similar to its smaller counterparts of the 3rd Dynasty. However, in Sneferu's desire to surpass his predecessors, it was made 50 percent larger. Once this king began to build, his ambition knew no bounds. His first major work probably began at Meidum, just 6 miles (10 km) west of Seila. Although it eventually became a geometrically true pyramid, its transformation took three building stages. In its present ruined state, the pyramid is little more than an enormous rectangular tower of three great steps rising at 75 degrees.[4] These are the remains of eight such steps spaced in height about 26–36 feet (8–11 m) apart—other steps having been removed as quarry stone over the centuries (**5.2**).

Table 5.1

CHRONOLOGY OF THE 4TH–6TH DYNASTIES, 2613–2181 BCE

4TH DYNASTY	DATE (BCE)	5TH DYNASTY	DATE (BCE)	6TH DYNASTY	DATE (BCE)
Sneferu	2613–2589	Userkaf	2494–2487	Teti	2345–2323
Cheops (Khufu)	2589–2566	Sahure	2487–2475	Userkara	2323–2321
Djedefre (Radjedef)	2566–2558	Neferirkare	2475–2455	Pepi I	2321–2287
Chephren (Khafre)	2558–2532	Shepseskare	2455–2448	Merenre	2287–2278
Mycerinus (Menkaure)	2532–2503	Raneferef	2448–2445	Pepi II	2278–2184
Shepseskaf	2503–2498	Niuserre	2445–2421	Nitiqret	2184–2181
		Menkauhor	2421–2414		
		Djedkare Isesi	2414–2375		
		Unas	2375–2345		

After Ian Shaw and Paul Nicholson, *The Dictionary of Ancient Egypt*, 310. A different estimate gives the 4th–6th Dynasties as 2575–2152 BCE (John Baines and Jaromír Málek, *Atlas of Ancient Egypt*, 36).

Figure 5.2. Meidum Pyramid remains as a tower of three great steps.

Initially planned as a seven-step pyramid, Meidum was constructed like its 3rd Dynasty counterparts, by layering inwardly inclined rectangular blocks against a central core, so that their end faces formed a plane (**5.3**). In this way, it reached a height of 197 feet (60 m), with a square base of about 330 feet (100 m) on each side, about the same size as the large pyramids of the 3rd Dynasty. As the layers diminished in height from the center outward, their tops formed seven steps of the first building phase (E1). These steps were built with a slight difference from the pyramids of Djoser, Sekhemkhet, and Khaba: instead of each step being formed by two 8-foot-thick layers as in the earlier structures,

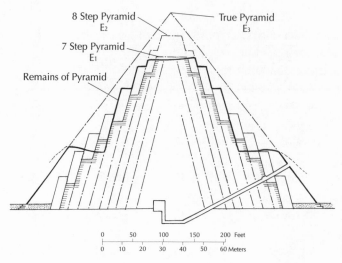

Figure 5.3. Section of Meidum Pyramid showing how the structure grew from seven to eight steps before becoming a true pyramid. The dark outline indicates what can be seen today.

the steps at Meidum were made of a single homogeneous layer of stone 16 feet (5 m) thick. Although the blocks used for the stepped layers were roughly squared, poorly laid, and had their joints filled with sizable globs of mortar, they were hidden by a facing of well-fitted and smoothly dressed limestone (**5.4**).

With the addition of another inclined layer of stone forming an eighth step, the structure was heightened to 262 feet (80 m) in a second building phase (E2). The smoothly dressed and well-fitted layer of facing stone covering these steps indicates that they also were intended to be final. The third phase (E3), which increased the size of the base to 482 feet (147 m) per side and the height to a bit over 300 feet (91 m), transformed the stepped structure into a true pyramid. In this final effort, after packing stone was placed in the steps to produce a pyramidal shape, the entire structure was covered with a smooth outer facing of casing stone. Using a building procedure that has since puzzled generations of investigators, the four sides of the Meidum pyramid were made to rise at an uninterrupted angle (51°52') and meet at a distant point in the sky.[5]

Figure 5.4. One of the great steps of Meidum Pyramid shows carelessly laid blocks covered by a single layer of smooth casing.

Although the inner structure of the pyramid is hidden from view, an exploratory tunnel by G. A. Wainwright cut through the masonry shows that the first two structural phases were not built around a rocky knoll, as some later pyramids were, but rest instead upon a carefully leveled rock foundation. He also found a radical change in the third building phase. Rather than making use of inclined layers as in the first and second building phases, the final phase was built of horizontal courses of masonry supported on a separate foundation outside the bedrock. Consisting only of stones and compressed sand, such seemingly inadequate foundations have continued to support buildings in Egypt for thousands of years. Indeed, many of the smaller pyramids have only one or two courses of blocks placed in a foundation trench dug into the desert conglomerate. In a continuing effort to keep the cultic traditions shown at the Temple Oval at Khafaje in Mesopotamia, and at the oval mound in Hierakonpolis, the foundation trenches of temples were regularly provided with clean, specially sieved desert sand. At times the clean fill was used only to adjust and level the stones; at other times it is seen as a layer 20 inches (0.5 m) thick. It is thought that in Egypt, this was done with the intention of establishing a pure "primeval hill" of sand during the foundation ceremonies.[6]

While it is certainly more prudent to support the entire pyramid on bedrock, foundations holding the mantle stone in the desert conglomerate bear less weight than one might imagine. In the case of Meidum, for example, only the lowest courses of the outer fill and casing stones would rest directly on the conglomerate. As the courses grow in height, and recede with the slope of the pyramid, the greatest mass of stone would rest on blocks that transfer their weight straight down to the bedrock. The carefully dressed faces of the first two building phases indicate that while the true pyramid was not originally planned, all three phases were built fairly close together in time, the larger interval being before Sneferu transformed the step pyramid into a true pyramid (**5.5a, b**).

The buildings associated with Meidum include at least one subsidiary pyramid, an enclosure wall as protection from drifting desert sands, and two temples—the same sort of structures found in all Old Kingdom pyramid complexes. A small temple adjacent to the

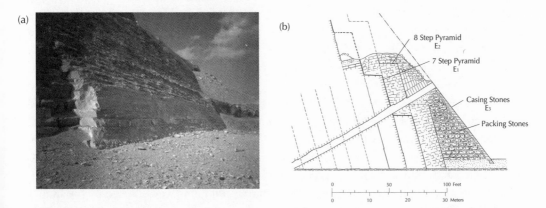

(a)

(b)

8 Step Pyramid
E₂

7 Step Pyramid
E₁

Casing Stones
E₃

Packing Stones

0   50   100 Feet

0   10   20   30 Meters

Figure 5.5. (a) North side of Meidum Pyramid. Compare the newly uncovered casing with the scarred and pitted stone, the result of years of exposure to the elements. (b) Detail of Meidum Pyramid showing the inclined masonry of the inner steps and the horizontal masonry that transformed the step structure into a true pyramid.

Figure 5.6. View from the east side of Meidum Pyramid shows the upper temple and stelae in the foreground and the causeway leading to an area of cultivation in the background.

east side of the pyramid is connected by a sloping causeway to another temple lower in the valley (**5.6**). When connected by a canal to the Nile, the valley temple enabled the funerary procession to arrive by water and walk to the high ground of the king's tomb along a prepared roadway. Placed within view of an area of cultivation and its populace, the pyramid of Meidum may have served two purposes: as a daily reminder linking the life and death of the king to that of the sun, and a means of signaling the approximate time of the inundation.

The Bent Pyramid

North of Meidum, the Bent Pyramid of Dahshur, with a present height of about 334 feet (101 m) and square base of 619 feet (189 m) on each side, covers a much larger area than that of the pyramid of Meidum. Before attaining its present size it also went through a number of design changes. Originally built at a 60-degree slope, by the time it reached about one third of its present height, a number of cracks (still seen shored up with cedar timbers in an upper chamber) seem to have appeared in the chambers and passages. In the vain hope of reducing further damage by lightening the weight, the base was enlarged and the slope reduced (54°31'). When the problems persisted as the structure reached about halfway to its present height, its outer slope was lowered (43° 20'), and this became the slope the rest of the way to the summit (**5.7**).[7] The nucleus of the Bent Pyramid is supported on compacted clay, and the backing and casing stones are held by an outer platform of limestone blocks. Similar cracks seen in the nearby pyramid of Ammenemes III, situated on a like foundation, suggest that the structural faults were caused by the inability of the clay to withstand the accumulated weight of the pyramid. Interestingly, the preventative measure used by the builders—enlarging the base—may actually have aggravated the problem by increasing the number of courses bearing directly down on the inadequate clay foundation.

Figure 5.7. The Bent Pyramid still covered by much of its casing stone.

Due to the retention of much of its backing and casing stone, it is not possible to see if the Bent Pyramid has the same internal layering or steps found in earlier structures. However, when the pyramid was used as a quarry, the blocks that were removed provided a unique vista into the remaining masonry. Unlike the earlier steep accretion angles, this structure has courses that are essentially horizontal (**5.8**). These courses were given only a slight incline toward the core of the pyramid, averaging 6 degrees near the bottom of the pyramid and about 3.5 degrees near the top. The casing stones, which were cut to the outside slope of the pyramid, appear in section as right-angle trapeziums. Slots on their lower side edges show that they were placed in position with levers—the probable slots on the front faces having been removed with the final dressing. A foundation block on the corner of the pyramid still holds the incised lines that were used as a guide for laying the first course (**5.9**).

Because of the difficulty of raising stone, both the casing and backing stones (those stones directly behind the casing stones) are seen to diminish progressively in height from bottom to top. The casing stones near the bottom are of finer material and have better joints than those near the top—Egyptian masons always paid more attention to work easily seen. The casing stones near the ground are also very large. Set as headers, their ends showing in the face of the pyramid, some of the lower casing stones reach to a depth

Figure 5.8. The deep casing stone of the Bent Pyramid used as headers.

Figure 5.9. The Bent Pyramid foundation platform shows incised guidelines for placement of the casing stone.

of 6.5 feet (2 m). A few courses near the bottom are 6 feet high, but sometimes to reach this height it was necessary to place one block upon the other. On nearing the top, the courses are carelessly laid and are only about 18–20 inches (50 cm), in height. Several blocks bear inscriptions or quarry marks identifying the work gang that hauled the block. One such block contains the Horus name of King Sneferu, builder of the pyramid.[8]

A small subsidiary pyramid oriented to the same north-south axis as the Bent Pyramid lies a little to the south. With a base of 173 feet (53 m) per side and a slope close to that of the top half of the Bent Pyramid (44°30'), the smaller structure had an estimated final height of 84 feet (26 m). Having lost almost its entire casing, it reveals that its nucleus blocks, as at Meidum, are roughly laid (being dressed only on the bedding surfaces) and have poorly fitted joints filled with globs of mortar and limestone chips. On the other hand,

Figure 5.10. Remains of subsidiary pyramid of Bent Pyramid.

the casing stone still in place on the north face is well-laid white limestone of workman-ship equal to that of the main pyramid, although individual blocks are much smaller—about 18 inches high (50 cm). The pyramid was built on a foundation platform that extends beyond the casing and rests on two or three courses of blocks placed one upon the other in the desert conglomerate.[9] (**5.10**).

The Red Pyramid

Built by King Sneferu, the North or "Red" Pyramid of Dahshur—an appellation acquired because of oxidation of the fossilized shells in the limestone blocks—has the same hori-zontal casing observed at the Bent Pyramid and the pyramid of Meidum. At 345 feet (105 m) high it is roughly the same height as the Bent Pyramid. Its larger base, about 722 feet (220 m) on each side, is a result of the entire pyramid being built with about the same shallow angle (43°22') found in the upper section of the Bent Pyramid (**5.11**). Due to the low angle and the ease with which the stone could be quarried, most of the fine casing stone of the Red Pyramid has been removed. The backing stone remains untouched, being of a lesser quality. The remains show a pyramid of well-made regular horizontal courses of packing stone, which average about 35 inches (90 cm) high at the base and about 24

Figure 5.11. North or Red Pyramid of Dahshur with the low top angle of the Bent Pyramid.

Figure 5.12. View of Red Pyramid with a reassembled pyramidion (perhaps from another as yet undiscovered pyramid) at its base.

inches high (60 cm) near the top.[10] It is not known if the packing stone covers a stepped core similar to that of Meidum or if the foundation of this pyramid is supported on bedrock. The probability of the structure having had a complete coat of smooth casing stone was thought to be affirmed when the German excavator Rainer Stadelmann found an uninscribed limestone pyramidion (capstone). Broken in its fall, it has been painstakingly pieced together and now sits at the base of the pyramid (**5.12**). The capstone disclosed faces that slope at about 54 degrees—more than a 10-degree difference from the slope of the Red Pyramid, its supposed location. Noting the different angles, Stadelmann suggests that the discrepancy was a deliberate attempt to make the top portion of the pyramid more visible from the ground, in effect giving the pyramid a bend so that its shallow and steep faces are opposite to those of its southern neighbor, shallow near the bottom and steep on the top. This is questionable, since remains of the Red Pyramid do not exhibit the underlying masonry that would be required to support the steeper top.

Stadelmann's suggestion is also questioned by Corinna Rossi, who has investigated this anomaly. Finding it to be similar to the two which survive from the Old Kingdom, she suggests that the capstone was originally made for the second building stage of the Bent Pyramid but was discarded and brought to the Red Pyramid site when a change of angle was decreed. She claims that the slope of the pyramid was established before beginning the work, and the capstone was completed in advance to act as a guide for the final smoothing of the pyramid.[11] Instead, I will show that the pyramidion could not have acted as a guide, since evidence at Abusir shows a pyramidion with a fine gold finish being celebrated as the very last architectural component needed for a completed pyramid. Clearly, if the limestone pyramidion is not from the Bent Pyramid, it may be of a yet undiscovered Old Kingdom pyramid—Middle Kingdom pyramids more usually having inscribed and decorated pyramidions of dark stones, such as gray or black granite.

Transition from Accretion to Horizontal Layers

The experiments that led Sneferu to create the true pyramid can be traced by the chronological changes found in the masonry of the various structures. They show the early exclusive use of accretion layers, followed by the tentative introduction of horizontal courses, and finally the complete abandonment of accretion layers—the last pyramidal structure to have used accretion layers was Meidum. From that time forward all pyramids were constructed with courses that are essentially horizontal.[12] By abandoning their further use, Sneferu seems to have recognized an inherent fault in building a pyramid with inwardly inclined layers of stone.

As I show later, whether a pyramid is built with a core of inclined layers or with horizontal layers, each method provides a steplike inner structure that supports the casing stone. Egyptians rejected the use of inclined layers when it was found that horizontal courses were easier to erect and made for a more substantial structure. According to Kurt Mendelssohn, pressure on the high points of the blocks at Meidum caused the poorly squared masonry of the accretion layers to be forced outward at the sides, causing collapse of the structure.[13] Although this did not result in the collapse of the pyramid, even a slight sideways movement of the blocks would have formed cracks easily seen when the faces of the steps were dressed—the smooth finish accentuating the defects. If such cracks appeared in the first two stages of the Meidum pyramid, at a time when they were interrupted by steps, they would have been even more pronounced on the smooth flat faces of a true pyramid—an observation that may have persuaded the builders to adopt the new construction method.

Using horizontal courses, and filling spaces in the roughly squared blocks with a mixture of mortar, limestone chips, and rubble, seems to have prevented the lateral stone movement Mendelssohn described. The greater stability of these courses is a result of the role played by gravity: instead of the stone being pushed outward by a component of force acting at an angle, as in the accretion layers, the overhead pressure of horizontal layers is directed straight down to the ground, where it is distributed onto the foundation. This is an important consideration for pyramids with portions of their foundation in the desert conglomerate supporting their outer stonework, as at Meidum. The new building system also precluded the need to fill the saw-toothed top of the inclined layers (an unavoidable result of their use), instead providing a horizontal work surface on which to walk or move stone (**5.13**). All in all, it seems to have worked so well that once it had been tried, all future pyramids were made with horizontal courses.

A comparison of the major pyramidal tombs completed in the 3rd and 4th Dynasties shows a steady growth in size from Djoser's Step Pyramid at Saqqara to the true pyramid built by Cheops at Giza (**5.14**). The effort by Chephren to match the size of the Great Pyramid evidently depleted a royal treasury already drained by his predecessor. Although this may have forced the next king to reduce the size of his tomb, Mycerinus made up for it with a greater use of granite and the excellent workmanship it still displays. As the high point of Egyptian pyramid building, the majesty achieved in the 4th Dynasty, at Giza, would make all future pyramid building efforts pale by comparison.

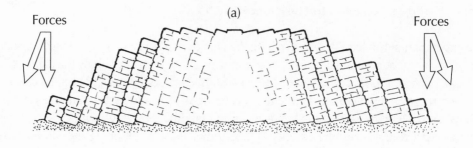

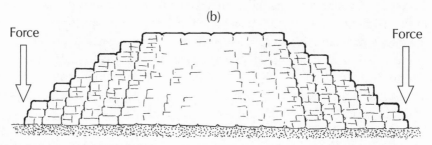

Figure 5.13. Comparison of accretion and horizontal masonry. (a) Accretion-layered masonry has forces acting at an angle and has a saw-toothed top surface. (b) Horizontally laid masonry provides a flat surface and has its forces acting vertically.

The Puzzling Number of Sneferu's Building Projects

Judging by its layered construction, and its similarity to the small step pyramids, it seems reasonable to conclude that the first structure erected by Sneferu, developer of the true pyramid, must have been the small step pyramid of Seila. The chronology of the remaining structures, Meidum, Bent, and the shallow-angled Red Pyramid, is uncertain. Also uncertain is the question of how one king in his 23 regnal years could muster the men and material for three major pyramids. The total amount of stone used in these undertakings is more than one third greater in volume than that used at the pyramid of Cheops, a structure that in itself seems overwhelming to present-day investigators.[14] Sneferu's accomplishments also involve the time and material required to prepare the site, mine the quarries, and erect all the usual temples, causeways, and enclosure walls that constitute a pyramid complex. In the case of the Bent Pyramid, even its subsidiary pyramid with a base of about 174 feet (53 m) and a height of about 85 feet (26 m) would be a major undertaking today, considering the lost skills.

When we assess Sneferu's many projects, their numbers seem to suggest that some efforts attributed to him were actually built by other kings. Indeed, it has been argued that Huni, an immediate predecessor, was the builder of the seven- and eight-stepped portions of the Meidum Pyramid, the only Sneferu contribution being its final transformation to a true pyramid. However, with no mention of Huni found in the entire complex of Meidum, and with the ancient name of Meidum pyramid being Djed Sneferu (Sneferu endures), this seems to be an argument designed to escape from an untenable position. Not only did

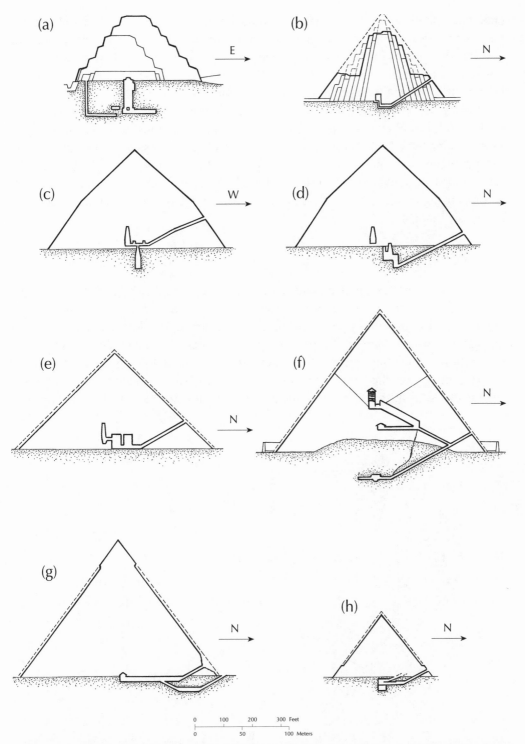

Figure 5.14. Comparison of the completed 3rd and 4th Dynasty pyramids. (a) Djoser's Step Pyramid. (b) Sneferu's pyramid at Meidum. (c, d) Sneferu's South or Bent Pyramid at Dahshur with its two entrances. (e) Sneferu's North or Red Pyramid at Dahshur. (f) Pyramid of Cheops. (g) Pyramid of Chephren. (h) Pyramid of Mycerinus.

graffiti by visitors of the 18th Dynasty attribute the small chapel of Meidum to King Sne-feru, but symbols of the same work gangs are written on blocks of the lower part of the Red Pyramid of Dahshur, a definite Sneferu project, and on blocks that came from the upper part of the Meidum Pyramid.[15] Graffiti left by masons also have dates showing that both pyramids were under construction at the same time.

In view of these puzzling findings, Stadelmann feels that the reign of Sneferu as recorded in the Turin king-list is too short and should be amended to 34 years. However, even granting the king 11 more years of working time, as suggested by Stadelmann, and assuming that the stepped portion of the pyramid of Meidum was built by Huni, it still seems almost beyond belief for one king to have built the two Dahshur pyramids with their accompanying installations—unless, of course, the building system took less effort than previously thought.

The Upper Temple

Each pyramid complex had two sacred areas: the valley temple, where the funerary cere-mony began, and the upper temple (generally referred to as a mortuary temple), where burial rites were supposedly performed next to the pyramid. In addition to the building of the first true pyramid having occurred in the time of Sneferu, a major change in the solar cult is shown by the placement of the upper temple on the east side of the pyramid.

This meant that the temple structure was made to face the rising sun instead of the circumpolar stars in the north, as at the pyramid of Djoser.[16] A study of such temples at

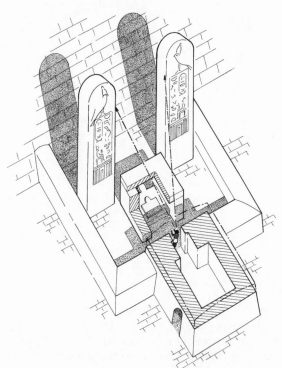

Figure 5.15. Upper temple of the Bent Pyramid, showing priest viewing inner side faces of the stelae for changing shadows.

the three pyramids indicates that the structure at Meidum is a later development than that of the Bent Pyramid (**5.15**).[17] It also suggests that the most recent of the three temples was built at the Red Pyramid.

Ruins of the Bent Pyramid temple indicate that it was built in several stages on an exact east-west axis, the first stage consisting of a pair of tall (30 foot [9 m]) round-topped benben stones, like those found at Heliopolis. One such stone is inscribed with the name Sneferu, the planned occupant of the tomb. In front of the stelae is a low altar, which in the second building phase was enclosed by side walls, and possibly a roof, as protection from the drifting sands.[18] A temple building was built in a third stage, and an enclosure wall was added in a final building phase to protect the entire temple complex from sand (**5.16**). The subsidiary pyramid at the Bent Pyramid has a similar temple on its east face.

One of the building differences suggesting that the temple at the Bent Pyramid is an earlier construction is the use of mud brick there versus use of stone at Meidum—stone being a building element used for temples at a later time in Egypt. There were occasions, however, such as at the temple of Mycerinus, when mud brick was used as a cheaper and faster way of completing a project. The separate construction stages seen at the Bent Pyramid temple are in contrast to those at Meidum, where the entire temple complex was built at the same time. Indeed, the temple at Meidum shows all its accouterments—stelae, altar, enclosure wall, and temple building—already in place, although the temple wall is only partially dressed and the stelae are uninscribed.

The serpentine entrance at Meidum is also an improvement in the design of the upper temples (**5.17a, b**). It is a more sophisticated development for keeping out wind-blown sand than the simple entrance shown at the Bent Pyramid temple. Although both entrances

(a)   (b)

(c)   (d)

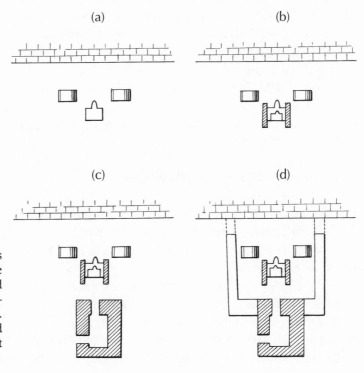

Figure 5.16. Building stages of the upper temple of the Bent Pyramid. (a) Stelae and altar. (b) Side walls to protect altar from drifting sand. (c) Temple structure behind altar. (d) Enclosure wall built around the entire complex.

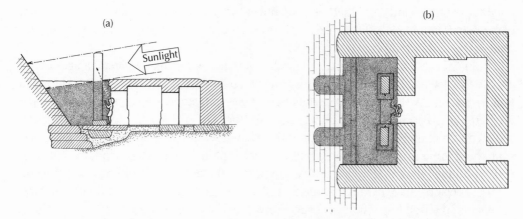

Figure 5.17. Upper temple at Meidum. (a) Cutaway showing priest viewing the changing shadows of the stelae. (b) Plan of temple.

may once have held wooden doors, the serpentine entrance of Meidum would more effectively prevent filling of the temple interior with sand blown in around the edges of the door—a problem soon clear to anyone ever caught in a sand storm.

Stadelmann's recent clearing of debris from the east side of the Red Pyramid shows the foundations of a larger and more complex upper temple than had ever before existed. Besides its several buildings, there is also a change in the major cult object. From this temple forward, the round-topped stelae seem to have been replaced with the same style of niche or false door used earlier on the tombs at Saqqara. However, instead of being located outside the temple, as before, it was placed on an inside wall, as in the temple structure on Level XVI (4900 BCE) at Eridu, Mesopotamia. In Egypt, however, the niche was oriented toward the equinox instead of the somewhat solstitial orientation of the Mesopotamian temples (**5.18**). The temple of the Red Pyramid was constructed of mud brick instead of limestone. While mud brick is a material that indicates an early date, Stadelmann believes that as with the Mycerinus temple, this one was hurried to completion after the death of Sneferu. This observation is confirmed by the pillared court, which suggests it to be not only a later temple than at Meidum or the Bent Pyramid but also a similar and immediate predecessor to Cheops' Upper Temple.

Sneferu's Burial Place and Chronology

In the absence of discovery of the king's sarcophagus, there is great uncertainty over which of Sneferu's three major pyramids became his eventual burial place. Although the earliest royal stone sarcophagus known was ascribed to King Sekhemkhet, of the 3rd Dynasty, none of Sneferu's pyramids is known to have contained a stone mummy case.[19] By contrast, all the kings of the 4th Dynasty who reigned after Cheops were equipped with sarcophagi—an addition that Edwards considers to have been brought about by the emergence of the Heliopolitan cult. Indeed, according to the Pyramid Texts, this creed indicates that the dead king was assimilated into the sun-god Atum-Re by entering the mouth of the sky goddess Nut every evening at sunset, passing through her body during the night, and

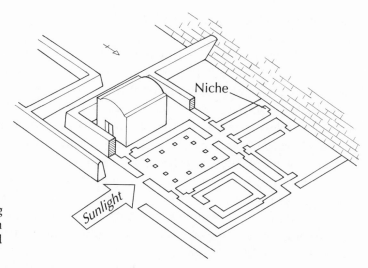

Figure 5.18. The east-facing niche used as a cult object in the upper temple of the Red Pyramid.

being reborn every morning. Other Pyramid Texts reveal that the sarcophagus could serve as a substitute for the actual body of the goddess.[20]

Even without a royal sarcophagus, we can logically expect Sneferu's remains to have occupied that pyramid with the most recently built upper temple. This is because the temples were added only at the final construction stage, while the casing stone of the pyramid was being applied or shortly afterward. Therefore, if we use the normal development of architecture as a chronological gauge, the more primitive temple of the Bent Pyramid shows it to be the first attempt at building a true pyramid. The Red Pyramid, with its more sophisticated temple layout, indicates it to be the last pyramid and final resting place of Sneferu.

To account for the pyramid of Meidum while allowing Sneferu's Red Pyramid to have been built with the chronology suggested, we can speculate that having built the first stage at Meidum equal to the height of the large step pyramids of the previous dynasty, Sneferu had it enlarged by 25 percent to show his greater power. In a stroke of genius, he then became inspired by the vision of a true pyramid. Unpracticed in its execution, the king moved to a new location to build the Bent Pyramid—a structure that in its three different angles (including the 60° initial slope) seems to show an experiment in progress. Dissatisfied with its interior cracks and awkward shape, Sneferu moved again to a new location in the valley and began construction of the Red Pyramid with the lower, safer angle and more stable horizontal courses. Perhaps, while the core of the Red Pyramid was under construction and before the packing stone was applied, he devised a way of bringing the fill of packing stone closer to the smooth plane of the pyramid face than had previously been possible. Not only would this newly discovered method regularize the outline of the packing stones; it would permit the casing stone to be laid as stretchers, with their long edge parallel to the pyramid face. Before attempting the new building method in a tomb he expected to occupy, Sneferu saw an opportunity to gain experience by installing the packing and casing stone on Meidum, a structure where an eight-step core had already been built.

True Purpose of the Upper Temple

The true function of the upper temple is uncertain. According to Felix Arnold, the purpose of all the cult buildings was to provide a framework for rites that would transform the human and mortal king into an immortal and divine being—a belief now applied to the lower temple. While it was once thought that the body of the dead king was received in the lower temple, where it was embalmed, it is now believed this temple acted as a quay for the gods when they arrived in their boats to join in festivals with the dead king.[21]

The same uncertainty exists regarding the purpose of the temple next to the pyramid—the so called mortuary temple. Separated from its counterpart in the valley by a causeway—and some causeways had walls that were decorated and roofed—it is unlikely to have been used for mortuary purposes.[22] Indeed, imagine the difficulty of carrying an encased corpse through the serpentine entrance of Meidum's temple. Further, its orientation suggests that the structure served to deify the king and enable him to participate in the daily journey of the sun. Clearly, while the primary focus of the temple may be on the dead king, the stelae or false door it contains would signal arrival of the equinox—an unavoidable result of the temple facing due east.

An awareness of this special period of the year is indicated by an astronomical chart from the Royal Tombs of Thebes (**5.19**). It shows the sky goddess Nut, her exaggeratedly long body bent over and touching the ground, head to the west and legs to the east, as she ingests the sun, which travels nightly through her body to be reborn at sunrise. Standing below Nut is Horus, the falcon-headed god. He holds a vertical line that bisects the sun's path between east and west—a line that seems to represent the equinoctial meridian. The chart also shows Horus, embodiment of divine kingship, with the life-giving power of the sun—a religious thought that increasingly grew until it was firmly established by the 4th Dynasty. Although this scene comes from a period later than the Old Kingdom, it is one of the few that record ancient Egyptian thought on the heavens.[23]

Relating the time of the equinox to the stelae on the east face of the pyramids raises some interesting possibilities. It suggests that although the broad faces of the stelae would be more or less lighted at sunrise all during the year, a priest standing at the temple altar would see the side faces of the stelae change in brightness at periodic intervals. This change would

Figure 5.19. A scene from the Royal Tombs of Thebes shows the sky goddess Nut as she swallows the setting sun and later gives birth to the sunrise. The path of the sun is bisected by a meridian line held by the falcon-headed god Horus.

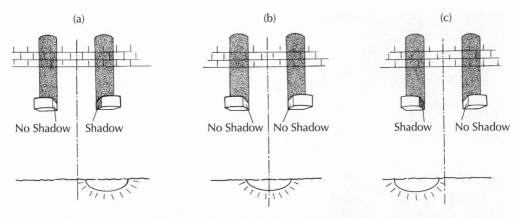

Figure 5.20. (a, c) Shadow falls on inside wall of stelae as the sun marches from solstice to solstice. (b) Absence of shadow when the sun rises at the equinox.

occur as the sun, in its march toward the solstices, crossed the imaginary east-west equinoctial axis. At that time sides that had been illuminated for six months of the year would fall into shadow for the next six months (**5.20**). Later in the year, as the sun moved toward the opposite solstice, the same event would occur in reverse. For a period at the time of the equinox as it rose due east, the sun would illuminate the side faces of both stelae equally.

These shadows would change in a comparatively short time because the sun moves more quickly (a full diameter each morning) during the equinoctial period than during the rest of the year and because, for all practical purposes, the light rays from the sun are always parallel. Presumably at a time when both inner side faces were equally lighted, offerings would be made to signify unification of the sun with the dead king. At the Red Pyramid, the same event would be signaled on the side walls of a niche or false door, when it eventually replaced the stelae as a cult object. While remains of one such niche are still visible at the temple of the Cheops Queens (G1-b) Pyramid (**5.21**), others are said to have been placed in various pyramid temples.

Among these others, the French archaeologist Jean-Philippe Lauer postulates a similar but more elaborate niche on an inside wall at the so-called mortuary temple of Cheops (**5.22**).[24] In this case, the back wall of the niche is a passageway that opens to a terminus chamber in the form of a T, like those found in Mesopotamia (**3.10**). In Egypt, five statue shrines are often placed in the rear chamber of such temples. Having the passage niche oriented to the east, as was often the case, allowed the rays of the equinoctial sun to enter the passage twice a year and transform the king into Horus by illuminating his statue. Called the "gate of Nut" in temples of later kings, the passage niche is decorated with scenes of goddesses nursing the young king and of gods welcoming him.[25]

The finding of devices that signal the position of the sun seems to confirm that the appellation *mortuary temple* is a misnomer. If anything, such a structure should be referred to as a solar temple. Indeed, the small structures at Meidum and the Bent Pyramid probably had more to do with the solar cult and deification of the king than with any attempt at preserving his body. Further evidence at the Bent Pyramid shows that cultic stelae were erected well before being accompanied by the temple structure in which the king's body

Figure 5.21. Remains of niche at the upper temple of the Queens Pyramid G1-b of Cheops.

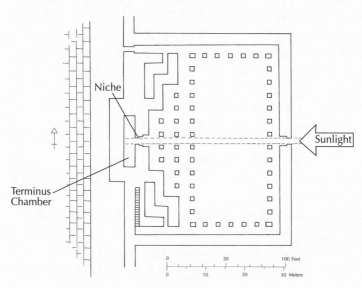

Figure 5.22. Niche and terminus chamber in the upper temple of Cheops when illuminated by the rising sun.

was supposedly purified. Such cult objects help to confirm the temple as a place for the dead king to receive offerings. Even if temple structures are yet found to have been used for some form of mortuary purpose, the presence of a niche or false door in the temple shows that they also would herald the sunrise.

The Sphinx temple has taken the upper temple one step further into its new identity as a solar temple. Not only does it have a niche that faces the rising sun—it has a second niche located on the same axis, facing the setting sun (**5.23**). In this case, at the time of the equinoxes (21–22 March and 21–22 September), the rising sun would illuminate the western niche and the setting sun, the eastern niche.[26] Even when, due to a change in

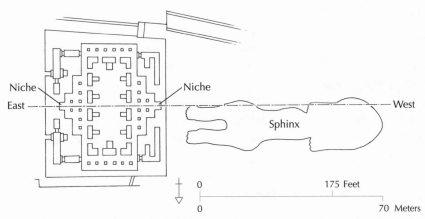

Figure 5.23. The Sphinx temple has two niches on its central axis. One faces the rising sun and the other faces the setting sun.

theology, later funerary temples reverted to the more solstitially oriented directions of the Early Dynastic tombs, the same architectural configuration shown at the pyramid temples was essentially retained. Dieter Arnold notes: "The combination of pillared court and door niche with statue shrines in the back is consistently repeated in Egyptian funerary architecture, surviving until the gigantic Theban tombs of the Late period. In the latter, the ancient pillared court seems to be retained in the form of an open, underground light well. An offering table for the mortuary offering was a feature of the light well which served as the juncture between the realms of day and night, symbolized by Re and Osiris. In the rear wall of the court, a high, deep vaulted niche leads into the interior parts of the tomb, which contained the statue shrines and burial apartments."[27] To heighten the effect of sunlight as it entered to illuminate the statue of a god, early temple buildings of the New Kingdom were designed on a single axis, the floor gradually rising, the ceiling lowered, and the rooms becoming smaller until reaching a dark terminus sanctuary where the statue of a god was kept.[28]

Nabta Playa

Although the niche found in these temples is a solar device that can be traced to Mesopotamia, the same cannot be said of the stelae. In Egypt, the early beginnings of these vertical slabs can be found at Nabta Playa, an area about 62 miles (100 km) west of Abu Simbel. Playas were temporary lakes formed by the summer monsoons about 11,000 years ago. Signs of desert inhabitants from 8,000 years ago were found at this location by investigators J. McKim Malville and Fred Wendorf. This is the oldest known monument yet found to have been built with astronomical considerations in mind. Following several years of field work, Wendorf considers the site to have been used as a ceremonial center to mark the onset of the rainy season—knowledge essential to desert dwellers living during a time when the climate began to change, from being fairly wet to becoming completely dry.

The general complex, about 1.8 miles by 0.75 miles (3 km × 1.2 km), consists of slabs 9 feet (2.7 m) high, rock-lined ovals, burial sites for cows, and a calendrical circle of stones. This 13-foot (4 m) circle of recumbent stones contains four sets of upright slabs. Two such sets, which Wendorf calls "gates," form a sight line to the horizon on an azimuth almost exactly to where the first gleam of the summer solstice sun (63.2°) would have appeared 6,000 years ago. The start of the monsoons, signaled by the day of the summer solstice, would be significant to desert cattle herders. The other sets of gates in the astronomical circle form a straight line that comes within 2 degrees of true north (358°). Indeed, Nabta Playa being located on the Tropic of Cancer, the behavior of the sun becomes doubly interesting. On the two days it crosses the zenith, about three weeks apart, slabs set in a vertical position will not cast noon shadows—a time of great significance and mystery to all people of the tropics.[29]

The Pyramid as a Seasonal Clock

The increasing influence of the Heliopolitan cult, with its emphasis on the east-west points of the compass, suggests that the pyramid itself may also have been used to indicate the position of the sun—an unavoidable result of its orientation, and a probable reason for the change from building pyramids in the general direction of the solstices to erecting pyramids that face the equinox—midpoint of the sun's travels along the horizon.

By facing the pyramid sides to the cardinal points, several anomalies are produced; at about the time of the equinox, the pyramid would appear to swallow the sun as it slowly set in the west directly behind the monument. Dorothea Arnold suggests that a similar scene is incised on the shaft of a copper chisel from Deir el-Bahri (11th Dynasty), showing a winged sun rising or setting on the apex of a pyramidion (**5.24**). A modified form of the symbol is also shown at a later time, on the Greek island of Delos.[30] At high noon, the shadow cast north of the pyramid, the "stride of Re," would each day draw closer to the base until it was completely ingested by the pyramid (**5.25**). This method of shadow signaling is similar to that used by the Chinese when at high noon on the day of the summer solstice, the shadow cast by a gnomon was swallowed by the wide base on which it stood (**1.16**). The length and angle of shadows falling north of the pyramid were so important a means of judging the passing seasons that a line a few centimeters long was centered on the pavement north of Cheops pyramid. On measuring the line (not a joint in the pavement), the investigator S. M. Cole found it to be only 2.75 inches (71 mm) off the central axis of the side of a pyramid over 9,000 inches (22,860 cm) in length.[31]

Figure 5.24. (a) The setting sun slowly disappears directly behind the pyramid at the time of the equinox. (b) Part of a copper chisel from Deir el-Bahri that shows a winged sun rising or setting on the apex of a pyramidion. (Photo courtesy Metropolitan Museum of Art [27.3.12])

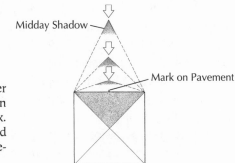

Figure 5.25. As the midday shadow draws closer each day to the north base, the pyramid will be seen to swallow its own shadow at the time of the equinox. A centerline of the meridian, which may have helped to judge the shadow, was found incised in the pavement at the base of the pyramid.

There is yet a third way for the pyramid to signal the time of year. The pyramid shadow falling in a westerly direction at sunrise, moves along the ground daily until it falls directly behind the pyramid at about the time of the equinox (**5.26**).[32] In 1853, the French archaeologist Mariette used just such a signal from the Great Pyramid to determine the approximate arrival of the vernal equinox. Mariette said the inhabitants of all neighboring villages in the 1850s knew that the rays of the setting equinoctial sun would graze the faces of the pyramid and that the extremity of the 2-mile-long (3 km) shadow would terminate in the east near a granite rock a quarter of an hour before sunset.[33]

Cotsworth, a 19th-century calendar reformer, went a great deal further, claiming that the Great Pyramid could be used to measure precisely the length of a tropical year and to calibrate the solar year. There is no evidence to support this contention. Many of his calculations were based on pyramid shadows thought to have matched inscribed calibration lines on the surrounding paved surface at the north face of the pyramid. While a 268-foot-long (82 m) shadow would have been cast north on the date of the winter solstice, the pavement ends 33.5 feet (10 m) from the pyramid's base at the vestiges an old wall. It is not thought that the pavement ever extended past this point. Cotsworth also thought shadows at the north base of the pyramid would disappear on the vernal equinox, only to advance later down the face before reappearing on the pavement at the autumnal equinox. Further investigation showed that the minimum shadows do not occur at the equinoxes but 14 days before the vernal equinox and 14 days after the autumnal equinox.[34]

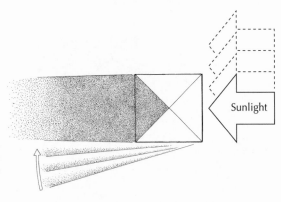

Figure 5.26. As the sun moves to the solstice, the changing angle of its shadow gradually becomes aligned with the side of the pyramid.

If the Great Pyramid did not provide the astronomical precision required for finding the exact length of a year, it certainly filled the purpose and needs of the period. Evidently, in the Old Kingdom a link was made between the equinoctial sun and the east-facing niches or stelae of the upper pyramid temples. At the same time as these cult objects were illuminated, a shadow from the opposite pyramid face would fall west toward the land of the dead. Without discounting the theological forces behind construction of the pyramids, or the need to place the king's body in the primeval mound, it seems the structures were much more than tombs for dead kings. Not only does the entire pyramid complex provide a forum to deify the king; inevitably, the pyramid acts as a seasonal clock, wrought in stone and representing eons of human thought and observation.

CHAPTER 6

THE GNOMON

The ability to construct a pyramidal tomb that could also act as a seasonal indicator required years of observation before the sun's cycles were fully understood. Once these were mastered, however, the sun's movements virtually dictated that the pyramid sides be squared, the pavement be leveled, and the structure be oriented to the cardinal points. Yet the knowledge and skills required for this undertaking were not achieved for architectural purposes but instead were developed at an earlier time for a purpose required by the state.

Due to a land tax imposed on agricultural properties by size, there was a constant need to reestablish boundary lines and settle disputes caused by the annual floods, the frequency of which resulted in development of a class of skilled surveyors at an early time in Egyptian history. Indeed, by the 3rd Dynasty, a list on the wall of the tomb of Methen shows that surveyors had already established a method of measuring land and computing the area of properties.[1] The Palermo Stone also bears witness to advanced accounting skills needed by the early Egyptians to reconstruct property rights after each flood. The list shows Old Kingdom records of annual flood heights along with a periodic enumeration of the population.

Although little evidence exists of the ancient surveying methods, the tools they used are pictured on the wall of Menna, a land overseer and inspector of the boundary stones. In a scene depicting a cornfield being measured, men are shown with a rope knotted at intervals of about three feet. Others carry extra coils of rope terminating with a ram's head, identifying them as officials of Amun-Re. The surveyors also exhibit writing materials, food, and a stafflike object called a *was*-scepter (**6.1**). At times considered a scepter for the gods and symbol of dominion, the was-scepter is an object variously described as a device to capture snakes, a water carrier, cattle prod, hook, walking stick, or weapon.[2] Although it was possibly used for all these purposes, scenes from the New Kingdom show the *was*-scepter

Figure 6.1. Scene from the Theban tomb of Menna showing a cornfield being surveyed.

also employed as a surveying instrument. One such scene shows a man holding the device over a boundary stone at the edge of a field as he utters the oath: "As the great god who is in heaven endures, the (boundary) stela is exact as it stands, O my father."[3] With instruments such as these and mastery of the surveyor's art, ancient Egyptians were able to place provincial boundary stones accurately at great distances apart—from 15.5 miles (25 km) apart east-west across the river valley to 9.3 miles (15 km) north-south along the Nile.[4]

Needless to say, such measurements would require the basic criteria of a survey—length, elevation, and geographical direction—to be made accurately with the tools of the Menna scene. A fairly close measure of length can be found by counting the number of equally spaced knots in a cord; elevations can be attained with great accuracy by sighting over two leveled rods to a third rod, some distance away. Less obvious and more difficult to achieve are the geographical directions. But once one direction is found, it serves as a reference from which other bearings are taken. According to 1st Dynasty texts and drawings associated with the sky and the cardinal points, the was-scepter pictured in the Menna scene seems to have been an advanced form of portable gnomon.[5] Not only can shadows cast by this odd-looking device indicate the approximate time of day; the length of the shadows can also give the general direction of true north. However, before describing its unique benefits, a brief background should be given on gnomons, in general.

Gnomons Measure Length

Classical literature is filled with references to the height of a pole and the length of its shadow. Although a gnomon may be used in a sundial, this is not its true purpose. The sundial is a device that measures the *direction* of the shadow, while the gnomon instead measures its *length*. Based on observations in the first century of the Christian era, the Roman scholar Pliny the Elder says: "Travelers' sundials are not the same for reference everywhere, because the shadows thrown by the sun as they alter, alter the readings at every three hundred or at farthest five hundred stades. Consequently in Egypt at midday at the day of the equinox the shadow of the pin or 'gnomon' measures a little more than half the gnomon itself whereas in the city of Rome the shadow is one-ninth shorter than the gnomon, at the town of Ancona one-thirty-fifth longer, and in the district of Italy called Venezia the shadow is equal to the gnomon, at the same hours."[6]

Together with other ancient historians, such as Vitruvius and Strabo, Pliny shows a keen awareness of the sun and the results of its most distant movements north and south along the horizon during the year.[7] Among the reports, he cites observers in the town of Syene (Aswan) who found no shadow cast at noon in midsummer—a deeply dug well to test the oddity showed that light would reach its very bottom. On an island in Meroe, Sudan, shadows would disappear twice a year when the sun was in the 18th degree of Taurus and in the 14th of Leo (time of the summer solstice). A nearby mountain named Maleus is reported as casting its shadows southward in summer and northward in winter. According to Pliny, the science called gnomonics was discovered by Anaximander, who first exhibited a timepiece called "Hunt the Shadow."[8] Anaximander's earliest philosophical work in the Greek language, *Upon Nature* (547 BCE), describes how the solstices, equinoxes, and the obliquity of the ecliptic were determined with a gnomon obtained from Babylon.[9] Findings such as these suggest that astronomy had long since passed its primitive beginnings. Indeed, the Babylonians had already reached an advanced state in astronomy by the 2nd millennium BCE, and by this time, China, independent of others, had already established an observatory.[10]

Often depicted with tall staffs, travelers of yesteryear did not keep the devices merely to serve as walking sticks. Also functioning as gnomons, they are described in *Chapman's and Traveller's Almanack*, a 1712 English pamphlet (**6.2**):

> For the ready finding of the Hour of the Day by this *Dial*, you must provide a straight Staff or Ruler, which must first be divided into Ten equal parts, and then each of those into Ten other smaller parts, so will the whole Staff or Ruler be divided into 100 equal parts, which may be numbered by 10, 20, 30, etc. to 100 and so it is fitted for use. Now when you would find the Hour, you must erect your Staff or Ruler perpendicular, that is, set it upright upon some plain level Ground Floor or Table, and note the place where the end of the Shadow did fall, and with your Staff measure the length of the Shadow in Staves lengths, and hundred parts of the Length according as it is numbered. *Example*, Suppose that on the 16th day of *January* I do erect my Staff perpendicular, and measuring the length of the Shadow thereof, I find it to be exactly 3 times its length, whereof finding, the 16th day at top of the month of *January*, I find 3,0 to stand against the 16th day, and the top to find XII, which tells me it is then just 12 a Clock. . . . After several such examples it concludes with; a little practice will make all this plain.[11]

Accordingly, a staff with a scale marked in one hundred equal parts is held erect on level ground. After noting the end of the shadow, the staff is tipped to the ground and the shadow is measured against the scale (**6.3**). The time of day is found by comparing the length of the shadow with monthly tables appearing in the pamphlet.

The gnomon was adapted from a time when the human form itself was used as a shadow device. To find the direction of Mecca, for example, a standard Arab measure for daily prayer was to note the length of one's shadow and step off the distance heel to toe.[12] Telling time by estimating in paces the length of one's own shadow was ancient and widespread. A table for this purpose was given at about 700 CE by the Venerable Bede, an English historian and theologian.[13] Descriptions have also entered the realm of literature: in the *Assembly of Women* by Aristophanes, Praxagora says to her husband: "When the stoicheion

The English

Chapman's and Traveller's
Almanack,

For the Year of CHRIST, 1712.

Wherein all the Post-Roads, with their several Branches and Distances, the Marts, Fairs, and Markets in England and Wales, are Alphabetically disposed in every Month; so that the Place where, and the Days on which any of them are kept, is immediately found out.

To which is added,

A TABLE of ACCOUNTS
READY CAST UP,

For the Buying or Selling of any Commodity by Number, Weight, or Measure, from One Farthing to Ten Pounds; and of any Quantity, from One to Ten thousand.

WITH

A Sun-Dial, and other Tables and Things useful for all Travellers, Traders, and Chapmen of what kind soever.

ALSO.

The rising and setting of the Sun and Moon, the Tides, the Length of Days, Increase and Decrease of the Days throughout the Year, and whatsoever else is necessary for an Annual

ALMANACK.

LONDON, Printed by E. James for the COMPANY of STATIONERS. 1712.

A Brief Chronology, in 1712.

THE Conquest of England by Duke William,	646
The Invention of Guns,	335
The Art of Printing was Invented,	362
The Infectious Sweating Sickness,	361
The Massacre in France,	140
The whole Heavens seemed to burn with Fire,	138
The General Earthquake in England,	132
The Camp at Tilbury in Essex,	124
The Gun-powder Treason,	107
The Voyage to the Isle of Ree,	81
The Duke of Buckingham Murthered,	80
The Plantation began in New England,	80
The Third part of London Bridge burnt.	80
The Earl of Stafford was Beheaded May 12,	71
The Irish Rebellion began October 23. 1641,	71
The Fight at Edge-hill, October 23. 1642,	70
The Fight at Brainford, November 12. 1642,	70
The Scots entered England, January 16.	69
The Fight at Newberry,	69
Marston-Moore Fight, July 2,	67
The great Fight at Naseby, June 14. 1645.	67
King Charles was Murthered, January 30.	64
The Scots routed at Dunbar, November 3.	62
The great Fight at Worcester,	60
King Charles II. returned to London, May 29,	52
King Charles the II. was Crowned April 23,	51
The strong Tempestuous Wind, February 18,	49
Three Blazing Stars appeared, .	47
The last great Plague in London,	47
A great Fight between the English and the Dutch,	46
The great Fire in London, September 3, 4, 5, 6,	46
King Charles the II died February 6, 1684.	38

Fairs in January.

Bristol	6 and 25	Gravesend	25	Llangihony	7
Churchingford	25	Hickford	5	Llondysfel	31
Derby	13	Llanibither	3	Salisbury	6

The use of the Sun-Dial.

January hath XXXI. Days.

Figure 6.2. Page from *Chapman's and Traveller's Almanack* (1712) describing the method of telling the time of day.

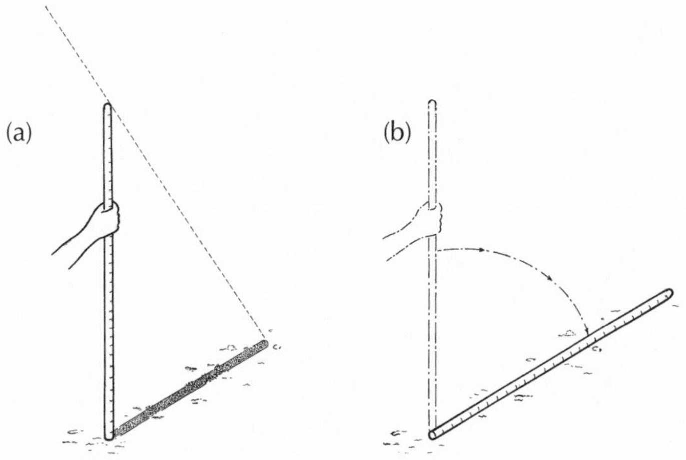

Figure 6.3. (a) The staff, with a scale marked along its length, is held erect on level ground. (b) Noting the end of the shadow, the staff is tipped over and the distance measured against the scale. The time of day is found by comparing the length of the shadow with monthly tables appearing in the pamphlet.

[length of one's shadow] is ten times as long as your foot, . . . perfume yourself and come to dinner."[14] In the 14th century, Chaucer wrote:

It was four o'clock, according to my guess,
Since eleven feet, a little more or less,
My shadow at the time did fall,
Considering that I myself am six feet tall.[15]

Knowledge of shadow reckoning in Egypt helps explain a Middle Kingdom prophecy that refers to the sun's shadow. In a rendering by James Allen: "The sun will be separating himself from people. Though he will rise when it is time, no one will know when noon comes, no one will distinguish his shadow."[16]

The connection between shadow length, time, and geographical direction is the result of countless years of observing the natural phenomenon that as the sun rises and travels through the sky to its setting position, the shadow an object casts changes its angle and length, the shortest shadow always pointing to the north, at noon. While it is possible for high noon to be visually identified by the practiced eye of farmer or sailor, other times of the day are more difficult to find. For millennia, the device used for this purpose was a simple straight staff. Used as a portable gnomon by travelers, it cast shadows that could be measured via markings on the shaft of the gnomon. This is done by gauging the shadow's length and comparing it to previously compiled tables, templates, or other mnemonic devices giving the shadow length of each hour for different times of the year.

Despite its almost universal early use, the staff was not free of problems. When readings are taken at most latitudes, the shadow of the noonday sun is long enough to be measured, but this changes as one nears the equator. In lower latitudes the shadows grow ever shorter, disappearing completely at the summer solstice when the noon sun is directly overhead at the Tropic of Cancer (23° 27' north latitude). Problems arise in Egypt, where the summer sun is at a very high angle overhead at Cairo (it would have been 83° 56' at noon in 2700 BCE) and is almost directly overhead at Aswan (89° 57').[17] Indeed, in parts

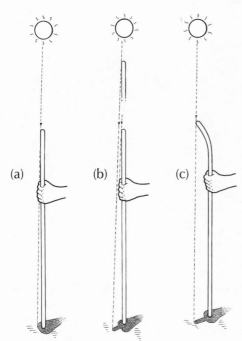

Figure 6.4. (a) In Egypt, the shadow of the high summer sun cannot be measured by a straight staff due to its short length. (b) Elongating the staff would lengthen its shadow, but would make it impractical to carry. (c) Egyptians solved the problem by bending the top of the staff toward the sun.

of Egypt the shadow becomes so short as the summer sun increases its overhead angle that the very hand holding the staff obscures the noon shadow cast by the top of the staff (**6.4**). The problem can be remedied by greatly increasing the height of the pole, but this not a desirable solution.

The Bend in the Gnomon

Instead of elongating shadows by increasing the height of the pole, a far simpler solution was provided by the Egyptians—the top of the pole was bent to face the overhead sun. These bends are found to range from 15 to 90 degrees off the vertical shaft (**6.5**). Use of such a staff as a portable gnomon is shown in a scene of Amenophis II with the same type of markings along his shaft as are later described in the English almanac.[18] Such staffs are similar to the Egyptian hieroglyph *renpet*, ∫ ∫, a shape supposedly taken from a bent palm branch and sometimes shown with tally marks along its shaft—seemingly the remaining stems of missing fronds.[19] However, Old Kingdom descriptions and an 18th Dynasty scene from the tomb of Ti show that the bent shafts were man-made, not a product of nature. The scene from Ti shows a straight pole fixed to a yoke while force is applied to the far end (**6.6**). The accompanying caption reads: "Press well! It is an oiled staff that is in it." No doubt, on achieving the desired bend, it was held in position until the oils dried.[20]

Symbols of the bent shaft, when used in hieroglyphic words that mean "time," ⌐⌐{⊙, or "year," {°, were probably derived from its use as a gnomon—a use that may also explain the phrase "he who is the mouth [voice]," which Egyptologist Henry Fischer found so odd when applied to a staff.[21] Although he feels it was an adage suggesting that instructions were sometimes given by beating rather than talking, a different interpretation may also

Figure 6.5. Egyptian scenes that typify various staffs: (a) slight bend, (b) 90-degree bend, and (c) Amenophis II holding a staff with scale markings similar to those mentioned in the English almanac 4,000 years later.

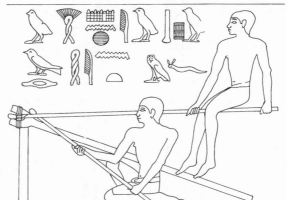

Figure 6.6. The method by which staffs are bent is shown in an Old Kingdom scene from the tomb of Ti.

be applied: the staff may be thought of as possessing a voice if it imparts information about the hour of the day.

The Was-Scepter

The bent shaft has problems of accuracy—the length of its shadow is dependent on the user's ability to hold it perpendicular to the ground. Tilting the shaft while assessing the shadow will change the length of its shadow. This problem was ingeniously solved by the Egyptians with the invention of the was-scepter, a straight staff provided with a bifurcated foot, later given a metal insert to reduce wear (**6.7**), and a short downturned head at the end of its bent top. Being of equal length, the tines on the bottom kept the staff perpendicular in the fore and aft plane (**6.8**), and the downturned head signaled the slightest lateral deviation. This occurs because a shadow cast by the downturned head is only aligned with the shaft when the was-scepter is held perpendicular to the ground. If the shaft of the device is tilted to the side, the downturned portion casts a separate shadow, which appears as a bump in the shadow of the shaft. Although the divergent shadow depends on the degree of tilt, the slightest tilt off plumb can readily be seen.[22] While the was-scepter later took on symbolic shapes devoid of all utility, in its original and practical form it was the

(a)   (b)

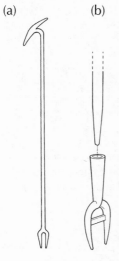

Figure 6.7. (a) The was-scepter, with its angled head and forked bottom. (b) Forked inserts of metal were sometimes placed on the bottom of the staff to prevent unevenness due to wear.

(a)   (b)   (c)

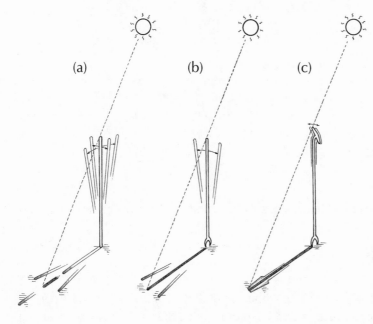

Figure 6.8. Shadow patterns from various staffs. (a) The straight staff has unrestricted movements both fore and aft and side to side. (b) The forked bottom stabilizes the staff fore and aft but permits movements side to side. (c) The angled head of the was-scepter indicates the slightest side-to-side movements by means of a diverging shadow.

most accurate shadow caster of any portable staff, including those used some 4,000 years later in England.

The Shadow Clock

The was-scepter seems to be uniquely Egyptian, but use of the simple gnomon led Egypt and the entire Near East to the use of more advanced shadow-measuring instruments, as is shown in the Old Testament (Kings II, 20:8–11): "And Hezekiah said unto Isaiah: 'What shall be the sign that the Lord will heal me, and that I shall go up unto the house of the Lord the third day?' And Isaiah said: 'This shall be the sign unto thee from the Lord, that the Lord will do the thing that He hath spoken: shall the shadow go forward ten degrees, or go back ten degrees?' And Hezekiah answered: 'It is a light thing for the shadow to decline ten degrees; nay, but let the shadow return backward ten degrees.' And Isaiah the prophet cried unto the Lord; and he brought the shadow ten degrees backward, by which it had gone down on the dial of Ahaz." The terms *degrees* and *dial* have been loosely interpreted. As the Swiss archaeologist L. Borchardt shows, the Hebrew word *Ma'alot* translates more accurately into "lines" or "steps." Although Borchardt suggests that King Ahaz is referring to a shadow cast from a roof to a staircase, the description more aptly refers to the shadow of a gnomon falling on the steps of a shadow clock.[23]

A simple version of the biblical shadow clock is shown in Egypt. Basically, it is a small instrument shaped like an L lying on its back. Instead of reading the shadow by tipping the staff to the ground, this device gave the time of day by the user pointing its head toward the sun and measuring the shadow falling on a scale marked along its horizontal bar **(6.9)**. Designed to also be handheld, it is kept level when a plumbline fixed to the top of the vertical bar is made to overlie a vertical line scored on its side.[24] Designed with a scale bar and gnomon of equal width, it allowed a shadow to cover the scale completely when the instrument was faced directly to the sun. Improperly aimed, however, it permitted a sliver of light to appear on the scale bar. Although primarily a timekeeper, as a by-product it can also be used to find direction—its tail pointing north when the shortest shadow of the day is found.

Allen provided a translation of an inscription about its manufacture and operation from the tomb of Seti I (1295–1186 BCE) **(6.10)**:

. . . know the hours.
    Make a shadow clock with a plank 5 palms long, [with a head on one end . . .] high, [and a crossbar] 2 fingers high [and . . . long] on the head of this shadow-clock.

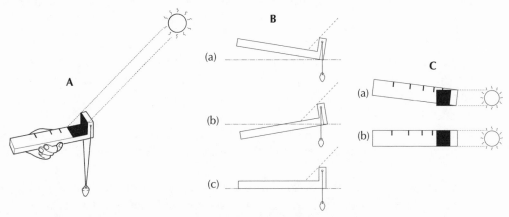

Figure 6.9. (A) When the shadow clock is pointed by hand toward the sun, shadows that fall on a scale can indicate the time of day. (B) The scale bar is made level by aligning a plumb bob to a vertical line on the side of the shadow clock: (a, b) bar not level, line exposed; (c) bar level, line covered. (C) The shadow clock is faced directly to the sun when the gnomon's shadow matches the width of the scale bar: (a) it is misaligned to the sun when a sliver of light appears on the scale bar; (b) it is aligned to the sun when the scale bar is in full shadow.

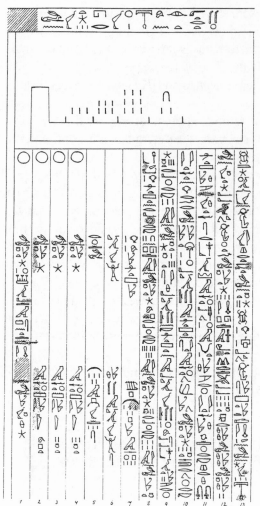

Figure 6.10. Roof inscription titled "Knowing the hours of the day and night," from the tomb of Seti I. Near the middle of column 11 are bull's horns for the phrase "after the sun has come to stand in the apex of the crossbar."

[You have to divide] these 5 palms into four parts, [each one] branded on this shadow clock. You have to put 12 rules on it for the first hour, you have to put 9 on it for the second hour, you have to put 6 on it for the third hour, and you have to put 3 on it for the fourth hour.

Now align this shadow clock in alignment with the sun, with its head, on which the crossbar is, to the east until the sun's shadow is exact on this shadow clock.

Now after the end of the fourth hour, you have to turn this shadow clock, with its plank, to the east. After the sun has come to stand in the apex of the crossbar, you have to count these hours again until the sun enters four hours according to the first rule.[25]

The instrument was later provided with an inclined scale to define the shadow more clearly and to help register what would ordinarily be long early morning and late afternoon (a)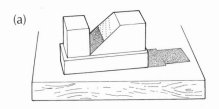

(b)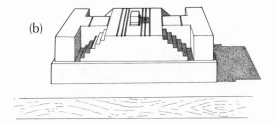

Figure 6.11. To help register the long early morning and late afternoon shadows, the face of the scale bar was raised to capture the sunlight. (a) Shadow lengths for different months are given by the slanted scale of dots. (b) Shadow clock with a scale of steps.

shadows (**6.11a**). A further development was the stepped shadow clock mentioned by the Hebrew prophet Isaiah.[26] Although shadow clocks, a more advanced reckoner, may have existed together with and served the same function as the was-scepter, different stages of technology are often found side by side; some future archaeologist may discover a sundial in the garden of a modern home also containing analog and digital timepieces.

The Festival of Min

Not only were the gnomonic arts known long before Anaximander and before there was even a country known as Greece; they were probably also used long before Egyptian history. This knowledge, acquired by countless years of observing the sun, was put to good use in agrarian societies dependent on the start of the planting season or the rise and fall of a river. Blessed with almost constant sunshine, Egyptians and others gathered this information by observing changes in the direction and length of shadow patterns. With the knowledge that such changes repeat each year at the same time, it became possible for them to predict cyclical events by matching the changing shadow lengths of any fixed object. For example, the shortest shadow of the day, at noon, changes its length in an annually repeating pattern from being longest on the day of the winter solstice to being shortest on the day of the summer solstice.

The importance of these shadows is widespread. Tribesmen in Borneo used and perhaps still use pegs to mark shadow lengths as they move along a template (**6.12**).[27] In China, for several days before an expected time, a calibrated bar called "the gnomon shadow template" was used to measure shadows of a pole 8–10 feet (2.5–3 m) high. In addition, the Chinese devised an instrument somewhat analogous to the Egyptian shadow clock, but instead of lying on its back, the L was placed upright. The shadow cast by the gnomon would fall on the short bar fixed to the bottom, which served here as a template (**6.13**).[28] The Chinese also made use of the aforementioned gnomon with the shadow shortening and being swallowed by its pedestal at the summer solstice (**1.16**). Indeed, at times sun clocks have been formed of the most primitive of devices; until recently field workers in the Midwest were called for their midday meal when a shadow reached a mark scratched near a south-facing farmhouse window.[29]

One of the earliest gnomonic devices to make use of these changing shadow lengths was employed in a ceremony called the festival of Min. Ancient Egyptian scenes of this

Figure 6.12. Tribesmen in Borneo track the length of the sun's shadow by placing pegs alongside a shadow template.

Figure 6.13. The Chinese measured the summer solstice using a gnomon operating on the same principle as the Egyptian shadow clock.

festival are often accompanied by an odd-looking shrine or hut (*shn.t*), the shape of which may be compared to a bowling pin (**6.14**). In later iconography, such as at the 12th Dynasty Chapel of Senwosret I at Karnak, these huts acquired Egyptian-style entrances.[30] When this occurred, the hut was usually accompanied by a mast showing mounted the horns of a bull containing a coil of rope, which represents the sun. Indicating a common relationship, a line from the sun connects the horns, mast, and hut—devices that all represent Min, one or another being more prominently displayed, as illustrated in figures 2.4(**k**) and 6.14(**c, d**).[31] In some early period, the hut, sometimes with a line supporting

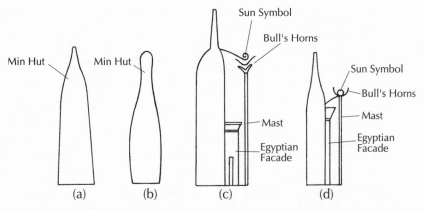

Figure 6.14. (a, b) In its early form, the Min hut is strikingly similar to the white crown of Upper Egypt. (c, d) Min's hut with an Egyptian facade, pole, horns, and sun disc.

the spiral symbol of the sun, seems to have been adopted by the king as the white crown of Upper Egypt (**2.17, 6.15**).

The strangest of gods, Min is identified with a group from some unknown foreign land that settled in the Wadi Hammamat. His companions are the people from the south, perhaps from Punt, a geographical area not yet identified. As an ithyphallic god, he is variously described as "Lord of foreign mountains"; "who opens clouds"; "Lord of the earth, creating their life, insuring their nourishment." As "wind of the river" he is "the great one who carries (rain) on the fields" and is linked to the "gathering of the waters."[32] When he first came upon the Egyptian scene, the three statues of Min had marine symbols, strange to Egypt, that seem to have originated in the Red Sea rather than the Mediterranean. Min's possible connection to the Near East is shown by his appearance (bald head and full beard). Not only is he connected with the sky, but any study of Min always encounters

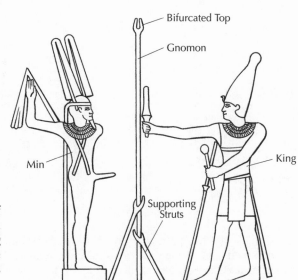

Figure 6.15. Scene from the pavilion of Senwosret I (12th Dynasty) showing a gnomon with a bifurcated top. The king pays homage to the gnomon and the god Min, shown here with a flail in his upraised arm.

a pole of one sort or another—it seems to be the very essence of his worship. For example, he is called "Lord of the *snwt*," an Egyptian word describing the sacred flagstaffs fronting the pylons of a sanctuary.[33] Indeed, the very festival scene in figure 6.15 bearing his name shows an upright gnomon supported by struts.

Unique to Min's gnomon is a bifurcated top reminiscent of the horns of a bull shown at the hut entrances. When fixed in position to frame the sunlight, either device—the forked top of the gnomon or the horns of a bull—aid in an interesting function: they can help to read the changing shadows of the sun as it moves each day from sunrise to sunset. The shadows they cast also help to track the seasons of the year. Seemingly difficult, this task becomes possible because as the shadows cast by the devices change in shape according to the time of day, those previously distorted become symmetrical when the sun arrives at a point perpendicular to the faces of one or the other bifurcated device **(6.16)**. Occurring only once a day, these symmetrical shadows fall along a straight line; thus their length provides a daily record of the sun's position as it moves from solstice to solstice. Although the face of the devices may be turned in any direction, the more closely the forked top faces the midday sun, the shorter will be the length of its shadow and the more pronounced its definition. For increasing accuracy, it is necessary to make the surface of the ground smooth and level—a probable reason why descriptions of Min's festival are often accompanied by a foundation scene.[34]

When the changing lengths of symmetrical shadows of past years are matched, it becomes possible to find empirically the approximate time of an anticipated rainy season or inundation. Such advanced knowledge would have allowed people time to prepare for the rising waters by clearing irrigation ditches of silt from the previous season, a necessary action for a successful crop. Indeed, the importance of Min's festival to the planting season is shown by an event that also occurred at the coronation of the king—a time when

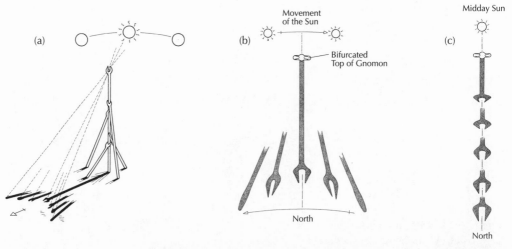

Figure 6.16. (a) View of the changing shadow cast by Min's gnomon in the course of a day. (b) The distorted shadows become symmetrical as the sun moves to face the forked top of the gnomon. (c) Symmetrical shadows occur only once a day, their changing lengths helping people to judge the coming inundation.

four birds were released to the corners of the earth.[35] At the coronation, the birds were released to proclaim the king's ascension to the throne; at the festival of Min, they were released to spread welcome news of the rising Nile.

The bull's horns, as used in Min's bifurcated gnomon, can also be used to gauge a general passage of time—the link being shown by *wpt-rnpt*, ⚭, ⚭ (New Year's Day), where the bent gnomon, sun disc, and bull's horns are combined in a single hieroglyph. The symbolic relationship of the bull's horns to the sun disc is also reflected in the headdress of Hathor, mother of the sun god (**6.17**). Further confirmation of use of the bull's horns as an indicator of time is given by Allen, who points out that the shadow-clock text from the tomb of Seti I shows the horns of a bull used for the phrase "after the sun has come to stand in the apex of the crossbar" (**6.10**).[36]

The symbols attributed to Min seem to show the line of shadows found by the bifurcated gnomon in schematic fashion. These symbols appear in various forms as one or more opposing arrowheads on the same shaft, some having flat ends, others with a bolt-like appearance that some interpret to mean a shrine or sanctuary (**6.18**).[37] At times, the arrowheads are seen to overlie a gnomon having a bent top, as seen in figures 2.3(**k**) and 6.18(**a–c**). At other times, possibly in an earlier version, the bent gnomon is shown as a bent feather. The symbolic drawings of Min's festival mast shown in figure 6.18(**d–f**), which have similar arrowheads, suggest direction, or shadows cast by Min's gnomon, as they move along a straight line.

Figure 6.17. Mother of the sun-god, Hathor, shows the sun aligned with the bull's horns of Min's gnomon.

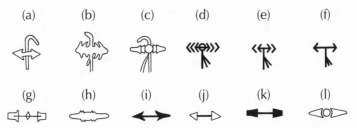

Figure 6.18. (a–c) Opposing arrowheads overlying bent gnomons are suggestive of direction or the shadows' changing length. (d–e) Shown on Min's gnomon, the arrowheads seem to issue from its very top. (g–l) Min's symbols are often represented by what are essentially two opposing arrowheads.

Although the line of shadows, indicated by the arrowheads, required generations of observation to understand, its study may have begun by pure serendipity in a settled community of Min-style huts.[38] Yet, while the shape of the hut would show the repeating shadow patterns, it would provide no means of measuring their length. This critical omission may have been rectified by discovery of symmetrical shadows cast by the chance mounting of the horns of a bull. Their importance to those dependent on water from the inundation or the seasonal desert rains would indelibly fix the devices in the iconography of the Egyptian people. Interestingly, we may still retain a word that reaches back to that distant past. Used at the end of a prayer or a statement to express approval, the word *amen*, a possible derivation of *aman* or Min, has ancient roots going back to the Greek *amën* and Hebrew *ämën*.[39] The word *aman*, a Libyo-Berber word that means water, may also point to a possible connection between water, *aman*, and Min.[40] Many of the Libyan gods were so ancient that they were already dying out by the Old Kingdom. Perhaps because of his identification with water, the essence of life and growth, Min may later have developed into Amun, the chief god of imperial Egypt.

Considering that the chief purpose of the device was to signal a time for the rising of the Nile, it is startling to see a gnomon at the festival of Min, an event considered to be a harvest festival—a disclosure made clear by a scene depicting the king cutting and consecrating a sheaf of emmer.[41] The time of harvest is obviously determined by the status of the crop, an occasion when no external indicator like a gnomon would be required. Clearly, a reason for their joint appearance is in order.

In northern climes, we generally think of the harvest as an autumnal event, determined by seasonal temperatures. In Egypt, however, harvest time is in the spring, from the end of May to the beginning of June. It occurs at this time because the planting season is not decided by seasonal rainfall but by the overflowing Nile. As reported by Breasted:

> The marvelous productivity of the Egyptian soil is due to the annual inundation of the river, which is caused by the melting of the snows, and by the spring rains at the sources of the Blue Nile. Freighted with the rich loam of the Abyssinian highlands, the rushing waters of the spring freshet hurry down the Nubian valley, and a slight rise is discernible at the first cataract in the early part of June. The flood swells rapidly and steadily, and although the increase is usually interrupted for nearly a month from the end of September on, it is usually resumed again, and the maximum level continues until the end of October or into November. The waters in the region of the first cataract are then nearly fifty feet higher than at low water; while at Cairo the rise is about half that at the cataract. A vast and elaborate system of irrigation canals and reservoirs first receive the flood, which is then allowed to escape into the fields as needed.[42]

Due to well-organized water management, Egyptians were able to extend the planting season from October to mid-December and thus produce a harvest of emmer that lasted about seven weeks—most of April and May—almost running into the time for the next spring inundation.[43] To find a shadow indicating when the Nile began to rise required preparation. Therefore, before the approaching spring shadow, the ground must be leveled and the gnomon raised into position, events which would start in late May or early June in upper Egypt. This was also a time of the end of harvest, when the king cut and offered the gnomon the last sheaf of emmer, thus giving back the field some of that which had been taken.[44]

The custom of returning to the fields that which has been taken is not restricted to the last of the harvest; sometimes the first fruits are involved. According to anthropologist Winifred Blackman, in some parts of Egypt, before any of the corn is cut, villagers even today go into the fields to pluck the finest ears by hand and plait them into a special form called the "bride of the corn." They place this object on the heaps of grain after winnowing is completed, as a charm to secure a good harvest the following year. Tradesmen sometimes hang such charms in their shop windows, believing these will bring them a steady flow of customers. The bride of the corn is also depicted in several Theban tomb-chapels of the 18th Dynasty and can possibly be traced back to the Old Kingdom in a different form.[45]

Some of Min's festival scenes show the gnomon braced with struts and include groups of men holding ropes while others climb toward the top, as in a contest (**6.19**). This depiction seems to suggest a scenario in which after successfully heralding the rising waters, men would compete to reach the forked top and the magical properties it was thought to possess. Judging by their head feathers, they may be Libyans or Nubians, perhaps reflecting an early time in the Epi-Paleolithic Period (7000–3000 BCE) when increased rainfall enabled desert inhabitants to establish more permanent settlements in locations such as the Wadi Hammamat.[46] However, during what were still arid conditions, it was essential

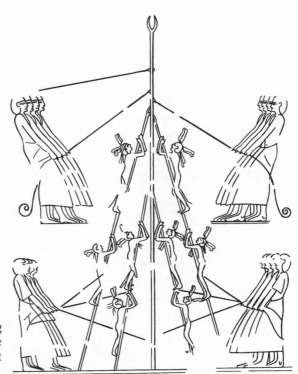

Figure 6.19. Min festival scene showing men climbing, as in a contest, toward the top of the gnomon, while others support the structure with ropes.

Figure 6.20. (a) Facing a tilted gnomon, Min receives offerings from the king. (b) Tilted gnomons were needed in the high sun of Upper Egypt to lengthen the shadow and to define its penumbra better.

to keep a close watch on the rainy season. As Michael Hoffman says, "Rainfall, when it does occur in arid or semiarid regions with any regularity, is restricted to a particular season of the year. The livelihood of peoples in such areas, therefore, depends on a rather precise knowledge of when such rains will come—this kind of timing is absolutely critical to survival."[47]

As the climate grew more arid, the rains decreased to the point that life in the desert could no longer be sustained. To survive, the population had little choice but to move to the river valley and face the overflowing Nile. At that time the river was a dangerous, unmanageable, and useless torrent. Only through years of building canals and reservoirs, and by means of discovering the gnomonic arts or borrowing these from another culture, were the new arrivals able to survive and prosper. Those who settled in the north made use of the upright gnomon (**6.15**); those in the south learned to contend with the high summer sun and its shortened shadow by placing the Min gnomon at an angle (**6.20**).[48] This expedient not only made measurements possible but helped to define the penumbra (the area between complete shadow and complete illumination) by having the fork of the gnomon directly face the sun.[49]

The Navigational Gnomon

The sun was important to travelers on the waters as well. Gnomons are also found on extant models of Egyptian ships. Probably used in navigation, these so-called solar ships display bent gnomons pivotally mounted to a block located on the centerline of the vessel. The block also holds a knifelike member on the centerline, pointing to the bow and acting as a lubber line to indicate the direction in which the ship is headed (**6.21**).[50] In use, the bend of the gnomon is turned until it casts the shortest shadow of the day at high noon. The midday shadow always points to the north, and its length is always the same for each latitude around the world in the northern hemisphere. Considering this, a helmsman can correct his course and steer to a steady parallel by relating the position of the lubber line to the lie of the midday shadow (**6.22**). Although gnomons were of great help

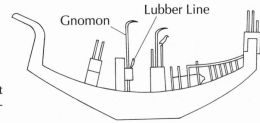

Figure 6.21. Model of a solar ship with bent gnomon and upstanding knifelike member acting as a lubber line.

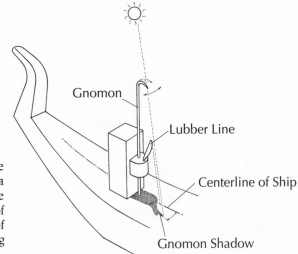

Figure 6.22. Method of finding the direction of solar ships by means of a gnomon. North, located by turning the gnomon to the short midday shadow of the day, is compared to the heading of the ship, as indicated by the upstanding lubber line.

to ancient mariners, knowledge of longitude was required to find distant lands with accuracy—a discovery not made until recent centuries.

Instead of displaying only one lubber line, some more advanced solar ships have two such devices in vertical alignment, the upper one pointing to the bow of the ship and the lower one toward the deck. The supporting block, which also holds the gnomon, has lines on its surface that divide it into four quadrants—an arrangement somewhat analogous to the hieroglyph *shems*, 𓍞, meaning to "follow" (**6.23**).[51] As in the monthly records of *Chapman's and Traveller's Almanack*, the hieroglyph suggests that the lubber line points to a scale on the deck (in the Egyptian fashion, details normally seen in plan are turned up to the viewer) giving the length of the midday shadow for each month of the year. According

Figure 6.23. Solar ship with gnomon, two lubber lines, and four quadrants. The quadrants probably represent a scale on the deck giving the length of noon shadows for different times of the year.

to Cheryl Haldane, an American marine archaeologist, these archaic symbols are often associated with symbols of Min, the early patron god of desert travelers.[52] Min was evidently the patron god of seafarers as well.

Navigation by the heavenly bodies has been practiced since people first ventured past the coastal waters. Indeed, the position of the sun was used for everything from the most casual to the most important maritime observations. The saying "sun over the yardarm," the approximate time a ship's officers would slip below for their first drink of the day, is based on the sun being over the foreyard of a ship by 1100 hours in northern latitudes. With the aid of a chronometer, later navigators used the sun to locate longitude by comparing local noon (the meridian) to Greenwich time; every hour of difference accounted for 15 degrees of longitude. Before the advent of fixed satellites, a method of finding local noon was to halve equal altitudes of the sun with navigational aides, such as a sextant. However, long before invention of the sextant, Vikings and others found the height of the sun with calibrated sticks, outstretched arms, or by comparing the sun's altitude to the ship's rigging. On a constantly rolling ship, the inevitable errors were reduced by using the mean of several readings. On overcast days, Vikings located the sun by use of the light-seeking properties of double-refracting Icelandic feldspar crystals.[53]

Although more art than science, navigational gnomons were a considerable aid to navigation.[54] I. E. S. Edwards gives a modern example of their use: as a passenger in a convoy of forty ships in the Atlantic during the World War II, he spent five weeks at sea between Scotland and West Africa. Despite evasive action of the convoy, with his watch set to Greenwich time, Edwards was able to predict his arrival at Freetown to within a few hours by measuring the shadow of an upright iron bar until it was at its shortest.[55]

The discovery of Egyptian model ships containing gnomons raises questions of an interesting nature. The sole purpose of such a gnomon was to help people cross a body of water beyond visible landmarks. It would be of questionable value to people sailing the Nile or the coastal waters of the Mediterranean or Red Sea. Long before Sneferu (2575–2551 BCE) sent 40 ships along the coastal waters to Byblos to trade for cedar wood, Neolithic inhabitants of Crete (3000 BCE) crossed the open sea to export obsidian, a volcanic flint suitable for the manufacture of edged implements and weapons, to Egypt.[56] The presence of solar ships suggests that Egyptian sailors also ventured farther than has yet been imagined—possibly to Náxos in the Cyclades. This island, known throughout the ancient Mediterranean for its great quantities of the "iron stone" (emery), may have helped produce some of the great Egyptian works in basalt, granite, and other hard stones. A voyage of this nature would probably follow the coastal waters to Turkey, island hopping along the parallel of Náxos, and crossing at most about 35 miles (56 km) of open sea—child's play when compared to the thousands of open miles crossed by Polynesians in their long canoes. Indeed, as seaman and scholar Douglas Phillips-Birt notes:

> Always to be remembered is the fact that what modern man has gained in philosophical ability has been won at the cost of atrophying some useful and once instinctive powers—accurate observation, memory that did not require records, sense of direction and locality that had no need of instrumentation or maps, smell often so invaluable to the seaman. . . . In our own day we have the examples of

the unlettered men who, a generation ago, were often placed in charge of steam-trawlers that remained at sea for weeks on end, and yet they never thought to consult the charts provided by the owners which remained in their first folds year after year. These men when making a landfall in thick weather, could identify it though they may have faced it last a decade or more before.[57]

Calendar

Although heat and light from the sun enabled the ancient cultures to survive, it was the shadows the sun produced that them helped to systematize their lives. As previously mentioned, in an agrarian society it is of prime importance to know when the planting season is due to begin. Today we simply refer to the calendar, and it is common to associate holidays with different seasons of the year. However, ancient Egyptian calendars were so inaccurate that festival dates shifted through the seasons from year to year. The changing festival cycle resulted from the early use of a lunar calendar that did not correspond with the solar year. As a result, except at rare intervals, the official lunar calendar was completely different from the natural calendar of farmer and shepherd. To keep the seasons in place, the Egyptians were forced to add a 13th intercalary lunar month every two or three years.

The beginning of the inundation is variable, in terms of the solar year, occurring at any time within a two-week period from the end of May to the beginning of June. In some exceptional years the period may even spread over two months.[58] Nevertheless, Egyptians would start the year with the lunar month immediately after the Nile began to rise and would then use the heliacal rising of Sirius to adjust the lunar calendar. Identifying Sirius as the goddess Sopdet (Sothis), the Egyptians imagined her as rising with the rising Nile and so linked her appearance to New Year's Day. However, due to irregularities between the two events, the rising of Sirius coincided with the Egyptian New Year only every 1,460 years. Because the Roman author Censorius recorded the simultaneous events in 139 CE, they are calculated to have coincided previously about 1317 BCE and 2773 BCE.

By the early third millennium BCE, the irregularities of this variable calendar gave birth to a twelve-month year of 30 days for each month. This was further divided into three seasons of four months; *akhet* (inundation), *peret* (winter; emerging growth), *shemu* (summer; harvest). Because this totaled only 360 days, five additional days were needed to make a 365-day year. These "epagomenal" (added) days were considered birthdays of the deities Osiris, Horus, Isis, Seth, and Nephthys.[59]

It is uncertain how the Egyptians decided on a year of 365 days. Among the theories is one that the number of days was supposedly counted between successive risings of Sirius, and adverse weather conditions that interfered with sightings were dealt with by averaging over a period of years. Alternatively, it is suggested the total number of days was averaged over several lunar years.[60] Considering their uncertainty, both methods are questionable. In whatever way it was accomplished, the new civil calendar did not wholly replace the older lunar calendar, which continued to be used for religious festivals. People continued to use the moon for an excellent reason—to celebrate festivals simultaneously throughout a country with limited means of communication, nothing can surpass a heavenly body that changes in appearance on a regular basis. To this day, starting with the ancient Israelites, all religions from the Near East have the start of some of their holidays (Passover, Easter, and Ramadan) controlled by the phases of the moon. Because this lunar-stellar calendar had 365 days as against the solar year of 365 ¼ days, they separated by one day every four years, or 25 days every century. It was 3,000 years before Julius Caesar reformed the calendar in 46 BCE with an added day every four years (leap year).

Although it has been postulated that the Egyptians were able to establish a 365-day year by use of Sirius, evidence suggests that New Year's Day and the number of days in a year were originally found by observing shadows cast by the sun—the rising of Sirius representing the New Year at a later time in Egyptian history. As with the moon, Sirius probably came to represent New Year's Day because its heliacal rising served as a better herald for the Egyptian populace than did the word-of-mouth results of some carefully observed priestly shadow event. This is supported by Egyptian hieroglyphs themselves, a written language with roots closer to physical reality than in one based on an alphabet.

Hieroglyphic writing shows "the going up of Sothis" (Sirius) as represented with the symbol of a star, 𓇳𓏤𓇼; however, the same star symbol does not appear in the hieroglyphs that refer to "daily," 𓏤; "time," 𓂝𓏲𓇳; or "New Year's Day," 𓇳. A symbol of the star also does not appear in hieroglyphs that stand for the seasons: "inundation," 𓇳; "winter," 𓇳; and "summer," 𓇳. Instead, the solar connections of these hieroglyphs are shown by the use of a sun disc as a determinative.[61] Indeed, the timing of the inundation itself lends support to this view—the river starts to swell at a time closer to the summer solstice in mid-June than to the heliacal rise of Sirius in mid-July.[62]

The natural year of 365 days can be more readily found by the sun than by any means previously suggested. Any day of the year may be used as a reference point, provided that the solar event occurring on that day happens only once during the year. The event may be as simple as the number of consecutive days between when the first ray of light enters a darkened chamber, as the rising sun moves toward the solstice, and the next such occasion. No doubt, this is the very reason that the 24-hour day of Egypt runs from sunrise to sunrise instead of moonrise to moonrise, as in the calendars of most ancient people, or the midnight-to-midnight day of our own calendar.

Besides the important role it played in the everyday life of Egypt, the gnomon became itself an object of worship when formed as an obelisk. By causing people to observe and record shadows, this simple stick became an important basis of much science; it also set the stage for the incredibly accurate orientation of the Great Pyramid of Cheops.

ORIENTATION

As the solar cult of Heliopolis became more embedded in Egyptian thought, by the 4th Dynasty, the need to acknowledge the primacy of the sun became increasingly important. The rulers of Egypt became "Sons of Ra," adopted a solar disc as their symbol, and regarded the sun as the source of all life. Yet their belief in the sun was not restricted to theology. The effect of this creed on the funerary architecture of Egypt was profound, causing the pyramids, burial chambers, and coffins within the structure to be oriented to the cardinal points.[1] The greater the accuracy of this accomplishment, the more closely Egyptians felt the tomb would equate the life and death of the king with that of the rising and setting sun.

Table 7.1 shows that the effort toward a perfect orientation was not always successful. While some pyramids are oriented to the cardinal points with astonishing precision, others, such as the 3rd Dynasty pyramid of Djoser, are not. However, as the earliest of these unique structures, Djoser's 3-degree departure from perfection suggests an orientation procedure not yet fully realized. If this monument is eliminated from consideration, the 4th and 5th Dynasty pyramids would disclose an average deviation of only about 30 arcminutes from true north (each angular degree is made of 60 arcminutes; each arcminute is made of 60 arcseconds). The Giza pyramids are an outstanding example of the ancient skills. They range from the 3-arcminute error of Cheops (an average of its four sides), to the less accurate but still remarkable 14-arcminute error found at the pyramid of Mycerinus.

Of the small deviations in Cheops pyramid, table 7.2 shows the north, east, and west sides of Cheops pyramid to be astonishingly close to the cardinal points, deviating by only a couple of arcminutes, the greatest error off the cardinal points occurring on the south side. The findings were made in a 19th-century survey by W. M. Flinders Petrie and later confirmed by J. H. Cole. Their surveys and those of all present-day surveyors judge direction by relating angular measurements to true north. This direction was contrary to that

Table 7.1

ORIENTATION OF MAJOR 3RD AND 4TH DYNASTY PYRAMIDS

KING	DYNASTY	PLACE	DEVIATION FROM TRUE NORTH	
Djoser	3	Saqqara	3°	east of north
Sneferu	4	Meidum	0° 24' 25"	west of north
Sneferu	4	South Dahshur	0° 09' 12"	west of north
Sneferu	4	North Dahshur	0° 05' 00"	west of north*
Cheops	4	Giza	0° 03' 06"	west of north
Chephren	4	Giza	0° 05' 26"	west of north
Mycerinus	4	Giza	0° 14' 03"	east of north
Sahure	5	Abusir	1° 45"	west of north
Neferirkare	5	Abusir	0° 30'	east of north
Niuserre	5	Abu Gurab (Solar Temple)	1°	west of north
Unas	5	Saqqara	0° 17' 28"	east of north*

After Zbyněk Žába, *L'Orientation astronomique dans l'ancienne Égypte*, 11–12.
* Measured by Joseph Dorner.

Table 7.2

ORIENTATION OF THE SIDES OF THE GREAT PYRAMID

PYRAMID SIDE	ORIENTATION	
North side	2' 28"	south of west
East side	1' 57"	west of north
South side	5' 30"	south of west
West side	2' 30"	west of north

After J. H. Cole, *Determination of the Exact Size and Orientation of the Great Pyramid of Giza*, 7.

sought by the Egyptian surveyors, whose major interest was an orientation extending from east to west, the rising and setting positions of the sun. Interestingly, the tables also show evidence that may help to resolve questions about the method employed by Egyptian surveyors to achieve their extraordinary results. For one thing, the tables indicate that a deliberate attempt was made to orient the pyramids to the cardinal points. They also disclose that while there were differences in orientation, the pyramids stayed within parameters of about 30 arcminutes. Considering this, it seems reasonable to assume that any method of orientation suggested that does not account for the errors observed was probably not one that was employed by the Egyptians. One may also assume that in a society devoid of precise measuring instruments, once found, the same orientation procedure was used in all cases.

A possible early use of the magnetic compass would not have given the observed results; indeed, had the ancient surveyors been acquainted with the device, the magnitude of error would have been much greater. North magnetic pole, which the needle seeks, is not on the meridian (a line that extends from pole to pole) but varies according to the place and time the readings are taken. The cardinal points are geographical directions defined by the axis of the earth and therefore constant. The sun and the stars are used as devices to find the axis. Accordingly, any method proposed for the Egyptian surveyors must make use of these heavenly bodies.

Narrowing the field of inquiry, the celestial object chosen for the task should be one that has a repeating cycle of movement that discloses an accurate direction when its path is measured. This requirement makes the moon, which has an 18.61-year cycle, a questionable candidate. Its rapid movements from rising to setting, its changing shape, periodic disappearance, and the difficulty of observing the moon in its frequent daylight ascents would prove handicaps in any ancient method of orientation, particularly if great accuracy were sought. To these difficulties may be added the maximum positions reached, north and south, during the moon's monthly and yearly cycles.[2]

If we eliminate use of the moon, Egyptian surveyors seem to have been restricted to one of three possible astronomical methods of orientation: they could sight to a star and bisect the angle between its rising and setting positions; they could bisect the extreme positions of a circumpolar star; or they could use the shadows cast by the sun.

Orientation by the Rising and Setting Stars

As the earth rotates, the stars seem to rise and set along different points of the eastern and western horizon. Some also rise heliacally. A heliacal star is one that disappears from the nighttime sky for a period, and briefly reappears, keeping close to the path of the rising sun before being overwhelmed by its intense light. Sirius, a prime example, is represented as the goddess Sothis (*Spdt* in Egyptian), adorned with a headdress of a star. These morning stars do not stay in the same position on the horizon. With every passing dawn, each rises higher in the sky until another heliacal star takes its place. Using this natural phenomenon, Egyptians selected a different morning star or constellation to represent the first day of each of the 36 ten-day weeks and five epagomenal (added) days that made up the 365-day year in their civil calendar. In addition, they divided the night with star charts into twelve time divisions by selecting heliacal stars called decans, which rise each hour on the eastern horizon. The star charts were used for religious rituals, such as the passage of the sun-god traveling from sunset to sunrise through the underworld.[3] The Egyptian word for hour is written with both star and sun symbols.[4]

Among those favoring the use of stars for orientation, Edwards suggests a means of sighting a star and bisecting the angle between its rising and setting positions. For this task, Edwards claims:

it was clearly only necessary to fix one axis; the other axis could be determined by the use of a set square; contemporary buildings with corners forming a perfect right angle prove that an accurate instrument for this purpose must have been available to the pyramid builders. East and west could have been discovered approximately by observing the rising and setting of the sun on the two equinoctial days every year, and north by an observation of the Pole Star, but in each case the resultant error (even after allowance has been made for a change in the position of the pole in relation to the Pole Star in the course of about 4,500 years) would have been greater than the amount revealed by at least the two main pyramids at Giza. To judge from the instrumental and representational evidence so far found, it seems more likely that the high degree of accuracy was achieved by astral than by solar observation.[5]

Due to irregularities in the terrain and to atmospheric refraction, which causes rising objects to appear higher than their actual position, Edwards realized that it is not possible to find direction by bisecting the angle of a rising and setting star as it breaks the horizon. He therefore postulates a high circular wall to act as an artificial horizon.[6] This would permit an observer to sight over a centrally located pole and to mark the position of a star as it rose and set at the top edge of the wall. Transferring the points to the ground with plumb lines, Edwards claims true north can be found by their bisection with the center pole (7.1).

Everything Edwards says is true, theoretically. As a practical matter, however, the difficulty of erecting a large-diameter masonry wall in a precise circle, that is exactly level, would be a task beyond the ability of the most expert of the king's masons. Considering the great distances to stars and the material of which the wall would be constructed, even a slightest deviation in the wall's radius or the smallest imperfection in its level would greatly affect the results. More questionable than the lack of supporting evidence, and the unattainable perfection of masonry construction required, is the ability of an observer to sight the rising and setting positions of a star accurately from the exact center of the circle;

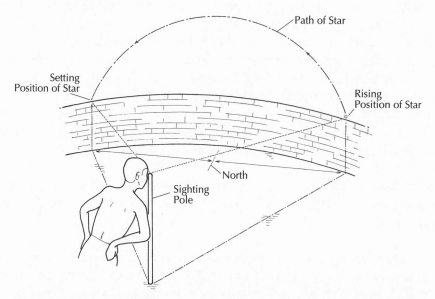

Figure 7.1. For accurate orientation by the stars, Edwards proposes erecting an artificial horizon and marking, when viewed from a center pole, the rising positions of a star as it appears or disappears behind the wall. True north is found by bisecting their positions.

the events occur many hours apart. Even with the pole exactly located, and the observer immobilized in position for the required length of time, the slightest movement of head or eye when the star finally intersected the wall would change the sighting angle and, considering the distance being measured, would lend substantial error to its outcome.

Bisecting the Extreme Positions of a Circumpolar Star

During the age of pyramid building no star was fixed on the pole that was visible to the naked eye, therefore none could have been used as a stationary target. The closest star at the time was Alpha Draconis (Thuban), a circumpolar star, at 1° 40'.[7] Although circumpolar stars may appear stationary to the casual observer, they circle the north celestial pole with varying diameters. Called "imperishable spirits" by the ancient Egyptians, they were approximately aligned to the entrances of 4th Dynasty pyramids to aid the spirit of the dead king in his ascension to the sky.[8]

The sighting of circumpolar stars varies with latitude, their numbers increasing with distance north from the equator. These distant sky specks can provide an accurate method of finding true north if the extreme positions of the circular paths of the stars can be bisected. However, since the eastern-most and western-most positions are twelve hours apart, this problem is more difficult than one would imagine. Indeed, just viewing the positions requires 12 hours of darkness—a possibility reserved for equinoctial nights. Compounding the problem is the ever present morning mist, today exacerbated by industrial smoke. Early mist is a natural phenomenon caused by the rising sun as it heats the moisture condensed on the surface of the desert during the cool nights. Even assuming the absence of mist, the great distance and the small target would require precise measuring instruments unavailable to ancient people. And if all these problems could be overcome, the results still would not provide the roughly 30-arcminute error in orientation shown by the existing pyramids.

Despite the difficulties, the Czech scholar Zbyněk Žába favors the use of circumpolar stars for the orientation procedure. He postulates that the circular path of Eta, a star in the Great Bear constellation, can be bisected with an apparatus consisting of a plumb line and a *peseshkef* mounted on a small block. A *peseshkef* is a flint knife with a bifurcated blade shaped like a fish tail used in a ceremony called "opening of the mouth," a magical rite that supposedly returned to the deceased the use of their senses. According to Žába, to view the extreme positions of the star orbiting the north celestial pole, a block holding the peseshkef is shifted east and west, the block being guided by a slat fixed to a level surface. At each extreme, the peseshkef is sighted to the target star across a distant plumb line centrally located north of the slat. Žába claims that a bisection of the two extreme positions of the shifted block supplies the direction true north (**7.2**).[9]

Although seemingly well planned, the described procedure is not possible. Along with the questions already mentioned for bisecting the rising and setting positions of a star, the method of achieving an exact east-west orientation for the slat and the means of centering a distant plumbline due north before either direction has been found are not explained. Assuming again that all the problems were overcome, despite these objections, the procedure also would not account for orientations that fall within the roughly 30-arcminute error shown by the pyramids of table 7.1.

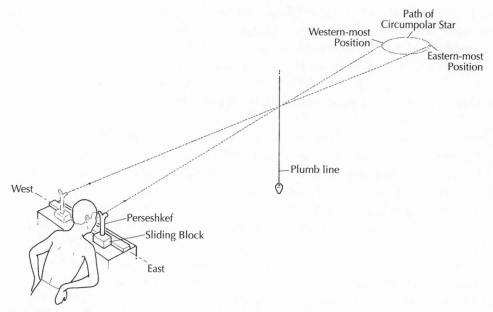

Figure 7.2. To find true north, Žába suggests finding the extreme east-west positions of a circumpolar star. The star's positions are sighted over a perseshkef, a device borrowed from the "opening of the mouth" ceremony. A bisection, providing true north, is made after shifting the position of the device relative to a distant plumb line.

The Sun

The sun, by contrast, is overpoweringly visible in Egypt and has played a preeminent role throughout the long history of its people, such close attention being paid to this body that deities were assigned to represent the sun's every movement. Gods of the morning sun, represented by a beetle, were called Herakhty and Khepri; those of the midday sun, Ra or Re, were represented by a sun disc. The evening sun was either seen as Atum or as one of the ram-headed gods, such as Khnum. At a later time other symbols were used, the first two hours of the morning sun being pictured as a child rising from a lotus blossom and the last two hours of the evening sun as a ram-headed old man with a cane.[10] The sun in the form of a beetle is seen in chapter 42 of the Book of the Dead, a funerary tract of the New Kingdom: "I am he who is constantly appearing, whose real nature is unknown; I am yesterday; 'He who has seen a million years' is one name of mine; I pass along the ways of those sky-beings who determine destinies; I am the master of eternity, ordering how I am fated, like the Great Beetle."[11]

The means by which the sun was propelled through the sky puzzled the Egyptians, engendering several schools of thought. One belief held that the sun traveled the sky in a boat, either moved by magic or rowed by the god Re. A different manifestation shows the sunrise propelled by the wings of a falcon. Yet a third was the link made between the morning sun, Khepri, and a giant scarab beetle pushing a ball of dung; the Egyptians seem to have equated the dung ball with the daily rebirth of the sun, and indeed the beetles lay eggs within the dung such that their larvae feed on the dung ball.[12]

Discounting the use of other heavenly bodies for the orientation process leaves the sun as the one remaining candidate, but what an ideal choice it turns out to be! Gone are the problems of a nighttime sky and the need for false horizons or moving contrivances. By use of a simple stick, every movement of the sun—from summer to winter solstice and from sunrise to sunset—is registered directly on the ground, without the need of plumb lines. This advantage is claimed by no other heavenly body. Considering this, the pyramids could have been oriented by one of two possible methods: bisecting the shadows of the rising and setting sun, or finding the shortest shadow of the day. Both methods have the same theoretical basis. The sun rises and sets in almost equal but opposite angles to the meridian—the time it reaches its highest point in the sky and therefore casts its shortest shadow of the day.

Bisecting Equal Angles of the Rising and Setting Sun

Using the sun with the first of the two methods mentioned, the Italian scholars V. Maragioglio and C. Rinaldi suggest a gnomonic procedure that bisects the equal angles of the rising and setting sun:

A pole was fixed vertically in the leveled rock, for example in the point chosen as the south-east corner of the pyramid. When the sun rose and set in the same day the shadows made on the ground by the pole were traced and continued on the other side of the pole itself. It is evident how the shadows would have indicated the exact east-west direction only in the equinoctial days, when the evening shadow would have been in line with the morning one. It seems, however, the ancient Egyptians' astronomical knowledge was not advanced enough to enable them to fix the exact date of the equinoxes and the solstices. In any case, the method could have been used in whatever day of the year: in fact, the lines of the shadows and their extensions would have formed angles with the pole as the vertex, the bisection of which would have given a quite precise east-west direction and therefore, in this case, the orientation of the pyramid south side. Lines drawn at right angles would have then easily determined the direction of the other sides.[13]

Although it is theoretically possible to find true north by tracing shadows from the rising and setting sun on the ground, as described, the procedure has practical difficulties. In addition to the problem of refraction, which gives a mistaken position for the sun as it breaks the horizon, differences in the height of the terrain cause the shadow angles to register false readings (**7.3a, b**).

The American Egyptologist O. Neugebauer, who supports use of the sun for the orientation process and who obviously recognizes the shortcomings of Maragioglio and Rinaldi's method, suggests a change in the procedure:

It is therefore perhaps permissible to suggest as a possible method a procedure which combines greatest simplicity with high accuracy, without astronomical theory whatsoever beyond the primitive experience of symmetry of shadows in the course

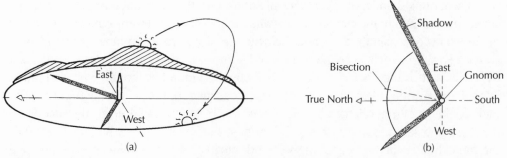

Figure 7.3. (a) To find true north, Maragioglio and Rinaldi suggest bisecting the equal and opposite shadows cast by the sun as it rises and sets on the horizon. (b) Unequal horizons produce a false reading.

of one day. In short, one can use the shadow of a pyramid as an excellent instrument for orientation. All one has to do is to place an accurately shaped pyramidal block (e.g. the capstone of the pyramid under construction) on the accurately leveled ground which will eventually carry the monument. Let its square base be oriented according to a reasonably accurate estimate of the SN/EW directions. Then one observes the path of the shadow cast by the apex of the pyramid from some time before noon to some time after noon. This path describes a curve which will intersect first the western, then the eastern base of the pyramid or a straight continuation in a northerly direction. If these points of intersection are at different distances from, e.g., the south corners (AC and BD respectively), then the orientation is not yet correct. A slight turn of the base and repeated observations on the next day will improve the situation. Not only can this process be repeated many times until high stability is reached but by waiting some weeks one utilizes different tracks and thus in effect averages small errors of individual observations. For example, observations scattered over half a year would lead to a neat set of mid-points between the two parallel base sides providing the desired SN direction.[14]

Although Neugebauer's system of measuring the sun when it is high in the sky would produce more accurate results than the method described by Maragioglio and Rinaldi, it has practical problems that make its use questionable. He proposes measuring the corners of the capstone from a sun path that has yet to be found. The method also requires readings to be made by the axial rotation of a heavy pyramidion with an apex that is equiangled and equidistant from the corners of its base (**7.4**). The necessity of shaping a stone of this size within a millimeter of perfection makes the Neugebauer suggestion impractical—especially since the pyramidion found by Stadelmann at the Red Pyramid seems to be anything but symmetrical in shape.

Indian Circle Orientation Method

An easier and proven method to find direction with shadows that fall shortly before and after the midday sun has been long known in India and elsewhere. The Indian circle procedure

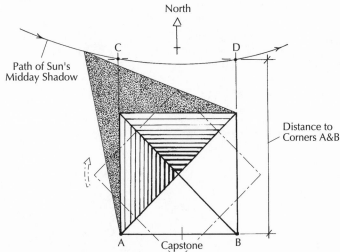

Figure 7.4. The Neugebauer system of finding true north: before and after midday, the shadows of a pyramidion are measured against a path previously generated by shadows of the sun. To find true north, the pryamidion is turned each day until the distance from A to C matches the distance from B to D.

avoids the need to contend with heavy objects, uneven horizons, or refraction of the rising or setting sun. It also affords the advantage of providing shadows that are more clearly delineated by the intense midday sun.

In use, the method requires a circle or arc, acting as substitute horizon, to be drawn around the base of a gnomon. Accordingly, when the sun rises in the sky, and the long shadow of the gnomon shortens, its tip is marked as it intersects the circle. It is again marked in the afternoon, when the gnomon's shadow lengthens and leaves the circle.[15] The two marks on the circle represent the equal and opposite altitudes of the sun as it passes the meridian. When both marks are connected with a straightedge, or cord (derivation of the chord of a circle), they lie in an east-west direction. As the midpoints of the sun's yearly travels along the horizon, they represent the directions sought by Egyptians in the Pyramid Age (**7.5**). If a direction to the north is required, it may be found with a set square or by joining a line from the middle of the two points on the circle to the base of the gnomon.

Due to the apparent movements of the sun, and regardless of the care taken, directional lines produced by this method will seldom lie exactly due east and west. Although the differences are small, they are a result of the slight changes in the sun's declination between its rising and setting positions. This is best understood by imagining the sun rising in one latitude and setting with a fractional difference in another latitude—a result of the time of year the procedure is made and its period of time between sunrise and sunset. These differences cause the high point of the midday sun to deviate slightly from the north-south axis of the earth.[16] True direction occurs only when the high point of the sun is directly on the axis of the earth—most of the year it is on one side or another (**7.6**).

The sun appears to change declination rapidly at the equinoxes, about one degree per day. If the interval between equinoctial sunrise and sunset is about 12 hours, there will be a difference between the sunrise and sunset declinations of about half a degree, or 30 arcminutes. The solstices produce different results; the sun seems to dwell on the horizon before reversing its course. Indeed, the word solstice comes from the Latin for "sun stand still." At this time the declination is significantly reduced, the sun changing in declination

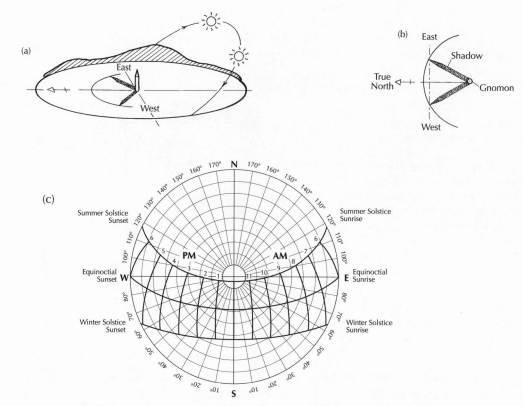

Figure 7.5. (a) The Indian circle method of orientation: when the sun is high in the sky, the entry and exit points of a shadow are marked on an arc drawn around a gnomon. (b) The directions east and west are found by joining the points with a straight line. (c) Movement of the sun, as plotted at 28° north latitude, approximately central Egypt.

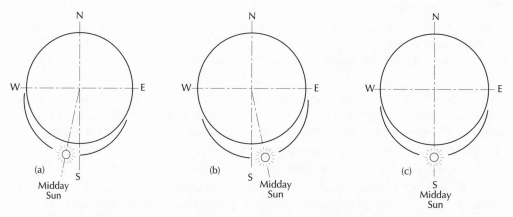

Figure 7.6. Relationship of the sun's apparent motion as it relates to the meridian. (a) Sun reaches high point of arc after it passes the meridian. (b) Sun reaches high point of arc before it reaches meridian. (c) The high point of the sun's arc as it coincides with the meridian.

about 12 arc*seconds* a day before and after the solstice. By four days before and after the solstice, the difference approaches 3 arcminutes. On the winter solstice, when the daylight hours are much fewer than in summer, the declination may be as little as 4 arcseconds. In summer, with more daylight, it is closer to 8 arcseconds. However, for this kind of precision one would need to know the solstice to the day.[17]

Less precision is required to achieve the accuracy shown in Egyptian pyramids. Indeed, if the orientation procedure took place within a week of the winter solstice, it could duplicate the results shown at Cheops Pyramid. Taken at other times of the year, the procedure would supply varying results up to the 30-arcminute error at the equinoxes—the very range of error shown by the average orientation of a number of pyramids (**table 7.1**).[18] Accordingly, the results produced by apparent movements of the sun suggest that shadows and the gnomonic arts were used to orient the pyramids.

Of course, other factors enter into the orientation procedure. At times, diffraction caused by haze or wind-blown dust may result in false readings. It should be remembered, however, that all errors can move as much toward an exact bearing as away from one. Although most accuracy could be achieved if the orientation procedure took place at the winter solstice, the summer solstice has a different advantage—the rays of the sun would be high above the gnomon and more intense. Indeed, coming near the start of the inundation and the New Year, it would be a propitious time for a building project of such great importance to the king.

There are strong indications the so-called Indian circle method was used in the royal city of Meroë, about 120 miles (192 km) northeast of Khartoum in Sudan, at a latitude of 17 degrees north. Due to its location in the tropical zone, the shadows of the sun would fall in a southward direction for a number of days during the year. Exploring the site in 1914, a mathematician and scientist named Garstang found graffiti of crude drawings purported to contain astronomical observations. Among the drawings is one that seems to show the sun shining upon an upright gnomon located in the center of a circle. Graffiti on a wall also include a record of a series of observations that seem to have been taken about the time of the summer solstice—the very time the Nile began to swell at the start of its annual inundation. Dated to about second century BCE, the graffito appears at the southern-most location with which Egypt and the more technically advanced nations had some form of regular communication.[19]

Orientation by Use of the Meridian Shadow

Another method of orientation is based on finding the shortest shadow of the day. Although it is akin to the procedure at the festival of Min, which signaled the approximate time for the rising Nile, its demands are more exacting. The intention of the Min festival was to search for symmetrical shadows cast by a bifurcated gnomon and then compare their length, as measured from the base of the gnomon, to those of previous years. The proposed procedure differs from that of orienting the pyramids to the directions east-west in that it endeavors to find those shadows which fall on or close to the meridian, an imaginary line that circles the poles in the position of the gnomon or observer.

At noon when the sun is high in the sky and casts the shortest shadow of the day, this shadow is governed by the declination of the sun and generally falls on one side of the

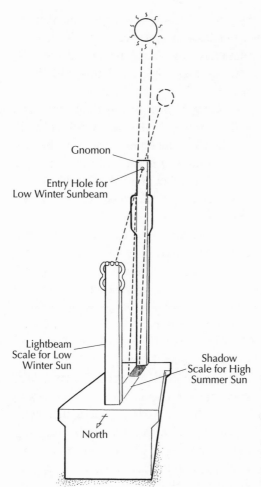

Gnomon

Entry Hole for
Low Winter Sunbeam

Lightbeam
Scale for Low
Winter Sun

Shadow
Scale for High
Summer Sun

North

Figure 7.7. A Chinese gnomon from the Ming Dynasty. The high summer sun is registered as a shadow on a horizontal scale. The low winter sun is registered as a beam of light, thus shortening the distance and accentuating an otherwise weak beam by bringing it perpendicular to the surface.

meridian or the other. Although these shadows can be recorded on a daily basis, tracking them over a period of time and averaging the results will more likely provide a true direction for the meridian. Yet, even assuming perfect conditions—a clear day and a smooth, level surface—it is difficult to register shadows with precision due to their poorly defined edges and the speed at which they move (factors that are inversely proportional). Long shadows are easy to track, but they move fast and have fuzzy outlines; short shadows are sharp and move more slowly, but the small changes are hard to follow. These difficulties were recognized by other ancient cultures.

The Chinese followed the movements of heavenly bodies with great care, believing a close association existed between these bodies and the emperor. Penalties encouraged their attentiveness; the court astronomer who failed to predict an unusual event, such as a solar eclipse, would pay with his life. Having learned, perhaps from the Jesuits, that a sunbeam could be read more accurately than a shadow, the Chinese devised ingenious means to track the path of the sun. One such device, a circular disc with a small central hole, made the beam of light easier to see when surrounded with the circular shadow of the disc.[20] Using the light beam principle during the Ming Dynasty, they produced a broad flat gnomon having a small hole just below its top. This clever device would serve a double purpose; in addition to registering the shadow of the high summer sun on the usual horizontal scale, it would direct the low winter sun to fall as a beam of light on a vertical scale opposite the hole. The upstanding scale not only shortened the distance of what would ordinarily be a very long light beam but also made it possible to read the beam with accuracy by forming it into a small circle.[21] Indeed, the more perpendicular incident light (or shadow) is to its source, the more defined it becomes (**7.7**).

Faced with the need for increased accuracy, the Chinese built Chou Kung's Tower, a tall structure designed solely to support a gnomon. The carefully leveled gnomon, round in section, was placed horizontally across a narrow vertical opening in the structure about 40 feet (12 m) above the ground (**7.8**). The *Yuan Shih*, a history of the period (1260–1368 CE), gives the reason for this unusual construction and a general analysis of the gnomonic problems:

> When a gnomon is short, the divisions on the scale have to be close together and minute, and most of the smaller divisions below feet and inches are difficult to determine. When a gnomon is long, the graduations are easier to read, but the inconvenience then is that the shadow is light and ill-defined, making it difficult to get an exact result. In former times, observers sought to ascertain the real point by using sighting tubes, or a pin point gnomon and a wooden ring, all devices for easier reading of the shadow mark on the scale. But now with a 40 foot gnomon, 5 inches (12.7 cm) of the graduation scale corresponds to what was only 1 inch (2.54 cm) previously and the smaller subdivisions are easier to distinguish.[22]

The *Yuan Shih* also describes a shadow definer—a small rectangular leaf of copper having a pinhole in its center. Used in conjunction with the horizontal gnomon, it is mounted on a frame that permits it to be moved along a carefully leveled 128-foot-long (39 m) scale located on the ground. The description continues: "The instrument is moved back and forth until it reaches the middle of the (shadow of the) crossbar, which is not too well defined, and when the pin-hole is first seen to meet the light, one receives an image no bigger than a grain of rice in which the cross-beam can be noted indistinctly in the middle. On the old methods, using the simple summit of the gnomon, what was projected was the upper edge of the solar disc. But with this method one can obtain, by means of the cross-bar, the rays of the sun without any error."[23]

Although a great distance from the gnomon, the ingenious device overcomes what would ordinarily be a fuzzy shadow. Utilizing the principle of the pinhole camera, a device familiar to Chinese scientists for the prior three centuries, a copper leaf projects a tiny but precise image of the gnomon onto the scale. The shadow definer enabled the Chinese to find the exact position of the sun in the sky and helped them to find the summer and winter solstice shadow with an accuracy of four decimal places—the greatest accuracy ever found with solstice shadows.[24]

Others supplied their own solutions to the poorly defined shadow of the gnomon. In an effort to solve the problem by use of large instrumentation, Jai Singh II, 18th-century Maharaja of Jaipur in India, built stone sundials up to 90 feet (27 m) high. He angled the

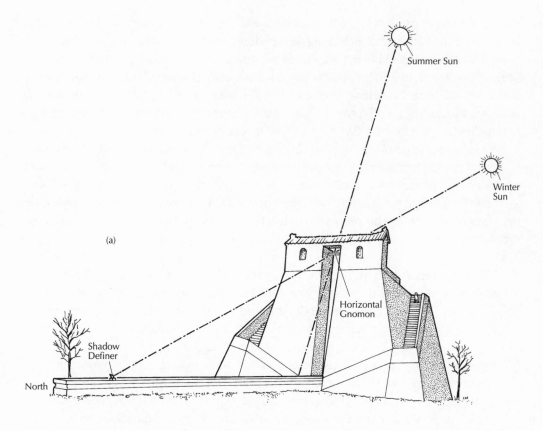

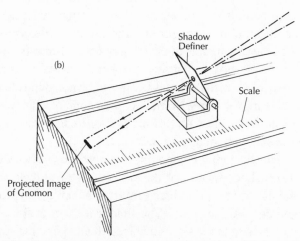

Figure 7.8. (a) Chou Kung's Tower, which shows the summer and winter sun in relation to a horizontal gnomon high in the tower's vertical opening. (b) Acting as a pinhole lens, the shadow definer casts a small image of the gnomon on the ground scale.

style (gnomon) toward the pole star in the latitude of the instrument, making it perpendicular to the ecliptic. To sharpen the incident shadow, he raised the scale to the plane of the ecliptic and curved its face, thus making it parallel to the top surface of the style (**7.9**). The enormous size of the scale, and the sharpness of the shadow, enabled Jai Singh to read the changing shadows to 2-second increments.[25]

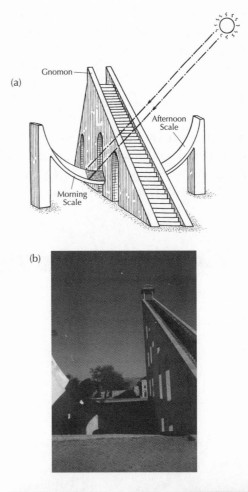

(a)

Gnomon

Afternoon Scale

Morning Scale

(b)

Figure 7.9. (a) The 90-foot-high gnomon of Maharaja Jai Singh II. (b) Angled to the pole star, the shadow of the style (angled gnomon) always falls perpendicular to the curved scale. (c) It forms a sharp and easily read image in two-arcsecond increments.

The ancient Egyptians dealt with fuzzy shadows in several ways; they raised the scale of the shadow clock (**6.11**), bent the top of the gnomon (**6.4**), or, as in the case of the Min festival, they tilted the gnomon (**6.20**). Not only were these measures taken to sharpen the shadow by facing it directly to the sun, but they helped to increase the length of shadows cast by a high sun. The Egyptians also used an instrument called a *bay*, a device made of the middle rib of a palm leaf cut to a roughly shaped V at its broad end (**7.10**). Inscribed as an "indicator for determining the commencement of a festival and placing all men in their hours," this device was previously thought to be a means for sighting stars. Although it may also have been used for that purpose, when placed notch down and used as a frame to block the surface reflections, it helps to clarify the shadow.[26]

Stretching of the Cord Ceremony

In an experiment somewhat akin to that of Žába, Austrian Egyptologist Josef Dorner suggests that the device shown in the "stretching of the cord" ceremony was used by the Egyptians for orienting the pyramids (**7.11**). He claims that if used as an elongated compass—one pole fixed and the other movable—the device could be used to find the culminating

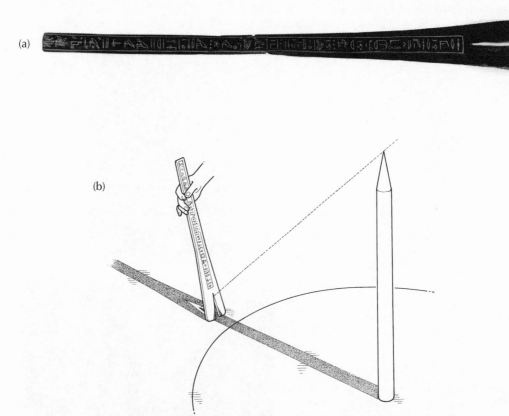

Figure 7.10. (a) An Egyptian instrument called a bay, made of the middle rib of a palm frond. Photo courtesy Ägyptisches Musem, Berlin. (b) The bay is used to define the shadow of a gnomon by framing its tip and blocking the surface reflection.

Loop of Cord

Poles

Figure 7.11. The god Thoth and goddess Seshat face to face, holding poles by which they stretch apart a loop of cord. They also hold clubs to hammer the poles into the ground.

east-west points of a circumpolar star. Dorner suggests that the positions can be found by sighting over a plumb line until both poles are aligned with the star—the movable pole being placed by an assistant under the direction of the observer. Accordingly, when both extreme positions of the star are located, their bisection will be true north.[27]

As with other apparatus for observation of stars, Dorner's suggestion must contend with several difficulties; the poles must be kept perpendicular and on the same level as they move to each position, the slightest misalignment being greatly multiplied. Seen at a great distance, the star is smaller than the thickness of a pole, making its alignment uncertain even with additional plumb lines. Dorner's suggestion requires a lengthy period of darkness and the ability to see well enough in the dark to direct a distant pole into position. In sum, all nighttime orientation procedures are more complicated than using the sun's shadow in the daytime, and their results do not account for the roughly 30 arcminutes of error shown in the pyramids.

There may be a different meaning in the cord-stretching scene than the one Dorner suggests. However, some theoretical aspects of the rite should be considered before explaining its practical application, which is shown later in discussion of preparing of the pyramid site.

I believe it unlikely that stars were used for measurements in the orientation procedure, but this assumption seems to be contradicted by descriptive texts and scenes at the temples of Edfu and Dendera. In particular, the texts found at these locations indicate that some monumental Egyptian structures were sited by means of both stars and shadows.[28] Although the scenes having these descriptions come from long after the Pyramid Age, the procedure described as the stretching of the cord can be traced back to the 2nd Dynasty.[29] Scenes show the king and queen, representing the god Thoth and the goddess Seshat, standing face to face and holding poles by which they stretch apart a loop of cord.[30] They also hold clubs, which they seem to use for pounding the poles into the ground. In Edfu the scene is accompanied by an epigraph:

> I hold the peg. I grasp the handle of the club and grip the measuring-cord with Seshat. I turn my eyes to the movements of the stars. I send forth my glance to Ursa Major. . . . [Thoth?] stands beside his merkhet. I make firm the corners of thy temple.[31]

Another scene says:

> He (the king) has built the Great Place of Re-Herakhty in conformity with the horizon bearing his disk; there the cord was stretched by His Majesty himself, having the stake in his hand with Seshat; he untied his cord with He-who-is-south-of-his-wall, in perfect work for eternity, being established on its angle by the majesty of Khnoum. He-who-makes-existence-run-its-course stood up to see its shadow, it being long in perfect fashion, wide in perfect fashion, high and low in accurate fashion, finished with work of excellent craftsmanship furnished with everything required, sprinkled with gold, decorated with colors; in appearance resembling the horizon of Re.[32]

The first epigraph speaks of glancing at a constellation while standing beside a device called a *merkhet*. The word *merkhet* is elsewhere said to be an instrument that either means "indicator" or "object used to recognize"; operating it is said to require knowledge and skill.[33] Since the word *merkhet* is also used when referring to the short vertical bar of the shadow clock, an object already shown to be a gnomon, it would seem to be a gnomon in the context of the epigraph.[34] The presence of a gnomon also seems to be implied in the second epigraph by the phrase "He-who-makes-existence-run-its-course stood up to see its shadow."

Yet the gnomon is a daytime device and does not seem to have a connection to Ursa Major, the nighttime constellation of the epigraph. However, this seeming contradiction may have a different intent. The positions of constellations in the sky were often used to alert ancient observers to anticipated solar events, such as the solstices or the equinoxes. Ancient builders could use such prior knowledge to level the ground for the gnomon and the orientation ritual, and by referring to both the sun and the stars, they could pay homage to the heavenly bodies that played such important roles in their theology.

Although shadows were used by many ancient cultures, seldom were they employed to greater advantage than when meeting the theological and practical needs of the 4th Dynasty. Only by understanding shadows were the builders accurately able to site a pyramidal structure linking the tomb of the king to the life and death of the sun. Moreover, as one explores the difficulties facing early builders, the orientation procedure turns out to have been among the least of their many problems.

CHAPTER 8

PREPARING THE SITE

The difficulties facing the pyramid builders reached far beyond questions of orientation and leveling: it is one thing to survey an open area but quite another to form an accurate survey around an outcropping of rock. Yet, with varying degrees of success, this is exactly what was accomplished at the pyramids of Cheops, Chephren, Djedefre (Abu Roash), and Senwosret II (Illahun). The exactness achieved was not accidental. Indeed, the method used by the Egyptians for leveling the site was such that the inclusion or absence of a central rocky core was irrelevant. Their leveling improved with experience, as is shown by the deviations of less than 5 inches (12 cm) from a level plane at Meidum pyramid, less than 2 inches (4.6 cm) at the Bent Pyramid, and within 0.75 of an inch (2 cm) at the pyramid of Cheops.[1]

The advantage of building a pyramidal structure around a rocky mound is obvious. With over 50 percent of the total volume of a pyramid in its lower quarter, the rock mass provides stone that need not be quarried, transported, raised, or set into place. Further, the natural formation is a stable mass unaffected by the exigencies of poor engineering. However, these benefits are somewhat offset by the problem of leveling and orienting to the cardinal points a square built around an object that does not allow the diagonals to be measured (matching diagonal dimensions indicate a geometric square). According to Mark Lehner, making an accurate layout of the pyramid is akin to the classic chicken-and-egg problem: "The survey of a true square oriented to the meridian is most accurately done on a leveled surface, but where the surface is to be so finely leveled depends on the exact position of the true square."[2]

Despite the suggested paradox, Egyptian builders did a commendable job, particularly at the Great Pyramid of Cheops, where a narrow square of paving was formed around a rocky core that is seen at one place to rise about 23 feet (7 m) above the ground. Made of almost regularly shaped and fitted white limestone paving blocks almost 2 feet (55 cm)

Casing Blocks   Fine Paving   Surrounding Court

Figure 8.1. The north side of Cheops Pyramid shows the bottom edge of the casing blocks near a line of fine paving. As shown in the foreground, the fine paving meets the surrounding court in a straight line. The level bedrock under the missing paving stone is shown in the background.

thick, this square, the most accurately leveled area of the entire pyramid, was made to support all the casing of the first course except the corner blocks, which were placed directly on the bedrock. While most casing blocks have long since disappeared, the pyramidal mass of stepped courses remains in place. The pavement consists of lesser and finer grades of limestone, the poorer grade being hidden under the pyramid. At some locations, such as at the northeast corner, the poor grade of paving meets the rocky core. Laid at the same level but outside the poor grade, the square of fine paving ends an average of 1.33 feet (40 cm) beyond the foot of the casing blocks, where it meets the surrounding court (**8.1**). The idea, once held, that the sockets cut into the bedrock for the corner stones were meant to counteract the downward thrust generated by the corner of the pyramid has been abandoned. This is due to their varying depths and the absence of a socket on the southwest corner.[3]

While Egyptians may have been inspired to orient the pyramids by religious beliefs, the smooth and level pavement found under the structure was made for a more practical purpose, as I presently show—it helped when maneuvering the heavy casing blocks into position as they floated on a bed of mortar. The pavement of the Great Pyramid is so accurately leveled that it departs from perfection by only 0.75 of an inch (2 cm) as it slopes down from the northwest to the southeast corner. No other levels on the Great Pyramid reached this almost flawless horizontal plane. The top of the first course of casing stones, for example, deviates by 1.25 inches (3 cm) from a level plane. Although such leveling may be readily accomplished on a floodplain or river bank by channeling water to the building site and using its surface level as a gauge, it is a remarkable achievement for a desert site. Various theories explain the results.

Figure 8.2. Englebach's suggested method of achieving a level is by flooding an area surrounded by an embankment and cutting the bedrock a given distance below the water surface.

R. Engelbach suggests as a method flooding an area surrounded by a mud embankment and cutting the bedrock to a given distance below its surface.[4] This procedure does not consider the enormous quantity of water required and the near impossibility of measuring and cutting stone without disturbing the very surface upon which the level depends **(8.2)**. Recognizing this, and noting the troughs and postholes that surround the pyramids of Cheops and Chephren, Lehner suggests a different approach. He proposes that the builders set about filling the trough with water and placing a line of wooden pole markers on a level with its surface to serve as datum points **(8.3)**. In this way, the water would remain isolated and undisturbed while providing a level by which the surrounding bedrock could be reduced—a great advantage over flooding the whole area, especially on a site high above the Nile.[5]

Yet, even assuming the Lehner method as a workable system, it does not address, for example, the small Queens Pyramids of Cheops, erected on slanting ground. Queens Pyramids is a term used for the satellite pyramids at Giza. These structures are not built on top of a level terrace, like the pyramids of Chephren and Sekhemkhet; instead, their level was achieved by adding more courses downgrade and blending courses into the terrain upgrade **(8.4)**. If used at this location, Lehner's leveling system would require an unusually deep trough (which does not exist) carrying a large amount of water with attendant problems of evaporation and loss to the many crevices in the bedrock. The system is cast further into question by the more probable use of the postholes for scaffolding and the discovery of similar troughs that are certainly drainage ditches around the pyramid of Illahun.[6]

If Egyptian surveyors used water for leveling a desert site, surely it would have been employed differently. Water seeks its own level and is not affected by the width of the troughs in which it is carried. Instead of the vast flooded area Engelbach suggests or Lehner's wide shallow ditch, the narrowest of trenches would be adequate to provide a level. Not only would the narrow trough require less water—it would expose a smaller surface to the evaporating rays of the sun. With a little imagination, a commodity with which

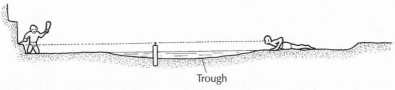

Trough

Figure 8.3. Lehner suggests that the water could have been confined to troughs surrounding the pyramids of Cheops and Chephren. Posts placed in the water could use its level to establish a sighting line.

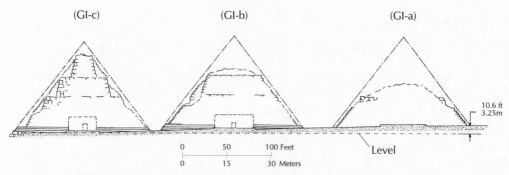

Figure 8.4. The three Queens Pyramids of Cheops are built on slanting ground made level by adding more courses downgrade and blending them into the terrain upgrade.

the ancient builders were well endowed, they may also have employed a tubing device still used on occasion by builders when lacking a transit: a rubber or plastic tube having open ends can transfer a level over a considerable distance when filled with water. Absent flexible tubing, Egyptians could use the long hollow stalk of *Silphium*, a North African species of *Ferila*.[7] With water containers at each end, the tapered stalks of this umbelliferous plant could easily have been interlocked, sealed, and made to extend for long distances (**8.5a-c**).

Fancy aside, other ancient cultures developed portable leveling instruments with little water: the Roman *chorobates*, the Babylonian *dioptra*, and the *shui phing* from China were devices on which spaced sights were leveled by being floated on a tube or a water channel of wood (**8.6**).[8] A level was achieved when the tops of the floating members were

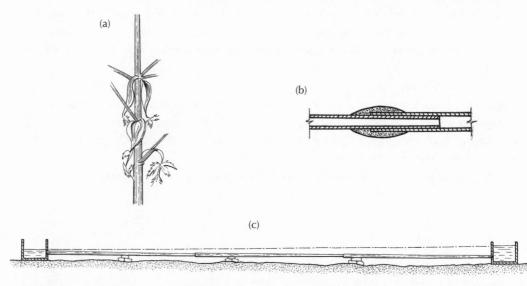

Figure 8.5. A tube with open ends can transfer a level of water over a considerable distance. (a) In the absence of flexible tubing, Egyptians may have used the long hollow stalks of a marsh plant. (b) Its long tapered stalks have ends that can be interlocked and sealed. (c) With a container of water at each end, a level can be made to extend for long distances.

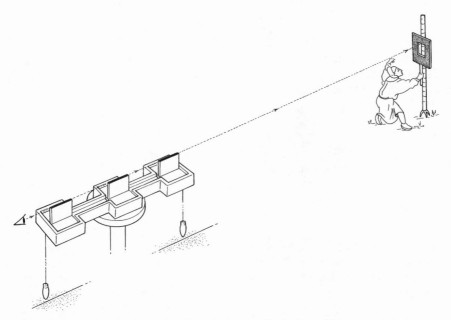

Figure 8.6. A Chinese water leveling device in which three floating members were brought into horizontal alignment when sighted to a distant target. Opposing plumb lines hanging from the device permit the instrument to be aligned with an existing ground line.

in alignment. Sighted over the tops, a baseline was established with plumb lines hanging from the apparatus. Simplest of all, and until recently employed by Chinese agricultural cooperatives for irrigation works, is a device thought to have ancient roots. It consisted of a short length of split bamboo, made level by floating it in a rice bowl on a meniscus of water. A sighting level was achieved by peering over its septa sights to a distant measuring rod (**8.7**).[9] Water was also used sparingly in India. Dripped from a pinhole in the bottom of a container over the area being worked, it enabled stonecutters to reduce the high points until the surface was evenly wetted (**8.8**).[10]

Due to arid conditions at the construction sites, and despite an almost universal appeal of water as a leveling means, the ancient Egyptians made use of an instrument based on the principle of gravity. This square-level, in the form of a wooden capital A with a plumb line hanging from the apex, is the equal of any modern bubble level (**8.9**).

Figure 8.7. A leveling device used until recently by Chinese cooperatives. A short length of a split bamboo is made level being floated on a meniscus of water in a rice bowl.

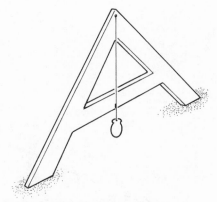

Figure 8.9. Instead of using water for leveling, the ancient Egyptians used a square-level operating on the principle of gravity. When the plumb line of the device is made to overlie a mark on the crossbar, the seats of the legs are at the same level.

Figure 8.8. In India, small areas were leveled by allowing water to drip from a container. This enabled stonecutters to reduce the high points until the surface was evenly wetted.

Interestingly, the square-level works even with legs of slightly different lengths—a deficiency of manufacture addressed when the device is calibrated: while standing on a surface, the square-level is marked at the exact point where the plumb line crosses the horizontal bar. The device is then reversed in place, and the position of the plumb line is recorded once again. If the legs are of equal or unequal lengths, and the surface on which the device stands is level, the plumb line will fall in exactly the same place on the crossbar. If the surface on which the device stands is not level, the plumb line's positions will fall slightly apart when the level reversed in place, whether or not the legs have equal lengths. Having marked both positions of the plumb line, the difference in their spacing is divided by an estimated center point **(8.10)**. The location of the point is tested once again by reversing the square-level. If the plumb line does not fall on the same point when reversed, the differences are repeatedly divided and tested until a common center point is reached. Despite any unevenness in the legs, once the square-level has been so calibrated, it will indicate a level surface whenever the plumb line falls on the center point. As described later,

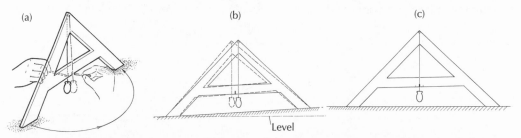

Figure 8.10. The square-level may be correctly calibrated even if it has legs of unequal length and is standing on a surface that is not level. (a, b) Marking the plumb line where it falls, and again when reversed in position, a center is found by dividing the distance between the marks. (c) Thereafter, the square-level will indicate a level surface whenever the plumb line falls on the centerpoint.

the Egyptians used the method of reversing the level and halving the difference to an exact center to achieve the great accuracy shown in several of their building practices.

Establishing an Orientation Station

Before making use of the square-level to establish an orientation station, the area surrounding the site would probably be roughly evened by clearing it of sand and gravel and by cutting the most obvious high spots in the bedrock. This can be accomplished by leapfrogging three stakes of equal length, cutting drafts in the bedrock, and sighting over their tops until they are all on the same sight line. When rough measurements show an area large enough to encompass the rocky mass, which will be left in the core of the pyramid, an orientation station can be prepared (8.11). According to the projected size of the pyramid, the location of the station becomes a factor to be considered. For example, a station in the corner of a small pyramid has the advantage of addressing two adjacent sides from the same place. In a large pyramid, such as at Cheops, a greater advantage would be to locate the orientation station in the approximate center of the north or south sides.

Dieter Arnold discovered a probable orientation site at the complex of Senwosret I. Located at the southeast corner of a small subsidiary pyramid, the gnomon probably used in the orientation process was held erect by a circular hole cut into a small limestone block. The block was embedded under the surface of the cornerstone.[11] The station was probably placed on the corner of the pyramid to help orient a line that extends to the west and north sides of the structure. Although the southwest corner may once have held a similar block, it has not been found.

To level the small area selected for the orientation station, drafts are cut in the bedrock to accommodate the legs of the square-level (8.12). Made deep enough to anticipate a final level for the site, the two drafts leveled by the gravity device are used as a basis for cutting additional drafts—a minimum of three being required to establish a plane. The area between the drafts is flattened and brought to their level by reducing the intervening stone. This may be accomplished with the help of a wooden straightedge or a string

Figure 8.11. Used for an orientation station, a small area located near the perimeter of the pyramid is made level by cutting level drafts in the bedrock. Three drafts are required to establish a plane.

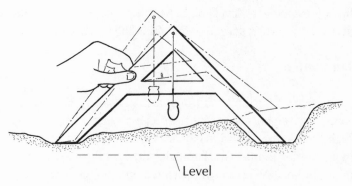

Level

Figure 8.12. The square-level, as it is used to test drafts cut in the stone.

stretched between the drafts until enough stone is removed to allow a straight line (**8.13**). At times, Egyptian masons also made use of a "boning rod," two pegs of equal length attached at the top by a string. When pulled apart and stood upright on a surface, as with the drafts, the taut string on top of the pegs establishes a datum line above the rough surface. A third peg of equal height placed at different points under the string allows additional drafts to be cut to the same level. To avoid formation of a catenary curve, the string of the boning rod is limited to short horizontal spans as shown in figure 8.13(**c**).

With the small orientation area leveled by use of the means described, a gnomon is made vertical by use of another ancient device (**8.14**). Operating on the same gravity principle as the square-level, the plumb device consists of two blocks of equal dimensions fixed to a flat vertical slat. A weighted line hanging from the top block tangentially touches the lower block, a short distance below, when the device is held against an object that is truly vertical (**8.15**). Although it is possible to plumb a vertical object such as a gnomon with only one device, the task is facilitated if two such devices are held against the gnomon at right angles to each other. Once the gnomon is vertically positioned, an arc may

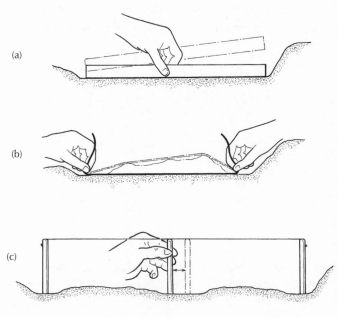

(a)

(b)

(c)

Figure 8.13. The drafts are joined by use of one of three devices: (a) a straightedge, (b) a string, or (c) boning rods.

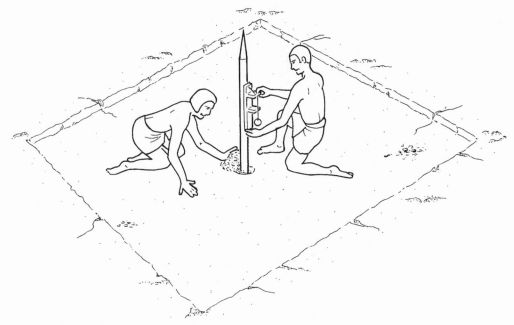

Figure 8.14. When the orientation station is made level, a gnomon is erected perpendicular to the surface with a plumb device.

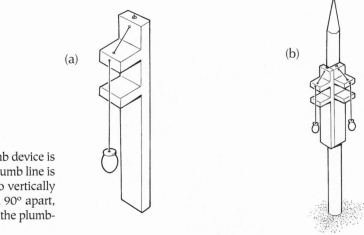

(a)

(b)

Figure 8.15. (a) The plumb device is perpendicular when the plumb line is tangent to the edge of two vertically spaced blocks. (b) Placed 90° apart, two such devices facilitate the plumbing procedure.

be struck around its base with the aid of a compass in the form of a cord or, for greater accuracy, with a rigid object such as a wooden slat. The slat may have a V notch that pivots against the round base of the gnomon, as the other end holds a marker to strike the arc **(8.16)**.

Having located an east-west direction by use of the equal angles of the sun's midday shadow, as described earlier **(8.17)**, the next step is to join the points on the arc by a line extending along the ground to the limits of the small orientation area **(8.18)**. This line serves to guide a template, the purpose of which is to help position posts at each end. The

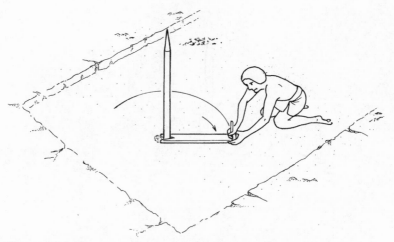

Figure 8.16. To prepare for the orientation procedure, an arc is made by rotating a compass slat around the gnomon.

Figure 8.17. Equal altitudes of the midday sun are made as the shadow of the gnomon intersects the arc.

Figure 8.18. The points of intersection are joined by a chalkline to establish an east-west direction.

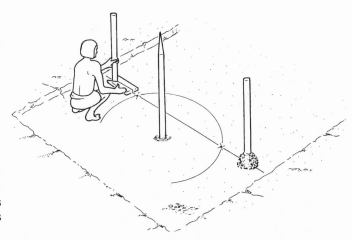

Figure 8.19. A template helps locate two opposing posts exactly on the chalkline.

template used for this may be a flat wooden rectangle having a triangular cutout at one end and a line centered down its length. When the centerline of the template is placed directly over the line on the ground, it forms an angled seat to receive and center a round post on each end of the east-west line (**8.19**).

The reason for raising the directional line is obvious. Not only is the surrounding terrain still rough and uneven at this stage of preparing the site, but to anticipate a final level around the rocky mass, the orientation station should be placed somewhat below ground level. When both posts are erected and plumbed, the east-west line, originally located on the ground, is accurately elevated. Although the directional line found by this method is much too short to represent the side of a pyramid, the positioning of the posts is the first step in the process.

Extending the Direction Found by the Orientation Station

As with other Egyptian rituals, the previously described stretching of the cord ceremony has a practical purpose—it helps to transfer the short direction found by the orientation process to a distant location with equal accuracy. This is cleverly and simply accomplished by stretching a loop of cord around two posts with the use of levers (**7.11**). Although the two figures in the cord ceremony scene are shown close together, in actual practice they would stand a great distance apart. If the levers they hold are aligned with and are of equal diameter to the two upstanding posts of the orientation procedure (**8.20**), the loop of cord extending from the levers will form two straight and parallel lines that are exactly tangent to the posts. They will remain parallel even if the posts are far apart, and even if a catenary curve is formed by the cord—provided, of course, that the dip in the cord does not touch the ground.

If the cords are not perfectly aligned with the posts, a space will appear between the cord and either side of one or both upstanding posts. The space indicates that the extended loop of cord does not follow the short but carefully found line of the orientation procedure, the slightest misalignment being easily seen. However, simply moving one or both lever poles laterally to the posts can close the space and correct the misalignment (**8.21**). The

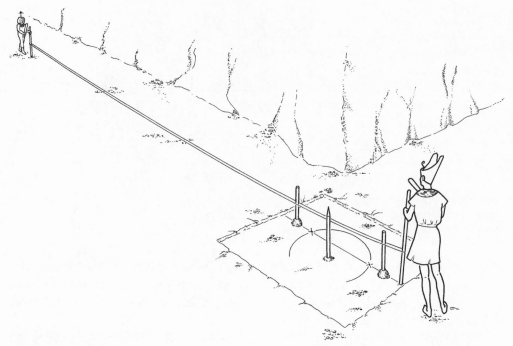

Figure 8.20. The king impersonating the god Thoth in the stretching of the cord ceremony. The queen, or a priestess, takes the role of the goddess Seshat. The goal of the rite is to raise the carefully found east-west line of the orientation station above the rough and uneven bedrock.

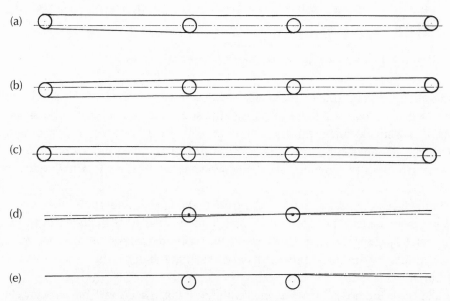

Figure 8.21. Schematic showings of the various relationships of cord to the posts: (a) both levers on one side of the posts; (b) levers on opposite sides of the posts; (c) levers aligned with the posts. Using a single cord, (d) it may deviate imperceptibly when stretched over center points or (e) it may deviate imperceptibly when made tangent to only one side of the posts.

remarkable accuracy achieved by this procedure cannot be duplicated by stretching a single cord over the center of the posts or by making it tangent to one side of both posts. A slight deviation or bend in the single cord would probably go unnoticed and become greatly amplified by the time it reached its terminus position, some distance away.[12]

If the distance between the levers is great enough to cause the catenary curve to touch the ground, causing a possible error, the procedure may be accomplished by a series of short steps using additional posts at each terminus position. In whatever way this is done, it results in having a line oriented and accurately lengthened. However, it would not yet be accurately dimensioned for the side of the pyramid. So as not to interfere with ongoing construction, the terminus points of the line may be marked on batter boards located well outside the possible work area. Such boards are even used today in the building trades. Once this directional line is established and safely fixed, another procedure makes it possible to bring the terrain along the entire directional line to the same level previously made on the surface of the orientation station. To accomplish this, however, requires that a different form of leveling device be installed in the orientation station.

The Leveling Station

A leveling procedure that I devised and that may have been used by the ancient surveyors was successfully employed in a field test with Dieter Arnold in Egypt. At Lisht, it was found possible to duplicate the accuracy displayed at the Cheops and Chephren pyramids with two stakes placed about 6.5 feet (2 m) apart. Held in a vertical position with rubble, they were brought to exactly the same height by placing a square-level on a board that bridged the tops of the stakes. A third stake, acting as a target, was placed 154 feet (47 m) away, a distance limited by obstructions at the test site. Using the top edge of the board as a straight rod, a sight line was established to a movable marker on the target stake. Tested with a theodolite, the sight line was found to be within 0.375 of an inch (1 cm) of the height of the board at the distant leveling station.[13]

Although the Lisht experiment tested the feasibility of extending a sight line accurately, the procedure described is different than that required by the ancient surveyors. Instead of moving a marker on the target stake to match the height of the sighting board, as at Lisht, marks on the stakes would be brought to a level with the sight line by cutting drafts in the rough and irregular terrain. To accomplish this, the target stake would initially be placed next to the top of the sighting board and marked (**8.22**). Brought to a distant location, drafts would be cut beneath the stake until the mark could be seen on a level with that of the sighting board. With the level at a remote location equal to that of the leveling station, the same procedure is used to backsight from the sighting station to a second target stake in the opposite direction, thus doubling the distance. In this way, a number of spaced drafts on the same horizontal plane may be cut along the entire length of the previously established directional line. The drafts may then be joined into a narrow corridor by reducing the intervening stone with any of the several means already described—straight edge, stretched cord, or boning rods.

A remarkable survey of the Great Pyramid by Petrie in 1883 showed that regardless of their length, all the dimensions in the monument are well within the range of the human

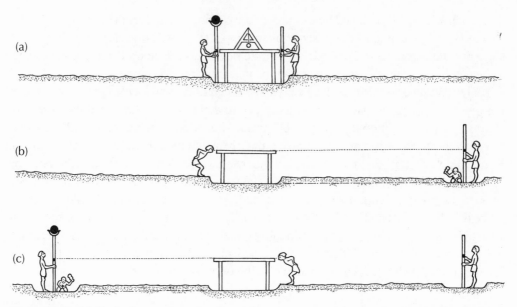

Figure 8.22. Method of extending a level to a distant position: (a) mark target stakes to each end of a level sighting board; (b) reduce the bedrock until the mark on stake coincides with the sight line; (c) backsight to second target and reduce bedrock to the same level.

eye. By using a straight rod as a guide to the eye—the same method as that described for leveling—Petrie was able to see variations in the optical plane of the pyramid across the middle of the face, up an edge, and along the base that were as small as 1 inch (2.54 cm).[14] The impressive accuracy he achieved in his survey left little room for improvement by later surveyors.

The human eye is so remarkable an organ that accurate sight lines at great distances are taken for granted in the military. An accomplished rifleman is able to hit repeatedly a target with a 10-inch (25.4 cm) bull's-eye at 900 feet (274 m)—a distance the army considers to be a short range. Some marksmen, familiar with the firing characteristics of their weapons, are able to group shots close enough to have them touch—this despite the fact that bullets do not travel in straight lines, their paths taking a greater or lesser trajectory according to the distance traveled. Indeed, a rifle is supplied with an adjustable rear sight to help compensate for changes in windage and distance. Given normal eyesight, the problem of the marksman is not in seeing the distant target but in correctly aligning the front and rear sights while holding one's breath, squeezing the trigger, and not anticipating the recoil. None of these factors affects an aim governed only by a sight line. Incidentally, for best visibility, the target should be black on a white background, and the target should be toward the north.[15]

Although we confirmed with a theodolite the results of our leveling test at Lisht, one may wonder how ancient builders were able to check the accuracy of the same leveling method without the use of such instrumentation. Here too, as when calibrating the square-level, a reversing procedure was probably employed. In this case it could be readily accomplished by switching positions of the marked target stakes and resighting them from the same central station—a procedure that would exaggerate the slightest of errors

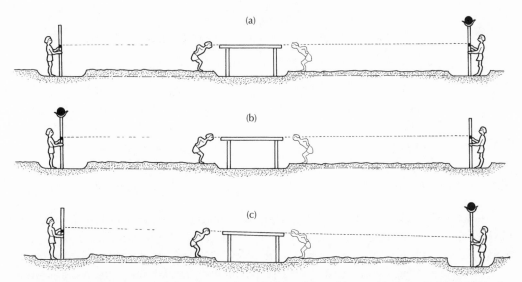

Figure 8.23. Method of checking the accuracy of a level found by a sight line. (a, b) If level, the marks are seen aligned with both sides of the sighting board even when the targets are switched. (c) If marks are not level, any error will be accenuated when the targets are switched.

(**8.23**). Repeated sightings and switchings could be undertaken until, regardless of which side the target stakes were located, their targets would be aligned with the sighting board. Limited only by the human eye, the procedure makes it possible to level the entire 755-foot (230 m) length of the Great Pyramid with perhaps two or three such stations on each side.

The same methods described for leveling the pyramid may have enabled ancient surveyors to establish nilometers in every important town from the delta to the First Cataract. Nilometers helped prepare the fields for a new crop by gauging the height and speed of the flooding river. The usefulness of the nilometer is seen by markings on a wall adjacent to steps leading down to the water's edge, markings that still retain indicia indicating the various heights of the rising river. These markings are inscribed with the numerals of ancient Egyptians as well as those of their Greek and Roman conquerors. The Irrigation Service of Egypt, later surveying the stations, discovered that the ancient planners had been sufficiently exact to establish a slope of 1 in 14,440, as compared to the actual 1 in 13,700 found by more modern methods—a commendable feat considering use of the rudimentary devices described.[16]

Establishing Lengths for the Pyramid Sides

Having established a narrow corridor in the bedrock, the entire length of a pyramid side may be dressed to a smooth level just wide enough to establish an accurately measured dimension on its surface. Although measurements of Cheops show the dimensions of the pyramid sides to be less exacting than those given by the leveling and orientation procedures, they are still fairly close, the greatest error being the 7.9-inch (20 cm) difference between the north and south sides.

Table 8.1
LENGTH OF THE GREAT PYRAMID SIDES

PYRAMID SIDE	LENGTH
North	9,065.1 inches
South	9,073.0 inches
East	9,070.5 inches
West	9,069.2 inches
Mean	9,069.45 inches

After J. H. Cole, *Determination of the Exact Size and Orientation of the Great Pyramid of Giza*, 7.

As with all ancient building techniques, the methods and devices used for accomplishing linear measurements must have been simple and straightforward. Although wooden cubit rods are preserved only from the New Kingdom (1540–1075 BCE), some evidence suggests their use before the 4th Dynasty. However, with its large divisions—the Royal Cubit of 20.62 inches (52.5 cm) is divided into seven palms, and these into four digits—it is of doubtful utility for fine measurements. Considered to be ceremonial objects, cubit rods had inexact divisions that have been found to vary not only in different dynasties but at times within the same dynasty. They became more exact only later in Egyptian history, when stone examples were found with digits subdivided into halves, thirds, quarters, and sixteenths. Some cubit rods were also found with astronomical data. While the longest yet discovered is a two-cubit wooden rod, longer ones were probably available.[17]

Instead of using cubit rods for measuring, two or three hardwood sticks with flat ends could have produced the same results found on the side of the Great Pyramid if placed end to end (**8.24**). No evidence exists for this procedure in ancient Egypt, but its simplicity

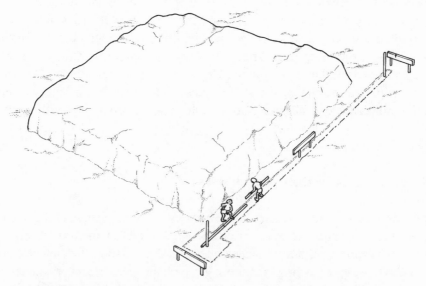

Figure 8.24. Finding the length of a pyramid side by placing two or more wooden rods end to end.

lends weight to the suggestion that it was known from earliest times. The accuracy resulting from use of such sticks was displayed in a field test when Engelbach placed a pair of
cubit-size hardwood rods end to end 25 times and returned them to exactly the same starting point.[18] In Roman times, 10-foot (3 m) rods were given flat bronze disks to reduce wear
when butted end to end.[19]

Although the use of a measuring cord from the corners of a side would produce a greater
variation than is shown at the Great Pyramid, its precision might be improved somewhat
if it were stretched from an estimated center of the pyramid to each corner. Draftsmen are
still taught to measure from both sides of a central axis to achieve accurate dimensions, no
different from those of yesteryear who used stone instead of paper. Indeed, examples are
found in ancient Egypt of measurements made from a central axis to both sides of a room
with measuring rods, the points being scratched with flint tools.[20]

The problems of measuring the comparatively short sides of a pyramid make one wonder how Egyptian surveyors were able to place accurately the previously mentioned provincial boundary stones at such great distances—15.5 miles (25 km) apart east-west across
the river valley and 9.3 miles (15 km) north-south along the Nile, as noted. The terrain in
those areas is not level enough for butting rods together, and distances are too long for
stretching a cord. Could the short knotted lengths of palm or fiber rope shown at the tomb
of Menna (6.1) have been used for this purpose? Differences in elevation may have been
determined by sighting to a series of vertical rods and establishing a plane by measuring
the distance between the rods. A series of short measurements erring on the plus side as
often as on the minus side would tend to compensate for one another, possibly making
the net result of accidental errors small enough to have set the ancient boundary stones.[21]
Considering this, perhaps the measurements found on the sides of the Great Pyramid were
also the result of a series of short measurements along the leveled side with a knotted rope.

Establishing the Corner Angles of a Pyramid

With a line on one side of a pyramid oriented, leveled, and measured, it remained only for
a right angle to be formed at each of ends—a seemingly uncomplicated task, yet one that
is easier said than done. Even if the Pythagorean triangle were used, with its proportions
of 3:4:5, Josef Dorner does not think the method of making it would be precise enough to
lay out the square of the Cheops Pyramid.[22] As with all the other measurements in the Great
Pyramid, whatever method was actually used, the right angles of its corners are made with
remarkable accuracy.

Engelbach successfully tested a possible procedure for producing a right angle. It
entailed the use of a large builder's square with pegs fixed at the joint and at the end of
each leg. By aligning one leg of the square to a baseline, a sighting could be made over the
joint peg and the peg at the end of the perpendicular leg. At Engelbach's direction, a target post was placed on the sight line about 300 feet (91m) away. The builder's square was
then rotated around the joint peg, and its previously perpendicular leg was aligned to the
baseline. With a second sighting from the same joint peg, this time over the newly positioned perpendicular leg, a second target post was positioned. If a faulty builder's square
caused the distant targets to be spaced apart, their differences would be divided, and a

Table 8.2
CORNER ANGLES OF THE GREAT PYRAMID

CORNER	ANGLE
Northeast	90° + 3' 2"
Southeast	90° − 3' 33"
Southwest	90° + 0' 33"
Northwest	90° − 0' 2"

After Somers Clarke and R. Engelbach, *Ancient Egyptian Masonry*, 66.

line extending from the joint peg to the center of the two target stakes would be perpendicular to the baseline (**8.25**). Indeed, according to Engelbach, no field test of this device had an error exceeding 1.5 arcminutes from a right angle, a result well within the range found at Cheops Pyramid.[23]

For the ancient surveyors to have established the east side of the subsidiary pyramid of Senwosret I, where Arnold found the corner orientation station, it would first be necessary to find the direction north. This may be accomplished by locating the exact center between the east-west points on the arc formed by the aforementioned orientation procedure. It would also require the ability to measure the distance and halve it with great accuracy—a task more exacting than that of simply halving a cord stretched from one point to the other (**8.26**) or, for that matter, using a cubit rod with its widely spaced markings. At a later time, however, limestone cubit rods with their closely spaced divisions may have been used for this purpose.

Any method used to find the center of an arc that does not produce exact results will result in errors that become greatly exaggerated when extended over a long distance. These errors can be avoided with a simple wooden straightedge and the aforementioned reversing and dividing procedure. Placed across the arc, the straightedge is marked at the points

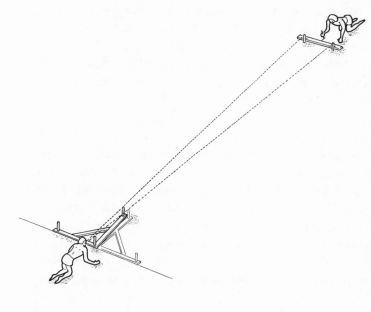

Figure 8.25. A method proposed by Engelbach to find a right angle. A large builder's square with posts at each end is sighted to a distance, and a target is placed in the ground. The builder's square is rotated and a second post is sighted and positioned, If the target posts are spaced apart, the distance is divided in half. A line from their midpoint to the post around which the builder's square turns will be perpendicular to the baseline.

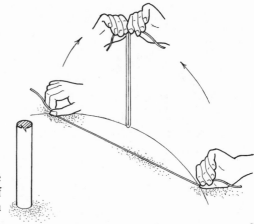

Figure 8.26. Stretching a cord and halving the distance is an obvious but inaccurate method of finding the distance between two points of a circle.

where it overlies the two shadow intersects. A center, estimated between the two points, is marked both on the ground and on the straightedge. If the estimate is correct, when the straightedge is reversed and repositioned over the shadow intersects, the center marks will again match; if not, the difference is halved and the process repeated until they coincide (**8.27**). Once the point is located, a cord is looped around the base of the gnomon and stretched over the newly found center (**8.28**). The short but accurate right angle can then

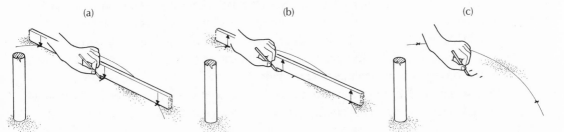

(a)   (b)   (c)

Figure 8.27. The distance between the two points of an arc is more accurately found with a slat of wood. (a) First mark an estimated center on the straightedge and on the ground. (b) Reverse the straightedge and mark the ground again. (c) If the marks are spaced apart, repeated reversals will establish a center point.

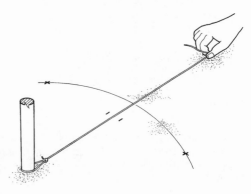

Figure 8.28. A right angle can be found by looping a cord around the gnomon and extending it over the center point.

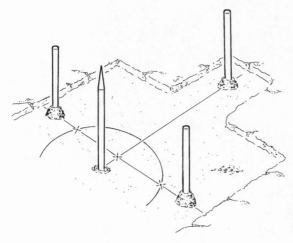

Figure 8.29. If a post the same diameter as the gnomon is placed on the centerline, a right-angle line to the north can be established with the cord-stretching ceremony.

be lengthened without any loss of accuracy by adding a post of the same diameter as the gnomon and using both posts in the aforementioned cord-stretching procedure (**8.29**).

Having established a narrow square band around the rocky mass of the pyramid site, the level may be given a final check by aiming from sighting boards to stakes around the perimeter. The accuracy of the sight line can be judged by matching the final sight line registering on a corner stake with the point at which it started (**8.30**). The area surrounding the narrow level band may then be expanded to the rocky core in preparation for the actual construction of the pyramid. However, before proceeding, a curious anomaly should be mentioned. Although the leveling and orientation procedure is here described as taking place on the bedrock of the Giza plateau, the most exact level found at the site of the Great Pyramid is on top of the fine limestone pavement.

This suggests that preparations described as occurring on the bedrock may instead have taken place directly on the paving and would mean that the paving stone would need

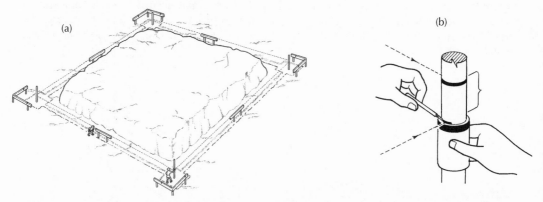

(a)

(b)

Figure 8.30. (a) The bedrock can be checked for level by sighting from stakes around the narrow perimeter. Accuracy is determined by comparing the terminus point of the sight line with the starting position. (b) Detail showing a sliding target sleeve registering a sight line below that of its starting position.

to be thick enough to account for differences when reduced to a level. It is also possible that an initial leveling and orientation procedure on the bedrock was followed by a second and more exacting procedure directly on the paving stone. This suggestion is supported by a slightly altered orientation found between building the core and fixing the sockets of the casing corners.[24] These findings suggest that the pyramid was constructed in at least two stages—a central pyramid core was raised either directly on the bedrock or on a poorer grade of paving, then a new orientation and leveling procedure was made on a finer layer of paving stone.

In present-day terms, the duplication of a building procedure may seem needless and redundant. However, if anything in Egyptian technology can be viewed as a "building secret," it was to make each step of construction more exacting than the last. Indeed, in this case there is a twofold advantage; reestablishing the layout square on a layer of close-fitting, fissure-free blocks of fine limestone would considerably increase the accuracy attainable. It would also avoid the damage likely during building and during transport of the stone that constituted the central core of the pyramid, so as to provide an unblemished surface exposed to public view on completion of the project.

Contrived with little more than sticks, shadows, and a bit of string, the four points that define the base of the pyramid were not only the first step in the actual construction; they were among the most important aspects of the entire undertaking. The ability to locate the parameters of a pyramid before it is completed is as important as the means by which the stone is raised. But having said this, a geometrically true pyramid consists of five points, not just those at the base. The genius of King Sneferu was the method by which he was able to position the distant fifth point.

CHAPTER 9

THE NUCLEUS

Locating the four base points of a pyramid was not an easy task, but it pales by comparison to the difficulties of placing the fifth point of the pyramid, high in the sky. The method by which this was accomplished, considering the primitive instruments available to the ancient Egyptians, is the key feature of all true pyramid construction and the most difficult to comprehend. Before delving into the problem, however, it may be an advantage to review other pyramidal structures of the period.

True pyramids of the Old Kingdom that are in an advanced state of disrepair show a nucleus having a number of regular tiers, or large steps, each rising at a steep angle and ending in a set-back—somewhat similar in appearance to the step pyramids of the 3rd Dynasty. These internal structures are visible not only in pyramids built of horizontally laid courses, as shown at the Queens Pyramids at Giza; they are also seen in the accretion-layered nucleus of Meidum. Also shown inside pyramids of later dynasties, the steps seem to be an essential stage of construction.[1] To discover if such tiers exist in the major pyramids at Giza, it is helpful to examine minor contemporary structures at the same location **(9.1)**.

All three Queens Pyramids of Cheops **(8.4)**, aligned north to south, were originally built to be true pyramids almost 100 feet (30 m) high.[2] Used as a quarry and having lost almost all their outer stone, they show a nucleus, or core, which consist of tiers that vary in number from two to four. Although the northern Queens Pyramid (GI-a) has only two tiers now, it certainly once held a third, as does the central pyramid (GI-b), or even a fourth, as in the southern pyramid (GI-c). The face of each tier consists of a number of large and small roughly squared blocks that are well fitted and bonded with mortar.[3] They are given an outer slope of about 75 degrees by having each upper course set slightly inside the one below **(9.2)**. The stones inside the tiers, which form the bulk of pyramid masonry, are small and poorly fitted compared to those on the face, some near the center of the nucleus being

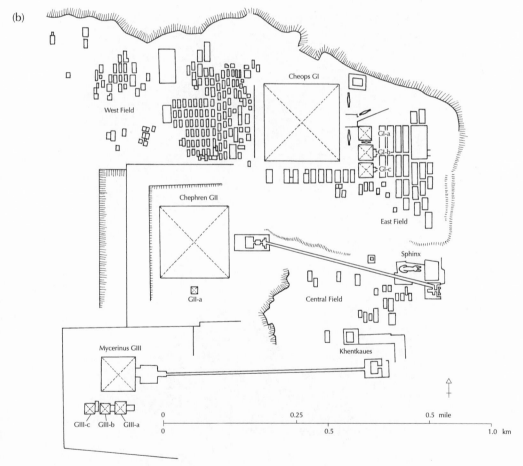

Figure 9.1. (a) View looking north with Queens Pyramids of Mycerinus in foreground and pyramid of Cheops in background. (b) Map of Giza Plateau.

Figure 9.2. Queens Pyramids of Cheops: (a) North Queens, GI-a; (b) Center Queens, GI-b; (c) South Queens GI-c.

placed almost haphazardly. Although the northern pyramid (GI-a) has only one casing stone left, the other two Queens Pyramids still contain a number of these blocks together with their backing stones, those stones placed directly behind the casing blocks. All the stones on these small pyramids are laid on generally horizontal beds.

Similar to those of Cheops' queens are the three Queens Pyramids, aligned east to west, just to the south of Mycerinus (**9.3**). Despite their present state of disrepair, the eastern structure (GIII-a) has retained enough packing stone for it almost to form a true pyramid. Its nucleus is not visible, but according to the investigators Reisner, Rinaldi, and Maragioglio, one probably exists deep inside the monument.[4] Although the entire pyramid was once encased with a mantle of smooth limestone rising at an angle of about 52 degrees, as at the king's pyramid, the granite casing blocks that form the first course have never been dressed. The center pyramid (GIII-b) has four large tiers, their outer slopes made from four to five courses of well-fitted blocks. By setting each course back from the one below, as at the Queens Pyramids of Cheops, the same rising angle is found at the Queens Pyramids of Mycerinus. The Egyptians measured the slope (*seked*) just as we do today, as a horizontal distance from the top of a vertical line. Our vertical line is one foot high, their line is one cubit high (20.62 inches or 52.5 cm)—we use feet and inches for the horizontal distance, they used cubits, palms, and fingers.

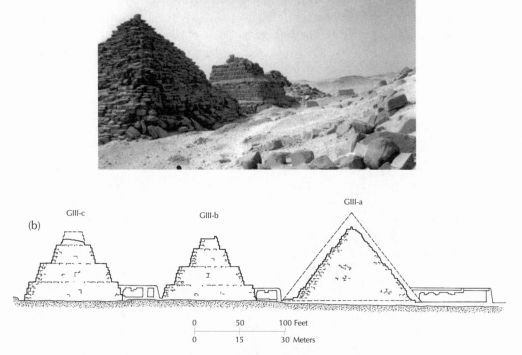

Figure 9.3. (a) View of Queens Pyramids of Mycerinus from the east. (b) Elevation from the south.

Because the center pyramid has the same size base (100 feet [30 m]) as its western neighbor, of which only three incomplete steps remain, it is thought that all three pyramids once had internal structures of the same size. If this is true, the combined packing, backing, and casing stones outside the nucleus of the east queen's pyramid (GIII-a) would have been about 20 feet (6 m) deep on each side. However, when this thickness is added to the cores of the central (GIII-b) and western (GIII-c) pyramids, there would be little room for the addition of a mortuary temple on the east side. This and the unusual care given to fitting the nucleus of both central and western structures suggest that GIII-b and GIII-c were meant to be completed as step pyramids and never intended to be true pyramids.[5]

On examining the mass of stone that makes up the tiered nucleus of the Queens Pyramids of Cheops and Mycerinus, it is found that to make each into a smooth-sided true pyramid, two additional building procedures seem to have taken place: first, a thick layer of packing stone was laid outside the tiered faces of the nucleus to bring the structure closer to a pyramidal shape; and second, the small steps left by the packing stones was covered with a smooth mantle of casing stone (**9.4**). Interestingly, the same form of tiered internal structure found in the Queens Pyramids appears to exist in the larger kings' pyramids at Giza.

Two of the three large pyramids of Giza also seem to show signs of a step nucleus. The breach made by the Mamelukes on the north face of Mycerinus enabled investigators to identify at least three large steps on the inside of the structure—the first tier can be seen extending vertically to about the eighth course of granite casing. Each tier, about 32 feet high and about 17 feet deep (9.75 × 5 m), is made of seven or eight set-back courses of good quality stone. Although the roughly 52-inch-high (132 cm) courses are faced with well-squared stones of uniform height, the blocks behind the facing stones are smaller and not as well formed.[6] Four tiers of a central nucleus can also be seen through the remaining packing stone when viewing the northeast corner of Chephren's pyramid in profile (**9.5**). As shown by their even spacing and clear outline, these tiers are not an accidental

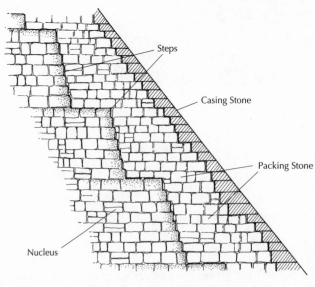

Figure 9.4. The Queens Pyramids of Cheops (GI-c) and Mycerinus (GIII-a) are generally constructed in the same way. The casing is supported by packing stones held by the stepped outer faces and setbacks of the stepped nucleus.

Figure 9.5. View of the northeast corner of Chephren, which indicates the existence of at least four steps in the nucleus.

result of later quarrying. Although no signs of a step nucleus can be seen at the pyramid of Cheops due to its covering of stone, it would be unusual for this pyramid to be built differently from all others since it is the finest example of a structural style that had been slowly developed over the years. Whatever else these internal structures may signify, the nucleus seems to be an essential part of the pyramid-building process. This appears to be true whether structures were made of the small roughly squared blocks of the 3rd Dynasty, the huge, well-squared blocks of the 4th Dynasty, or the smaller blocks to which the builders of the 5th and 6th Dynasties reverted.[7]

Abusir

According to Czech Egyptologist Miroslav Verner, the pyramids built at Abusir by Sahure, Neferirkare, and Raneferef, the second, third, and fifth kings of the 5th Dynasty, follow a scheme that is yet to be fully understood. They all were equinoctially oriented, and they seem to have been positioned according to a preconceived plan. If a diagonal line touching their northeast corners is extended, it intersects at a distant point with a similar diagonal line coming from the southeast corners of the three largest pyramids of Giza. Interestingly, the point of intersection is at the ancient site of Heliopolis, now an eastern suburb of modern Cairo. Iunu (Heliopolis) is the most sacred spot in Egypt—a place where the benben, the first matter thought to exist in the universe, was kept in the "holy of holies."[8]

Of the group of 5th Dynasty pyramids, the works of Niuserre, sixth king of the dynasty, show an unusual familial devotion. In his 30-year reign, he seems to have completed the

Figure 9.6. Pyramid of Neferirkare at Abusir. The ruined 360-foot-square
(110 m) 5th Dynasty pyramid has a nucleus reminiscent of the Step Pyramid of Djoser, built some 200 years earlier.

true pyramid of his father Neferirkare, which was 236 feet (72 m) high, with a nucleus of
six tiers (**9.6**). This is a much larger pyramid than his own 164-foot-high (50 m) structure. He also completed the small pyramid (56 feet [17 m] high) of his mother, Khent-
kaues, and the pyramid that was barely begun by his brother, Raneferef. Perhaps tired
of building for others, Niuserre simply faced the one core step completed by Raneferef
with limestone and left it in the form of a low square mastaba, like Djoser's first building
stage at Saqqara.[9]

The briefest study of Egyptian masonry, from the simplest stone walls to their ultimate
triumph, the true pyramid, shows that masons generally did not pay great attention to work
that was not visible. Using a building technique that resulted in a great savings of time
and skill, they often placed a well-fitted skin of good quality blocks outside each building
stage to hide the ill-fitting, poor quality stone of the interior. In each building stage—
stepped nucleus, packing, and casing stone—only the outer face seems to have regular
well-fitted stone. Assuming the internal masonry would remain unseen, the builders
worked some of it so carelessly that some internal blocks do not even show evidence of
being held together with mortar.[10] For example, in the masonry behind the facing stone of
Cheops Pyramid, which is visible in the compartments and passages inside and outside
on the faces, some joints are so large that were it not for the mortar, a closed fist could be
introduced without fear of scraping a knuckle—and indeed, at times the joints even lack
mortar (**9.7a, b**).

Based on these observations, it is fallacious to think that the Great Pyramid is composed of two million or so finely fitted blocks averaging 2.5 tons in weight—a statement
repeated so often that it seems to be accepted as fact. As with all pyramids, while this one
may possess a large number of such large blocks, especially on the outside at the lower levels, and while it may contain some truly enormous blocks, as at the pyramids of Chephren

Figure 9.7. Detail of Cheops Pyramid showing carelessly laid masonry behind the facing stones on the (a) north face and (b) south face.

and Mycerinus, the great internal mass of the structure more likely consists of smaller blocks and common fieldstone showing irregular joints filled with chips, rubble, and mortar. Having observed this masonry technique, Petrie was successfully able to argue against the widely accepted accretion theory of pyramid building. The theory held that the finest work of a pyramid occurred when the king was in his youthful prime and that it began to deteriorate badly when the structure was hastened to completion as he neared death. Petrie noted just the opposite at the first two pyramids of Giza, where the finest work is on the outermost parts. This building technique is not restricted to Giza; even King Djoser's Step Pyramid at Saqqara has an interior composed of rubble but an outer stepped casing as fine as any seen in Egypt.[11]

For his great undertaking, Cheops not only had the benefit of architects, stonemasons, and laborers who kept improving their skills over time; he also had many artisans who had been directly involved with the works of his father, Sneferu, developer of the true pyramid. It is uncertain whether the Great Pyramid was built with the same technique used at Meidum, that of erecting a step nucleus before the outer masonry was applied. The question can only be answered by addressing the two most puzzling aspects of pyramid building: the method used for lifting the stones, and the means by which they were positioned to meet at a far-off point in the sky.

Theories for Controlling Slope

It is sometimes suggested that the stones were accurately positioned and brought to a distant point in the sky by completing each course before the next was applied and using diagonal measurements from corner to corner to control the shape of each rising square. It is also suggested that the corners of the square were aligned and prevented from twisting by visually relating them to outside datum points. Although it is true that the outside corners can be aligned to outside reference points, it would have been impossible to form the slope of a pyramid by controlling the individual courses with the instruments then available. According to this method of pyramid building, the precision of the whole depends on the exactness of its parts.

To form a pyramid with a series of squares, each course must be accurately leveled and must have perpendicular sides of equal dimensions. Approximations will not produce the required results. Although a course can be made into a square even if it is not level, the tilt of the course would become cumulative, as one course was laid on another, and would prevent the faces of the pyramid from joining at a distant point. Yet, despite the need of great accuracy, a survey by Petrie established that almost no course in the Great Pyramid is truly level. Indeed, by only the second course from an almost perfectly leveled pavement, the difference between the southeast corner and the southwest corner is already 5.7 inches (14.5 cm).[12] At the pyramid of Chephren, corrective leveling can be seen on the west side of the fifth course and on the entire tenth course. These, however, are minor differences compared to Queens Pyramids of Cheops, which have sides that are neither parallel nor at right angles to each other. For example, the bedrock on which the northern one (G1-a) is built slants from north to south and from east to west, making the northwest corner of the monument about 6.5 feet (2 m) higher than the southeast corner (8.4).[13] Clearly, if the casing stone were measured with a series of squares having each corner at a different height at the very bottom of a pyramid, the succeeding courses would greatly compound the error and prevent the faces from meeting at a point in the sky (9.8).

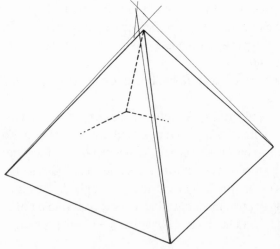

Figure 9.8. Errors in the size or level of casing courses near the bottom of a pyramid would be greatly multiplied and would prevent the four faces from meeting at a point in the sky.

Lacking any other means to control the rising angle of the pyramid, some continue to espouse the theory of exact superincumbent courses. To form the nucleus, these advocates claim, when reaching a course, stone was made to extend outwardly from the center in an even square until arriving at the face of the nucleus. To account for the small setbacks of the courses, the sides were said to be so carefully squared and measured that the facing blocks could be laid over a lower course with enough accuracy to permit the steps of the nucleus to rise at 75 degrees. It is also further claimed that once the facing blocks of the nucleus were set, the courses would continue to be expanded until nearing the outside face of the pyramid. At that time, the casing blocks, their rising joints earlier cut and fitted on the ground (some claim the angles of their faces were also made on the ground), would be placed in position. Completed in this manner, the casing would be dressed to a smooth plane, as outside supply ramps and foothold embankments used to raise the blocks were disassembled from the top down **(9.9)**.[14]

Others found that level indications placed on the blocks by the Egyptians were too roughly made for calculating or accurately scribing a square on each course. Recognizing that the some 200 and more courses in the Great Pyramid would have led to cumulative errors, they suggest reducing the number of measurements by the use of very long plumb lines. Employed to find the proper horizontal distance, they claim, plumb lines could have been dropped into pits formed in the surrounding foothold embankments. Since the mantle of a pyramid results from a rise of 14 on a horizontal distance of 11, this approach would require a minimum 40-foot-thick (12m) embankment with a 51-foot-deep (15.5m) pit. By use of such devices, these advocates claim, only ten shifts would be needed to build the Great Pyramid accurately. To prevent an overall twist, they also propose visually aligning the corners of the pyramid to preformed squares on the base. The squares of each course, as defined by spots carefully dressed along their sides, could then be measured against diagonals and axes previously projected up onto the course from outside datum points with the use of sighting poles **(9.10)**.[15]

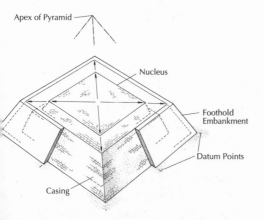

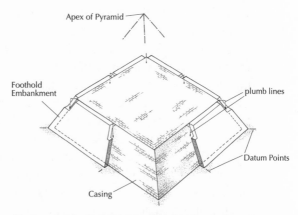

gure 9.9. Building a pyramid by completing each
yer from the ground up. The faces of the stepped
cleus are supposedly established by measuring the
agonal of each course in relation to outside datum
ints.

Figure 9.10. Establishing the facing angles of a pyramid by dropping a series of 51-foot-long (15.5 m) plumb lines along the edges of a 40-foot-deep (12 m) foothold embankment.

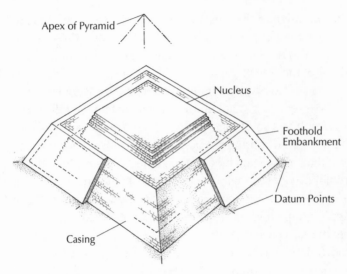

Figure 9.11. Building the faces of the nucleus in advance of the rest of the course would be self-defeating as it brings to each course an obstacle similar to that of the rocky core.

Considering the stated difficulties, others suggest that the nucleus must have been built by several layers above the rest of the pyramid course. The set-back faces of the nucleus could then be more carefully controlled and the angle of the casing more accurately measured. Needless to say, this approach is self-defeating. It would bring to each layer an obstacle similar to that of the rocky core, the very object that had previously interfered with the diagonal measurements of the foundation and that required considerable effort to overcome (**9.11**). But even if we accept that a pyramid could be built to its angled faces by carefully controlling the measurements of each square, what then would be the purpose of making an internal stepped structure having regular rising angles and set-back courses when only the top surface of each course of the nucleus is visible to the stonemasons?

The set-back nucleus does exist. Once we acknowledge the existence of a stepped internal structure, the reasons for its presence will become clear. Indeed, many advantages spring from erecting the nucleus before the rest of the pyramid: its rising angles can be viewed and controlled; containing the great bulk of the pyramid, it can be made of smaller, more manageable stones, which can be placed with less time and care; it provides an elevated structure having set-back levels that provide staging areas at different heights above the ground for men and material; it forms a stable structure to support the outer fill of packing blocks and casing stone. The small set-back courses on its outside face provide the "tooth" to prevent a sliding plane from developing between the nucleus and the packing stone, and the stepped core allows a carelessly built inner structure to be adjusted later by a later and more exacting outer coat.

An example of this adjustment is seen at the pyramid of Meidum. Although it is a geometrically true pyramid, the faces of its nucleus are out of square, and the summit of the first stage is a 30 × 49 foot (9 × 15 m) rectangle.[16] The large steps of the nucleus are of unequal heights, and each single step does not even have the same height around its perimeter. In addition to the depth of treads not being uniform or equal to each other, they are not horizontal or even parallel to each other. Yet, despite the poorly planned and executed nucleus, the casing that covers Meidum Pyramid is almost as accurately laid as that of Cheops.[17]

Citing the lack of modern surveying equipment, Mendelssohn, who credits engineering colleague T. E. Connolly for his insights, gives another reason why it is impractical to build a pyramid without first constructing a central core:

> Whereas in a step pyramid slight errors of alignment are hardly apparent and can always be corrected at the next step, the same is not the case for a true pyramid. Its edges must be straight and, at the same time, meet in one point which, in the early phases of construction, is high up in the sky and unattainably far away from the building operations. . . . For a building of the size of the great Giza pyramids a tiny error of only 2 degrees in the alignment of the edges will result in a mismatch of over 49 feet (15m) at the top. Since the edges had to be straight from the outset, they could not be corrected later and had to be accurate to a fraction of a degree.[18]

Before suggesting the manner in which the stepped core was built, it may be helpful to describe the method a modern mason uses to erect a wall. Starting with a level foundation, the length of a side is measured to locate the corners. Using a spirit level and straightedge, a corner is laid with great care several courses in advance. A stick, called a story-pole, placed against the corner and marked with the height of each course, is used as a gauge to enable opposing corners to be built to the same height. If the corners of the wall are not distant, the mason simply stretches a cord from one course to another and lays block to the line. However, if the distance is great, a catenary curve, which cannot be eliminated even with great tension, will be formed. Caused by the weight of the line, the sag in the cord must be supported at intervals by temporary piles of blocks that hold line-pins. The height of these line-pins is also gauged by the story-pole. As the course is filled toward the temporary blocks holding the line-pins, they are transferred to the closing course, thereby continuing to support the cord until the distance is sufficiently reduced (**9.12**).[19]

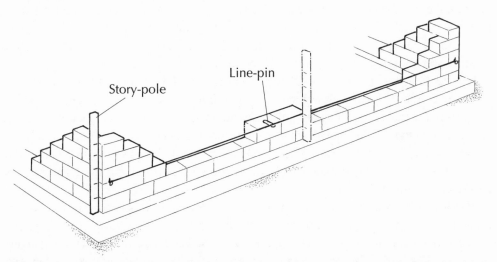

Figure 9.12. Establishing level courses of an ordinary masonry wall by marking the height of each course on a story-pole and transferring the height elsewhere along the wall.

(a)

(b)

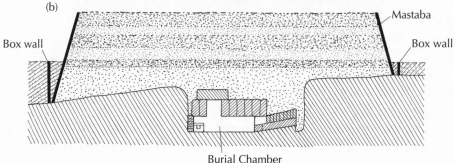

Burial Chamber

Figure 9.13. (a) Mastaba 17 at Meidum. (b) Section showing walls of structure founded on slanted bedrock.

The simple procedure of building a wall becomes much more complicated when applied to a nucleus with corners rising at an angle. A method used by the Egyptians to facilitate the problem is shown at Mastaba 17 at Meidum (**9.13**). Excavated by English archaeologist G. A. Wainwright, the inwardly leaning faces of this 3rd Dynasty mastaba have vertical box walls that are spaced close to each corner. Due to the slanting bedrock on which they stand, the four right-angle box walls were built to different heights—3, 4, 5, and 21 feet (0.9, 1.2, 1.5, and 6.4 m) below the surface of the ground. On the inside face of each wall, the Egyptians drew a system of grid lines to help establish equal slopes for the faces of the mastaba. Calculated by the builders in terms of rise to run, the slope was marked at an angle of 76 degrees with a double red line that runs from the bottom inside corner to the top outside corner (**9.14**).[20] By following the double red line with a cord stretched from one wall to another, the builders could transfer to the faces of the mastaba the slope drawn on the box walls.

Among the wealth of early building techniques found at Mastaba 17 is a method to discourage tomb robbery by isolating the sarcophagus. Cut into the bedrock, the main hall of the burial chamber is lined with limestone blocks and covered with great roofing beams of 38 tons. The burial chamber, being encompassed by the outer walls of the mastaba founded on the same bedrock, does not provide an outside entrance. For additional secu-

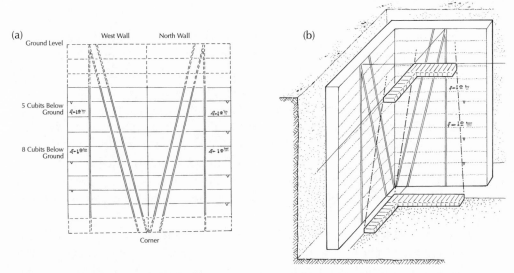

Figure 9.14. (a) Box walls found at each corner of Mastaba 17. (b) Method of using such box walls to lay corners that rise at an angle.

rity, the entire 172 × 343-foot (52 × 104 m) overhead structure was filled with a loose aggregate of about 100,000 tons of limestone chips and marl taken when the nearby pyramid of Meidum was constructed. Interestingly, instead of simply dumping the aggregate within the walls, it was carefully placed in level layers across the inside by matching them to stone walls erected for that purpose.[21] No doubt, the level of aggregate rose as the mastaba was constructed and helped to level its outer walls. A similar procedure at the 12th Dynasty pyramid complex of Senwosret I, at Lisht, shows a somewhat irregular grid of low brick walls to provide a level for the interior court.[22] These examples indicate that simple, proven building methods changed little in Egypt over the centuries.

The reason for the elaborate building plan at Mastaba 17 was to cause an endless flow of loose aggregate to block any passageway cut into the side of the monument by tomb robbers. It was an obstacle that caused Wainwright great difficulty; he excavated an enormous pit to contain the flow. On arriving at the burial chamber, he found that it contained an 8.5-ton sarcophagus for which the only means of entrance must have been by rope through the roof of the chamber. Imagine his surprise on discovering that the supposedly secure chamber had already been entered by ancient intruders. The robbers, doubtless having worked on its construction, completely by-passed the loose aggregate by cutting a tunnel directly through the bedrock. Despite the limited space, once inside the burial chamber the intruders were able to lift the 3.5-ton lid with a lever made of a 6-foot (1.8 m) branch of acacia, a hardwood native to Egypt. The 2.5-inch-diameter (6.3 m) lever, sharpened to a chisel point at one end, was similar to that used for opening the sarcophagus of Horemheb.[23] The confidence bred from moving enormous roofing beams, lowering heavy sarcophagi with rope, and lifting the heavy lid of the sarcophagus with a short piece of wood shows the matter-of-fact nature of stonework in ancient Egypt at that time.

Meeting at a Distant Point

Although providing sloping sides to a structure with a truncated top, as at Mastaba 17, was not a difficult task, box walls could not be used successfully to bring the four faces of a pyramid to a distant point in the sky. For example, it is estimated the Great Pyramid would require a minimum of fifteen 33-foot-high (10 m) walls—each closely spaced on the corners of the pyramid as these were aligned on a continually rising embankment.[24] Erected individually, all the box walls would have to be perfectly plumbed, with carefully calculated angles; the smallest discrepancy in any of the 60 required corners, with their 120 adjacent sides, would result in the kind of cumulative error that would prevent the pyramid corners from meeting at the top. Considering the difficulties here and elsewhere, it seems prudent to avoid building with a series of small steps when forming the facing angles of a smooth-sided pyramid.

The pyramid of Meidum, laid over a highly inaccurate nucleus, indicates a method of pyramid building radically different than those previously proposed. The pyramid seems to have been built in separate building stages that allowed material to be raised while still providing an overview of the structure being erected. Meidum also indicates an exactness reached by remeasuring the site after the eight-step nucleus was built, thus lending support to the finding at the Great Pyramid, which shows slight differences between the azimuth of the packing stone and that of the casing stone.[25] These differences suggest that the nucleus, and perhaps also the packing stone, somehow helped to establish the final pyramidal form.

A possible method by which this was accomplished stems from a discovery in the late 19th century by M. A. Robert, a French surveyor. While establishing a geodesic point for a survey of the Fayum area, he reached the summit of the now exposed nucleus of Meidum Pyramid after a difficult climb. Satisfied to be the first to have ventured to this point since its ancient destruction, he observed a round hole 6 inches in diameter and 12 inches deep (15 × 30 cm) in the center of the level top. Assuming the cavity once to have held a pole, Robert planted his own 10-foot (3 m) sighting staff topped by a red and white flag.[26]

If this hole was cut by the ancient builders, as is likely, its probable purpose was to support a shaft of considerable length.[27] Being centrally located on the flat summit sug-

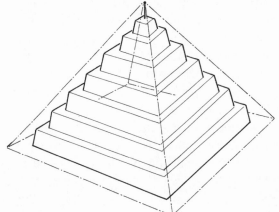

Figure 9.15. Mounting a sighting target on the stepped nucleus to establish the sky point of a pyramid before the packing or casing stone is applied.

gests that it may have been employed to support a target, representing the apex of the pyramid—a target no larger than one of the round black pots of the period.[28] Perhaps this device was used for that distant point in the sky mentioned by Mendelssohn. Indeed, as a sighting target it would have given Sneferu the means to convert the completed but inexact step pyramid of Meidum to a more pyramidal shape (**9.15**). Only an afterthought at Meidum, it would provide future builders the simplest means of building a true pyramid. While it is probable that similar targeting devices were used on other pyramids, the only evidence found to date is the hole on top of Meidum. Nevertheless, it is possible to position target staffs without placing them in holes—for example, a staff set up with struts on the summit of Cheops Pyramid, erected for astronomical purposes by the Transit of Venus party in 1874, was later used by Petrie for measuring the pyramid.[29]

The ability to see a small pot at a distance of 700 feet (213 m) from datum points on the ground was confirmed while examining the casing seat at the northwest corner bedrock of Cheops Pyramid. Looking skyward along the edge of the pyramid to the apex, I watched several hawks circling the staff of Venus—one choosing that very moment to perch on the staff (**9.16**). The silhouette of a hawk with its wings in a folded position, although not larger than a pot, could be clearly seen with the naked eye from the corner socket. All this aside, postulating the means to form a pyramidal structure before describing how the stone may have been raised into position is getting ahead of ourselves.

Ramps

After preparing the site for the pyramid of Meidum, preparations were probably made for erecting the nucleus. The number of tiers or steps used would depend on the contemplated height of the structure and the judgment of the builders. Initially built as a step pyramid, the seven-layer Meidum structure was enlarged in a second building stage to eight steps

Figure 9.16. Hawk perched on top of the Transit of Venus staff as seen by the naked eye from the northwest corner casing socket of Cheops Pyramid. Another hawk is seen to circle left.

by adding another layer to the outside, the steps being spaced in height about 36 feet (11 m) apart. Although built with steps, as at Sinki, Meidum Pyramid, probably due to a more advanced building method, does not display signs of the same ramps shown at the earlier structure.

A desert roadway east of Meidum Pyramid is often suggested as the remains of a linear ramp over which men pulled stone-laden sledges for constructing the second stage of the stepped core. This is contradicted by the evidence. Depressions on the fifth and sixth steps, said to be a seat for interlocking the ramp with the pyramid, are wider at the top than at the bottom, just the reverse of a possible ramp.[30] The depressions are also about the same width as the 13-foot-wide (4 m) roadway in the desert—making an impractical construction for a 210-foot-high (64 m) mud brick or stone ramp. Its high vertical sides and narrow width would make it very unstable. Indeed, no possible ramp could attain this height without being widely buttressed on its sides, a construction that would have left even more signs of its presence than those found of the roadway.[31] Despite this, if the ramp somehow did exist, its measured angle of 9–10 degrees would bring it only to the second step of the nucleus.[32] All this conjecture is moot, however, since the sequence of materials deposited on the desert roadway indicates that the supposed pyramid ramp was instead used to transport material to the plateau for earlier mastabas, and it seems to have been abandoned before the pyramid was even begun.[33]

The erection and subsequent destruction of ramps of the three construction stages at Meidum, each to be about as high as the structure itself, is the most convincing argument Maragioglio and Rinaldi can imagine against the supposed use of linear ramps for constructing the pyramid. As each stage was begun at the bottom, the preceding ramp would be an obstacle to enlarging or encasing the pyramid and would have to be leveled.[34] Further, all construction would have to stop as the ramp was being raised between courses. A wider ramp would avoid the problem by permitting half of the roadway to be raised while the other half remained in service for transporting stone; however, this would add considerably to the already enormous volume of material required. If a ramp such as this were used for bringing the estimated 7-ton capstone to the 500-foot (152 m) top of Cheops, while keeping to a reasonable working angle of a 1-foot rise to a 10-foot run (10 percent gradient), it would require a length of about 4,900 feet (1,500 m). The enormity of this undertaking would cause the ramp to pass completely over the quarry south of the pyramid, from which the limestone blocks destined for the pyramid were said to have been taken. A ramp of such enormity would have a volume of about seven times that of the pyramid itself and would require about 300,000 workers from an estimated population of 1–2 million for its construction.

Ramp-Building Material

A discussion of ramps requires consideration of the materials used for their construction.[35] Although native wood was used to make tools, furniture, and boats, it was largely an imported item and in short supply. Even assuming unlimited shipments, a wood ramp of the size required would probably denude the forests of Lebanon. Another suggestion has been that ramps were built of stone-chip waste cut from the pyramid blocks during shaping.

These chips would supposedly be combined with water and tafl, a natural claylike desert substance that forms a hard concretion when mixed with water. However, based on the volume of chips needed, a ramp for Cheops would require that each block placed in the pyramid somehow be made to yield about eight times its volume in waste chips.[36] Considering the height attained, if sand were used as a ramp, the size of the mound would dwarf the pyramid and cover much of the Giza Plateau. A clever method of modifying and heightening mounds is mentioned in a passage from the Anastasi Papyrus, which refers to the erection of a colossus. Here, a grid of upstanding mud brick chambers was built to contain the sand of a 79-foot-high (24 m) embankment.[37] Despite the ingenuity of this construction, mud brick has inherent limits that would prevent it from reaching the heights of the pyramid.

Although Egyptians made extensive use of mud brick (burnt brick was not employed by the Egyptians until Roman times) the maximum height a ramp using this material could attain before it would be crushed by its own weight is approximately 380 feet (116 m)—much less if the weight of the stone being transported is also considered.[38] Worse, the ramp would not only fail to support stone transported near its edges, but as it bore against the continually narrowing pyramid face, the roadway would simply run out of working room. If the road were made wider than the face, it would require the backing of an amount of earth as tall as but wider than the pyramid. Consider this in terms of the weather. While it rains infrequently in the desert, rain can be torrential when it does fall. This would subject a mud-brick ramp to serious erosion during the reported 20-year period it took to build the pyramid.[39]

Realizing these shortcomings, Petrie suggested placing a zigzag stone ramp on top of the linear mud-brick ramp for the highest 100 feet. However, a ramp of this nature could not reach the apex of the narrowing pyramid as each switchback became steeper; it would run out of space. Considering this, Petrie suggested levering up the remaining stone from pits left in the pyramid.[40] This building approach cannot be given serious consideration, especially when we take into account the impossibility of transporting the building blocks, much less the estimated 7 ton capstone up the increasingly steep ramps, and the lack of any evidence for the said pits or room for levering if the capstone were to arrive.

With no other materials available to the Egyptians, it would seem that only a linear ramp of fitted stone with mortared joints could possibly have been used for Cheops Pyramid—one wide enough to permit empty sledges to return and for workers to maneuver the pyramidion into position (9.17).Yet this too should be reconsidered. Herodotus states that it took ten years to build the 3,000-foot-long, 60-foot-wide, and 48-foot-high causeway (914 × 18 × 15 m) of stone leading to the Giza Plateau. Using that as a guideline, the time required to build the ramp for Cheops Pyramid, which is ten times higher, would extend well beyond the 23-year reign of Cheops.

Roads, Causeways, and Low Ramps

We have only to consider the three major pyramids built by Sneferu in his 24-year reign to realize the impossibility of any kind of linear ramp. The Meidum and Bent pyramids alone are known to have undergone the kind of major revisions that would have required several ramp reconstructions. Indeed, despite the existence of almost 100 pyramids, the remains of a construction ramp large enough to reach to the top of a pyramid remain undetected to

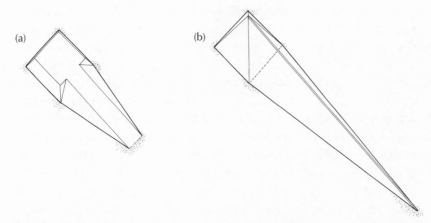

Figure 9.17. (a) The wide roadway of a linear ramp (b) disappears at the top of the pyramid. This system does not provide a path for returning emply sledges near the top. It also requires all work to cease as the ramp is heightened between courses.

this date. We need to reject the possibility of large construction ramps that scale to the heights of a pyramid.

There is, however, strong evidence for the use of ramps and causeways for the lower courses of a pyramid and for paths extending from the low desert to the pyramid sites. Indeed, low ramps, roads, and slideways have been found that run directly to pyramids, and in some cases they run in close proximity and parallel to the pyramid base. The northern pyramid of Sneferu at Dahshur, for example, has two wide causeways built of sand, which cross the desert and lead to a storage area in the southwest, about 500 feet (150 m) from the corner. Due to their width, the causeways are thought to have been used for transporting the large mass of local stone needed for the central core of the pyramid. Narrower roads from the east, which also end near the pyramid, were probably used for the finer

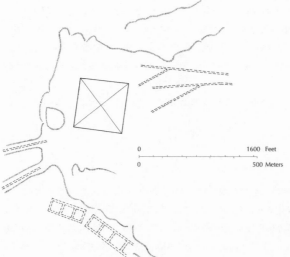

Figure 9.18. The Red Pyramid at Dahshur north showing roadways that carried masonry close to the base of the pyramid.

casing stone (**9.18**). At the Mastabat el-Faraun in Dahshur, supply roads 3,300 feet (1,000 m) long lead directly to the base of the 66-foot-high (20m) structure.[41]

Although the 12th Dynasty pyramids, with their skeletal framework, may have had ramps used differently than for their Old Kingdom counterparts, the newer pyramids also do not show signs of ramps reaching to their higher elevations. At the 12th Dynasty pyramid of Amenemhet I at Lisht, for example, a low 21-foot-wide (6.5 m) ramp with brick retaining walls starts at the valley temple, crosses the desert, and ends at an area near the northeast corner of the pyramid. Interestingly, just below the top surface of this mud-and-mortar road, Arnold found timbers salvaged from boats that were spaced across the axis of the roadway like crossties of a railroad. Similar timbers were also found embedded in the desert conglomerate near Senwosret I, at Lisht, a pyramid surrounded on all sides by roads, ramps, and stone-dressing stations. These timbers were used to reinforce the concretelike surface of gypsum and limestone chips. With the road topped by mud, friction between the hardened surface and the wood runners of the sledges could be reduced by frequent wetting.[42] Clearly, if building material is deposited near the foot of a pyramid, it is not reasonable to suggest that it would be moved again to the entrance of a distant construction ramp.

The horizontal transport roads, or slideways, that run parallel to the base of Senwosret I are at a distance of 66–164 feet (20–50 m) from the pyramid. The remains of two 164-foot-long (50 m) ramps perpendicular to the structure were also uncovered, but according to their gradient, they could only have reached the lower levels of the 197-foot-high (60 m) pyramid. The Senwosret complex also discloses what may be termed a jumble of stone delivery systems—slideways built under and in some cases over the remains of a sloping ramp leading to the center of the king's pyramid. Of the many ramps found at this location, most were less than 164 feet long (50 m), some built at an earlier time than others.[43] This indicates pyramid construction in different phases—a far cry from the generally held view of the use of a single ramp system delivering material to each course as it was being completed.

The Spiral Ramp

The discovery of roadways leading close to the base of the pyramid seems to suggest a type of ramp built directly on the structure. American Egyptologist Dows Dunham and other like-minded theorists claim that a ramp of this nature would start at a bottom corner and spiral up the pyramid, rising at a 10 percent grade—low enough to permit teams of men to pull supply sledges as the courses grew in height (**9.19a, b**).[44] Unfortunately, this delivery system has more serious problems than the proposed linear ramp. Other than the obvious difficulty of turning blocks around the many corners of the pyramid as they rise in height, the ramp would simply run out of space before reaching the top due to the converging pyramid faces. Indeed, at the upper reaches, the side walls supporting the spiral ramp would be forced to overlap the lower roadways and would become increasingly steep, even without providing a path for the returning empty sledges. Widening the ramp to provide a return path would simply worsen the overlapping problem. Nevertheless, a wider ramp could not be avoided, if only for turning the many corners with the 56 roofing beams of the king's chamber, each over 26 feet (8 m) long and weighing about 54 tons.[45]

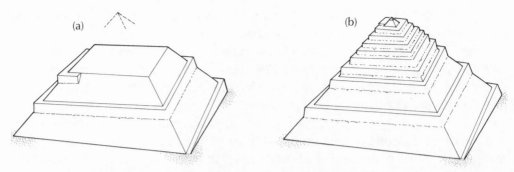

Figure 9.19. (a) A spiral ramp for the delivery of masonry to each course of the rising pyramid. (b) Near the top, the ramps would overlap and run out of room. This system does not permit all the casing to be set from outside and provides a torturous path for delivering the stone.

In an endeavor to raise the beams, the spiral ramp would completely cover the pyramid and make it even more difficult to bring it to a point than if the aforementioned linear ramp were used.

The spiral ramp was supposedly supported on steplike casing stones, which would have been dressed back progressively from the top down as the ramp was removed, giving a smooth, even slope from top to bottom.[46] Contrary to this, the undressed granite casing stone on the pyramid of Mycerinus remains with the same rough angle with which it was laid (**9.20**). Clearly, without stepped courses, this pyramid would provide no support for the spiral ramp. Yet, despite the angled faces on the lower 15 courses (54 feet [16 m] above the ground), the pyramid was built to completion. This is shown by scattered remains on the ground of smoothly dressed limestone casing from the upper levels. The granite casing on the lower courses, fashioned from boulders found at Aswan, was used to protect the pyramid from wind-blown sand. Due to the hardness of the granite and the probable death of the king before completion of the pyramid, the roughly angled faces at Mycerinus result from not completely dressing their bulbous shape when they were set

Figure 9.20. North face of Mycerinus, with lever bosses on the angled face of granite casing. They show that the blocks were set into place from foothold embankments outside the pyramid.

Figure 9.21. Boulders, from which granite casing stones of Mycerinus were formed, are shown loosely scattered around Aswan.

into place (**9.21**). Although it may be claimed that other pyramids instead employed step-like casing stones, thus making the building procedure less complicated, the method of constructing Mycerinus must be addressed if a solution to the pyramid problem is to be found.

It might be argued the roughly angled stones resulted from an interrupted final dressing process, but this cannot be true. The granite stones exhibit well-defined bosses on their outside faces—the only purpose of which was to take the points of levers when manipulating the blocks into position.[47] Similar means are seen in the other stoneworking cultures, such as at Sacsayhuaman and Ollantaytambo in Peru (**9.22**). This method of placing casing stones into position was not restricted to granite; evidence of similar means is seen at the southeast corner of the Cheops south Queens Pyramid (G1-c), a pyramid built entirely of limestone. Here, however, instead of employing bosses, the rough limestone blocks had cavities cut into their outer faces (**9.23**). Although all evidence of their existence was removed when the stone was later dressed, similar lever pockets can be seen on the side joints at the first course of Cheops. Ordinarily hidden in the side joints, these were exposed when almost all the casing stone was taken. The pockets were filled with mortar, as though to disguise their presence. There is not any logical reason to disguise a lever pocket that will never be seen, unless, of course, it is an unavoidable result of a building procedure— a matter to be discussed presently.

In common with all other Egyptian construction, these findings indicate that the casing stones of all pyramids were manipulated into position by simultaneously levering them from two positions—from the front, while standing on outside foothold embankments, and from the side, while standing on the course itself. These combined forces would best provide a tight fit against the adjacent stone while giving the ability to set the stone into the plane of the pyramid face. Indeed, this is the simplest and most practical way for setting the blocks. Any method of building the pyramids must therefore provide for foothold embankments that surround each course as the casing stone is laid. Paradoxically, however, controlling the shape requires that the pyramid be viewed as it rises—a contradiction that seems to add yet another layer of complexity to an already difficult building process.

(a)

(b)

Figure 9.22. Bosses are commonly used for setting masonry. Although generally removed when the stone was dressed, they may still be seen at various locations around the world such as (a) Sacsayhuaman and (b) Ollantaytambo, Peru.

Figure 9.23. South Queens Pyramid of Cheops (G1-c), showing lever pockets to manipulate the casing blocks from the outside.

Material Flow

The use of the aforementioned linear or spiral ramp raises the question of delivering an adequate supply of stone in a timely manner. With the practitioners long since gone, the best way to judge the efficacy of traffic flow on a ramp is to review what is thought to be practical when using a low causeway to bring material to the base of a pyramid. According to quarry dates on the casing stone, Meidum Pyramid took 17 years to build. Calculating its volume, Petrie estimated that it contained about 600,000 blocks averaging 2 tons each. Assuming a total of 6,000 working days in 17 years, blocks had to be hauled up the sloping causeway to the building site at a rate of 100 blocks a day. Estimating that a 2-ton block could be dragged up a gently sloping causeway 2 feet (61 cm) per minute (120 feet [37 m] per hour), it would take a day to deposit the required amount of stone near the base of the pyramid. Also to be considered is that with 100 blocks in transit, each pulled by four files of five men, the teams could not be closer than 40 feet (12 m) apart. Therefore, judging by its estimated length, only 20 or 25 blocks could be moved on the causeway. Under these conditions, some 2,000 men and four or five causeways would be needed for the required amount of stone, teams being crowded as closely as practicable.[48] Once the project began to rise, the restricted space prevented the use of draft animals.

Using as a basis the number of men required to haul stone-laden sledges on a gently sloping causeway, imagine the manpower needed if ramps with even slightly greater inclines were used at Cheops Pyramid. This structure, which contains four times the volume of Meidum, would require a minimum of 16 ramps, placed only on the north and south faces. These directions are the only possible locations if the king was to avoid the cemeteries to the west, which held his high officials, and to the east, where his royal relatives rested.

While it is possible to slide, roll, or tumble heavy weights along level ground with a comparatively small effort, it is more difficult to raise them to great heights by means of a ramp. For example, if 56 men are required to drag a sledge with a 2-ton load up a 10-degree slope, 77 men would be required for the same load on a 20-degree ramp, and as many as 96 men for a 30-degree ramp.[49] Although it might be imagined that fewer men would be needed if friction were reduced by wetting the surface, a new problem would arise; they would barely be able to keep their footing on the slippery surface if the teams followed at close proximity, as they must. Widening the ramp to establish adjacent dry paths for the teams would require that more ramp-building material be used for an already burdensome project.

Among further proposals for methods to bring stone to great heights is the reversing or switchback ramp. Apart from a lack of evidence for its use, this theory would fail because as each reversal became prohibitively steep, such a ramp would run out of room before reaching the heights. Leaning against the pyramid face as it rose would cause other problems. The ramp would be unable to cling to the roughly angled casing stone and would make it necessary for each new reversal to cover the preceding ramps—requiring the entire system to begin once again from the bottom (**9.24**). This waste of effort and material is almost incidental when compared to the most important consideration of all—the switchback ramp does not provide for surrounding foothold embankments to set the facing stones of each course.

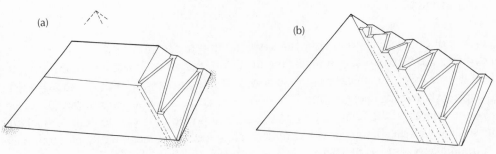

Figure 9.24. A switchback ramp requires being started anew with each reversal. (a) About halfway up the pyramid. (b) Nearing the apex.

Findings of supply roads close to the bases of pyramids seem to indicate the need for a radical departure in thought about pyramid building. To fill this need, Dieter Arnold proposes the use of a short linear ramp that starts close to an outside face and extends through the center of the pyramid almost to the opposite side. Falling short of the top, it gains additional height by being reversed with a construction on the pyramid itself. As this also fails to reach the top, Arnold proposes completing the pyramid with the aid of a staircase that starts about halfway up the outer ramp and rests against the previously made opening, now filled with masonry (**9.25**). Although an original and radical departure from all previous theories, the idea of cutting through the center of the pyramid does not allow for any means to control the size of the courses. It also does not provide for the possible presence of the stepped nucleus or for the foothold embankments for setting the casing blocks in place.

With problem piled on problem, we seem to be facing a dilemma that can only be resolved by a close examination of the essential building requirements. As previously mentioned, two primary problems must be overcome to erect a pyramid: stone must be raised to great heights and, once there, positioned with accuracy. These problems are obvious to anyone with even the most casual interest in the subject. Yet of the theories offered to date, the solution to one problem seems to cancel out the solution to the other. Specifically, in

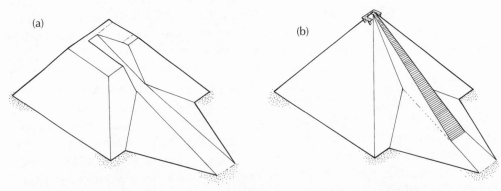

Figure 9.25. Suggested by Dieter Arnold, (a) a short linear ramp enters a cut through center of pyramid and gains additional height by a switchback ramp built on the pyramid. (b) After filling the cut, the top is reached by erecting a stairway on the outside ramp.

any ramp theory, by covering or cutting into one or more of the faces, the means to lift the stone becomes the very thing that prevents accurate measurement of the pyramid. To address this dilemma, a number of previously ignored construction questions should also be addressed. Therefore, before proceeding, let us list the more obvious difficulties with which the Egyptian architects would have had to contend:

1. A means to build a stepped nucleus while controlling the angle of its faces.
2. A means to raise a true pyramid around an inaccurately built nucleus.
3. A means to reassemble a material delivery system easily between building stages.
4. A means to raise building material from close to the base of a pyramid.
5. A stone-raising system with enough pathways to allow for timely delivery.
6. A means of placing stone into position from outside the courses.
7. A means of raising and setting a several-ton pyramidion and the long roofing stones of the Kings Chamber.
8. A means of blending of pyramid courses into slanted ground.
9. A means of bringing the four faces of a pyramid to meet at a distant point in the sky.
10. A means of abrading the rough casing stone into four smooth faces.

And they would obviously have needed to meet all these difficulties with the technology then available.

CHAPTER 10

GATHERING MATERIAL

Before the nucleus of a pyramid could be erected, great quantities of masonry had to be gathered and transported to the building site. Although some stone, such as the large granite roofing beams above the burial chamber of Cheops, the casing stone on the first course of the Chephren Pyramid, and the first sixteen courses of Mycerinus' pyramids, arrived from distant sources at Aswan, most of the limestone came from nearby quarries on the Giza Plateau. At times the stone was taken from open quarries, as shown by the gridlike area on the northwest side of the Chephren Pyramid. These grooves are mistakenly thought to have been used as water channels for leveling the pyramid site. The enormous quantity of material taken from just this one nearby quarry is best judged by comparing the present surface of the grid to the top of the bluff on the north and west side of the pyramid (**10.1**), a height of at least 18 feet (5.5 m). Signs of a similar grid can be seen peeking through the sand to the northwest of the queen's pyramid of Mycerinus, GIII-c, when viewed from the top.

When discovered in the 19th century by the English investigator J. S. Perring, the Chephren quarry had been protected for millennia by a covering of sand. On being cleared, the site disclosed remains of blocks, probably 3 feet high (0.9 m) and 9 feet square (2.7 m), that were separated by a gridlike network of 2-foot-wide (0.6 m) trenches. At the time of discovery, Perring made a sketch that shows the stone squares with flat smooth surfaces and well-defined edges.[1] The same smooth flat surfaces were observed a hundred years later by Maragioglio and Rinaldi when removing the sand that had once again returned.[2] Deprived of their protective covering, the stone surfaces are no longer smooth and the edges are no longer sharp. As with so many sites in Egypt, deterioration begins shortly after items are exposed to the ravages of people and the smoke of newly introduced industry—the primary reason some tombs are presently refilled with sand when studies are completed.

Figure 10.1. (a) Remains of a quarry for supplying stone and leveling the grade near the northwest corner of Chephren's pyramid (right background). The terrain originally reached the height of the bluff on the left. (b) Remains of a similar grid near the northwest base of the Queens Pyramid of Mycerinus (GIII-c).

Quarrying

Reports of an earlier smooth and level surface at the open quarry of Chephren seem to suggest that stones were quarried in ancient times by a unique procedure, somewhat akin to that of peeling stones, level by level, off the bedrock. For this task, a grid of trenches just wide enough for a stonecutter was used to separate blocks and cut them all to the same approximate depth. Starting from the end rows, each individual block was then split from the bedrock by wedging, using one of the many natural fissures in the bedrock. The wedge probably consisted of a hardwood such as acacia driven between two sheets of copper. On

Figure 10.2. The gridwork at Chephren suggests a procedure unique to open quarries. (a) First, a grid of trenches was first cut to the same approximate depth. (b) Blocks were then split from the bedrock and hauled away. (c) To prepare for the next layer, the remaining rough surface was made smooth by dragging large blocks over a layer of quartz sand.

removal of the split blocks, a thin layer of quartz sand was spread on the roughened surface, which was smoothed by dragging a large flat block over the bedrock (**10.2**). With the surface thus abraded to a smooth, level plane, trenches would be cut to the depth of another layer of stone with a long-handled adze or hard stone pick, and the entire process was repeated.[3] Wedged from the bedrock and split into smaller sizes, the blocks would require little additional dressing when placed in the nucleus smooth face down.

The fault lines that permitted the blocks to be parted from the bedrock are the result of a natural process occurring when the sedimentary rock was formed. Limestone is a soft calcite rock of many varieties, having colors that vary from gray to white according to its purity. Formed mostly by minute forms of marine life, some samples still show the remains of hard parts of ancient plants or animals. The chief characteristic of limestone is the layers of which it is composed, the top of one layer marking the bottom of another (**10.3**). As described by 19th-century mining engineer Halbert Powers Gillette:

> All rocks are more or less split up along vertical or nearly vertical planes, termed joints, which greatly assist in the quarrying. Joints are the result of stress, due to shrinkage of the earth's crust upon cooling. The shrinkage has produced great compression in some places and tension in others, resulting in cracking of the rock masses at more or less regular intervals. In limestone and in close grained shales the joints are often regular but so close as to be invisible until revealed by stress or weathering. . . . In sedimentary rocks there are generally two sets of joints running approximately at right angles, known as the dip-joints and the strike-joints. The "dip" of the rock is the angle that its bedding planes make with a horizontal plane. The "strike" is the line of intersection between an inclined plane and a hor-

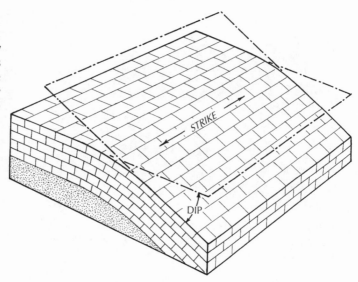

Figure 10.3. Sedimentary rocks generally have two sets of joints, dip joints and strike joints, running approximately at right angles. The dip of the rock is the angle that its bedding planes make with a horizontal plane. The strike is the line of intersection between the inclined plane and a horizontal plane. Together with other stresses, such as shrinkage of the earth's crust upon cooling, nature produced regular blocks of limestone practically loose on all six sides.

izontal plane; thus, if a sheet of cardboard be held at an incline in a basin of water, the line of the water surface along the face of the cardboard is the "strike." Since a quarry is usually worked to the dip of the rock, the strike joint, or "backs," form clean cut faces in front of the workmen as they advance; while the dip-joints, or "cutters," form the side faces of the benches in a quarry.[4]

Not only did nature produce regular blocks of limestone practically loose on all six sides, but according to the plane of the bedrock, knowledgeable quarrymen were often able to select the thickness of a layer to suit any particular need. Although it appears solid and massive, limestone is easily split by wedging, thus giving Egyptian quarrymen less difficulty than one might imagine. Still, it must have been brutal. One need only spend several days walking the limestone quarries of Zawiyet el-Amwat (Zawiyet Sultan), an area east of the Nile near the town of Minya, to realize how exhausting it must have been to work under the hot Egyptian sun. Whether credit is given to the workers for their perseverance or to their taskmasters, these well-worked locations show signs of quarrying by trenching in open and underground areas, following the limestone beds (**10.4**).

Contrary to the open quarries, which display row on row of blocks separated by trenches large enough to hold a man, evidence of underground quarrying in Egypt indicates that stone was removed in a steplike fashion. Except for the difference in tools, soft stone blocks were quarried long ago as they are today, by cutting great cavernous openings ever deeper into the side of a mountain and supporting the overhead mass with columns or walls left at spaced intervals. With the massive machinery of today, 25-ton blocks can more easily be extracted using a method called broaching. With this device, the vertical face of a stone block is outlined by a series of closely spaced holes drilled to the back plane of the block being removed. The block is set free by joining the separate holes with web-cutters and parting it at the back by pneumatic wedging.[5] Egyptian quarrying was more labor intensive.

Figure 10.4. (a) At Zawiyet el-Amwat, stone was taken by trenching in open quarries (foreground). Stone was also taken by cutting into the side of a rock face (background). (b) The narrow grid trenches are well over the height of a man.

Remains in the area of el-Babein and el-Siririya, also near Minya, show that roughly rectangular blocks were instead parted from the bedrock by being outlined with sizable shafts. Quarrymen would begin the procedure by driving a horizontal corridor along the top of the limestone, just high enough for a stonecutter to squat. From this awkward position he would cut into the bedrock with a stone that was hafted or handheld and struck with a mallet—an unenviable task. Accordingly, the tool would leave a surface dotted with impact points, or with a series of parallel and crosscut grooves. The horizontal corridor would be cut deep enough into the stone to allow a column to be isolated by sinking vertical trenches down its sides and back (**10.5**). The natural fissures in the column would allow layers of limestone blocks to be wedged off from the top down and tumbled down to a waiting transport crew. Continuing down layer by layer until ground level, adjacent

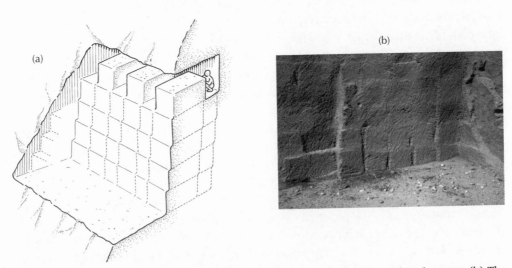

Figure 10.5. (a) Method of isolating columns to extract blocks from an enclosed quarry. (b) The signs of blocks removed from a quarry at el-Siririya.

columns would be attacked from the top in the same manner. Often footholds cut to support the workmen are found on a vertical face, others having been removed with the quarried blocks. Signs of wedges used to separate the blocks are found only on the lowest part of a face, the previous marks having been removed with the block.[6]

Cutting Stone

Judging from the rising joints found in various structures, Egyptians had little difficulty in cutting limestone with copper tools. Evidence of overcuts left on the courses suggests that they were able to cut blocks with a short, single-handed saw having a curved bottom and a blade width of about 0.2 of an inch (0.5 cm).[7] To work the surface with copper chisels, any of three basic strokes could have been used. The "carving stroke" makes shallow cuts on the surface when used at a low angle, producing stone shavings that might be compared to that of a wood plane. Used at an angle of about 45 degrees, the "mason's stroke" allows the chisel to cut deeper into the stone, leaving a series of sawtooth marks on the surface. When executed with light blows, the purpose of the "vertical stroke" is to stun the surface of the stone, breaking down its crystalline structure and permitting it to be more easily reduced with an abrasive.[8] The latter method seems ideally suited for abrading hieroglyphs in the hard stone faces of granite or basalt.

Although limestone was the principal building stone of the Old Kingdom, granite, an igneous rock, was sometimes used. While difficult to work due to its hardness, it had three natural cleavage lines almost at right angles, rift, grain, and head, which together formed stone into natural cubes. The rift can be seen with an experienced eye and is a comparatively easy joint to split; the grain splits with less ease and the head with much more difficulty.[9] Rock in its natural setting has established a temporary equilibrium with the external forces of erosion and weathering. For steep rock slopes to achieve the same equilibrium, they tend to degrade to a gentler angle.[10]

While some quarrying of granite may also have occurred, most of the stone used during the Pyramid Age was obtained by gathering loose blocks from what the German investigator Joseph Röder called a "rock sea," formed by nature's quest for equilibrium. The boulders parted naturally from their bed by "woolsack deterioration," a process caused by the effects of chemical and spheroidal weathering that penetrates deeply into the fractures of the granite bed. The resulting stone cubes often assume spheroidal shapes because the rate of attack on the corners is twice that of the sides.[11] As seen at Aswan and vicinity, the rock bed breaks apart in almost parallel layers, bringing round, flat, square, and beam-shaped blocks sliding down the face of the slope one upon the other like woolsacks or cheese balls (**10.6**).

The process of dressing granite was time-consuming and therefore restricted to special situations where the hardness of the stone, or its ability to span a great distance or support a great weight, was required. To produce granite casing, workers would start with boulders closest to their needs and shape them with dolerite balls, a natural tough stone found in the eastern desert valleys. Untold numbers of these handheld balls, ranging from 5 to 12 inches (13–30 cm) in diameter and weighing about 12 pounds (5.5 kg) on average, can still be found in the quarries of Aswan and in building sites all over Egypt. By use of

Figure 10.6. During the Old Kingdom granite casing was made from loose boulders formed at Aswan and vicinity by a natural process called "woolsack deterioration."

the dolerite hammer stone on a small area, Engelbach ran a trial in the trench at the unfinished obelisk at Aswan. He estimated that the ancient stoneworkers could have extracted 0.315 inches (8 mm) of granite every hour by pounding (**10.7**).[12]

In the Old Kingdom soft stone was sawn and chiseled with copper tools or drilled with spearlike points of flint rotated by a device consisting of an eccentric handle attached to

Figure 10.7. (a) Impact areas made by dolerite balls on the unfinished obelisk at Aswan. Recent field tests using (b) hafted and (c) handheld dolerite balls.

Figure 10.8. Interior of a stone vase drilled by a weighted device turned with an eccentric handle.

a weighted shaft (**10.8**).[13] Yet, while copper or bronze saws can be used to cut limestone, they cannot cut hard stones such as granite. Still, examples of such use have been found on the granite sarcophagus of Cheops, where a cut was made with a blade that, considering the size of the object, must have been at least 8 feet (2.4 m) long. Saw cuts have also been discovered on the basalt triads of King Mycerinus, where parallel, well-defined scorings on the back of the statues indicate a penetration of 0.125 inches (3 mm) with each stroke of the saw blade. Being too soft to cut hard stone, the metal blades must have had corundum, jewels, or even bits of diamond inserted in their edges.[14] Amazingly, even before historic Egypt, the hardest of stones could somehow be sawn and drilled with the linear strokes of a blade or the rotary motion of a drill.

Copper or bronze blades may simply have been used as carriers by which an abrasive such as sand, emery, or diamond dust was rubbed against the stone. Working along these lines, Deneys Stocks has experimentally cut soft stone with flint chisels and hard stone with dry granules of quartz sand carried by copper tools.[15] As the sharp cutting angles of the grains of quartz become worn, a new charge is placed in the kerf. Roger Hopkins, an American stonemason, has demonstrated the same ability with a two-handled bronze saw having a blade 0.250 of an inch (6 mm) thick with a flat cutting edge, the handles being wooden rods placed crosswise in holes on opposite ends. Finding that quartz sand cuts faster with the addition of water, Hopkins tilted the granite block slightly, put the slurry upgrade, and let it flow in to recharge the kerf whenever the blade was lifted. Driven by a tube of bronze, the same slurry was used to drill holes in granite or to polish its surface after shaping with dolerite pounders[16] (**10.9**).

Tubular copper or bronze drills were invariably used for hollowing out granite coffers. The process was to drill row upon row of tangential holes to the required depth and break down the intervening pieces and cores. The bottoms of some unfinished coffers can still be seen with the remains of broken off core stubs. Varying in diameter from 0.250 of an inch to an astonishing 18 inches (0.6–46 cm) the tubular drills seem to have had corundum or bits of jewels embedded in the circular cutting edge and on parts of their vertical surfaces. According to Petrie, enormous pressure was needed to produce the spiral penetration as the drill was rotated—perhaps one or two tons upon a drill of 4-inch (10 cm) diameter.[17] By this method, Egyptians were able to produce extensive cavities in the hardest of stone with a minimum of labor.

(a)

(b)

(c)

(d)

Figure 10.9. (a) Granite worked with a two-handed toothless bronze blade that acts as a carrier for a slurry of sand. (b) Cut made by the blade. (c) Brace and bronze tube using the same slurry to core granite. (d) Shallow cut made by the tube.

Leonard Gorelick and John Gwinnett found holes drilled in the ends of a granite sarcophagus lid using a tool that left closely spaced, well-defined spiral incisions.[18] On coating the holes with liquid silicone that hardened into a plastomeric substance, they were able to reproduce faithfully the marks of the cutting tool. Examining the marks under an electron microscope, the investigators experimentally attempted to duplicate the incisions found in the stone. The results showed that while quartz sand can abrade granite, it does not leave the same indentations as were shown by the ancient stone samples. However, when loose particles of emery were used in a slurry of water, or better yet, in olive oil, they exactly matched the ancient cuts.[19]

Much of the hard stone in Egypt was worked by bruising it into small projecting segments that could be easily broken away. For example, when the red quartzite in the quarry

Figure 10.10. At Mycerinus, the granite casing was probably brought to a plane by pecking it with a pointed hammer stone mounted to a springy flexible haft.

of Gebel el-Ahmar was found to be too hard for dolerite balls, Egyptian quarrymen used a series of 2-inch-deep (5 cm), closely spaced holes with a pick or dolerite chisel struck by a wooden mallet. The space between the holes was further reduced until the remaining ridges were small enough to be broken off with dolerite pounders.[20] This technique was also found in soft stone areas near the Sphinx. Working from the top down, the rock would be channeled into isolated humps with a copper chisel and bruised off with a heavy stone hammer. When found, the hammer stone still bore flecks of ancient copper.[21] The granite casing at the pyramid of Chephren also shows examples of stone bruised into ever smaller segments. The irregular top surface of each block was brought to a flat plane by being repeatedly pecked out with a pointed hammer stone, probably mounted on a springy wooden haft (**10.10**). Used with a slight wrist motion, it would cause the point, backed by a massive head, to bruise the surface with the springlike motion of a woodpecker. Slender, flexible hafts like these would enable repeated blows to be made with little effort and great control.

Until recently in Asia and Africa, to help ease the effort of pounding, stone was softened with fire. Its effects are also seen at the unfinished obelisk at Aswan, where Engelbach reports that burned granite could be picked up almost anywhere, and at Mastaba 17, where robbers used fire to enter the burial chamber.[22] In 19th-century India, a line of fire was placed in a groove cut a couple of inches deep, and water was dashed from pots all along the line after the ashes were swept away. Often, this was aided by beating along the intended line of fracture with heavy stones. In this way, blocks 6 feet square on a side (1.8 m) and upward of 80 feet (24 m) long were removed.[23] When water is poured on granite already heated enough to cause the stone crystals to split along natural cleavage lines, the granite becomes so crumbled that it can almost be broken away with the fingers. Since Roman times granite has been split with iron wedges that are flanked by two feathers placed in a series of closely spaced holes—the feathers conforming on the outside to the shape of the hole and on the inside to shape of the wedge. Pounding the wedges in sequence back and forth into the lines of holes causes the feathers to expand and the stone to fracture and part. This ancient method of cutting granite has been updated by the use of a flame torch, which is played on the surface, causing the stone to fracture and fly off in fragments (**10.11**).

(a)

(b)

Figure 10.11. (a) To split off a section of granite, feathers and wedges are inserted into a line of holes. (b) A flame torch is used to remove vertical grooves left by the drilled holes.

Moderate or light blows are easier to control and less tiring to workers when an entire day is spent cutting stone. Nevertheless, if the cutting tools do not help absorb the impact of the blows, the blows can cause a numbing effect to the arms. To avoid this problem, sculptors today use chisels with hard tempered points and soft iron shafts. When struck with an iron mallet, the top of the shaft absorbs some of the blow by peening over and flaking off—a process that also continually shortens the chisel. Speaking as a sculptor, this seemingly small and insignificant cushioning effect permits a full day of work without tiring. The same results can be seen as Egyptian mallets are bruised into an hourglass shape, or where both the dolerite hammer stone and the object being worked absorb impact by losing part of their surface material. When cutting stone, the built-up detritus should be brushed or blown off the impact area to permit the tools to cut effectively.

Although this is not generally known, freshly quarried stone is easier to cut than is stone that has been lying about for a time. Indeed, the easiest stone to shape, comparatively speaking, is that which is still attached to the bedrock.[24] This is due to large amounts of connate water contained in the "surface zone," the crust of the earth, extending to a depth of up to several tens of kilometers deep.[25] This "quarry sap" is present in all stone to varying degrees, but limestone and sandstone contain considerably more than do igneous rocks. Yet even granite becomes harder to fabricate if parted from the bedrock and permitted to overdry.[26] The probable reason is that quarry water contains in solution considerable cementing material, which, deposited when the water evaporates, firmly binds the particles together.[27] While a block parted from its bedrock will retain moisture for some time before this occurs, regardless of when the stone is carved, its durability will remain the same. Although it is an advantage to have water present when carving, it does not remain beneficial. Indeed, when set in place, stone should always be laid on its natural bed to prevent the entry of rainwater and the impurities it may carry—the major agent in the decay of stone.[28]

Transportation of Stone

Whenever animals have been available for heavy work, efforts have been made for their employment. The ancient Egyptians were no exception. Scenes from the 12th Dynasty tomb of Nakht at el-Lisht show oxen pulling a plow that is roped to wooden sticks tied across their horns.[29] An 18th Dynasty scene at the Ma'sara quarries shows them dragging a loaded sledge roped to their neck collars (**10.12**).[30] While evidence shows that the Egyptians made use of draft animals, the means by which animals were harnessed meant that they were not employed to their full capability.

Although the ox or bullock (a castrated male bovine) is larger and probably five times stronger than a man, the combined strength of multiple animals is needed for moving heavy loads. However, while large groups of people can easily be made to pull in response to a signal, such coordination is more difficult with teams of animals. This changed with the introduction, probably by the Romans, of the yoke, a device that is to oxen what rope is to men. Taking advantage of the prominent withers of the animal, people devised a crossbar fashioned with two U-shaped pieces made to encircle the necks of each pair of beasts (**10.13**). The center of the yoke was then pivotally attached to the tongue of a wagon or some such conveyance. This arrangement permitted the combined efforts of multiple animals to pull heavy weights, even if efforts of the individual animal were uncoordinated. The advantage of this invention is shown by the long trains of yoked oxen used to haul 50-ton loads on wheeled carts in the marble quarries of 19th-century Carrara.[31] Although

Figure 10.12. (a) Scene from the 12th Dynasty tomb of Nakht, which shows oxen pulling a plow roped to wooden sticks tied across their horns. (b) Scene from Ma'sara quarries shows oxen dragging a sledge by rope tied around their necks.

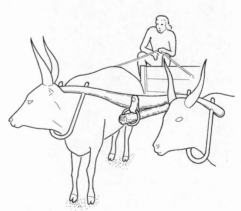

Figure 10.13. A yoke can tie paired oxen to a conveyance, greatly increasing their pulling power.

oxen were later replaced by horses, which were stronger and pulled at a faster rate, oxen remain superior draft animals on rough ground or mud.[32]

In ancient Egypt most heavy hauling seems to have been done by people rather than draft animals—they were more readily available and cheaper. Eating the same kind of food, as they probably did in Egypt, five men could survive on the amount needed for a single ox. Besides, men can do many things over a greater time because they are more adaptable and live longer (the working life of an ox is only about a decade).[33] Men can lift and deposit loads and can navigate terrain that would be impossible by other means. More important, men can be controlled so that at the beat of a chant, they can bring a thousand arms to bear at exactly the same moment. Making use of this force, the Egyptians were able to transport stones of immense weight over great distances—a skill no doubt acquired by years of experience with smaller blocks.

In Egypt as elsewhere, land transport started modestly with human portage. The earliest beasts of burden were women, a choice presumably justified on the grounds that the male had to be unencumbered to protect his family.[34] However, the drudgery of carrying burdens was not restricted to the female; men were generally used when loads became too heavy. The load limit was what the human back could bear; though difficult to comprehend in the industrial world, burdens like that of a porter in Korea as late as 1945 (**10.14**) may still be typical in much of the Third World. The porter is shown holding the wooden legs of a tripod that can be quickly assembled to support the load when he needs a rest.

At times the size of the weights carried was startling. Among the feats of Asian porters is the trekking of 360-pound (163 kg) loads of tea to distant markets over the mountainous terrain of the Sino-Tibetan border region.[35] To aid in the task, simple devices were developed, such as tumplines to help distribute the load between the forehead and the back or a yoke carried across the shoulders having burdens at each end.[36] A pole could support a heavy burden between two porters, and for heavier weights the hand-barrow was a 10-foot-long (3 m) open platform probably carried by four men.[37] In India and elsewhere, great weights supported by of hundreds of porters were moved for several miles on

Figure 10.14. Typical of loads carried in Korea, 1945.

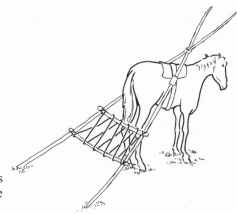

Figure 10.15. A travois is a pole device that supports a load in its center while being dragged along the ground, thus greatly reducing the weight.

cribwork of crisscrossed bamboo or logs.[38] Even today, at the Italian feast in Brooklyn for the patron saint Paulinus, 120 men carry a platform holding an 8,000-pound (3,629 kg) tower and a 14-piece brass band. The porters are choreographed into movements called the dancing of the giglio, during which the platform is raised, lowered, rotated, and even coaxed into a two-step.[39]

Although loads such as this may still be carried ceremonially, easier ways of moving weights were used from earliest times. This may be seen in the universal appeal of the travois and sled—vehicles that are serviceable over snow, steppes, rocky tracts, and deserts.[40] A travois is a pole-like device that supports a load at its center while being dragged along the ground, thus greatly reducing the weight being carried. It has taken in many forms. In the cattle regions of Africa a Y-shaped device is cut from the fork of a tree and dragged by oxen with rope from the stump, the branches used as runners; among the natives of North America, the travois took the form of a V-shaped device mounted to the back of a dog or a horse (**10.15**).[41]

Unlike the travois, which supports only part of the load, the sledge, which bears the entire burden on two runners, is so efficient that it has remained unaltered for millennia. Although the runners may vary from whalebone used in arctic dog sleds to the thick wooden beams of the Egyptian sledge, both forms serve to reduce frictional contact with the ground and to raise the platform above the uneven terrain. The low profile means this vehicle also has the advantage of being easily loaded—often blocks of stone can simply be tumbled onto it. Of the three Egyptian sledges found almost intact, one uncovered at Dahshur and now in the Egyptian Museum is a 14-foot-long (4.25 m) sledge used to carry a royal barge in the 12th Dynasty (**10.16a**). Sturdily built, its runners are joined by cross members having dovetail or mortise and tenon joints reinforced with pegs, one such cross-bar in front (now missing) having been attached to a rope by which the sledge was pulled forward. The many slots located on the sledge are intended to receive woven straps for securing the cargo. The front of each runner is upwardly curved to help the sledge over-ride small obstacles. On many sledges the back of the runners is cut at an angle to allow the introduction of a lever to help move the sledge forward.[42]

Among the several quarries in the Sahara region of Gebel el-Asr, a location 40 miles (65 km) to the northwest of Abu Simbel, is one from which stone for several life-size diorite

(a)

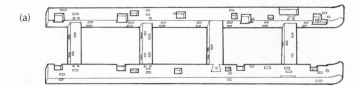

(b)

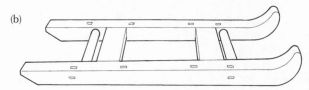

Figure 10.16. (a) A 12th Dynasty Egyptian sledge from Dahshur, used to carry a royal barge. (b) Sledge with back of runners angled to receive the point of a lever.

statues of Chephren was derived. Two stone-built loading docks found at the quarry are about 40 inches (1 m) high in front and taper back about 29 feet (9 m) to ground level. Perpendicular to the front of the dock are two parallel tracks lined with a hard marly substance, presumably made for the runners of sledges. The hoof print of a probable equid was also found nearby. The route that leads from Gebel el-Asr to the Nile, about 50 miles (80 km) away, is the longest surviving Egyptian quarry road.[43]

Despite the absence of wheeled vehicles, weights were brought from distant locations under the most trying conditions. Whether such transport was motivated by god, king, or clan, cultures advanced enough to organize have shown that if a block of stone could be moved an inch, with patience and effort it could be moved a mile. Examples of such efforts are seen around the world: the fortress of Sacsayhuaman near Cuzco not only contains several 200 ton-blocks, but they were placed together with amazingly close rising joints; a menhir at Locmariaquer in France, now broken, had an estimated weight of 350 tons when erected; the natives of Easter Island carved, transported, and erected volcanic rock statues of up to 80 tons; in addition to the 80 bluestones taken 124 miles (200 km) from Pembrokeshire to Stonehenge, each several tons in weight, the site contains 30-ton trilithons brought from a distance of 18 miles (30 km). The Romans set blocks of over 750 tons in the wall of the Temple of Jupiter at Baalbek in Lebanon. In an amazing feat of construction, these blocks, almost 70 feet long, 13 feet high, and 10 feet thick (21 × 4 × 3m), were transported and raised to a height of 26 feet (8 m) in order to rest upon the lower courses of regular-sized stonework. An even larger block of 1,000 tons remains hewn in the quarry.

The aforementioned stone-handling feats, commonplace for the ancient Egyptians, speak of a strong central authority in a display of power. For example, the colossi of Memnon, each estimated to weigh 700 tons, were transported overland to the plain of Thebes from Gebel el-Ahmar, a distance of 435 miles (700 km) (**10.17**). As shown by two 350-ton, 97-foot (29.5 m) obelisks of Queen Hatshepsut, monoliths were also moved aboard ships. These two monuments were not only transported but, arriving at their destination, were stood on end.[44] To give an example of the extraordinary effort involved to move such monoliths overland, some 2,000 men labored for three years to drag a monument weighing 580 tons from Aswan to Sais in the Nile Delta, virtually the entire length of Egypt.[45]

(a)

(b)

(c)

Figure 10.17. (a) The colossi of Memnon, each estimated to weigh 700 tons. (b) One of two 350-ton obelisks of Queen Hatshepsut, at Karnak. (c) The largest work ever attempted, the unfinished obelisk at Aswan would weigh 1,168 tons if completed.

The largest work ever attempted by any ancient culture seems to be the 137-foot (42 m) obelisk with a base almost 14 feet (4 m) square at Aswan. This monstrous stone, illustrated in figure 10.17(**c**), would have weighed 1,168 tons if completed; it was carved on three sides and abandoned in the quarry due to several fault lines. The task would never have been attempted were the Egyptians not confident that it could be moved and stood upright.[46] Indeed, they obviously succeeded in raising the now fallen statue of almost equivalent weight, the 1,000-ton colossus of Ramesses II, and this was possibly not their largest successful endeavor—fragments found at Tanis indicate the existence of four colossi with possibly greater weights.[47] Clearly, the increasing size of such monuments indicate an ongoing need of each king to overshadow the works of his predecessors.

The largest Egyptian monolithic monuments came from the New Kingdom, long after the pyramids were erected. Instead of displaying power with large carved objects, earlier kings of the Old Kingdom did it with pyramids—speed of placement being more important than the size of the stone. Nevertheless, large blocks were used at that time for special building needs: the 56 granite blocks, each of 54 tons, raised to great heights and used to roof Cheops' burial chamber; the enormous limestone blocks placed in the foundation platform of the Chephren Pyramid and in the temple wall of Mycerinus, some reaching 200 tons. The limestone, however, came from nearby quarries on the plateau.

Although a scene from the 5th Dynasty depicts wheels on a scaling ladder (**10.18**), evidence to date indicates the sledge as the only means of land transport for moving stone in the Old Kingdom. Perhaps, being a young technology, the wheel was not yet able to support the heavy weights required by the Egyptians—especially when mounted on a wooden axle. Indeed, wheeled conveyances are not known to have come into use in Egypt until the Second Intermediate Period (1640–1532 BCE), when the Hyksos introduced chariots. Regardless of their probable benefits, a recent development may help put the possible use of wheeled vehicles in perspective. An American company has just announced development of the largest truck in the world, a new mining dump truck roughly the size of a four-story brownstone house. Powered by a 3,400-horsepower engine and running on six tires, each nearly 13 feet tall and 5 feet wide, it has a 360-ton payload capacity. While

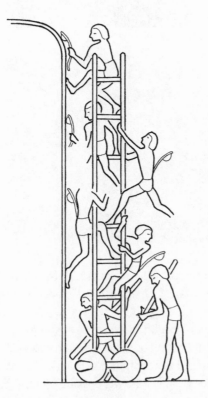

Figure 10.18. The scaling ladder with wheels from a 5th Dynasty tomb at Saqqara is the only representation of a wheel known in the Old Kingdom.

it is claimed that the bed of this truck can haul four blue whales, 217 taxicabs, or 1,200 grand pianos, it could not have transported the 500-ton obelisk quarried in Aswan, taken to Thebes, and erected by Tuthmosis IV.[48] In an age before mechanization, the obelisk was later lowered and transported, first to Alexandria and then to Rome, where it now stands in St. Peter's Square (**1.17**).

Sledges

The little evidence that exists to explain the method of transport for large stones is seen on Egyptian reliefs from a later time. But for two scenes showing ox-driven sledges with heavy building blocks, most show statues of the deceased, some probably made of wood, being transported to the necropolis.[49] During transport, a figure is usually shown pouring liquid from a vase in front of the runners to serve as a lubricant (**10.19**). Use in front of sledges carrying lightweight wooden statues may suggest that the purpose of the liquid was to serve as part of a purification ritual. However, in Egypt practice and ritual have often gone hand in hand, suggesting that the liquid probably also had a practical purpose. This is shown by the 58-ton colossus of Djehutihotep from the 18th Dynasty, the single example of a truly large stone sculpture depicted in transport (**10.20**). Standing on the massive knee of the statue is an overseer, who, according to the accompanying text, is beating time and crying praises to the king. The sledge is pulled by four hawsers and a total of 172 men on a roadway, probably made of stone chips reinforced either by wooden

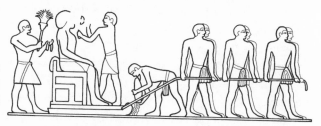

Figure 10.19. Scene from the tomb of Ti showing liquid poured from a vase to serve as a lubricant during transport of a statue.

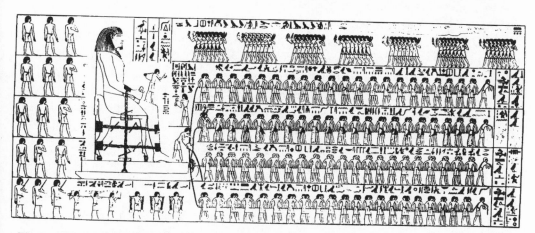

Figure 10.20. The single example of a large Egyptian stone sculpture in transport is the 58-ton colossus from a wall painting in the 18th Dynasty tomb of Djehutihotep.

Figure 10.21. Scene from the 18th Dynasty tomb of Maiherperi, which shows every means of transport then known, all employed to ensure safe passage of the deceased to the netherworld.

crossbeams or by a track of wood. It may also have been topped with silt to provide a slick surface, when wet, over which to pull the load. Filled with men, the scene shows some carrying sleepers, short beams of wood like railroad ties, perhaps to lay crosswise under the runners, as others carry additional vases of liquid lubricants.[50]

Rollers

Of all the evidence, none shows rollers being used to move weights except a scene from the 18th Dynasty tomb of Maiherperi, which depicts a funerary bark mounted on a sledge containing a naos (an enclosed shrine holding a statue) (**10.21**). However, this scene seems more symbolic than practical. Not only is the bark itself propelled by oars, but the sledge, which is supported on rollers, is shown being pulled by both men and oxen. The obvious emphasis of this improbable scene is to show every possible means of transport to insure safe passage of the deceased to the netherworld.[51] The Egyptians almost certainly made use of rollers, perhaps even entire tree trunks, for hauling. However, while rollers may be ideal for moving weights over short distances, they present serious difficulties to the movers in tight places. I have found problems with them when moving low tonnage blocks, both in Egypt and as a practicing sculptor, and others with experience in greater tonnage have likewise noted difficulties.

At Bougon, France, in a modern test of moving heavy weights, a team of men led by J.-P. Mohen pulled a 32-ton block a distance of 131 feet (40 m) over comparatively flat terrain. The block was rolled on closely spaced oak tree trunks, each 16 inches (40 cm) in diameter. These, in turn, were supported on a parallel track of oak beams laid end to end. As the block advanced, the distance was extended by bringing the rollers and tracks from the rear to the front. The initial movement of the block took the efforts of 230 men on four ropes as others pushed from behind with levers; once the block was in motion, only 170 men were required. Although the task showed that large stones could be moved successfully by groups of men, the skewing rollers caused the block to stray off course and required constant readjustment with a 33-foot (10 m) lever and 20 men.[52]

Much greater in weight are the two colossal statues of Ramesses found in Memphis and presented to Great Britain on condition that they be removed. The larger of the two, a 100-ton limestone monolith, was buried face down at an angle 17 feet below ground. After unsuccessful attempts and taunts by the press directed at the British Army then occupying the land, Major Arthur H. Bagnold, of the Royal Engineers, was sent to accomplish the task in 1887. Placing a platform of crossed sleepers under the statue, and using wedges and hydraulic jacks supported on timber blocks, he was able to turn the statue face up and raise it to ground level. The task completed, the smaller 60-ton pink granite statue of the king found nearby was also raised and moved some 400 feet away. As the colossus was pulled up a 60-foot incline with a capstan, the oak rollers, riding on rails, were crushed under the great weight. The movement was successfully completed by substituting greased skids for the rollers. In summing up, Bagnold states, "In hauling, whether up hill, down hill, or on the level, I think that greased skidding is superior to rollers, especially on soft ground."[53]

A bas-relief in the British Museum shows the method used for transporting the winged statues of the Assyrian king Sennacherib, more than 2,600 years ago (**10.22**). The statues, estimated at 45 tons, were transported on sledges pulled by four lines of men harnessed to hawsers, each thick as a man's arm. The runners of the sledge are shown to be moving on short pieces of wood. A past keeper in the Science Museum in London, C. Davison, cites several reasons why these could not have been rollers: while most have the regular shape of rollers, some scenes show them with the unmistakable outline of tree limbs; instead of being perpendicular to the sled runners, they are haphazardly scattered on the ground; unless the ground is very hard, wood under pressure would sink beneath the surface, making rollers inoperable; and use of rollers would have been dangerous when lowering the statue down the steep incline to the river. Instead, according to Davison, the short pieces of wood are actually sleepers used to reduce friction with the ground or to overcome small obstacles in the road.[54]

Showing the same concerns as Davison, Fitchen, an investigator of ancient technology, says:

Figure 10.22. A 2,600-year-old scene shows the transport of the winged statues of the Assyrian king Sennacherib. Estimated at 45 tons in weight, the statues were held on sledges that were pulled by four lines of men harnessed to hawsers, each as thick as a man's arm.

The fibrous materials of the Egyptians' hauling cables and ropes, of uneven quality at best, dried out and became brittle in the unremitting heat of the sun. Breaking without warning, the ropes would have released the ponderous blocks from all control if rollers had been inserted under them. Moreover, constantly retrieved from behind, and repositioned in front of the sledge as it moves along, the rollers could become skewed unpredictably despite the most careful attention to their placement and alignment. Again, unless the tracks under the rollers were kept absolutely and solidly level, without the slightest dip or rise, the great weight of the block could cause it to swerve and lunge about in response to gravity. Roller-less sledges prevented any of these mishaps and assured the haulers' constant control over the process of movement.[55]

Chevrier's Transport Experiment

The absence of rollers or sleepers in Egyptian transport scenes may be explained by an experiment French archaeologist Henri Chevrier conducted with a heavily weighted sledge. Having establishing a level roadway, he had it coated by a layer of mud packed down by the tread of human feet. At a signal, 50 men on two ropes energetically pulled the sledge holding a 5-ton block on the lightly wetted surface. Surprisingly, the heavily laden sledge moved forward so easily that all the men fell down—the sledge stopping only when it slid to a dry portion of the road. Finding so little friction, Chevrier gradually reduced the number of men until only six were needed to pull the 5-ton load.[56] Reflecting the accuracy of the Egyptian scenes, Chevrier's experiment showed that the sledge could be controlled to follow a given path by wetting the ground only in front of the runners.

Although Chevrier found one or two men enough to pull a sledge carrying one ton on a hard level road made slick with mud, the distance covered by the experiment required only short bursts of energy from the pulling team. To sustain such force on terrain that was not smooth and level would have required the three men per ton of an estimated 58-ton weight shown in the Djehutihotep scene. As the grade increases, walking is difficult enough without having to drag a heavy weight. For example, to haul a ton of weight up a grade of 9 degrees would require the efforts of at least nine men.[57]

Mud and ice surfaces are not the only means of reducing friction. Investigators Bryan Cotterell and Johan Kamminga found in an experiment that baked sweet potatoes mixed with a little water greatly reduced the friction between two wood surfaces.[58] A recent field test in Egypt showed that a sledge with a 2-ton block of stone could be pulled more easily if a wooden track were lined with banana skins (**10.23**). The possibility that Egyptians sometimes used wooden tracks is recorded by Ineni, the superintendent of the building projects of King Tuthmosis I. While giving an account of his great engineering feats, particularly the transport and erection of two great obelisks, he says: "I inspected the erection of two obelisks . . . and built the 'august' boat of 120 cubits in length and 40 cubits in breadth for transporting these obelisks. They came in peace, safety and prosperity, and landed at Karnak. . . . Its track (?) was laid with every pleasant wood."[59]

Due to the scarcity of wood, tree-trunk-sized rollers have not been found in Egypt, presumably having been made into other devices at the end of their useful life as rollers.

Figure 10.23. A recent field test at Aswan in Egypt where a sledge holding a 2-ton block of stone was pulled over a layer of banana skins laid on a wooden track.

To date, the only physical evidence of their existence are the short rollers found near sarcophagi or at the entrances of pyramid corridors—places where the stones could not be pulled by ropes but would have to be pushed into position from behind. The rollers found do not have equal diameters along their lengths; instead, they are slightly thicker at the center than at their rounded ends. One such roller 9 inches (23 cm) long from Deir el-Bahri has a diameter of 2 inches (5 cm) at the ends and three inches (7.5 cm) in the middle. While the convexity may be considered a result of wear, it may also have been intentionally produced so that blocks could be turned more easily while being maneuvered into tight places.[60]

The action of convex rollers is more readily understood if we consider the ease by which a fully loaded barrel can be turned and apply these observations to the roller: When a block is turned on rollers of uniform diameter, it is necessary to point the rollers toward the locus of the radius and to make the turn large enough to permit each roller to move before it goes askew and jams into its companions (**10.24**). The slight side-to-side imbalance

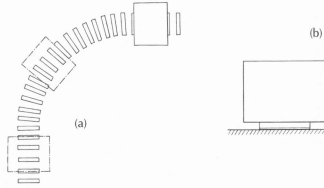

Figure 10.24. (a) Block supported on rollers of uniform diameter. (b) When a block is turned, the rollers should point toward the locus of a radius that is large enough to permit them to move without jamming.

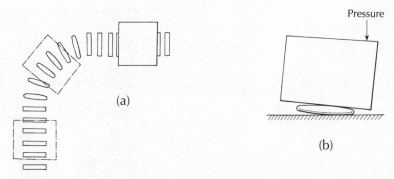

(a)

(b)

Figure 10.25. (a) Block supported on convex rollers. (b) The side-to-side imbalance enables the block to turn in a smaller radius by allowing the rollers to tilt and shift in response to overhead guiding pressures.

of convex rollers would, instead, permit the block to turn in a smaller radius by allowing the rollers to tilt and shift slightly in response to overhead pressures (**10.25**).

The convexity of the small rollers may also explain the true purpose of models of a wooden appliance from foundation deposits of the temple of Queen Hatshepsut at Deir el-Bahri and elsewhere (**10.26**). Petrie suggested that these cradles of wood were a means of raising blocks by alternately adding wedges to each curved end (**10.27**).[61] Instead,

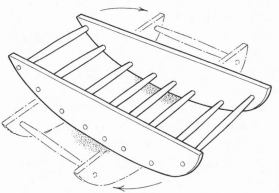

Figure 10.26. Model of a wooden appliance from a foundation deposit in the tomb of Queen Hatshepsut at Deir el-Bahri.

(a)

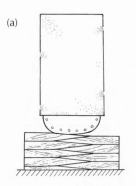

(b)

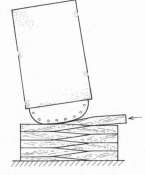

Figure 10.27. (a, b) Petrie suggests that the rocker was a means of raising blocks by alternately adding wedges to each curved end.

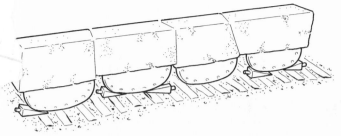

Figure 10.28. Engelbach suggests the rocker as a means to fit oblique blocks on the ground before they were raised to a course on the pyramid.

Engelbach considers them to be a means of support to fit oblique blocks together on the ground before they were raised to a course on the pyramid (**10.28**).[62] While such a cradle may have been employed for both these purposes, it may also have been used to turn blocks around sharp corners and tilt them into position. Interestingly, a block of stone that is difficult to turn while it is lying on a flat surface can readily be turned when imbalanced by having a small square of hardwood placed under its flat bedding face—a practice in common usage among sculptors (**10.29**). Although the weight may distort the small piece of wood, it will remain sufficiently intact to keep the center of the block higher than the edge on which it is resting. By just such means I have single-handedly turned a block of stone weighing about 1.5 tons.

With some experience, and taking advantage of balancing effects, stone handling is not as difficult as many imagine. As the work of the Egyptians shows, all it takes is years of practice and probably the best teaching experience of all—smashed fingers and toes.

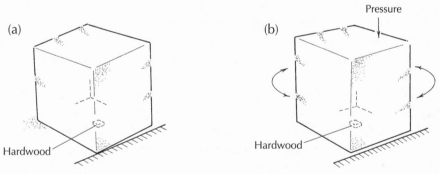

Figure 10.29. (a) A block imbalanced by a small square of hardwood in the center of its flat bedding face may be turned (b) by tipping it off the edge on which it is resting.

CHAPTER 11

BUILDING THE NUCLEUS

Once enough material is brought to the site, the matter of assembling the stones into a pyramidal structure can begin. Construction of this man-made mountain consists of three building stages. The first, which contains a probable 80 percent of the material in the structure, occurs with erection of the nucleus. This building stage functions much like the steel framework of a modern skyscraper; just as each floor of steel provides a framework to raise the structure to greater heights, an analogous means is provided by each tier of the pyramid nucleus. On completion of the nucleus, a fill of masonry and a mantle of casing stones combine to hide the roughly erected set-backs of the nucleus in the same way that a curtain wall or masonry facade hides the supporting steel of a modern building. The similarity ends, however, when the machines and measuring instruments available to modern builders are compared to those of yesteryear. Yet, even with these modern devices, the planning and execution of an average-sized pyramid of solid masonry would prove a greater problem to build today than does the highest of skyscrapers, due to the unusual architectural form of the pyramid and to our complete lack of experience at building with large stone blocks. Not so for the Egyptians. By the time of Cheops' pyramid, generations of improvements and refinements in a gradually evolving building procedure were available to the king.

As already discussed, once the four corners of the base have been found, the fifth point almost 500 feet in the sky must be set with a high degree of accuracy if the pyramid is to attain its required angle. However, to attain symmetry for the pyramid, finding the height of this point is not enough—a vertical axis must also be established that is centrally located relative to the four corners of the base. The builders must then bring the arrises, or corners of the pyramid, to the same point in the sky, seemingly an impossible task when the building method starts with a roughly built structure that does not quite reach the full height of the pyramid. Interestingly, none of these requirements need be met for the nucleus.

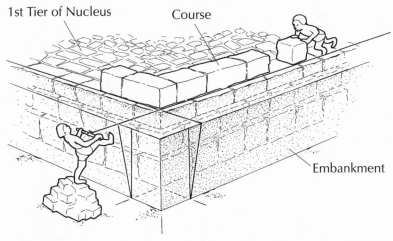

1st Tier of Nucleus

Course

Embankment

Figure 11.1. The facing angle for each tier of the nucleus was made by following angles on the corners of a surrounding embankment. Each course was
laid to a chalkline stretched from one corner to another.

While the primary purpose of the nucleus was to achieve height and mass without
undue pretensions of accuracy, evidence shows that the internal structure was not a simple pile of stone. Indeed, although the individual tiers may not have achieved a high degree
of dimensional accuracy, they were all roughly leveled, squared, and given an outer slope
of about 75 degrees. Doubtless, to achieve this, the nucleus was built with a surrounding
embankment made to rise with each course—the same kind of procedure used for constructing the mud-brick mastabas of Saqqara during the Early Dynastic period (**3.11**). The
75-degree slope for the individual tiers was marked at the corners of the embankment by
a line with its rising angle established, as at Mastaba 17, through use of a grid pattern
(**9.14**). By following the rising angle made on each corner, set-back courses such as those
seen at the Queens Pyramids of Giza were probably made by laying each course to a chalkline stretched from one corner to another (**11.1**).

The base of the nucleus would probably have had its corners aligned to a previously
made layout square. This square would be smaller than the final square of the pyramid to
allow for the additional thickness of packing and casing stone. It would also be marked at
the center of each side and on the diagonal of each corner. From this square, the courses
of the nucleus would be built until they reached a point that the builders deemed sufficiently high for the top of the first tier. The material by which the embankment was made
would then be transferred to the top of the tier and used to form a new embankment
around a second, smaller tier. As the tiers rose, one upon the other, their corners would be
roughly aligned by sighting over a plumb line to a mark on the ground (**11.2**).

While set-back levels provide stages above the ground for workers and material, they
also permit the builders to form a large central core that reaches almost to the height of
the pyramid while staying well within its final outline. In addition to producing a more stable structure, this would allow the large internal mass hidden deep within the pyramid to
be composed of stone that did not have to be cut and fitted with great care, yielding a considerable savings of time and effort. The set-back tiers would also provide the nucleus with

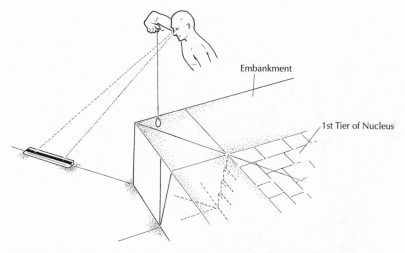

Figure 11.2. The corners of the tiers were roughly aligned by sighting over a diagonal line on the surface of each tier to a mark on the diagonal of the layout square.

deep indents to help interlock the fill of packing stones that would give the structure a more pyramidal shape in the second building stage.

Although it is true that ramps similar to those at Sinki may have been used to raise stone for the lower courses of the nucleus (**11.3**), the lack of evidence for high construction ramps suggests that a different method of raising stones was employed as the structure increased in height. Perhaps the kind of stairways Arnold suggested replaced or were added to ramps on each face of the nucleus. In all likelihood, the stairs were made to rise from one tier to another at an angle of about 52 degrees—the same angle as in the face of the true pyramid.

Made of stone, these stairways, would fit the description of Spell 267 of the Pyramid Texts: "A staircase to heaven is laid for him so that he may mount up to the heaven thereby." Laid at the same angle as the intended pyramid face, the stairs could be left in place and incorporated into the expanding monument when the packing stone was applied. Leaning on the set-back tiers (**11.4**), the stairs would also give the monument an appearance similar to that of the pyramids of Mexico, structures in which the courses were obviously raised by bringing masonry up the four stairways. The stairs at El Castillo in Chichén Itzá rise at an angle of about 45 degrees to provide access to the temple structures at the apex (**11.4**). Rising at an angle of more than 60 degrees, a much steeper flight of stairs is seen at Temple I, a Mayan pyramid in Tikal's Great Plaza.[1] Although it is frightening to contemplate the Mayan builders moving masonry up at so steep an angle, the ascent itself requires no special skills—anyone fairly fit can climb to the temple at the apex.

Used by Egyptian builders, and clearly defined when the pyramid was being built, the stairways are not always obvious to the present-day observer; still, investigators have sometimes commented on their appearance. For example, when studying the surviving part of the casing just under the summit at the pyramid of Chephren, Maragioglio and Rinaldi noted a nucleus formed of regular, clearly marked masonry courses that "formed an actual

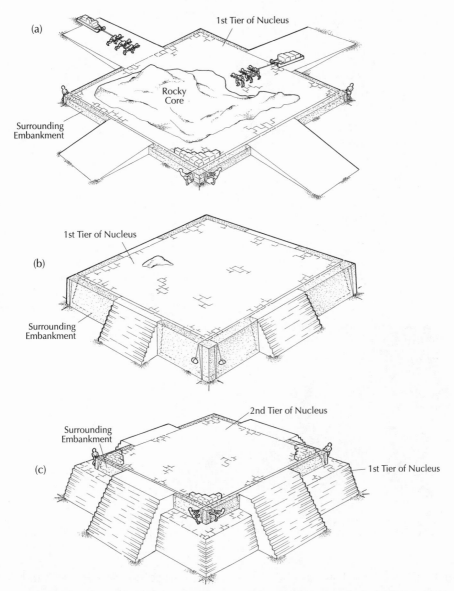

Figure 11.3. Surrounding embankments helped establish angles for each tier. (a) Ramps were used on the lower portions of the nucleus. (b) With increasing height, stairways replaced the ramps. (c) As the stairways rise with the same 52° slope, the embankment from the 1st tier is brought piecemeal to the 2nd tier.

flight of steps." They note that lower down, the steps were harder to distinguish due to the broken remains of the outer fill stone used to complete the pyramidal form.[2] Arnold, who first proposed the use of stairs in the construction of pyramids, discovered at the pyramid of Senwosret I the foundations of a wide, steep staircase that probably reached to its highest sections.[3]

The advantage of a stairway over any form of steep ramp is obvious; besides providing a means of ascent, the stepped surface can be used to support the movement of stone

(a)

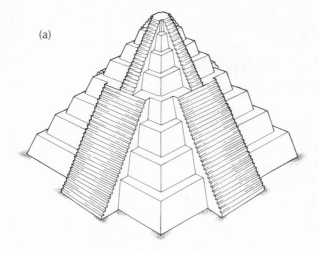

(b)

Figure 11.4. (a) Left in place on the completed nucleus, Egyptian stairways would be similar to (b) El Castillo, a 79-foot Mayan pyramid at Chichén Itzá, Mexico.

in different ways. Small stones and rubble can be passed up the steps by hand; larger stones, moved on two-, four-, or six-man litters, can be rested on the steps during the climb, the overhanging portions supported by rubble or wood. Sledges with runners can be used for smaller blocks; made to span two or more steps, sledges can either be dragged up a few courses at a time or boards made to span several steps can be used as slides over which blocks are pulled—the variations are endless.

While most pyramid masonry consists of stone small enough to be raised in the several ways mentioned, some blocks could have also been dragged behind teams of men pulling sledges up short low ramps in a manner often portrayed in popular conceptions. The method used, no doubt, would depend on the size of the block, the height to be reached, and the portion of the structure being built. With the great mass of small and moderately sized stone raised by the methods mentioned, the larger facing blocks, although more time-consuming to raise, would be only a small percentage of the great mass of stone needed for the nucleus. When all aspects of pyramid building are considered, any building plan that permits stone to be brought from all sides of the pyramid at the same time, and that uses the structure itself as the means of transport instead of requiring massive ramps to reach the heights, outweighs the attractions of previous theories. Yet, given the use of stairways, other means and devices must be employed for blocks too heavy to be lifted physically from step to step, such as those of the internal chambers, the nucleus, and the casing.

Levering

Larger blocks can be pulled by gangs of men assisted by levers, using the steps as fulcrums. Blocks can also be raised by alternately levering up their opposite sides and inserting rubble or wood cribbing in the spaces.[4] This method of levering and cribbing was tried in the course of a pyramid-building experiment for the television show *Nova*, where a 2-ton (1,753 kg) block of limestone was raised 30 inches (76 cm) from one step to another (**11.5**).[5] Although successful at the first try, the inexperienced crew took far too much

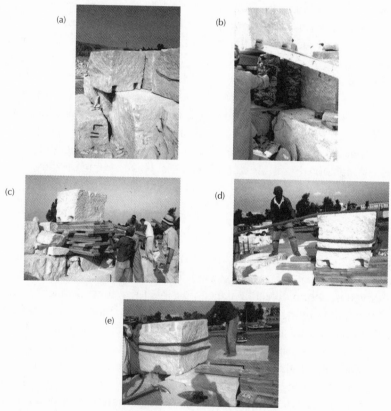

Figure 11.5. The procedure for lifting a 2-ton block of limestone from one step to another. (a) Although the block overhung the step, this did not affect the mechanics of the lift. (b) Used as a fulcrum, the trunk of a palm tree worked well and was easy to handle. (c) Cut for different purpose, the overlong planking caused unnecessary problems. (d) On reaching the required height, a board that overlapped the step kept the cribbing stable as the block was tumbled to its destination. (e) The block successfully placed.

time—an hour and a half—to make it practical. Assuming that experience might reduce the task to the also considerable time of 15 minutes, 15 such stations working simultaneously on the four stairways could supply a block to each course every minute.[6] This method is presently shown as a supplement to a more efficient delivery system that also makes use of levers.

As they bear against a fulcrum, levers work according to a simple formula; the effort, as multiplied by the distance of the force arm to the fulcrum, equals the weight multiplied by the distance of the weight arm from the fulcrum. In other words, 10 pounds of effort exerted on the force arm 10 feet from a fulcrum will raise 100 pounds 1 foot high on the other side (4.5 kg of effort 3m from the fulcrum raises 45 kg by 30 cm). While the gain does not come without cost—a large swing of the force arm will produce only a small swing of its weight arm—without this simple device, there would be no pyramids. Modern levers have become so efficient that a stevedore using a Johnson Bar, a 7-foot-long (2 m) wooden force arm having a wheeled fulcrum and a steel lip as a weight arm, can raise 2.5 tons off the ground 8 inches (20.3 cm). Two men standing on opposite sides can thus roll a 10,000-pound crate to its docking station with these levers.

According to the relationship of weight, effort, and fulcrum, levers are classified as "first kind," "second kind," and "third kind." Levers of the first kind have the fulcrum between the effort and the weight; the second kind has the weight between the fulcrum and the effort; and the third kind has the effort between the weight and the fulcrum (**11.6**).[7] Levers of the first kind, such as those found in the burial chambers of Horemheb and Mastaba 17, were reported to have been cut to a knife edge, a factor that gave the lever its own built-in fulcrum at the point where the angle of the knife edge meets the shaft, as illustrated in figure 12.6(**e**). Its efficiency was shown when a single 6-foot (1.8 m) lever of acacia wood enabled robbers to lift the 3.5-ton (3,175 kg) lid of a sarcophagus in the burial chamber of Mastaba 17, at Meidum. Interestingly, according to Pliny, the strength of acacia beams can be increased if they are first boiled in oil.[8]

Wedges

Nothing more than an inclined plane, the wedge matches the lever in simplicity, yet can perform incredible feats when properly used. This small piece of wood, cut to a shallow angle and driven under an object, makes it possible to lift tons of weight. When multiple wedges are used, their lifting power is enormous. As a sculptor, I had occasion to lift a 3-ton block of marble several inches off a surface for the insertion of rollers (**11.7**). The task was accomplished with surprising ease by use of six wooden wedges, three each on a side of the block. Magically, with each blow of a 3-pound hammer, the wedge was forced farther under the block, raising it off the ground. When so elevated, the block tends to stay in place due to the low angle of the wedge and the distortion of the wood fibers on its surface. Still, the block can easily be lowered by a side-to-side tapping of the wedge, which loosens its hold and permits gravity to do the rest. The most difficult part of the operation is to insert the knife edge of the wedge between the surface of the hard ground and the flat bedding face of the block—a problem sometimes solved with a shallow-draft cut under a lower edge, signs of which can frequently be seen at Egyptian building sites.

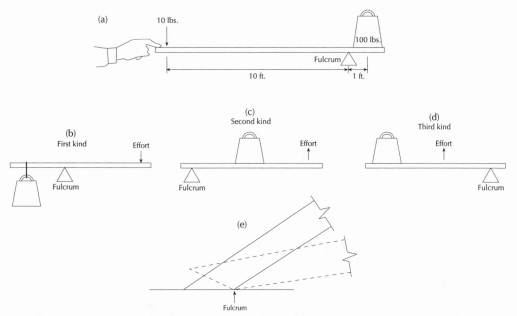

Figure 11.6. (a) Operating a lever: effort, as multiplied by the distance of the force arm to the fulcrum, equals the weight multiplied by the distance of the weight arm to the fulcrum. Levers are classified according to the position of the fulcrum, effort, and weight. (b) Lever of the first kind. (c) Lever of the second kind. (d) Lever of the third kind. (e) Placing the fulcrum close to the lifting end makes the knife-edge lever very efficient.

Figure 11.7. A 3-ton block of marble raised several inches off the surface by hitting wedges on opposite sides of the block with a 3-pound hammer.

A modern example illustrates the amount of weight that can be raised with wedges used in great numbers. When a ship's keel is laid on blocks, its full weight is held on the ground as it grows in size. To launch the completed vessel, a wooden cradle is built in two halves on each side of the ship, one above the other, the top half loosely resting on the bottom half. Thousands of wedges are then driven between the top half, built to take support of the ship, and the bottom half, which rests on greased tracks slanted toward the water. When the wedges force the upper cradle against the hull and take the weight of the ship off the keel blocks, it is transferred onto the bottom cradle, which rests on the greased tracks. The removal of stops on the track allows the cradle and ship to slide into the water together.[9] Clearly, if wedges can be used to raise a modern ship, they could manage the weight required by any pharaonic project.

Rope

Rope was as necessary a device for moving stone as were levers and wedges. Indeed, without a means to hoist, haul, lower, and tie, there would be no great stone monuments in Egypt. Rope making, like fire, is a universal skill practiced in the most primitive societies and using many things, from hair to the bark of trees. The earliest ropes were probably not man-made but consisted instead of twisted tendrils of vines. By imitating nature, people found that twisted strands could yield a stronger product and could also be made into almost indefinite lengths; ancient texts mention rope in lengths of 1,700–2,400 feet (525–735 m).[10] Egyptian rope from as far back as the Badarian period (4000 BCE) has been found, made of reeds, later specimens showing use of flax, various grasses, palm fibers, and strips of hide.[11] In its early manufacture, small-diameter rope was twisted by rolling vegetable fibers together by the palm of the hand on the bare thigh, a method still practiced in some parts of modern Egypt. Rope of larger diameter is made by beating vegetable fiber with a mallet and spinning it into yarn. Numbers of yarns were then formed into strands before being laid into rope and stabilized by twisting and countertwisting in patterns, such as three left-twisted strands formed into a right-twisted rope.[12]

As one of the earliest human tools, rope was used in virtually all crafts. The manufacture of webbing by braiding led to mat making, basket making, and weaving. The spinning of rope fibers led to the making of textiles.[13] Rope was also central to fishing and boating activity, in which it was used for making nets, rigging, and even for building boats, hulls of wooden planks being bound together with small ropes of twisted strands of fiber. Although fibers were also braided into webbing, few examples have been found other than a small piece of plaited linen cord from the 11th Dynasty.[14] However, judging from the narrow slots in the 14-foot-long sledge in the Egyptian Museum, webbing must have been used to secure blocks of stone or other objects being transported.

Three-strand papyrus ropes of uncertain date and with a diameter of 2.5 inches (6.4 cm) have been found in ancient quarries. Each strand has about 40 yarns and each yarn about seven fibers.[15] A slightly larger specimen from the 18th Dynasty, with a diameter of 2.75 inches (6.8 cm) was found at Deir el-Bhari. Generally, ropes of 2.25 inches (5.7 cm) in diameter had a working strength of 6–7 tons and a breaking point about three times higher. They were equal in quality to modern counterparts before the introduction of synthetics.[16] Domenico Fontana, the architect who moved the Vatican obelisk to St. Peter's Square, found that the almost 3-inch-diameter (7.5 cm) Foligno hemp rope he planned to use in 750–1,500-foot (228–457 m) lengths could not be broken with a pull of 25 tons.[17] With rope such as this, groups of men could be controlled so that at the beat of a chant, a thousand arms pulling at the same moment had the combined force to move large blocks for great distances.

Raising the Chamber Blocks

The use of stairways to deliver masonry up the sides of a pyramid also provides a number of methods for raising the 56 granite chamber blocks of the Great Pyramid, weighing some 50 tons each. These massive beams were used to relieve the pressure of the superincumbent stone above Cheops' burial chamber. Although they were unusually heavy, their great length provided the space for a number of levers, which could act in unison, thus allowing the amount of weight raised to be evenly distributed among the levers. Placing levers at one end at a time has the added advantage of contending with only half the weight of a megalith (**11.8**). For example, if a beam having a total weight of 100,000 pounds (45,360 kg) is to be raised just high enough to insert cribbing under its end, ten levers placed at that end need only lift 5,000 pounds (2,268 kg) each. During the levering process, if the treads of the stairway are too narrow to support the chamber blocks, they may be increased in depth by laying masonry across two or more of the steps. If necessary, the overhanging beam can also be supported on shallow stair treads by being chocked up with wooden beams or rubble. Some such lifting system seems to be confirmed by the fact that the beam surfaces still show signs of bosses for the points of levers, as also seen elsewhere in Egyptian masonry.

By planning the burial chamber in advance, as evidence seems to suggest, instead of raising the chamber beams on outside stairways, they could be raised incrementally, course by course, as the nucleus was built. For example, with the first course completed, the required

Figure 11.8. Stairways assist in raising the 50-ton chamber blocks of the Great Pyramid. Although deeper than the steps, they can be supported with masonry or wood columns.

number of beams could be raised up its 3- to 4-foot (0.9–1.2 m) height by use of the levering method described. When the second course was only partially completed but contained
enough surface area for storage, the beams on the first course could be levered to the top
of the second course. Never raised more than the height of a single course at a time, these
gigantic stone beams could be made to reach the king's chamber about 165 feet (50 m)
above the ground. Once they were set in place, the rest of the course would continue to
rise around the chamber, together with those megaliths destined for higher placement.[18]

As previously mentioned, Petrie suggests that the Egyptians may have employed a pal-
let with an arcuate bottom to lift stone by rocking, placing wedges underneath each side of
the device. To accomplish this, the long beam is centered on the rocker to allow its overhanging ends to act as levers activated in alternate directions by rope. Petrie also claims
the ends could be raised by balancing them, seesaw-like, on two closely spaced piles of
masonry cribbing. In this case, the beam would be tilted by the weight of men standing
alternately on each end, small stones being placed in the space opened above the opposite
pile of cribbing. Having raised a column up a stairway by this method, Petrie claims that
stones of enormous size could be raised from one course to the next by the use of cribbing.[19]

The cribbing described is still used even with the most modern lifting devices. Although
hydraulic or screw jacks are appliances of tremendous power, the small size of their bases
relative to the size of the loads being lifted tends to make them very unstable. To offset the
imbalance, safety supports of wooden cribbing are placed underneath the load, as it is raised
or lowered, to ensure that a displaced hydraulic jack does not become a disaster.[20] Using
two such hydraulic jacks and two tall piles of squared timber, the American naval com-
mander Henry Gorringe successfully lowered a 224-ton obelisk in Alexandria before having it shipped to New York, where it was erected behind the Metropolitan Museum of Art.[21]

Tumbling

When arriving on a level with each step, the chamber blocks could be transferred to the top
of the course by tumbling or with the aid of rollers, levers, and rope (**11.9**). Field experiments
show that five men can advance a block of about 1.5 tons by turning it end over end (**11.10**).
In this maneuver, when effort is applied opposite the corner on which it pivots, the block itself
acts as a lever of the second kind. When falling, the block will move forward at least the length
of its side, but with some impetus it will tumble twice that distance. The same physical rules
apply here as elsewhere; by lifting only one side, workers need cope with only half the weight.
The required effort is further reduced if the block is chocked up at an angle at the start of the
tumble—the higher the angle, the less the effort. Because the greatest effort in tumbling is
expended when the block is flat against the ground, it is generally made to fall on a stone. If
a lever is employed, the same block can be tumbled by only three men if one side is gradually
levered and chocked up with a pile of small stones. The most common method of tumbling
moderately sized blocks with rope is to tie a hitch so that the force applied to the rope is
directed to the corner diagonally opposite where it pivots, as illustrated in figure 11.5(**d**). The
force of this maneuver can be greatly multiplied by tying a stick of wood to the block. This serves
to lengthen the distance to the opposite corner, in effect making the entire apparatus into a lever
that extends from the pivoting corner of the block to the end of the wood beam (**11.11**).[22]

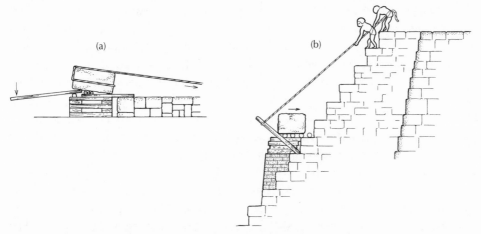

(a)   (b)

Figure 11.9. (a) Levers may be used to tumble the chamber blocks onto a course if they are raised with the nucleus. (b) Levers may also be used to roll the chamber blocks from the cribbing to a step if they are raised with a stairway.

Figure 11.10. Five men moving a large block by tumbling it end over end. A worker places a stone near its balanced edge to keep the block angled when it falls to the surface.

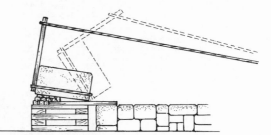

Figure 11.11. A wooden beam may be tied to the block to increase the turning force.

Slideways

The stairways outside the pyramid faces offer a possible means of raising stone by the use of long slideways, a means well-known and frequently used by the ancient Egyptians. Evidence of this is shown in the 18th Dynasty tomb of Rekhmira, where a scene shows a mud-brick ramp leading to the roof of a building under construction. It shows a roofing block held above the surface of the slideway by what appear to be wooden rails. The rails were probably lubricated with animal grease to help slide the block of stone to the top as it was hauled by men standing on the roof (**11.12**).[23] The remains of a temple at Qasr el-Sagha include a similar ramp. According to Dieter Arnold, the sockets cut into the ramp surface were for the insertion of wooden rails or poles that held large ceiling blocks as these were pulled into position, as shown in figure 11.12(**b**). Among other evidence, the Ramesside period temple (1307–1070 BCE) has a steep ramp of debris made firm with palm logs laid across the fill and retained with a wall of mud brick; the sliding was probably made easier by sprinkling water over a layer of mud in front of the blocks. In a further example in figure 11.12(**c**), considering the small size of the interior court, remains at the first Pylon at Karnak show what could only have been a steep ramp, constructed of brick chambers filled with debris. It seems to have been built with the same method mentioned in the Papyrus Anastasi I, where the scribe Hori writes of a ramp consisting of compartments covered with reeds and beams. The entrance to the tomb of the apis bull, at Saqqara, has a stairway on opposite sides of a central slideway similar to the platform of the primeval mound that holds the king's throne (**4.21**). Elsewhere in Egypt, to avoid the second cataract, sailors pulled wet boats along a 1.25-mile (2 km) mudway on sleepers, small-diameter poles embedded in the mud and set crosswise to the direction of the path.[24]

 Considering the frequent use of such slideways in other settings, it seems feasible to suggest that Egyptian builders also used them to haul the heavier blocks, with planks or poles fixed to the steep stairways of a pyramid. However, considering the steep angle and the weight of the blocks, the proposed system would probably need to be supplemented by simple mechanical devices, such as levers. Although slideways supported on the edge

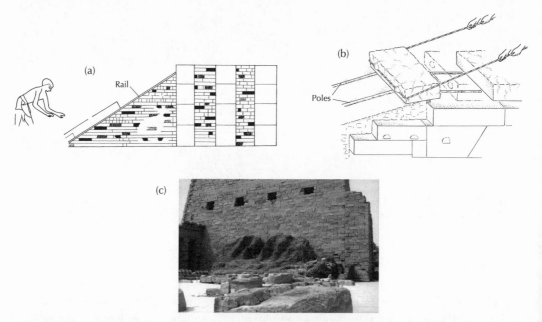

Figure 11.12. Egyptian ramps acting as slideways. (a) Scene from a tomb at Rekhmira showing a roofing block seated on rails. (b) The possible reconstruction and use from remains of a similar ramp at a temple at Qasr el-Sagha. (c) Remains of a steep ramp at the first temple at Karnak.

of a stairway or on a fill of aggregate placed at spaced intervals on the tiers of a nucleus may be viewed as employing a ramp, both its structure and the manner of its use would differ greatly from that of its conventionally imagined namesake.

Ramps described by past theorists were not considered to be practical if made to rise at an angle greater than one in ten due to the difficulty of dragging a heavy stone, and the not inconsiderable weight of the sledge holding it, while struggling to walk uphill. With methods suggested here, however, there is no need for sledges—the stone blocks would be attached by ropes and pulled up a slideway by groups of men who stood on firm footing (**11.13**). Although the sliding face of the block must be made smooth for this function, it is a known practice of Egyptian masonry to dress the bedding face of the blocks on the ground before they were raised into position.[25] As the block is incrementally raised with each collective heave, and as the rope shortens in length, its end is taken up and snubbed around a log—the same device said be used in Egypt while slowly lowering heavy sarcophagi and portcullis or ceiling blocks and also used to retain heavy weights in the *Nova* television show "Obelisk."[26] Having the short log fixed in a horizontal position upslope of the slideway would allow one or two men to hold the full weight of a stone with two or three turns around the log's circumference. Without the need to hold the weight of the block, workers expending their full effort in raising the

Figure 11.13. A block being raised along the face of a stairway. The block is supported on a lubricated wooden plank and pulled by a team of men assisted by levers. The rope holding the block is snubbed around a log. This enables the full weight of the block to be held between heaves of the rope.

load could rest between each collective heave on the rope and the next—a factor that makes a seemingly difficult task possible.

When a block of stone is supported at an angle of 52 degrees, with the proposed system almost one quarter of the weight is supported by the nucleus of the pyramid. A lower angle would take more of the weight, a higher angle less weight. For example, to raise a 4,000-pound (1,814 kg) block at a 52-degree angle with zero friction, about 3,125 pounds (1,417 kg) of effort would be required. If we assume the lowest pulling force of only 110 pounds (50 kg) per man, about 28 men would be needed to apply the required force and perhaps six or seven more to overcome friction and to provide for any unforeseen problems.[27] The number of men required can be substantially reduced if the pulling force is supplemented with levers. For fulcrums, the levers may pivot on cleated planks placed on opposite sides of the slideway (**11.14**). As the fulcrum device is moved to a higher position, or as the portable snubbing device (**11.15**) and short slide sections are leapfrogged up the side of the nucleus, the block may be chocked in place. The ability to support the block in transit would eliminate the need for long lengths of rope to the higher reaches of the nucleus.

To expedite the lift, instead of moving the fulcrum, a similar but longer device may be fashioned, having a number of such fulcrums fixed to planks on opposite sides of the slide-

Figure 11.14. In addition to supporting slideways, the stepped surface of a stairway provides a variety of methods for raising small and moderately sized stones.

Figure 11.15. Short pieces of wood make the snubbing device portable.

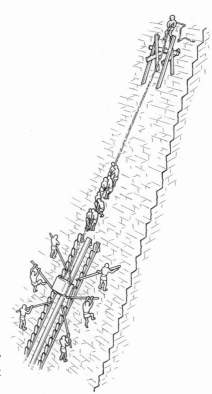

Figure 11.16. Fulcrums on both sides of a slideway would almost enable lever operators to pass the block from one pair to another.

way (**11.16**). This arrangement may extend for a short distance or from the bottom to the highest point of the nucleus. In the latter event, operators placed along the length opposite the fulcrums could assist the rope team by almost handing the block from one pair of levers to another—the rope teams and snubbing log providing a supplementary, but necessary, role in the exercise.

The Simple Pulley

Another method for raising the chamber beams requires the adaptation of the simple pulley or bearing stone, of which basalt and slate examples have been found from the 4th Dynasty, a time when the wheeled pulley was unknown. Its absence is indicated by scenes showing the sails of ships being raised by pulling on a rope slung over a yardarm.[28] Even if the wheel had been known, only wood or copper could have been used for its axle— both materials certain to fail under the enormous pressure to which it was subject. Not so with a solid block of stone. The semicircular top of the stone pulleys contain three grooves to act as guideways for ropes. Protruding from the flat bottom is a long tenon with a cross hole for locking the device into a post or wooden framework. Due to friction of rope sliding over the stone grooves, the device is less efficient than a pulley wheel turning freely on a shaft; however, the friction can be greatly reduced with a lubricant.[29]

When these simple pulleys were found on the Giza Plateau, the Egyptian archaeologist Selim Hassan realized that stones of enormous weight could be lifted if a number of these devices were used at the same time (**11.17**).[30] Mounted on frameworks near the edge of a course being laid, they would make it possible to raise multiton blocks of stone by redirecting a rope to the top surface of a platform on which groups of men could apply the required force (**11.18**). Although such frameworks would be restricted to the lower portion of the structure where there were surfaces large enough to hold the men, it was these lower levels that contained the greatest mass of stonework and that would benefit the most from the method.

Hauling weights up an incline while standing on a flight of stairs mounted to the side of a pyramid differs from hauling weights while standing on the horizontal platform of a course of masonry. Each has its own advantages. On stairs, a force directed in a straight

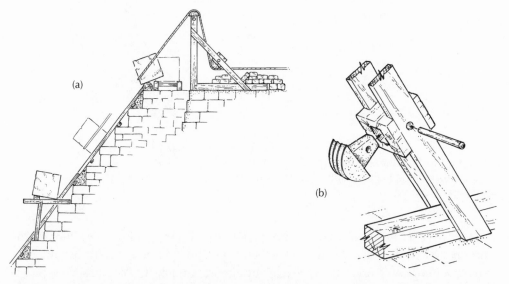

Figure 11.17. (a) Possible framework employed for the simple stone pulleys found at Giza and its use in redirecting the pull of a rope. (b) Detail of wooden framework made to hold a stone pulley.

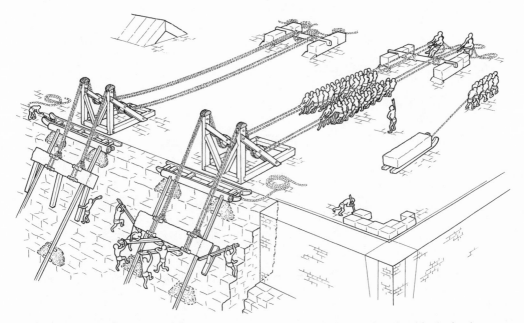

Figure 11.18. Possible use of several such frameworks to raise heavy chamber blocks for the pyramid of Cheops.

line from the block to the men would generate friction only between the wooden rails and the weight. Bending rope over a simple pulley and applying force from a horizontal position produces more friction, but it also provides a place for larger teams of men and gives them a better position from which to apply their efforts.

Interestingly, a similar method was used to raise weight on a much smaller scale several millennia later, in the 19th century. When excavating for a railroad, fully loaded wheelbarrows were raised from a deep ravine with a rope reeved over a pulley. The weight being pulled by a horse, the only task of a workman was to guide the wheelbarrow up a narrow ramp of wood planking (**11.19**). The basic difference between the two systems, ages apart, is the rotating pulley and the weight of the load.

In the Egyptian system, as the pyramid rose in height and the platform became too small to support large teams of men, it might have been possible to redirect the rope to others stationed on an opposite stairway (**11.20**). Indeed, with a second slideway added to the opposing stairway, large stone blocks could be counterweighted by a sledge filled with small stones (**11.21**).[31] Assisted in this way by gravity and a counterweight less than that of the block, a few men on the opposite slideway would be all that were needed for raising heavy weights. Instead of using rope, a somewhat similar principle was later employed to lift water for irrigation purposes with a counterweighted wood beam called a *shaduf*.

According to Herodotus, the lifting system used by the pyramid builders was described to him by Egyptian priests. Although they themselves had no firsthand knowledge of the event, the description acquires some importance since it is the only portrayal of the ancient building method. Herodotus was told: "When the workmen had finished the first tier, they elevated the stone to the second by the aid of machines constructed of short pieces of wood."[32] While tantalizing, the statement says little other than confirming the use of tiers

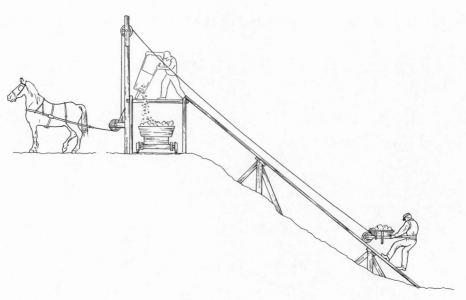

Figure 11.19. During excavation for a railroad in 19th-century England, fully loaded wheelbarrows were guided up a deep ravine with a rope reeved over a pulley and pulled by a horse.

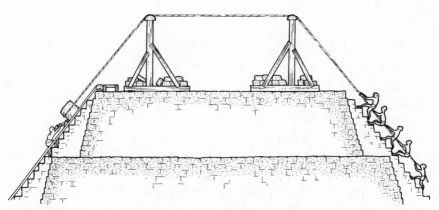

Figure 11.20. As the nucleus rises in height and the platform becomes too small to support large teams of men, the rope is redirected and pulled by men stationed on an opposite stairway.

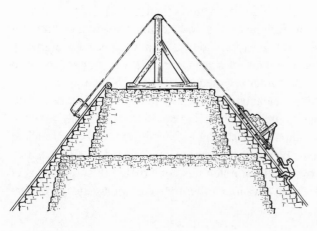

Figure 11.21. A few men can lift a heavy block that is counterweighted with rubble.

to construct the pyramid. The description of "machines" is vague enough to encompass almost any device postulated as an aid to a building system involving short pieces of wood.

The human struggles to build the pyramids and the almost casual attitude that must have prevailed in ancient Egypt toward the dangers of the undertaking may be difficult to understand, particularly in the safety-conscious, litigious, and fearful society in which we now live. Yet even in the past, with danger and disease part of everyday life, people were probably not casually expendable. However, accidents were then considered inevitable and more readily accepted. Although the riskiest tasks were doubtless reserved for those workers lacking the intelligence or special skills that would be missed, the deciding factor in any undertaking simply was that someone had to carry out the wishes of the king. Beside the rations of bread, onion, and beer given to the workers as builders of the tomb of their god-king, the honor of taking part in its construction was as at least as great as that later claimed by generations of workers who toiled on the great cathedrals of Europe.

Closer to our own time, the dangers associated with ancient building projects may be compared to those facing the builders of the Brooklyn Bridge. Characteristic of what was supposedly a more enlightened age, no figures on fatalities were kept. Nor were tallies made during construction of the Panama Canal, when thousands perished from disease alone. The Hoover Dam, completed in 1932, is a more recent example: workers hanging from cables would bounce themselves to and fro on a 700-foot (213 m) cliff to remove projecting rocks off its face with iron bars. Although over 100 men were killed in the effort and many others were injured, there were eager replacements during the Depression.

When George Simmonds, an engineer specializing in the erection of large sculptural pieces, studied the bas-reliefs of the Assyrian king Sennacherib, who transported large winged statues pulled by hordes of men, he was reminded of what he had personally observed. In 19th-century Carrara, stoneboats carrying blocks in excess of 25 tons were slid down slopes on wooden sleepers lubricated with grease or soap.[33] These enormous blocks were held from tumbling down the steep descent back by three hemp cables snubbed around clutch poles—short logs set in the ground about every 32 feet (10 m). Simmonds reports:

> Huge blocks . . . moved in almost exactly the same way [as Sennacherib], except that, their course being for the most part down hill, the cables are used to retard and control the movement of the sledge by a couple of turns being taken round heavy timber posts firmly and deeply embedded in the rocky soil; otherwise the picture is much the same. The vast mass of stone on its wooden sledge, the great cables, the long and ponderous lever bars, and last, though not least, the gangs of toiling, anxious men, some running ahead with sleepers, others laying them in order on the track, the man on the block giving orders, and others behind picking up the sleepers to pass them forward as soon as the sledge has gone over them whilst a number of others are hanging for dear life on the cables, or belaying one which has come to its end, whilst another is being bent around a post further ahead. Thus from post to post they progress, shouting, swearing, and working as . . . men work nowhere else, and giving us, in the nineteenth century, a living picture of what the Assyrian artist saw in his own country, and so graphically recorded nearly 3,000

years ago. Sometimes, though rarely, the cables slip or part, and then the fate of a gang of quarrymen is as tragic in the Carrara mountains as it could have been in Assyria in the days of Sennacherib.[34]

Despite the effort and the fatalities, the need of Egyptian kings for an eternal resting place and the competition to overwhelm their predecessors by its size not only took the treasure of the country but overcame all the physical obstacles of construction. However, completion of the nucleus was only part of the undertaking. The most challenging and ingenious aspect was King Sneferu's transformation of the towering mass of set-back stones into the four smooth faces of a true pyramid.

CHAPTER 12

THE SECOND STAGE

E recting the first building stage was basically a product of muscle. Its transformation into a true pyramid, not discounting the physical effort involved, was a product of the mind. Having already shown the impossibility of bringing a structure from the four corners of the base to a meeting point in the sky by measuring the squares of each course as they are applied, we are left with the question of how this difficult task could have been achieved with an inexact nucleus. As previously mentioned, the summit of Meidum Pyramid is a rectangle, its tiers have unequal heights, and the depth of its set-backs varies such that they are not equal, horizontal, or parallel. Although these deficiencies may be overcome by mounting a sighting target on top of the nucleus, signs M. A. Robert found in his survey, this is not enough. To achieve an angle of about 52 degrees, two conditions should be met; the target must be placed at the exact height of the proposed structure, and it must be located where the vertical axis of the pyramid meets the center of the layout square on the base.

King Sneferu solved these problems when deciding to convert the step pyramid, a standard configuration of the 3rd Dynasty kings, into one with four smooth faces. Clearly, the undertaking required careful planning. Indeed, the pyramid was probably laid out on a small-scale grid drawing, such as that found from a later time at Meroë by F. W. Hinkle, director of the East German Expedition. He found that half the vertical side of a pyramid was laid out by drawing it over a gridlike pattern incised on the wall of a nearby chapel. When Hinkle matched the horizontal and vertical divisions of the grid to a small nearby pyramid, he found that the ancient builders had planned the structure on a scale of about 1:10. The only difference discovered between the scale drawing and the actual pyramid was in the angle of the slope, but the difference was a matter of no more than 3 arcminutes—a discrepancy that may be attributed to the poor condition of the pyramid and the difficulty of drawing a 5.6 foot-high (1.7 m) plan over several courses of sandstone blocks.[1]

Positioning the Target

Regardless of the care given in the preparation of any small-scale drawing, only the most limited technology was available for accurately positioning the target on the apex of its full-size counterpart. Yet, considerable ingenuity devoted to solving this problem was a key feature of pyramid construction. In the 4th Dynasty only two methods could have been used for this purpose, the more obvious being to measure the height of each tier and arrive at a total. As noted, however, considering the set-backs and their badly leveled surfaces, the results would probably not give the required accuracy. A less obvious but more exact procedure involved the use of shadows. Although the method of measuring height by use of shadows is attributed to Thales (636–546 BCE), a pre-Socratic Greek philosopher of Miletus, it was probably in use long before; credit is usually given to those who first record a procedure.

There are two possible methods for measuring the height of a nucleus by use of its shadow, both employing a pole (gnomon) erected perpendicular to the ground. The shadows of the pole create triangles, geometric figures that include the height of the pole, the length of its shadow on the ground, and the angle of shadow cast from the tip of the pole, which forms the hypotenuse. As we know, all triangles are made up of three angles that total 180 degrees. Of these, the right angle at the base of the pole is already known. The study of these gnomonic shadows and the angles they cast was doubtless the basis of geometry and contributed greatly to the world of the mathematics.

The simplest method of finding the height of the nucleus requires observation without need of any of the aforementioned knowledge—simply that on two days of the year when the sun is at 45 degrees above the horizon, the length of its noon shadow will equal the height of the object from which it is cast. Therefore, with the height of a pole used as a radius, an arc is made around its base. At the very moment that the shadow of the pole reaches the arc, the nucleus is casting a shadow equal to its own height. The height of the nucleus may then be found by measuring the length of its shadow to one half its base.[2] The base of the nucleus is halved because the true length of its shadow does not merely extend to the stone at the edge of the nucleus but to its vertical axis, which lies in the center of the pyramid. This procedure can be used on several other days of the year using a noon shadow of easily measured lengths, such as half or twice the height of the pole (**12.1a**).

Instead of waiting for certain days, Thales used a triangle rule that allowed him to measure the Great Pyramid at noon on any day of the year. The rule states that triangles are equivalent if all their corresponding sides and all their corresponding angles are equivalent. For this, he placed a pole at the tip of a shadow cast by the nucleus at midday and measured the length of the pole's shadow. Since the two shadows occur at the same time, the height of the sun would cause the shadow of the nucleus and the pole to form triangles with equal slopes and equal angles. Being aware of geometry, Thales knew that the ratio of their corresponding sides would be the same—the known height of the pole would be to the known length of its shadow as the unknown height of the nucleus was to the known length of its shadow (**12.1b**).[3] Here too, the shadow of the nucleus is measured to one-half the base.

At this building stage, it should be noted that both aforementioned methods measured shadows from a nucleus having a flat top—one below and not central to the point where

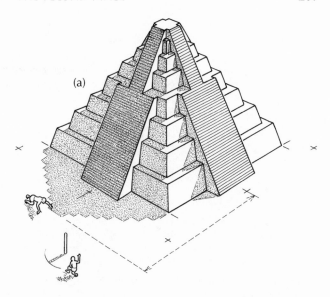

(a)

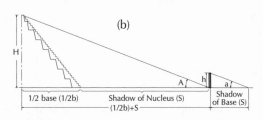

(b)

Figure 12.1. (a) On two days of each year the height of a gnomon is equal to the length of its midday shadow. At that time, the distance from the center of the nucleus to the tip of its shadow is equal to the height of the nucleus. (b) At noon of other days the height of the nucleus can be determined by comparing the length of its shadow to that of a gnomon of known height. The proportion of shadow length to height is always equivalent.

the four sides would join in a true pyramid. This is a seemingly inaccurate yet necessary procedure. Indeed, while one may consider that this distance could be closed with the previously mentioned target on a pole, the small size of the target and its great distance from the ground would cause its shadow to be lost in the bright sunlight—unlike the well-defined shadow on the flat top of the nucleus. Considering this, only after the shadow of the nucleus is measured can a target pole of a length representing the apex of the pyramid be placed on the nucleus.

Having established the target at a height that represents the very tip of the capstone, it must then be centrally located to the four corners at the base. Accordingly, a goal would be for observers positioned on adjacent sides of the nucleus to help direct the target on the axis of the structure by locating it, so to speak, in the crosshairs of their respective sight lines. This may be accomplished by the use of fixed plumb lines located on the centerlines extending from the base on two adjacent sides of the nucleus. Two observers on the ground would then be able to view the plumb lines, the centerlines of the layout square, and the target on the nucleus at the same time. Directions given to the target handlers on top of the nucleus could be indicated with flag or arm signals or, considering the distance, by moving

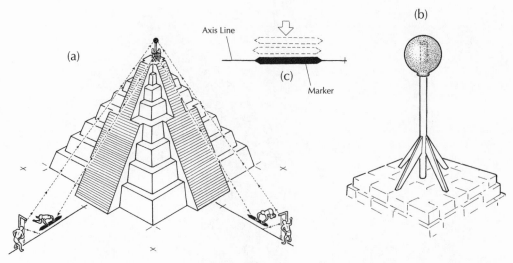

Figure 12.2. (a) Observers on the ground communicating with obsevers on the apex can cooperate to place a target in the center of the nucleus. This is done by moving the target on the apex (b) in response to markers (c) moved on the ground until they overlie the axis lines on two sides of the nucleus. The movements are guided by an observer peering across a plumb line fixed over each axis.

a large marker to the left or right of the centerline on the ground. If the signals on the ground were mimicked by observers in control of the target on the nucleus, the pole could be progressively brought into axial alignment with the two adjacent centerlines on the layout square (**12.2**).

Egyptian Mathematics

For the procedure Thales used about 2,000 years after the Great Pyramid to have been employed by the ancient Egyptians requires that they had some knowledge of geometry and the ability to work simple ratios. Perhaps they did. The Rhind Mathematical Papyrus, which contains examples of ancient mathematics, is a document with the largest variety of subjects treated. It shows that the Egyptians knew how to determine areas and proportions of buildings and how to calculate the batter on pyramids and walls. Basically, Egyptian mathematicians were devoted to practical matters; that is, they worked out the slope of a pyramid and determined the areas and proportions of buildings. They could also do simple equations, knew the concept of squaring and extracting the square root, and could work out the area of a circle and triangle. They could also find the volume of a cylinder and a truncated pyramid. All in all, Egyptians had the ability to solve any problem that might be encountered in constructing a pyramid, temple, or wall or in finding the weight of the volume of the material used.[4]

Whether the Egyptians knew of the right angle triangle having sides with a ratio of 3:4:5, the so-called sacred triangle, has long been a matter of conjecture. This triangle is made of three angles, 90°; 53° 07' 48"; and 36° 52' 12". According to Dieter Arnold, "The application of the 'sacred triangle' would have been a revolutionary improvement in surveying, but it is not clear when the Egyptian surveyors discovered and used the 'Pythagoras.'"

No written sources exist on that subject, so we can only infer its application from buildings that show the typical proportion (3:4:5)." Evidence leading to the use of these proportions has been found by Egyptologists in the Djoser complex and in the pyramid temples of the Old Kingdom.[5]

A study by Dušan Magdolen, an Egyptologist from the Slovak Republic, shows that despite the differences in measurements among Old Kingdom pyramids, some have in common the ratio of 3:4 between what was once the height of the pyramid and half the base. These make up two sides of what we know as the Pythagorean right triangle. He considers the third side, the hypotenuse or slope of the pyramid, to have been found by the angle formed as the shadow falls from the tip of a gnomon upon a flat surface, noting:

> The principle of a constant vertical height and a changeable horizontal distance is similar or even the same as in the slope of a pyramid, i.e., *cqd* (seked) in the Egyptian language. It is the distance given horizontally for every rise of one cubit in vertical height. Three examples from the Rhind Mathematical Papyrus, i.e., RMP 57, 58, and 59, deal with the ratio 3:4. In the first case, the length of the sides and the slope of the pyramid is known and the vertical height is calculated. In the second and third case, the slope of the pyramid is unknown. In all three examples, the slope of the pyramid equals 5 palms and 1 finger. Such a slope corresponds with the angle 53° 07' 48" which is the same as the angle in the "sacred triangle."[6]

Magdolen suggests that the frequency of the Pythagorean ratio in Old Kingdom monuments implies deliberate intention rather than haphazard coincidence, especially since the 53° 07' 48" angle is seen in the slope of pyramids from the 5th and 6th Dynasties. One could dispute that a pyramid could be so accurately measured in its ruined state, but they are close enough to warrant giving Magdolen's findings serious consideration.

According to Magdolen, the angle of slope was probably found at a location just south of Heliopolis (29° 07'), the center of the sun cult, prior to the 1st Dynasty. In 3000 BCE, at that location, the shadows of the sun culminated at 53° 07' 48" on the winter solstice (**12.3**).

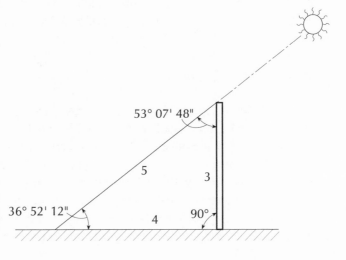

Figure 12.3. At the winter solstice, the shadow of a gnomon from the midday sun forms the angles and sides of a Pythagorean triangle.

Table 12.1

SLOPES OF MAJOR 4TH–12TH DYNASTY PYRAMIDS

KING	DYNASTY	PLACE	SLOPE
Sneferu	4	Meidum	51° 50' 35"
Sneferu (South)*	4	Dahshur	54° 27' 44"/43° 22'
Sneferu (North)	4	Dahshur	43° 22'
Cheops (Khufu)	4	Giza	51° 50' 40"
Djedefre	4	Abu Roash	52°
Chephren (Khafre)	4	Giza	53° 10'
Mycerinus (Menkaure)	4	Giza	51° 20' 25"
Userkaf	5	Saqqara	53° 07' 48"
Sahure	5	Abusir	50° 11' 40"
Neferirkare	5	Abusir	53° 07' 48"
Niuserre	5	Abusir	51° 50' 35"
Djedkare Isesi	5	Saqqara (South)	52°
Unas	5	Saqqara	56° 18' 35"
Teti	6	Saqqara	53° 07' 48"
Pepi I	6	Saqqara (South)	53° 07' 48"
Merenre	6	Saqqara (South)	53° 07' 48"
Pepi II	6	Saqqara (South)	52° 07' 48"
Amenemhet I	12	Lisht	54° 27' 44"
Senwosret I	12	Lisht	49° 23' 55"
Senwosret II	12	Illahun	42° 35'
Senwosret III	12	Dahshur	56° 18' 35"
Amenemhet III	12	Dahshur	57° 15' 50"
Amenemhet III	12	Hawara	48° 45'

After Mark Lehner, *The Complete Pyramids*, 17.
* Bent Pyramid

Although the slopes of earlier pyramids have angles that differ, they suggest a period of experimentation before arriving at a standard. Middle Kingdom pyramids did not follow this slope.[7]

The Corners of the Pyramid

Once the sky point is firmly identified, either by placing the pole in a hole, as at Meidum, or by supporting it with a wood stand or rubble, the five major points that constitute the outline of a pyramid are positioned, a major step in construction. But refinement is still required. The final shape of the pyramid depends on how accurately the lines between these points can be filled with masonry. Although the approximate 52-degree angles of the sides are cited whenever statistics are given on the Great Pyramid, they are of secondary importance to the approximately 42-degree angles at the corners of the structure. The 10-degree difference between the two angles is due to the hypotenuse of the triangle formed by the vertical axis of the pyramid with the corners being longer than the hypotenuse of the triangle formed by the vertical axis and the face.

The reason corner angles of a pyramid are more critical in construction than face angles is that face angles are a product of corner angles being carefully laid before the rest of the course is filled—a procedure similar to that of a mason carefully building the corners of a wall before filling the intermediate sections. However, pyramid corners are more difficult to form and require more care for several reasons: to come to a point, the corners must rise at the same angle; properly placed, they establish the parameters of each course and help in its construction; and imperfections that would be lost in the vast expanse of each pyramid face can easily be seen at the corners, which are silhouetted against the sky.

Establishing the corners of a pyramid appears to be an impossible task, especially at this stage, when the outline of the structure consists only of imaginary lines extending from the four corners of the base to the target on the apex. Whatever the means, the task was successfully accomplished by the Egyptians. Before disclosing the possible method, it is worth describing in greater detail the outer coating of masonry that gives structures of the 4th Dynasty their pyramidal shape.

Pyramid Masonry outside the Nucleus

The few casing blocks remaining at the base of the Cheops Pyramid show them carefully fitted to the blocks directly behind, called backing stones. Behind the backing stones, which are generally of the same height as the casing stones, one can see a thick fill of masonry called packing stones. All the stones in this fill seem to have irregular sizes and wide joints. It is generally thought that courses of the irregular packing stones extend back to the face of the nucleus. While it seems reasonable to assume that all the masonry outside the nucleus was laid together as a unit, this did not occur at the pyramid of Chephren, where a second building stage seems to exist between the tiered nucleus and the casing.

Despite the lack of casing stone, all the major pyramids of Giza—Cheops, Chephren, and Mycerinus—show corners that seem to run straight and true for their entire length, being interrupted only by missing blocks (12.4). This observation was confirmed in Petrie's survey of the Great Pyramid in the 19th century, sighting with a straight rod across a face of the pyramid now devoid of its outer layer of casing stone. Looking up an edge, across the middle of a face, or even along the base, Petrie found that the mean optical plane touching the most prominent points of all the remaining stones had an average variation of only one inch (2.54 cm).[8] At the time these sightings were made, the entire base of the pyramid was covered with sand and rubble except for the occasional shafts cut through the sand for taking measurements. Despite the covering, the accuracy of his measurements at the pyramids of Giza stands as one of the great Egyptological achievements of the 19th century. Clearly, if such close measurements of the sides of the pyramid could be achieved by sinking occasional pits to expose the base, his findings on the uncovered portions of the pyramid must be assumed to be at least as accurate.

Such underlying faces are even more pronounced at Chephren, a structure which still retains much of its casing on the top 148 feet (45 m) of the pyramid. Visible between the top casing and the remains of masonry, which is irregular in appearance due to differing

(a)

(b)

(c)

Figure 12.4. The pyramids (a) Cheops, (b) Chephren, and (c) Mycerinus seem to show that a regularized pyramidal structure exists underneath the casing stone. This is particularly evident at Chephren, which has retained much of its casing stone on the top portion of the pyramid.

depths and broken faces, is an area of regularized stones. Of this area, which Maragioglio and Rinaldi call the nucleus but which I refer to as the second stage, they state: "The nucleus is seen to be formed of regular, clearly marked masonry courses, which form as it were an actual flight of steps. Below this what remains of the face seems to be very much coarser, as if it had suffered more from the ravages of time. This, however, does not seem to be the case, and the irregular superficial layers is perhaps due to detritus or the remains of backing stone still in situ, while in the regular part these remains have fallen or been removed."[9]

Even more interesting, the regularized area of masonry shows straight lines of courses that extend across the entire face of the pyramid to the opposite corner. Along their upper

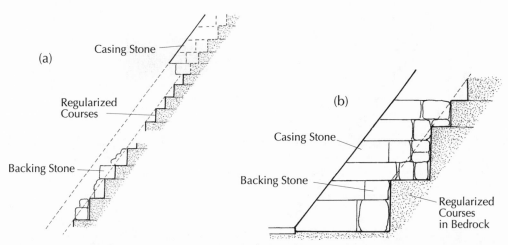

Figure 12.5. The (a) upper and (b) lower sections of Chephren show stepped courses with upper edges lying at the same angular plane as the casing stone.

edges these courses form a plane that is deeper inside but parallel to the angled face of the final layer of casing stones (**12.5**). Such regularity is also seen on the lower northwest corner of Chephren, where the steps of the courses are cut directly into the bedrock (**12.6**). These courses, which have remained undisturbed even when stripped of their outer mantle, appear to be a lower part of the regularized courses seen higher up. At the pyramid of Mycerinus surveyors also found that the face of backing stone rises at the same angle as the face of casing stone (**12.7**).[10]

Refinements at the Second Stage

The remains of Chephren show that even when it is freed of casing, a well-formed pyramid exists inside the outer mantle. This would not be possible if the masonry behind the

Figure 12.6. Regularized courses are cut into the bedrock at the base of Chephren Pyramid.

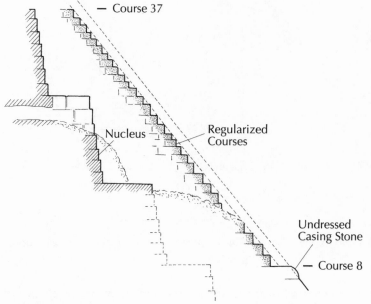

— Course 37

Nucleus

Regularized
Courses

Undressed
Casing Stone

— Course 8

Figure 12.7. A section of the pyramid of Mycerinus also shows a regularized structure under the casing stone.

casing stone, seen elsewhere on the pyramid to be of different sizes, had been extended back to the nucleus. On the contrary, if each course were laid from the face of the pyramid back to the nucleus, and some stones were later removed, as is the case, this would show on the corners now exposed. They would reflect the different sizes of stones of each course by indents and protrusions, instead of the regularity seen. It is a regularity indicating that a second building stage must have been constructed after the nucleus was raised and before the casing was applied; there can be no other explanation. Further, this was an intermediate building stage of the pyramid, serving to bring the nucleus one step closer to its final form, each stage being made more exact than the last—a standard building practice of the Egyptians.

At the pyramid of Cheops, Petrie discovered an anomaly in his survey that confirms the proposed second building stage. He found that the pavement sockets for the corners of the final face formed a more perfect square than the square established for the core of the pyramid (his definition of the core being what I call the second building stage). He also found that the entire square of the second stage was slightly twisted relative to the final square of casing stones—the mean difference in azimuths between the two being about 1.5 arcminutes (**12.8**). By establishing that the Egyptian surveyors made two separate layout squares at the base of the pyramid, he was forced to conclude that the orientation of the pyramid's casing was slightly altered after the core (second stage) was put into place.[11] To compensate for the twist at Cheops Pyramid, the square of casing stones would have to vary in depth. In some places they would be joined directly to the square of the core, while elsewhere, additional masonry would be placed to fill the greater distance between the two squares.

Accepting the premise that a second building stage was used when constructing the major pyramids does not obviate the question of how the three large Giza pyramids achieved the straight corners extending from base to apex and how each course was built to a reasonable level. It simply adds another layer of complexity.

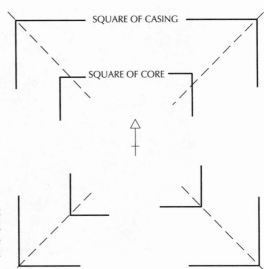

Figure 12.8. Petrie found that the pavement sockets for the final face of Cheops Pyramid formed a more prefect square than that of the core, which is twisted in a slightly counter-clockwise direction.

Laying Pyramid Masonry to an Outline

The most obvious method of forming a pyramid is to erect a pole having four cords extending pyramidally from its apex to the ground, a setup whereby the space within the corner boundaries can easily be filled with masonry to form four flat faces meeting at an exact point in the sky. Indeed, by use of this device, it is possible to form a symmetrical pyramid even if the ground is not level—a factor that might tempt one to explain construction of the Queens Pyramids of Cheops, built on a sloping grade. While this method may be feasible for a small structure, such as that of a monument for a downed German pilot in North Africa, it is unacceptable for even the smallest of Egyptian pyramids.[12] Laying masonry to a cord would reproduce the catenary curves of the cord, which would still be visible along the corners of the pyramid from the apex to the base. Clearly, other means must have been used by the Egyptian builders.

A clue to how this may have been accomplished is found at Cheops Queens Pyramids. Although these small pyramids have great numbers of their corner stones missing, both the center (GI-b) and south (GI-c) Queens Pyramids exhibit holes of about 2 inches (5 cm) in diameter on those few corner packing stones that still remain in place (**12.9**). Most such holes appear on the horizontal surfaces, but some may also be seen along the vertical corners, as in figure 12.9(**e**). One block on the northeast corner of GI-c has an arrowhead (**12.9d**) incised on its horizontal surface that points to the corner hole about seven feet (2 m) away. Appearing at key points of a pyramid, these holes may once have supported a pole-like device that held a straight rod, such as Petrie used in his survey of the Great Pyramid. Employed for the same purpose by the pyramid builders, it would enable the ancient surveyors to establish a line from the target on the apex to each corner of the base—the target, as previously mentioned, being an ordinary 10-inch diameter (25 cm) black bowl. Yet the problem of forming a pyramidal shape does not reside in the ability to sight to a small target accurately along the 718-foot length of the corner; it involves the ability to lay stone exactly to the line of sight.

Figure 12.9. The Queens Pyramids of Cheops, GI-b and GI-c, exhibit holes on their corner blocks. (a) An overview of G1-a showing two holes and an arrowhead, which points toward the corner hole. (b) Enlarged detail of the upper hole. (c) Enlarged detail of the lower hole. (d) Enlarged detail of the arrowhead. (e) Pyramid GI-c shows a hole on the vertical corner of the block.

This endeavor can be assisted by mounting a straightedge device on a movable stand near each corner of the layout square (**12.10**). With the angle of the device made adjustable, the straightedge can be aimed, from opposite ends, up to the target mounted on the apex and down to a corner marker on the roughly paved layout square. The straightedge can be incrementally moved until, without further need for adjustment, the target on the apex and the marker on the ground are seen to be in perfect alignment. Fixed in position at the base (**12.11**), the straightedge can then be used to align similar sighting devices on the corners of each tier of the nucleus by sighting from stations at the base to the target on the

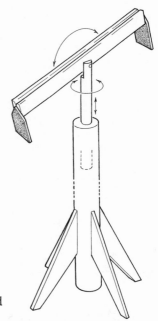

Figure 12.10. An adjustable straightedge device that may be used for aligning the corners of a pyramid.

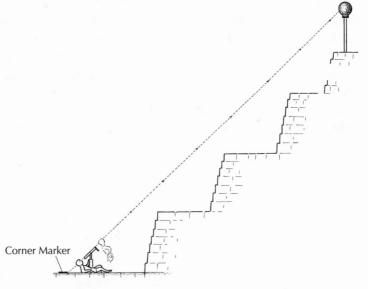

Figure 12.11. The straightedge, placed on the base of each corner, can be aimed from opposite ends to a target on the apex and to a corner marker on the pavement.

Corner Marker

apex (**12.12**). The height and angle of these intermediate straightedges can be aligned by sighting to their leading and trailing edges. These edges can be accentuated by easily seen markers. Once so aligned, the poles may be held in position on a stand with rubble or by inserting them in the aforementioned holes. Placing such devices on each corner of each tier has the advantage of retaining a line of sight along the corners of the pyramid even as some devices are removed during the building process.

With the sighting stations secured in place, packing stones can be placed around the nucleus—the stones becoming larger and fitting better as they extend to, and slightly past,

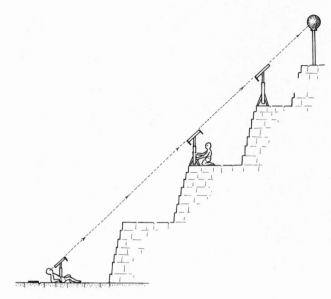

Figure 12.12. Once aligned, the straightedge can help position similar sighting devices on each corner of the nucleus.

the sight lines at the corners of the second building stage (**12.13**). Once in position, the corner stones can be brought to the same level by means of the previously described story-pole. To help cut the oversize corner blocks to the line of sight, markers directed by observers sighting from the stations on the first tier are moved to exactly where the sight lines intersect the corner blocks (**12.14**). Once the height of the first course is established, a narrow ledge at the same level as the corner stones is cut all along the outer edge. To align the outside of the course and bring it to a vertical plane, a line stretched from one corner point to another is supported on the horizontal ledge. Incised, or marked with a chalkline, the excess stone on the outside is cut to the line. Once this is accomplished, the rest of the course can be brought to the level of the ledge by use of the previously described square-level device.

Figure 12.13. The sighting stations can help to set the courses of stone in the second building stage, which give the nucleus its pyramidal shape.

Figure 12.14. With the edge of a course made level, the corners of a pyramid may be found by moving a marker until it is seen to intersect the sight line.

The efforts described will result in forming the first course—a perfect square filled with stone and located some distance outside the base of the nucleus. As the courses continue to be built, one upon the other, perhaps losing their level in the process (at the Great Pyramid, few of the courses are truly level), they may be reestablished by the occasional use of the same leveling procedure used earlier for establishing the layout around the rocky mass at the base of the pyramid. When the courses of packing stone reach to the height of the first tier, the sighting stations may be removed as the sighting chores are taken by the higher stations at the corners of the second tier (**12.15**). In this way, course upon course of stone can be accurately laid almost to the very top tier of the nucleus, thus filling out the tiers and providing regular indented seats to support a final mantle of stone. This second stage establishes the pyramid form we now see at the remains of Cheops and at much of Chephren.

With some additional masonry, the proposed building system allows continued use of the same stairways employed for raising the nucleus. In the second building stage, however, they would serve a twofold purpose. Not only would they help transport material up the side of the structure; they would also blend into the structure and become part of the fill bringing the nucleus to a more pyramidal shape (**12.16**). They would eliminate the need to assemble and disassemble the high construction ramps often said to have been used for pyramid building. This approach is of particular importance in the case of Meidum, where three such ramps would have been required. Indeed, the benefits of the proposed building system are manifold; instead of having embankments supported only by the set-backs of each tier, as on the nucleus, the indented steps formed by the superincumbent courses would provide the means to support a surrounding embankment at any level the builders chose.

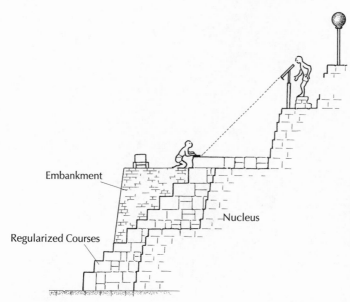

Embankment

Nucleus

Regularized Courses

Figure 12.15. As the courses rise in height, and as a surrounding embankment covers the lower sighting stations, the corner of the pyramid can be identified by sighting stations fixed at higher levels.

Due to the angle of the pyramidal structure, the horizontal work surface of the surrounding embankment becomes increasingly wide as its height increases. Made of mud brick or masonry, and rising with each course of the pyramid, the embankments provide a surface for the transportation of stone to any position along the course. They also provide a place for lever operators to stand as they push the facing stone into place from the outside. Although openings may be left in the embankments for the transport of stone, once the required amount of masonry has been delivered, the opening can be filled, providing an uninterrupted horizontal work surface around each course.

When the embankments become too high, or as the need arises, they can be moved to a higher level by disassembling and reusing the materials taken from the lower embankment. Indeed, if the embankments are built of small, easily handled stone, any excess masonry left as they are made to leapfrog over each other, decreasing in size as they gain in height, can be used as fill for the rising pyramid. As the courses of stone rise past the top tier, they may be built around the target pole on the apex. Better yet, if the target is supported by four converging poles placed on the previously cut corner stones, the target pole can be removed. The latter method would allow stone to be raised to courses having ever smaller work surfaces without interference from the upstanding pole. After the last sighting station has been removed, the four poles located on the corners would supply four rigid guides against which the remaining few course corners can be gauged when being put into place (**12.17**).

A Curious Anomaly

The courses of fill that make up the second stage of the pyramid are not of the same height; instead, they diminish in size from bottom to top. This reduction in the size of blocks is a general characteristic of all pyramids, and it is a natural thing to do because it takes a

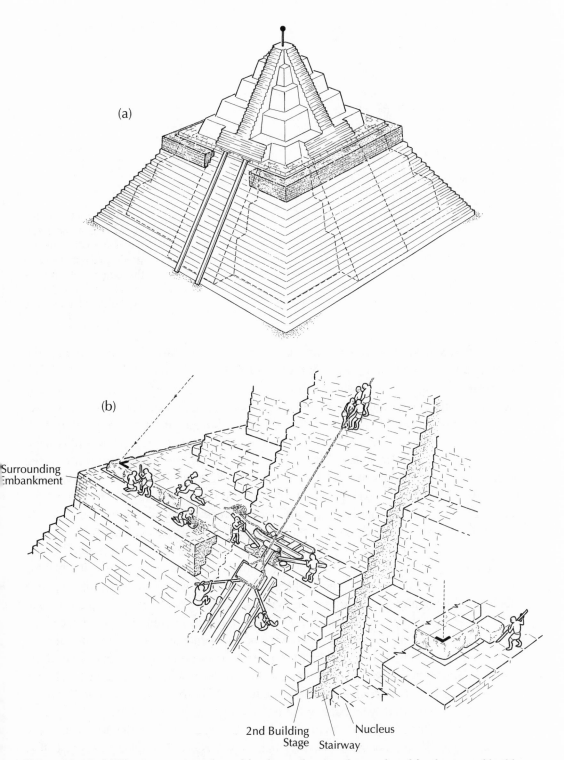

Figure 12.16. (a) The same stairways used for the nucleus can be employed for the second building stage. (b) Openings in the stairways may be filled when a required amount of stone has reached the course.

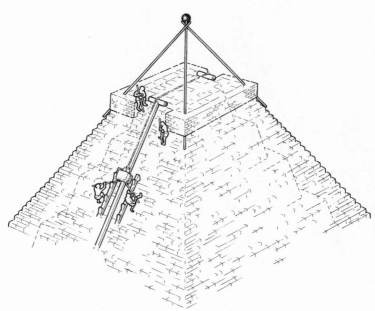

Figure 12.17. As the courses near the apex, the pole holding the target may be removed and the target instead supported by four converging poles placed on the corners.

greater effort to raise large stones than small stones. An example of this can be seen at the Great Pyramid, where though little of the casing remains, the height of the course coincides with the height of the missing casing stone. While the 5-foot-high (1.49 m) first course indicates a probable 7-ton casing stone, the stone in the 1.75-foot-high (0.54 m) courses near the top had a weight of no more than 1 ton.[13] Although the courses of packing stone vary in height and size, Petrie discovered a curious anomaly in the thickness of courses at the Great Pyramid. He states: "Thicker courses were perhaps intentionally introduced where the area of the course was a multiple of 1/25th of the base area; this system accounts for nearly all the curious examples of a thick course being suddenly brought in, with a series above it gradually diminishing, until another thick course occurs."[14]

Some scholars have suggested that the periodic decreases mean available stone from a quarry was used up before a new supply was drawn upon.[15] This explanation is based on the unlikely coincidence of 25 successive quarries having a progressively diminishing supply of stone. It also suggests that the thick stone taken when the quarry was first opened yielded to thinner and thinner stone, although the capacity of the quarry could not have been known in advance. While the thicker blocks in Cheops Pyramid are not spaced the same distance or number of courses apart, they occur repeatedly. Yet, even as they appear, blocks begin to diminish in size with subsequent courses until the next time, so that the general effect is both an overall and a periodic diminution of stone thickness (**12.18**). This seems to suggest that although forced for some reason to introduce the thickened courses, the builders immediately went back to the natural manner of laying stone.

Considering this, Jürgen Brinks proposes an association between the thickness of the courses and the position of the tiers in the nucleus of the Great Pyramid. He suggests that if the last course used to reach the top of a nucleus step were thin, it would be followed by a thicker course, and as noted by Dieter Arnold, it would therefore be a proportionally deeper stone (**12.19**). This is to enable the casing stone to overlie the tier step at those

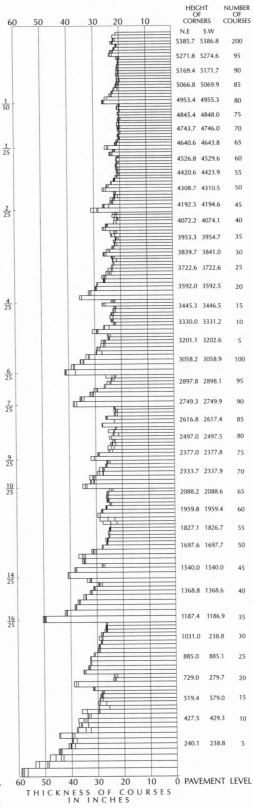

Figure 12.18. Petrie's chart shows that thicker courses seem to be introduced at regular intervals.

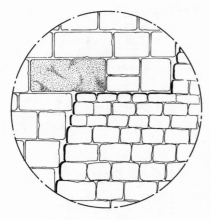

Figure 12.19. Arnold postulates that if the Great Pyramid has tiers, and if the last course of packing stone to reach the top of a nucleus is thin, it would then be followed by a thicker and therefore proportionally deeper stone.

points where the corners of each tier of the nucleus, which rises at a 75-degree angle, near the 52-degree angle of the pyramid face. This would help key the two building stages together.[16]

The mystery of the thickened courses has proven problematical for latter-day theorists, but I submit that these courses must have been functional rather than incidental. If, as I suggest, they helped to support a surrounding embankment that allowed casing stones to be placed in position from outside the pyramid, the thickened courses represent one of the most inspired of Egyptian building methods.

CHAPTER 13

THE FINAL BUILDING STAGE

Although the second building stage was an important conceptual and architectural feat, even this was still only part of the solution devised by King Sneferu for building a true pyramid. Transforming the stepped courses into a pyramidal structure with four smooth faces that met at a point in the sky was the most perplexing problem of all. This achievement was made especially difficult when one considers that, as at Mycerinus, courses of casing stone may have had outside faces that were angled instead of the steplike supports of both earlier building stages. At the pyramid of Cheops, this mantle of stone is estimated to have consisted of 115,000 blocks, with an average height of 29 inches (0.75 m).[1] The thickness of this masonry required the new layout square for the final building stage; the combination of casing stone, backing stone, and any additional fill obviously made the structure larger than the square of the second building stage. Adding to the problem, a more accurate orientation was made at Cheops, and perhaps at other pyramids, before the casing stone of the third building stage was applied.

To accommodate the slight twist between the two layout squares, more stone would have be placed along the wider part of the final square than along the narrow part. According to Petrie, at the northeast side of Cheops Pyramid, the distance between the outside edge of the casing stone and the plane of the core (second building stage), as it forms a square on the pavement, is 61.8 feet (18.8 m). At the southwest side the difference between the two squares amounted to only 50.4 feet (15.3 m).[2] The change of orientation also required that the sighting stations used to establish corners for the corrected square be slightly displaced from their earlier positions.

Skillful Side Joints

Even without the reorientation, other steps must have been taken to accommodate the additional masonry that constituted the final building stage. Indeed, just keeping the same rising angle as in the second building stage required the target on the apex to be elevated. The new square also required the four key stones at the base to be large enough in their raw state to contain the corners and facing angles of the pyramid when dressed down to size. In the peculiar manner of Egyptian masonry, the corner stones, as well as the faces of all the casing blocks in the pyramid, were laid as if by a sculptor instead of a stonemason; that is, they were shaped after being set into the course.

Egyptians never seem to have accepted the value of producing regular sizes of masonry with square joints. As mentioned, only the bedding and rising surfaces of stones were dressed before blocks were laid—the top surfaces were dressed only when being readied for the next course, and the outer faces were dressed only once all the stone had been laid.[3] This rule is shown with startling clarity in walls of Egyptian masonry. Meeting at right angles, two walls have their inside corners fashioned from single blocks that are part of both walls, instead of the blocks meeting at the corner and forming a joint with adjacent blocks. Also found in walls are blocks of different height, which produce six corners as they intersect with other blocks. While these have a fleeting resemblance to Inca masonry, as exemplified by the famous twelve-cornered stone in Cusco, the Egyptian style does not approach the intricate fit of Peruvian stonework.

Instead of being perpendicular to each other, the side joints found between Egyptian pyramid blocks (and walls) are often cut at oblique angles to the front, or to the bedding face.[4] This was probably a labor-saving device, the builders endeavoring to make maximum use of the raw blocks at whatever angle they were split from the quarry bed—a method that proves particularly useful when dealing with valued masonry such as Tura limestone or with casing stones made from hard granite boulders. The main difference between the masonry used in walls and that used in pyramids is found in the courses; pyramid courses were always brought to the same height, even if this sometimes meant two blocks were needed. The reason is obvious: level courses formed flat work surfaces. In a wall, only the top surface was required to be flat.

During Djoser's time when blocks were of a smaller dimension and masonry skills were not as well developed, builders were satisfied if the rising and bedding joints made contact with adjacent blocks for only a short distance along the front edge, the open gap of the rest of the joint being filled with mortar.[5] These poor beginnings evolved in the 4th Dynasty to the point of the casing stones on the north side of the Great Pyramid being worked so accurately that the entire joint area was separated by only a thin layer of mortar. Petrie described the joints upon first uncovering them in 1880–82:

> Several measures were taken of the thickness of the joints in the casing-stones. The mean thickness of the joints of the north-eastern casing-stones is 0.02 inches; and therefore the mean variation of the cutting of the stone from a straight line and from a true square is but 0.01 on a length of 75 inches up the face, an amount of accuracy equal to the most modern opticians' straight-edges of such a length. These joints, with an area of some 35 square feet each, were not only worked as finely as this but cemented throughout. Though the stones were brought as close as $1/50$ inch, or, in fact, into contact, and the mean opening of the joint was but $1/100$ inch, yet the builders managed to fill the joint with

cement; despite the great area of it, and the weight of the stone to be moved—some 16 tons.[6]

This skillful but time-consuming effort was reserved for those places where the work could be seen by an appreciative audience. The audience remains and grows, but the casing stones, unfortunately, are now few and far between. Signs of their removal in recent centuries for building projects in Cairo can be seen at the pyramids of Chephren and Mycerinus, where granite blocks were split into smaller pieces before being carted off. The ancient builders, however, had mastered the ability to manipulate blocks of exceedingly large dimensions. Among the advantages of larger stones, once experience had improved stone-handling skills, were that fewer stonemasons could dress one large block than would be needed for many small blocks and that the use of large blocks lends a structure stability.

Shifting Stones into Place

Setting the multiton corner blocks of the third building stage of Cheops Pyramid required them to be dragged by sledge close to their final destination and then shifted onto the corners of the newly established layout square. This was probably done by the judicious use of levers (**13.1**). Small limestone blocks, commonly found in 3rd Dynasty masons' chip heaps at Meidum and Saqqara, may have aided in this endeavor.[7] These blocks have a number of sockets, the inside conical surfaces of which are incised with concentric lines, and the sockets being so close together they occasionally overlap (**13.2**). Although it is sometimes thought that the sockets resulted from placing the block under an object that was drilled completely through, this is unlikely. Evidence of partially drilled holes show Egyptian drills as metal tubes of the kind illustrated in figure 10.9(**c**) and (**d**). Clearly, if a tube were to penetrate an object, the underlying stone would be incised with a circular outline instead of a conical indent.[8] It is more likely that these blocks were used in conjunction with a long wooden lever, perhaps one having a peg beneath it used as a fulcrum.

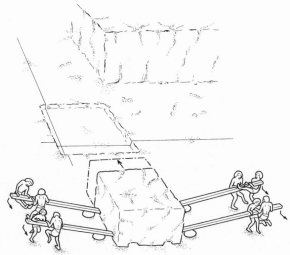

Figure 13.1. A corner casing stone being shifted into position by lifting and turning the lever on its fulcrum.

(a)   (b)   (c)

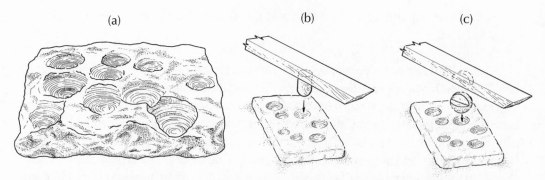

Figure 13.2. (a) Limestone block with a number of sockets cut into its irregular surface. (b) The concave sockets may have been the result of using a wooden peg as a fulcrum when shifting a block of stone into position. (c) A dolerite ball shaped to fit a socket in the lever may have been used instead.

With its use, Petrie says, "after taking a lift with it, under a boss or in a hollow of a stone, the lever was then turned on its fulcrum, and so drew forward the stone. Thus by turning the tail of the lever round two or three feet, the stone would be moved forward a few inches. This is the most effective way for a few men to move a large block which is beyond their direct powers, as I know practically in Egypt. After one lift and drag, the fulcrum was shifted forward, and the lever set on it for another lift."[9]

Instead of a wooden peg, it is also possible that the lever turned on a dolerite ball. The top of the ball may have been made with a flat stub to engage a complementary slot near the weight arm of the lever (**13.2c**). Several such devices placed on both sides of a corner block could have worked together to shift the block forward—the rotating ball incising the socket.

Establishing the First Course of Casing Stone

After being made level, the top surface of each corner stone would probably be marked from an upper sighting station by the same method used for the second building stage (**13.3**).

Figure 13.3. Once leveled, the top surface of each corner stone would probably be marked from an upper sighting station by the same method used in earlier building stages.

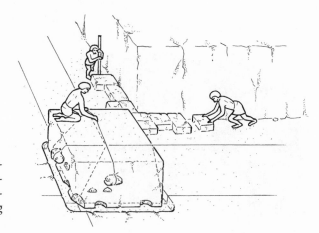

Figure 13.4. A line supported at intervals and stretched from corner to corner will establish a square that represents the top of the first course of casing stone.

This done, a line stretched from corner stone to corner stone, and supported at several points to remove the catenary curve, would help establish a square that represented the top of the first course of casing stone (**13.4**). This course would be located inside and higher than the square of the base. By removing the excess stone, and joining the mark on top of the casing stone to the corner of the base with a straightedge, the required corner angles could be established on each of the corner blocks (**13.5**). If this were done correctly, the angle on the corners of the casing blocks would exactly match the rising angle formed by the corners of the second building stage. Using the same procedure, the facing angles for adjacent sides of the pyramid could be made by cutting just enough material off the sides of the corner blocks to allow the upper and lower squares to be joined.

Signs of this procedure can be seen on the unfinished casing blocks of Mycerinus. Although they still contain bosses on their roughened faces for the points of levers, they also display chamfered edges that meet at the facing plane of the pyramid (**13.6**). While the bosses show that the blocks were set in place from outside the pyramid face, in many places they are mere nubs, encouraging some to suggest the impossibility of their having

Figure 13.5. Joining the mark on top of the stone with the corner of the base establishes the corner of the pyramid on each of the corner blocks. The facing angle of the pyramid is made by cutting just enough stone to join the upper and lower squares.

(a)

(b)

Figure 13.6. (a) North face of Mycerinus, which has casing blocks with angled faces, chamfered edges, and bosses for the points of levers. (b) Near the pyramid entrance, the facing plane of the pyramid is dressed to where the chamfered edges converge.

provided a seat for the point of a lever. However, their small size is the likely result of being reduced by stones that were rolled down the face of the pyramid when it was later used as a quarry. Indeed, the broken bosses show the wisdom of dressing the facing plane last—this protected the casing stone against damage during the building process and allowed for the placement of footholds and other such devices.

Using Chamfered Edges to Form a Plane

A closer look at the chamfered edges on top of the fifth course, for example, shows them to have been pounded to an indented line after the blocks were set into place (**13.7a**). Marked in this way, they formed the lines around each block (**13.7b**) that made it possible to establish a flat facing plane anywhere on the pyramid—even in those areas surrounded by

(b)

(a)

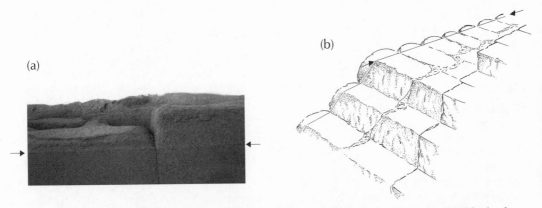

Figure 13.7. (a) Top edge of the fifth course on the north face of Mycerinus. The missing blocks disclose the chamfered edges ending in an indented straight line along the course. (b) Courses five to seven, showing the indented line that represents the face plane of the pyramid on the remaining blocks of each course.

undressed casing blocks, as at the north face. Although all the higher courses of limestone in the pyramid had already been dressed (and have since been removed), the time-consuming effort of abrading all the granite casing at the lower fifteen courses was probably abandoned at the king's demise.

Some theorists claim that the roughly angled casing is unique to the pyramid of Mycerinus, steplike casing blocks having been used on all other pyramids. They claim the steps would support the embankments needed for positioning the casing blocks as they were levered along the course and adjusted into place from the outside. Supposedly, the steps would also provide support for masons as the casing stone was reduced to a flat plane from the top face of the pyramid downward. Although this method is plausible, it does not address how the pyramid of Mycerinus, which does not have stepped casing stone, may have been built. Nor does it consider the advantages of angled casing stone: its reduced weight makes for easier delivery, and when arriving at their destination, the angled faces provide quick access and require less cutting in order to chamfer the edges for marking the facing plane.

Sliding Stone on Mortar

Although it is desirable to have angled stones on the facing planes of a pyramid, the four corner stones at the base, which do not have to be lifted, benefit more by having a flat top surface large enough to mark when sighting down to the newly oriented base square. When the corner blocks are positioned in the bedrock, the fine paving can be installed around the structure and dressed to the almost perfect level seen at the Great Pyramid (**13.8**). Once the pavement is leveled, all the casing stones of the first course can be placed on its surface and brought to the same height by means of the previously mentioned story-pole. Interestingly, the smooth top surface of the paving not only established a level for the first course

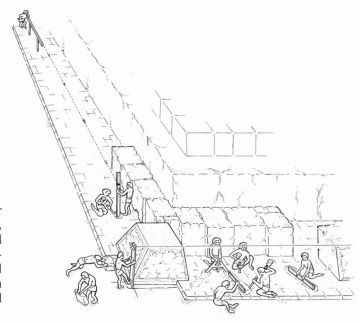

Figure 13.8. With the corner blocks seated in the bedrock, fine paving stone is placed around the base of the pyramid and made level. All blocks in the course can then be brought to the same level with a story-pole.

of casing stone; in an interesting way, it may have helped when moving the 16-ton blocks
into position.

The joints of the casing stone are adhered with a mortar consisting primarily of gypsum. Recombined after being heated to a temperature of 212° F (100° C), gypsum becomes
very hard when left to set. Indeed, after millennia, it is still difficult to flake mortar off the
joints of the stone. A stronger bond could have been made with the use of lime, a substance in plentiful supply in Egypt. But due to the shortage of wood and the high temperature required for lime production, 1,652° F (900°C), lime was not commonly used until
the time of the Greeks and Romans, when it gained currency because of the ineffective-
ness of gypsum in the wet climates of Europe.[10]

Mortar aside, the casing blocks on the first course in Cheops Pyramid are so large that
it would seem as if weight alone could keep them in place. However, the mortar served to
do more than cement the blocks together. It also acted as a lubricating bed on which blocks
could be floated into places inaccessible to lever operators. Had rollers been used in these
places, they could not have been removed after the block was positioned. Mortar served yet
another purpose: once set, it would fill any open space caused by a displaced paving stone,
thereby evenly distributing the overhead pressures on the casing stone to prevent them from
cracking. All in all, the blocks could not have been set without the use of mortar (**13.9**).[11]

Chevrier successfully proved that heavy weights could be transported easily on a
sledge pulled over a muddy track, but he did not test the possibility of moving a stone
block on the kind of flat surface formed by the paving stone. To help understand the problem, I conducted field tests with various lubricants and a 600-pound (272 kg) block of
stone. The results showed that regardless of how flat and smooth the bedding face of the

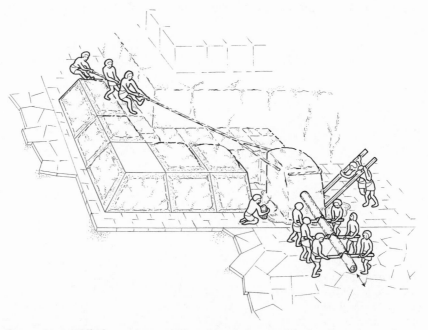

Figure 13.9. With the paving smooth and level, a casing block is floated into place,
and its edge is chamfered to the plane of the pyramid.

(a)   (b)

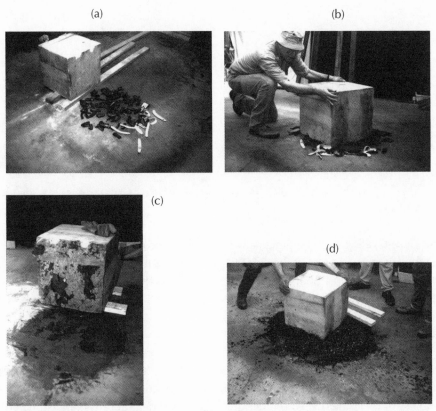

(c)

(d)

Figure 13.10. Use of different lubricants to move a 600-pound block on a smooth surface. (a) Bottom of block before being tumbled onto a layer of banana peel. (b) Block moved and turned with ease. (c) Even after extreme pressure, enough peel remained on bottom to keep the two surfaces separate. (d) The block moved on mud made of earth carefully sifted to remove pebbles.

block and the concrete surface on which it was moved were, liquid lubricants such as olive oil were ineffective. However, the ease by which a block could be moved on a thin layer of mud or banana peel was startling and unexpected—almost comparable to moving the object on ice. An examination of the residue after the test showed that regardless of the movement and pressure, enough of the lubricating mud or banana peel remained to keep the two stone surfaces from coming into direct contact (**13.10**).

Considering that the frictional force between two sliding surfaces is proportional to the force pressing them together and is independent of their contact area, a heavy block with a smooth bedding face can be made to slide as easily over a over a slurry of mortar on a smooth and level pavement as if the same weight were mounted on the sledge Chevrier used.[12]

The stone used in the field test was small by Egyptian standards, yet there is every reason to believe that similar results could be achieved with larger blocks and greater effort. The test also showed that a bed of mortar dams up in the direction of movement. The buildup may explain why the hidden lever pockets in the side joints of adjacent blocks are sometimes found to be filled with mortar although they were never meant to be seen. It may also explain how a thin layer of cement could be evenly spread on vertical surfaces that

(a)   (b)

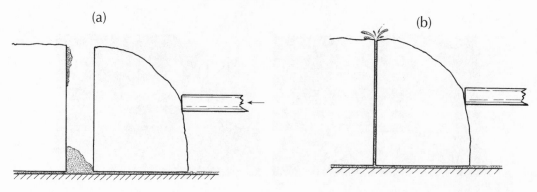

Figure 13.11. (a, b) The built-up mortar compressed as the moving block forcefully meets the stationary block.

were so close together as to be practically in contact. According to Petrie, merely to "place such stones in exact contact at the sides would be careful work; but to do so with cement in the joint seems almost impossible."[13] However, it becomes possible if the mortar compresses between the sliding block and the stationary blocks already in the course (**13.11**).

Marking and Shaping Blocks

At times control notes were written on the blocks. These concern the date, stage of transportation, work teams in charge of the stone, and destination (pyramids, pyramid temples, solar boats, or mastabas).[14] To protect the edges in transit, and to make stone easier to drag along the ground or to mount on a sledge, limestone blocks were probably dressed only on the bedding face when quarried. Roofing blocks, pyramidions, and stones meant for confined areas, narrow passageways, or tomb chambers seem to have been prepared on the ground and often marked with a destination in the pyramid. Such markings took various forms, some joints being paired by having the same hieroglyphic sign, others being marked with the same cardinal points or with the name of a course and a number. Such marks on the front face were removed during dressing, but some can still be seen in areas that remain unfinished.[15]

Given a mason's square and a stone or copper adze, it is not difficult to dress a limestone block. Indeed, if the roughened faces of a block are generally perpendicular to each other, a 3.5-foot (1 m) cube can be dressed on four sides in a single day.[16] But for one problem, it would probably take the same amount of time to dress a block with oblique side joints. Here, the difficulty lies in matching another block to the same angle, a task requiring a different measuring tool than the standard mason's square. While something similar to the adjustable-angle device used by the Greeks for their stonework may have been employed—two pieces of lath pivoted together at one end—there is no evidence for use of such a device in Egypt.[17] Yet the close oblique joints seen between many blocks make it likely they were somehow given a trial fit before being placed in a course.

Some suggest that a dressed oblique joint can be matched to an undressed block with a simple piece of string. Assuming the blocks are spaced apart, the string is used to span the distance from each corner of the dressed block to each corner of the rough block. The string having a length a little longer than the span, one end would overlap the rough block and define the depth of drafts to be cut into its corners. When joined, the drafts in the rough block will form a plane matching that of the dressed block.[18] Yet according to stonemasons, regardless of the success of the method when employed on vertical joints, accurate oblique joints could not be made without a preliminary fit. Given these findings, Engelbach postulates a system based on use of the rocker device—a means by which a train of blocks, their ends overhanging the rocker, can be pulled together and tested before being placed in a pyramid.[19]

Prefitting Casing Stones

Not taking issue with Engelbach, it is quite possible to prefit blocks without the use of rockers. Indeed, a procedure may be suggested in which only one side joint of each block would require careful fitting. For this, imagine a train of blocks outside but parallel to the course of their destination and spaced far enough apart to permit them to be worked simultaneously. Further, instead of string, imagine the corner drafts being transferred with a wooden pole having round or pointed ends—a device manipulated easily by one man (13.12). Also, suppose a series of rough casing blocks dressed on their bedding face and resting on rollers supported on level wooden planks. Labeling the blocks 1, 2 and 3, for purposes of identification, assume block 1 has a side that has already been matched to the last block mortared in the course.

To start the procedure, block 1 is rolled toward the block already mortared in the course and, by looking along the edge, adjusted until their matched faces can be sighted to a common plane. While block 1 is held in this position, the other side of it, previously dressed to some arbitrary oblique plane, is used as a pattern for the undressed near side of block 2. This is accomplished by using a pole slightly longer than the space between blocks to gauge and cut all four corners to the same depth. Being rigid, the pole is a better measuring device than the previously mentioned string. A plane is established on the rough face when the bottoms of the drafts are connected with a straightedge and all the intervening stone is removed. Together with these proceedings, the opposite face of block 2, the like opposite face of block 3, and perhaps other blocks in the train as well, are dressed to whatever arbitrary angle was formed when they were split from the quarry.

To test the matched faces while outside the course, block 2 is rolled to meet block 1. If the fit is not acceptable, it may be improved by any of several methods; with limestone, the high points of both surfaces may be reduced by drawing a saw blade through the joint.[20] With granite, a facing plane coated with red ochre may be used to note the high points, these being dressed until both blocks acquire red marks less than an inch apart when pressed together.[21] Presumably a match can be made with one preliminary fit, but if the situation demands, block 2 may be separated, reworked, and tried again. A method sometimes used in the Old Kingdom consisted of making a rough concavity on the face of a joint and fitting only its outer edges.[22] Generally, limestone blocks were trimmed with crisscross strokes of a chisel or an adze, which in the 2nd Dynasty was of flint but from the 4th Dynasty onward was of copper.[23] Being raised above the surface on rollers and planks, the bottom edges would always be accessible for dressing.

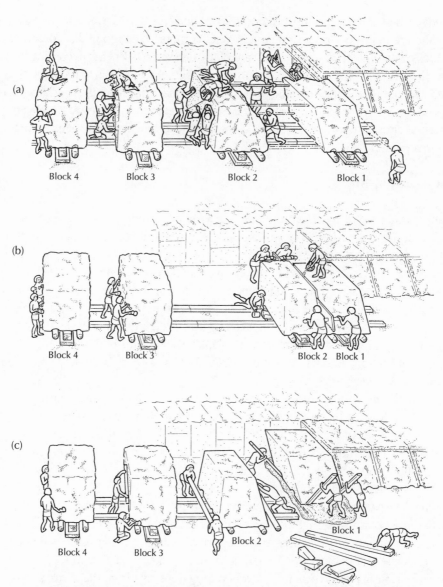

Figure 13.12. Method of prefitting a train of casing blocks with a pole, before setting them into the course. (a) The right side of block 1 is sighted to a plane common with a block already in the course. Its left side, already dressed to an arbitrary oblique plane, is used as a pattern for the undressed side of block 2. (b) Blocks 1 and 2 are joined and given a final fit with a copper blade and a slurry of sand. (c) After setting block 1 in the course, the procedure is repeated by sighting block 2 to a common plane with block 1.

If the fit of the joint is acceptable, the back of block 1 is dressed by gauging the pole against the backing stone already fixed in the pyramid. If the backs are curved, as in the granite blocks of Mycerinus or Chephren, they may still be successfully scribed by keeping the pole perpendicular to both faces with the aid of the square-level. Because the rear surfaces have been shown to be less accurate in Egyptian pyramids, a preliminary fit for them is not postulated. When block 1 is set into the course, its exposed side face becomes

Figure 13.13. The west face of Cheops Pyramid shows deep indents cut into the limestone casing stone by abrasive winds.

the basis for sighting block 2, now moved to a common sighting plane. Once block 2 is aligned, the other side of it becomes a pattern for the undressed rising face of block 3. Continuing in this way, a stream of blocks may be prefitted just prior to tapping out the wedges, lowering the fully dressed block in the mortar, and sliding it into position with levers, battering rams, or ropes that are placed in holes piercing the block or tied around the still undressed portion of its top surface.

Such time-consuming effort was limited to the lowest blocks in a pyramid, which could be seen by observers, the imperfections of higher courses being lost in the great expanse of the face. Despite the care given to perfecting the fit of the casing blocks, in a short time the wind-driven sands of the Giza Plateau seem to have abraded deep pockets into blocks on the first course of Cheops Pyramid (**13.13**). To counter this problem, builders planning the pyramid of Chephren, the next one to be built, laid hard granite casing stone on the first course. Finding that the cutting winds reached a greater height than anticipated, the third large pyramid of Giza, Mycerinus, was built with granite on the lower 15 courses; granite may also have been used for the pyramidion and for every corner on each course of the pyramid.

The First Course at Chephren Pyramid

Remains at the first course of Chephren Pyramid show that while granite successfully withstood the abrasive winds, its installation created a new problem for the builders: the method used to level the first course of casing stone had to be modified due to the difficulty of shaping the hard stone. Therefore, instead of being placed on top of a level pavement, the first course of Chephren was cut at various depths into the softer stone of the bedrock (**13.14**). As a result the most accurately leveled surface of the entire pyramid was made on the top surface of the first course. This was possible because the many large granite blocks, some about 8 feet (2.5 m) square, could easily have supported the required leveling stations. Cut from the bedrock, the low square foundation platform was so well planned that Petrie was able to use its outer edges to find the exact orientation of the pyramid. Regularly spaced rectangular cutouts around the edges of the platform show that levers were used to help set the first course of granite into position.[24]

Figure 13.14. Pyramid of Chephren shows a raised foundation platform with cutouts for levering the granite casing stones into position.

Regardless of the type of stone used in the pyramid, a large enough supply was probably always on hand to anticipate the needs of the builders. Supposedly, the stored blocks were raised only during the inundation, a four-month period when, unable to work the fields, farmers spent their time in the service of the king. The floods were also a time when heavily laden ships could be brought closer to the building site. At Lisht, however, work seems to have continued during all months of the year, although activity was greatest during the months of actual high water.[25]

Even assuming that the limestone casing blocks of Cheops Pyramid were given a preliminary fit on the ground, it is difficult to imagine 115,000 or so blocks being cut, stored, and transported in exact order some hundreds of feet up the side of the pyramid, much less that this occurred without the need of refitting. Indeed, the most experienced mason could not possibly cut and fit blocks with such exactness on the ground that they could match a distant course on the pyramid—especially since the length of each course changes with the rising structure. These problems, and the need to set the blocks into position from outside the course, confirm the need for an outside embankment around each rising level. With this platform, blocks approximately cut to fit on the ground and haphazardly raised could be recut or rearranged before being set in place. A platform would also permit undressed blocks to be raised and prefitted in front of each rising course, as earlier described.

Providing an Embankment for the Casing Stone

The need for a surrounding embankment raises the question of how it could be supported on casing stones that are not steplike but have irregular faces that are angled and would not provide the needed purchase. It has already been shown that although ramps were used on the lower levels, up to perhaps 50 feet (15 m), they are impractical for the higher reaches of the structure. Considering this, an embanking system must have been devised that did not encase the pyramid but would allow its shape to be carefully controlled as it rose. This would be especially critical at the final building stage, where the developing structure would be less forgiving of mistakes.

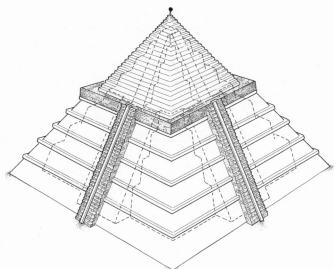

Figure 13.15. If the periodic thickened courses found at Cheops were to extend beyond the face of the pyramid by only a foot or two, they could support a surrounding embankment periodically made to rise with the courses.

An indication of the possible method used appears at the Great Pyramid. As previously mentioned, Cheops shows a regular pattern of thickened courses gradually decreasing in size until another such pattern begins. Thick and proportionally deep blocks that start each of these diminishing patterns are said to key together the nucleus with the casing stone of the pyramid. These thick stones may have played an additional role in the building process. If some courses in the pyramid were allowed to extend slightly beyond the face of the structure, they could be made to hold an embankment around the pyramid (**13.15**).[26] Rising with the courses, and being outside their face, the embankment would not interfere with sighting stations placed on upper levels of the pyramid corners (**13.16**).

This building system has many advantages: embankments would be deep enough to support work crews and to allow casing stones to be fitted before being set into the course;

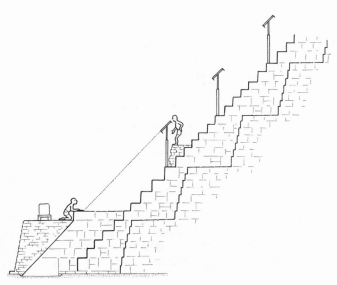

Figure 13.16. Being outside the courses, the embankment would not interfere with sighting stations placed on upper levels of the pyramid corners.

blocks elevated to the embankments could be positioned anywhere along a course from outside its face; the embankment would permit work teams outside adjacent faces to cooperate in laying the corner stones of each course—a problem never before addressed by any proposed ramp theory; by use of turning posts and rope snubbing devices stationed at the head of the stairways and the corners of the embankment, men could be distributed more effectively for lifting the blocks (**13.17a**). Although wood turning posts act as simple pulleys for the rope, the friction may be reduced by a leather sleeve rotating over a layer of grease—an early form of rotating pulley wheel (**13.17b** and **c**).[27]

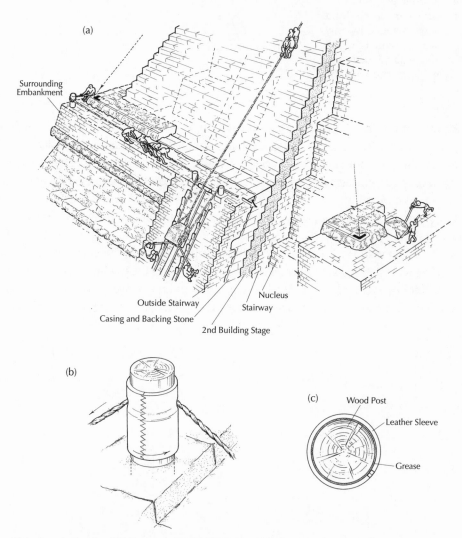

Figure 13.17. (a) Supported on a course of protruding stones, the surrounding embankment would provide the means to prefit and set the casing stone from outside the course. It also provides for posts to be stationed at strategic locations to assist in raising the blocks. (b, c) Friction normally generated on a turning post may be reduced with a leather sleeve rotating on a layer of grease.

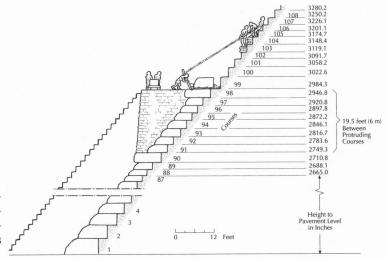

Figure 13.18. The embankment, as supported on a typical thickened course of Cheops Pyramid.

Assuming the 52-degree angle face of the pyramid to be the hypotenuse of a right-angle triangle, 1 foot (30.5 cm) of vertical rise for each embankment would result in a horizontal distance of 9.5 inches (24 cm). Accordingly, if an embankment were 25 feet (7.5 m) high, its work surface would be 19.5 feet (6 m) from the outside plane of the pyramid—certainly adequate for moving and levering blocks into place. In addition, if we consider the 3- or 4-foot (1 m) top surface of casing already in the lower course and the 1–2 feet (0.5 m) of the protruding thick stone, the actual work surface would be about 25 feet (7.5 m). Supporting the heavy embankment would be no problem since its greatest weight would be borne by the pyramid and not by the protruding stone (**13.18**).

This construction method has another important advantage; at the discretion of the builders, the embankment can be taken apart piece by piece and added to the next higher projecting course of casing stone. The disassembly may take place on reaching the projecting course, or the embankment may rise past the course until the top of the succeeding

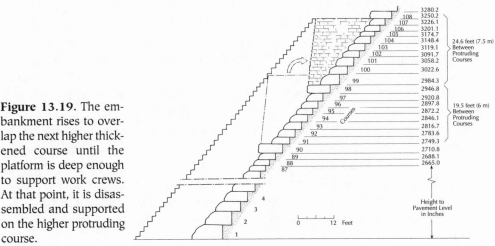

Figure 13.19. The embankment rises to overlap the next higher thickened course until the platform is deep enough to support work crews. At that point, it is disassembled and supported on the higher protruding course.

embankment is sufficiently deep for an adequate work surface (**13.19**). With embankments covering only one small vertical section at a time, the face of the pyramid is exposed enough to be observed and controlled. Due to the decreasing width of the pyramid as it rises, the encircling embankment would need an ever-diminishing amount of material, the excess being transferred to the very stairways that help to increase their height. Indeed, by leapfrogging the platform to the very top of the pyramid, the only extraneous material left on the pyramid would be the four shallow stairways on each face of the structure. These converging stairways could then be used to great advantage by combining them to form a platform on the summit large enough for workers to position the pyramidion in its rough or finished state (**13.20**). Since the pyramid corners are hidden by the converging stairways, it would be easier to establish the angles of the pyramidion if it was dressed before it was raised. Indeed, the twist of 1° 40' at the apex of Chephren's pyramid seems to affirm the problem caused by the converging stairways.[28]

The satellite pyramid of Cheops discovered recently by Zahi Hawass has some interesting features near the top. The pyramid had been capped and Tura limestone was used for all the upper courses. Found near the base of the structure, the pyramidion shows a slight convexity formed by four triangular faces cut into the underside. The stone just beneath the captsone is missing, but the third stone down is dressed with a bevel on its top surface. The bevel is made by following lines that run from each corner to the center. Obviously, the top stones were made to interlock with each other for stability against earthquakes or the settling of the pyramid. It is suggested that the diagonal lines found on the stone confirm the theory of forming a pyramid by controlled squares.[29] Instead, I believe the lines were provided as a guide for the masons to form the bevels. Speaking as a sculptor, the fastest and most accurate way to form the interlocking convex and concave stones found at the pyramid is by the use of diagonal lines.

While it may logically be assumed that some heavy blocks were placed on the first course and raised to their destination course by course as the pyramid rose in height, recently discovered evidence at the causeway of Sahure, a 5th Dynasty pyramid, suggests otherwise. On clearing the pyramid field at Abusir, researchers found among scattered stones from the causeway blocks that contain scenes showing the pyramidion as being the last architectural component to be placed on the pyramid. Although the pyramidion itself is not shown due to a missing block, there can be no doubt as to its presence. The extant causeway blocks show a group of men pulling a rope attached to a wooden sledge, with a man pouring water on the ground in front of the runners to ease its passage. An accompanying inscription reads: "(bringing?) the pyramidion (covered with fine gold) to the pyramid, 'The soul of Sahure rises in glory,' by both ship crews."[30] Nearby, dancers celebrate the last stone to be taken to a completed pyramid.

After raising the pyramidion using the various devices already described, the rough faces of the angled casing stone and the protruding courses, now minus their surrounding embankments, could be used as supports for wooden scaffolding. Working from the top down, the pyramid could be dressed to the plane marked by the chamfered blocks when they were set in place, one group of workmen probably trimming off the protruding parts as another group of workers, on a higher level, smoothed the surface to a plane (**13.21**).

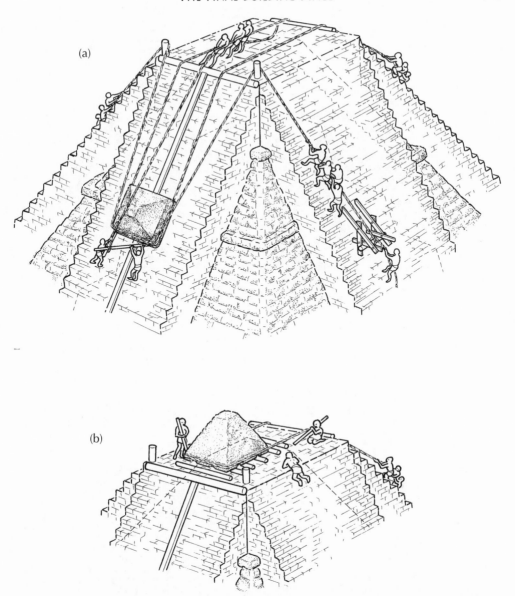

Figure 13.20. (a) The stairways on each face converge at the top to form a platform large enough to raise the pyramidion by use of levers, turning posts, and teams of men positioned on all four stairways. (b) Once on the apex of the pyramid, the pyramidion may be rolled into position.

Discoveries not yet made or devices not yet found may alleviate the absence of information describing the building method used by the Egyptians. However, a major factor in this lack of information was the separation in Egyptian society between the literate class and the craftsman class. With hieroglyphs, the literate class could write of the times, the gods, and the glory of the king. Stonemasons, builders, and surveyors, not being scribes, passed their knowledge from father to son by an oral tradition long since lost. This has left us with pieces of a building puzzle that has filled many lifetimes of investigation. Having used much of my life to investigate methods whereby a pyramid could be built around a

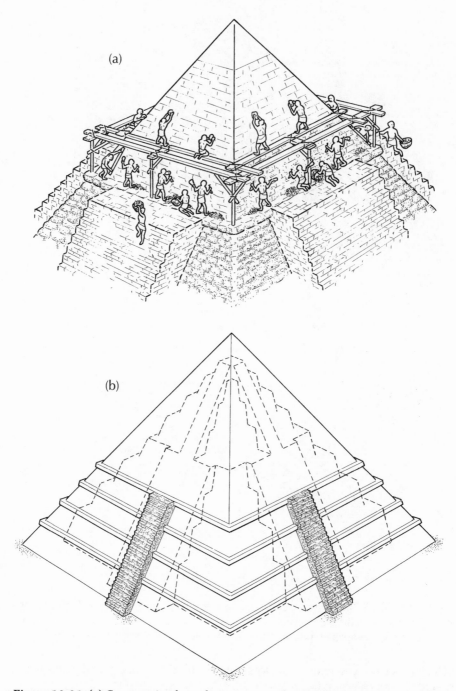

Figure 13.21. (a) Capstone in place, the stairway and projecting courses, now minus their embankments, can be used as supports for wooden scaffolding. The faces of the pyramid are finished to a plane from the top down—one group of workmen trimming off the projecting parts, another group smoothing the surface to a perfect plane. (b) With the face of the pyramid dressed, and the means of supporting the scaffolding removed, the pyramid is left with four smooth, flat faces.

nucleus—like an onion with two outer skins instead of like a more than 200-course layer cake—I find it pertinent to cite the method priests described to Herodotus when he visited Egypt over 2,000 years ago, keeping in mind that the pyramids were as ancient to him as he is to us:

> The ascent was regularly graduated by what some call crossae, or steps, and others bomides, or altars. When the workmen had finished the first tier, they elevated the stone to the second by the aid of machines constructed of short pieces of wood; from the second tier the stones were raised by a similar machine to the third; and so on to the summit. Thus, there were as many machines as there were courses in the structure of the pyramid; though there might have been only one machine, which, being easily manageable, could be raised from one layer to the next in succession. The summit of the pyramid was first finished and coated, and the process was continued downward until the whole was completed.[31]

Based on Herodotus, Petrie concluded that the pyramid casing was set starting from the top and working down to the foot of the pyramid. Arnold suggests that this is erroneous. In concurring with Arnold, that supporting stones cannot be placed under dependent courses, I interpret the last sentence quoted from Herodotus to mean that the casing was dressed (not set) from the top down; first the masons finished the casing by chiseling it to a plane, then they coated the casing by abrading and smoothing the surface.

In my efforts to change the prevailing thought on pyramid building, with its dependency on the use of major construction ramps, I have drawn upon a life of craftsmanship, particularly my experience as a sculptor and draftsman. My sculptural efforts gave me insights on how 2- to 3-ton blocks of stone could be maneuvered; my experience as a patent draftsman prepared me for the acceptance of new ideas and enabled me to illustrate what my mind's eye could see. Yet it is one thing to have a natural proclivity that helps one to analyze the Egyptian devices and building methods but quite another to fathom the minds of a society that would expend such enormous energy to provide a tomb for one man, king or god, and repeat the effort again, again, and again.

ABBREVIATIONS

AGMA	Pierre Amiet, *La Glyptique Mésopotamienne Archaique*
AJSLL	*American Journal of Semitic Languages and Literature*
Arnold, *Building*	Dieter Arnold, *Building in Egypt*
ASAE	*Annales du Service des Antiquités de l'Égypte*, Cairo
AM	Ashmolean Museum, Oxford
BdE	Bibliothèque d'Étude, Cairo
BEES	*Bulletin of the Egyptian Exploration Society*
BIFAO	*Bulletin e l'Institut français d'archéologie orientale*, Cairo
BM	British Museum
BSAE	British School of Archaeology in Egypt
CdE	*Chronique d'Égypte*
CEAEM	Somers Clarke and R. Engelbach, *Ancient Egyptian Masonry*
CPECAM	Joan Crowfoot Payne, *Catalogue of the Predynastic Egyptian Collection in the Ashmolean Museum*
EEF	Egyptian Exploration Fund
EM	Egyptian Museum, Cairo
Encyclopedia	*The Cambridge Encyclopedia of Archaeology*
GM	*Gottinger Miszellin*
HOA	G. Swarup, A. K. Bag, and K. S. Shulka (eds.), *History of Oriental Astronomy*
HT	Charles Singer, E. J. Holmyard, and A. R. Hall (eds.), *A History of Technology*
IFAO	L'Institut français d'archéologie orientale
JARCE	*Journal of the American Research Center in Egypt*
JCA	*Archaeoastronomy: Journal of the Center for Archaeoastronomy*
JEA	*Journal of Egyptian Archaeology* (London)
JESHO	*Journal of the Economic and Social History of the Orient*
KMT	*A Modern Journal of Ancient Egypt*
LÄ	*Lexikon der Ägyptologie*

MDAIK	*Mitteilungen des Deutschen Archäologischen Instituts, Abteilung Kairo*
MIO	*Mitteilungen des Instituts für Orientforschung*
MMA	Metropolitan Museum of Art
Needham, *Science*	Joseph Needham, *Science and Civilization in China*
Petrie, *Pyramids*	W. M. Flinders Petrie, *The Pyramids and Temples of Gizeh*
Piramidi	V. Maragioglio and C. Rinaldi, *L' Architettura della Piramidi Menfete*
RdE	*Revue d'Égyptologie*
SA	*Scientific American*
VA	*Varia Aegyptiaca*
WA	A. F. Aveni (ed.), *World Archaeoastronomy*
ZA	*Zeitschrift für Assyriologie*

NOTES

Chapter 1: Mountains of the Sun

1. Mellaart, *Earliest Civilizations*, 15.
2. Marshack, *Roots of Civilization*, 27–30.
3. Leach, "Primitive Time-Reckoning," *HT*, 1:116.
4. Orlove et al., "Forecasting Andean Rainfall," *Nature*, 403:68–71.
5. Frazer, *Spirits of the Corn*, 1:116, 309, 314.
6. Haddingham, *Early Man*, 107–8.
7. Ammarell, "Sky Calendars," *HOA*, 244–45.
8. Bernbaum, *Sacred Mountains*, 206–10; Zaphiropoulou, *Delos*, 5. To help simplify the text I have rounded out some of the measurements.
9. Bernbaum, *Sacred Mountains*, 111.
10. *New York Times*, 7 April 1999, A1.
11. Reinhard, "Sacred Peaks," *National Geographic* 181:91–92.
12. Degani, *Astronomy*, 144–47.
13. Aveni, *Skywatchers*, 62–63.
14. Stonehenge is a site once claimed to have been a virtual calendar of the heavens. This has since been challenged, especially by the findings of a possible second heel stone. The only reasonable statement that can still be made about Stonehenge is that the general layout of its axis was deliberately oriented toward midsummer sunrise and midwinter sunset (Ruggles, *WA*, 16).
15. Krupp, "The Cosmic Temples," *WA*, 68.
16. Vance R. Tiede, Astronomical Orientation of the Pyramid Mounds of China's Western Han Dynasty, Lecture at Yale University, 29 March 1996.
17. Schele and Freidal, *Forest of Kings*, 66.
18. Aveni, *Skywatchers*, 245–48, 277–79, fig. 100.
19. Ibid., 104, 248.
20. Dearborn and Schreiber, "Here Comes the Sun," *JCA* 9:23, 27
21. Aveni, *Skywatchers*, 64.
22. Zeilik, *WA*, 146.
23. Aveni, *Skywatchers*, 253.
24. Haddingham, *Early Man*, 176.
25. Schele and Freidal, *Forest of Kings*, 262.
26. Gallagher, *Exploring the Ancient World*, 134.
27. Gardiner, *Egyptian Grammar*, 489, n. 27.
28. Krupp, "Light in the Temples," in Ruggles, *Records in Stone*, 476, fig. 21.2; 492, fig. 21.11; 498.
29. Ibid., 484, fig. 21.7.
30. Ruggles, "Recent Developments ," *WA*, 14–16.

31. Firneis and Köberl, "Further Studies," *WA*, 430–35.

32. Younger, "Dayton: Crossroads of Indian Culture," *USAir Magazine*, Nov. 1992, 75–76.

33. Needham, *Science*, 3:284.

34. Ibid., 292–93, 297.

35. Habachi, *Obelisks of Egypt*, 10–12.

36. Snodgrass, *Symbolism of the Stupa*, 20, 164–66, 353.

37. Boorstein, *The Discoverers*, 86.

38. Lloyd, *Archaeology*, 17.

39. Ibid., 16.

40. Garrison, *History of Engineering and Technology*, 18–19, table 2-1.

41. Nissen, *Early History of the Ancient Near East*, 60.

42. Drower, "Water Supply," *HT*, 1:546.

43. Nissen, *Early History*, 60–61.

44. Schmandt-Besserat, "The Earliest Precursor of Writing," *SA* 53, 52.

45. Wenke, *Patterns in Prehistory*, 249.

46. Lloyd, *Archaeology*, 41–43; Kostof, *History of Architecture*, 55, fig. 3.15.

47. Frankfort, *Art and Architecture*, 18–22.

48. Saggs, *Civilization*, 56.

49. Frankfort, *Art and Architecture*, 18–19, fig. 3.

50. Lloyd and Müller, *Ancient Architecture*, 12.

51. Frankfort, *Art*, 23–24; Lloyd, *HT*, 1:462.

52. Lloyd, *Archaeology*, 54.

53. Drower, "Water-Supply," *HT*, 1:545.

54. Badawy, *Architecture in Ancient Egypt and the Near East*, 76, 78, 81.

55. Frankfort, *Kingship*, 313.

56. Ibid., 314, 322

57. Ibid., 320–23.

58. Gray, *Near Eastern Mythology*, 32.

59. Frankfort, *Art*, 22.

60. Frankfort, *Kingship*, 323, fig. 50.

61. Gray, *Near Eastern Mythology*, 32.

62. Crawford, *Sumer and the Sumerians*, 74–75.

63. Lloyd, "Building in Brick and Stone," *HT*, 1:467–68.

64. Burney, *The Ancient Near East*, 64.

65. Stronmmenger, *5000 Years of the Art of Mesopotamia*, 431–32.

66. Lloyd, *Archaeology*, 94–96, figs. 51–52.

67. Frankfort, *Art*, 22.

68. Lloyd, "Building in Brick and Stone," *HT*, 1:461.

69. Adams, *Predynastic Egypt*, 57, fig. 39.

70. Oates, "Emergence of Cities," *Encyclopedia*, 117–18.

71. Roaf, *Cultural Atlas*, 63–65; Lloyd, *Archaeology*, 85.

72. Algaze, *The Uruk World System*, 19–25.

Chapter 2: Egypt

1. Hoffman, *Egypt Before the Pharaohs*, 87–90, 97, 123.

2. Sherratt, "Beginnings of Agriculture," *Encyclopedia*, 105.

3. Hoffman, *Egypt*, 160–61.

4. Trigger et al., *Ancient Egypt*, 18.

5. Ibid., 21–22.

6. Hoffman, *Egypt*, 169–70, 175–76, 194–98, 201–3.

7. Ibid., 140–41.

8. Adams, *Predynastic Egypt*, 17.

9. Riley, *Origins of Civilization*, 28.

10. Adams, *Predynastic Egypt*, 48.

11. Trigger, *Ancient Egypt*, 32–33.

12. Hoffman, *Egypt*, 111.

13. Friedman et al., "Preliminary Report on Field Work at Hierakonpolis: 1996–1998," *JARCE* 36:5, 6.

14. Hoffman, *Egypt*, 143.

15. Adams, "Unprecedented Discoveries at Hierakonpolis," *BEES* 15: 29–31.

16. Ibid., 109–10.

17. Hayes, *The Scepter of Egypt*, 1:49–52.

18. Smith, *Egyptian Architecture*, 21–22.

19. Hoffman, *Egypt*, 202, fig. 54.

20. Ibid., 146, fig. 41.

21. Rice, *Egypt's Making*, 85–86.

22. Hoffman, *The First Egyptians*, 42.

23. Smith, "Making of Egypt," in Friedman and Adams, *Followers of Horus*, 235–36.

24. Algaze, *The Uruk World System*, 40, fig. 18H.

25. Smith, "Making of Egypt," 241–42.

26. Frankfort, *Kingship and the Gods*, 34.

27. Schenkel, *LÄ* 5:723; personal conversation with James P. Allen; *hrr*, "Flower" = *hrw*, Horus.

28. Kemp, *Ancient Egypt*, 74–77, fig. 25.

29. Quibell and Greene, *Hierakonpolis*, 2: 3–5, fig. 62.

30. Rice, *Egypt's Making*, 90.

31. Lloyd, *Archaeology*, 94–95.

32. Rice, *Egypt's Making*, 91.

33. Kemp, *Ancient Egypt*, 75.

34. Personal conversation with James P. Allen.

35. LeBas, *L'Obelisque de Luxor*, 2–3.

36. Aldred, *Egypt to the End of the Old Kingdom*, 64, fig. 55.

37. Lurker, *The Gods and Symbols of Ancient Egypt*, 128–29.

38. Saleh and Sourouzian, *Official Catalogue*, section 14, accession JE 32161.

39. Hawass and Verner, "Newly Discovered Blocks from the Causeway of Sahure," *MDAIK* 52:180.

40. Emery, *Great Tombs*, 2:102, fig. 105.

41. Trigger et al., *Ancient Egypt*, 39.

42. Payne, *CPECAM*, 13, pls. 1–5; Petrie, *Koptos*, pls. 3, 4; Kemp, *Ancient Egypt*, 81, fig. 28.

43. Emery, *Archaic Egypt*, 165–67.

44. Shaw and Nicholson, *Dictionary*, 157–58.

45. Breasted, *History of Egypt*, 6–7.

46. Davies and Friedman, *Egypt Uncovered*, 36.

47. Personal discussion with John Suh and Ji Kim.

48. Schenkel, *LÄ* 5:724–25.

49. Shaw and Nicholson, *Dictionary*, 219.

50. Görsdorf et al., "C Dating of the Archaic Royal Necropolis," 169–75.

51. Fischer, "The Origin of Egyptian Hieroglyphs," in Senner, *The Origins of Writing*, 59–62.

52. Wilford, "Finds in Egypt Date Alphabet," *New York Times*, 14 Nov. 1999.

53. Riley, *Origins*, 35.

54. Trigger, *Ancient Egypt*, 51.

55. Emery, *Archaic Egypt*, 105.

56. Ibid., 31–37.

57. Edwards, *Pyramids of Egypt*, 4–5.

58. Saggs, *Civilization before Greece and Egypt*, 274–75.

59. Emery, *Archaic Egypt*, 51, 120–21.

60. Gardiner, *Egyptian Grammar*, 72–75.

61. Personal conversation with James P. Allen.

62. Allen, *Middle Egyptian*, 79–81; Betrò, *Hieroglyphics*, 58; Shaw and Nicholson, *Dictionary*, 194; Clark, *Myth and Symbol in Ancient Egypt*, 232–33.

63. Cf. Gardiner, *Egyptian Grammar*, 453, D 28; Smith, "Making of Egypt," 239, fig. 22.

64. Emery, *Great Tombs*, 2:104–6, figs. 106–14.

Chapter 3: Early Monuments

1. McGovern, "Wine for Eternity," *Archaeology* (July–August 1988): 24–34.

2. Lehner, *Complete Pyramids*, 76.

3. Günter Dreyer, "The Beginning of Writing in Egypt: Discoveries in the Royal Tombs of Abydos," Lecture at MMA, 13 October 1999.

4. Hoffman, *Egypt*, 261.

5. Petrie, *Royal Tombs* 1: pl. 60.

6. Friedman et al., "Preliminary Report," *JARCE* 36:6.

7. Lehner, *Complete Pyramids*, 76–77.

8. Weeks, *Lost Tomb*, 39.

9. Emery, *Archaic Egypt*, 130.

10. Smith, *Art and Architecture*, 38.

11. Petrie et al., *Meydum and Memphis* 3:6, figs. 17–18.

12. Emery, *Archaic Egypt*, pls. 24a, b.

13. Wilford, "Early Pharaoh's Ghostly Fleet," *New York Times*, 31 October 2000, F1, F4.

14. Frankfort, "Monumental Architecture," *AJSLL*, 58:330–31.

15. Lloyd, *Archaeology*, 51.

16. Moorey, *Mesopotamian Materials*, 362; Emery, *Archaic Egypt*, 182–3.

17. Frankfort, "Monumental Architecture," 334.

18. Emery, *Archaic Egypt*, 48, fig 7.

19. Ibid., pls. 8–9.

20. Oates, "Emergence of Cities," 119, fig. 16.8.

21. Shaw and Nicholson, *Dictionary*, 189.

22. Watson, *Egyptian Pyramids*, 13.

23. O'Connor, "New Funerary Enclosures," *JARCE* 26:54, 82.

24. Arnold, "Royal Cult Complexes," in Shafer, *Temples of Ancient Egypt*, 36.

25. Emery, *Great Tombs*, 1:83–91, figs. 48, 51, 51AA–CC, 52.

26. Lloyd, *Archaeology*, 44.

27. Verner, *Forgotten Pharaohs*, 148–53.

28. Gardiner, *Egyptian Grammar*, 4, 5; Betrò, *Hieroglyphics*, 13.

29. Personal discussion with James P. Allen; Gardiner, *Egyptian Grammar*, 486, n. 7; p. 515, T 28, T 29.

30. Shaw and Nicholson, *Dictionary*, 85.

31. Seton-Williams and Stocks, *Blue Guide*, 577–79.

32. Emery, *Archaic Egypt*, 180–82.

33. Rice, *Egypt's Making*, 85–86.

34. Emery, *Great Tombs*, 2:3; 3:3–4.

35. Smith, *Art and Architecture*, 40–44.

36. In a personal conversation, David O'Connor claims the Abydos site is confirmed by recent findings as the royal cemetery; source for Saqqara is Watson, *Pyramids and Mastaba*, 13.

37. Frankfort, "Monumental Architecture," 332.

38. Petrie, *Egyptian Architecture*, 18–20, figs. 7:29A, 7:29B; Petrie et al., *Tarkhan 1 and Memphis 5*, 1–7, pls. 9–10:3, 10:4.

39. Frankfort, "Monumental Architecture," 340–43.

40. Reisner, *Development of the Egyptian Tomb*, 244–45.

41. Ward, "Relations between Egypt and Mesopotamia," *JESHO* 7:22–23.

42. Reisner, *Development*, figs. 129, 131–33, 140, 144.

43. Weeks, *Lost Tomb*, 40.

44. (Meidum) Michalowski, *Art of Ancient Egypt*, 478, fig. 837:2; (Dendera) Petrie, *Dendereh*, pl. 28; (Saqqara) Michalowski, *Art of Ancient Egypt*, 474, fig. 833, and Reisner, *Development*, 256, figs., 147–48; (Abydos) Peet, *Cemeteries of Abydos*, 2:30, fig. 8.

45. Smith, *Art and Architecture*, 80, fig. 72.

46. Shaw and Nicholson, *Dictionary*, 96.

47. Simpson, *The Mastabas of Qar and Idu* 2: pls. 29a–c, 27.

48. Smith, "Making of Egypt," 239, fig.22; Emery, *Great Tombs* 2:104–6, figs. 106–14.

49. Reisner, *Development*, 251.

50. von der Way, "Identification of Architecture," in Friedman and Adams, *Followers of Horus*, 218–19, figs. 2–4.

51. Ibid., 221.

Chapter 4: Step Pyramids

1. Edwards, *Pyramids of Egypt*, 37–38, fig. 6.

2. Lauer, *Pyramids of Sakkara*, 2–5, 11.

3. Emery, *Archaic Egypt*, 144–45, fig. 85.

4. O'Connor, "New Funerary Enclosures," *JARCE* 36:83.

5. A feature emphasized by Dieter Arnold during a personal discussion.

6. Swelim, *Some Problems*, 100.

7. With slight modifications, based on the description offered in Swelim, ibid., 103–4.

8. Swelim, "Additional Views," *MDAIK* 38:95.

9. Arnold, *Building*, 81.

10. Isler, "On Pyramid Building 2," *JARCE* 24:98–103, figs. 5–10.

11. Verner, *Forgotten Pharaohs*, 38.

12. Lesko, "Seila 1981," *JARCE* 35:233, fig. 22.

13. Swelim, *Some Problems*, 207.

14. Wilkinson, *Early Dynastic Egypt*, 243–44.

15. Edwards, *Pyramids of Egypt*, 70–71.

16. Petrie, *Royal Tombs*, 1:figs. 46:121, 46:134, 46:147, for example.

17. Allen, *Genesis in Egypt*, 13–14.

18. Frankfort, *Kingship*, 151–52.

19. Allen, *Genesis in Egypt*, 25.

20. Kemp, *Ancient Egypt*, 88.

21. Frankfort, *Kingship*, 153–54.

22. Allen, *Genesis in Egypt*, 59.

23. Clark, *Myth and Symbol*, 60–61.

24. Personal conversation with James P. Allen.

25. Kramer, *Sumerians*, 115.

26. Frankfort, *Kinghsip*, 152.

27. Clark, *Myth and Sumbol*, 38, 40–41.

28. Armour, *Gods and Myths*, 15.

29. Clark, *Myth and Symbol*, 41.

30. Frankfort, *Egyptian Religion*, 153.

31. Frankfort, *Kingship*, 152.

32. Ibid., 152.

Chapter 5: The True Pyramid

1. Frankfort, *Kingship*, 153.

2. Swelim, *Some Problems*, 152.

3. Needham, *Science*, 3:332–34

4. Maragioglio and Rinaldi, *Piramidi*, 3: pl. 2, fig. 2.

5. Ibid., 3:10–12.

6. Arnold, *Building*, 110–13.

7. Edwards, *Pyramids*, 82–83.

8. Maragioglio and Rinaldi, *Piramidi*, 3: 56–58.

9. Ibid., 74–76.

10. Ibid., 126–28.

11. Rossi, "Notes on the Pyramidion," *JEA*, 1999: 219–22.

12. Isler, "On Pyramid Building 2," *JARCE* 24:97–98.

13. Mendelssohn, *Riddle of the Pyramids*, 97–98, fig. 19.

14. Stadelmann, *Ägyptischen Pyramiden*, 105.

15. Maragioglio and Rinaldi, *Piramidi*, 3:134.

16. Edwards, "Pyramid Texts" in *Hommages*, 161.

17. Smith, *Art and Architecture*, 71.

18. Maragioglio and Rinaldi, *Piramidi*, 3: 80–82, pl. 8, fig. 8.

19. Wilkinson, *Early Dynastic Egypt*, 253.

20. Edwards, "Pyramid Texts," 162.

21. Arnold, "Royal Cult Complexes," 31, 51.

22. Hawass and Verner, "Newly Discovered Blocks," *MDAIK* 52:178–79.

23. Žába, *L' Orientation*, 2: pl. I.

24. Maragioglio and Rinaldi, *Piramidi*, 4: 62, 164; pl. 10; figs. 1–6, 9.

25. Arnold, "Royal Cult Complexes," 50.

26. Lehner, *Complete Pyramids*, 129–30.

27. Arnold, "Royal Cult Complexes," 50–51.

28. Weeks, *Lost Tomb*, 232.

29. Malville et al., "Megaliths," 488–90.

30. Temple, *Crystal Sun*, 407, pls. 63, 64.

31. Cole, *Determination of the Exact Size*, 8.

32. Cotsworth, *Rational Almanac*, 162–67, pl. 3.

33. Hale, "Oriental Ancestry," *Scribners*, 398.

34. Krupp, "Great Pyramid Astronomy," *Griffith Observer* 42:9–10.

Chapter 6: The Gnomon

1. Lyons, "Ancient Surveying Instruments," 132–33.

2. Lurker, *Gods and Symbols*, 127.

3. Gordon and Schwabe, "Egyptian *was*-Scepter," pt. 1, *Agricultural History* 62:74.

4. Lyons, "Ancient Surveying Instruments," 134–35.

5. Gordon and Schwabe, "Egyptian *was*-Scepter," 190.

6. Pliny, *Natural History*, 2:315–17.

7. Vitruvius, *Architecture*, 2:249–57; Strabo, *Geography*, 8:129.

8. Pliny, *Natural History*, 2:317, 319

9. Wheeler, *Herodotus*, 8–9, n. 2.

10. Needham, *Science*, 3:176; Zezong, "Ancient China's Astronomy," *HOA*, 38.

11. Cotsworth, *Rational Almanac*, section titled "The Pyramids of Egypt, Mexico, Etc.," 15–16.

12. Ibid., 186.

13. Waugh, *Sundials*, 2.

14. Rohr, *Sundials: History*, 12

15. Quoted in Waugh, *Sundials*, 2.

16. Personal communication from James P. Allen.

17. Personal communication from Leroy Doggert, U.S. Naval Observatory.

18. Davies, *Tomb of Ken–Amun* 1: pls. 16–17.

19. Gardiner, *Egyptian Grammar*, 479, M4.

20. Fischer, "Notes on Sticks and Staves," *Metropolitan Museum Journal* 12–13: 15–16, fig. 21.

21. Ibid., 6, 7.

22. Isler, "The Gnomon," *JARCE* 28:174; a later test on a computer program disclosed that the *was* scepter would produce a diverging shadow at a tilt as small as one degree.

23. Borchardt, *Zeitmessung*, B41, n. 1.

24. Isler, "Merkhet," *VA* 7:56.

25. Frankfort, *Cenotaph of Seti I*, 76–80, translation by James P. Allen. An earlier interpretation mistakenly claimed the shadow clock was fixedly faced to the east in the morning and to the west in the afternoon. Being immovable, Borchardt felt it would require the addition of a long bar to project shadows of the moving sun

(Borchardt, *Zeitmessung*). There is no evidence for this device. For a later and more detailed explanation see Isler, "The Gnomon," 176–78 or Isler, "Merkhet," 56–59, figs. 3, 6–8.

26. Borchardt, *Zeitmessung*, fig 13.

27. Needham, *Science*, 3: pl. 30, fig. 111.

28. Ibid., 286, 285, fig. 110.

29. Waugh, *Sundials*, 18.

30. Lacau, "L'Erection," *CdE* 28:21.

31. Munro, "Zelt-Heiligtum," *MÄS* 33–35; Wainwright, "Some Celestial Associations," *JEA* 21:164–66.

32. Lacau, 22; Badawy, "Min, the Cosmic Fertility God of Egypt," *MIO* 7:166–69.

33. Petrie, *Koptos*, 9, figs. 3–4; McFarlane, *The God Min*, 175, pl. 2, 3; Badawy, "Min," 177.

34. Lacau, "L'Erection," 17.

35. Frankfort, *Kingship*, 189–90.

36. My thanks to James P. Allen for these observations.

37. McFarlane, *The God Min*, 178.

38. Such huts are shown in Badawy, *Le Dessin Architectural*, chap. 5, figs. 1–12; Munro, "Zeit-Heiligtum," app. 3, figs. 1–22.

39. *The American Heritage Dictionary*, ed. William Morris (New York: Houghton Mifflin, 1973), 41.

40. Shaw and Nicholson, *Dictionary*, 31–32; Wainwright, *Sky Religions*, 13.

41. Frankfort, *Kingship*, 187–89.

42. Breasted, *History of Egypt*, 7–8.

43. Frazer, *Adonis*, 231–32 n.3.

44. Frazer, *Spirits*, 131–70.

45. Blackman, *Fellahin of Upper Egypt*, 171–72, 307–8.

46. Badawy, "Min," 169.

47. Hoffman, *Egypt*, 162.

48. Personal communication with Leroy Doggett, U.S. Naval Observatory: The height of the sun at summer solstice in 2700 BCE was 83° 56' in Cairo and 89° 57' in Aswan.

49. Lacau and Chevrier, *Une Chapelle*, 1: pl. 31, section 8.

50. Egyptian Museum, Cairo, Room 32, case E; Wilbur, *Tall Ships*, 66.

51. Gardiner, *Egyptian Grammar*, 513, T 18.

52. My thanks to Cheryl Haldane for these observations.

53. Jones, *History of the Vikings*, 192; personal discussion with Thomas H. McGovern, Hunter College.

54. Personal conversation with Captain George R. Sandberg, U.S. Merchant Marine Academy, King's Point, New York.

55. Personal communication with I. E. S. Edwards.

56. Goldsmith-Carter, *Sailing Ships*, 6.

57. Phillips-Birt, *History of Seamanship*, 14, 15.

58. Saggs, *Civilization*, 230–31.

59. Parker, "Ancient Egyptian Astronomy," in Hodson, *Place of Astronomy*, 52–53.

60. Parker, "Astrology and Calendrical Reckoning," in *Dictionary of Scientific Biography*, 707–8.

61. Gardiner, *Egyptian Grammar*, 203–5.

62. Breasted, *History of Egypt*, 7–8; Depuydt, "Consistency of the Wandering Year," *JARCE* 32:46

Chapter 7: Orientation

1. Arnold, *Building*, 15.

2. Burl, *Prehistoric Astronomy*, 18–19.

3. Parker, "Astrology and Calendrical Reckoning," 710–11.

4. Gardiner, *Egyptian Grammar*, 206.

5. Edwards, *Pyramids of Egypt*, 265.

6. Davidson, *Astronomy*, 48; Edwards, *Pyramids of Egypt*, 268, fig. 56.

7. Krupp, "Great Pyramid Astronomy," *Griffith Observer* 42:9.

8. Žába, *L' Orientation*, 22.

9. Ibid., 71.

10. Lurker, *Gods and Symbols*, 118.

11. Clarke, *Myth and Symbol*, 256.

12. Edwards, *Pyramids of Egypt*, 9.

13. Maragioglio and Rinaldi, *Piramidi*, 4: 100–102. (English translation is given beside the Italian throughout.)

14. Neugebauer, "Orientation of Pyramids," *Centaurus*, 24: 1–3, figs. 1, 2.

15. Singh, *Stone Observatories*, 34–35; Hogben, *Mathematics*, 55.

16. Waugh, *Sundials*, 18–25.

17. Personal correspondence with E. C. Krupp.

18. Summer solstice occurs about June 22; winter solstice, about December 22. Vernal equinox occurs about March 21; autumnal equinox, about September 23.

19. Depuydt, "Gnomons at Meroë," *JEA* 84:171–72, figs. 1, 6.

20. Rohr, *Sundials: History*, 6, fig. 4.

21. Swarup et al., *HOA*, 146.

22. Needham, *Science*, 3:298–99, figs. 115–17.

23. Ibid., 299.

24. Ibid., 99. In 1279 CE, the Chinese astronomers measured the solstice shadows as 12.3695 feet (3.77 m) in summer and 76.7400 feet (23.39 m) in winter.

25. Singh, *Stone Observatories*, 64, 90–91. A style is a gnomon set parallel to the axis of the earth, making it equal to the latitude of the location where the sundial is used.

26. Isler, "Ancient Method," *JARCE* 26: 198–99, figs. 5–7.

27. Dorner, *Orientierung*, 144–47.

28. Maragioglio and Rinaldi, *Piramidi*, 4:100.

29. Engelbach, "Foundation Scene," *JEA* 20, pts. 3–4; 183, pl. 24.

30. Žába, *L' Orientation*, 62.

31. Sloley, "Primitive Methods," *JEA* 17:170.

32. Žába, *L'Orinetation*, 60.

33. Ibid., 56

34. Isler, "Merkhet," *VA* 7:59

Chapter 8: Preparing the Site

1. Arnold, *Building*, 23, n. 35.

2. Lehner, "Some Observations on the Layout," *JARCE* 20:7.

3. Maragioglio and Rinaldi, *Piramidi*, 4:12.

4. Clarke and Engelbach, *Ancient Egyptian Masonry* (hereafter abbreviated as CEAEM), 62.

5. Lehner, "Some Observations," figs. 1–3.

6. Arnold, *Building*, 14.

7. Edwards, *Pyramids of Egypt*, 57, fig. 12

8. Singer, "Cartography, Survey and Navigation to 1400," *HT* 3:511–12; Needham, *Science*, 3:332, 4:570, fig. 245.

9. Needham, *Science*, 4:331–32, fig. 910.

10. Singh, *Stone Observatories*, 34–35.

11. Postulated by the writer (Isler, *JARCE* 36:198–99), and found by Arnold at Pyramid 8,

a subsidiary pyramid at the complex of Senwosret I; Arnold, *The Pyramid Complex of Senwosret I*, 3:38, fig. 12, pl. 48a.

12. Isler, "Finding and Extending Direction," *JARCE* 36:204–5, figs. 14–17.

13. Present with the writer at the trial in Lisht, in 1987, were Dieter and Felix Arnold. Günter Heindl was the surveyor.

14. Petrie, *Pyramids and Temples*, 37.

15. Personal experience; *Basic Field Manual* 3, Basic Weapons, Part One, Rifle Company, Chapter 1, Rifle Marksmanship U.S. Rifle, Caliber .30 M1903 (Washington: U.S. Gvt., 1938), 100–103. This manual was written when the chief infantry weapon was the bolt-action Springfield '03. During World War II, the U. S. rifleman carried the gas operated, semi-automatic .30 caliber M1. The earlier Springfield was considered to be a more accurate rifle.

16. Lyons, "Ancient Surveying Instruments," *Geographical Journal*, 69:136.

17. CEAEM, 63.

18. Ibid., 66.

19. Lyons, "Ancient Surveying Instruments," 138.

20. Arnold, *Building*, 11.

21. Breed, *Surveying*, 25, 94–95; personal conversation with Dorner.

22. Dorner, *Astronomische Orientierung*, 111–14.

23. CEAEM, 67–68, fig. 64.

24. Petrie, *Pyramids and Temples*, 41, fig. 20.

Chapter 9: The Nucleus

1. CEAEM, 119; Arnold, *Senwosret I*, 3:29, 37.

2. Maragioglio and Rinaldi, *Piramidi*, 4:78, 80, 84, 90, 92.

3. The mortar used in the lower courses of the Cheops Pyramid core masonry is similar to the gypsum mortar used to seal the 16-ton beams over the eastern of the two southern boat pits (Moores, "Stone-cutting Drag Saw," *JARCE* 28:139, n. 3, 5.). The pit had been sealed airtight by liquid gypsum plaster imported from the Fayum oasis and poured in all the cervices of the limestone blocks (Jenkins, *Boat beneath the Pyramid*, 65).

4. Reisner, *Mycerinus*, 56; Maragioglio and Rinaldi, *Piramidi*, 6:82.

5. Maragioglio and Rinaldi, *Piramidi*, 6:88, 90, 128, 130.

6. Ibid., 6:94, 34.

7. Arnold, *Building*, 159.

8. Verner, *Lost Pyramids*, 135.

9. Ibid., 141.

10. Mendelssohn, *Riddle*, pl. 19.

11. Petrie, *Pyramids and Temples*, 164.

12. Ibid., fig. 8, 41–42.

13. Maragioglio and Rinaldi, *Piramidi*, 4:76, 78.

14. Edwards, *Pyramids of Egypt*, 282–84.

15. CEAEM, 125–28.

16. Maragioglio and Rinaldi, *Piramidi*, 3:34, 36; CEAEM, 122.

17. Robert, "Quelques Graffites Grecs," *ASAE* (1902), 77–79; Maragioglio and Rinaldi, *Piramidi*, 3:16.

18. Mendelssohn, *Riddle*, 116.

19. Isler, "Concave Faces," *JARCE* 20:28.

20. Petrie, *Egyptian Architecture*, 9; Petrie et al., *Meydum and Memphis*, 3:3.

21. Petrie et al., *Meydum and Memphis*, 3:13.

22. Arnold, *Senwosret I*, 3:97.

23. Petrie et al., *Meydum and Memphis*, 14.

24. Badawy, "Periodic System," *JEA* 63: 52–58.

25. Petrie, *Pyramids and Temples*, 126.

26. Robert, "Quelques Graffites Grecs," 77–79.

27. Although Egyptians were able to make flagpoles that reached heights of 197 feet (Arnold, *Building*, 70), a much smaller distance would be needed for a target pole.

28. A likely candidate is a 3rd–4th Dynasty pot (Kelly, *Pottery of Ancient Egypt*, pl. 11.2, item 75).

29. Petrie, *Pyramids and Temples*, 43.

30. Maragioglio and Rinaldi, *Piramidi*, 3:14.

31. Arnold, *Building*, 82.

32. Maragioglio and Rinaldi, *Piramidi*, 3:48, 50.

33. Petrie, *Meydum and Memphis*, 6–8.

34. Maragioglio and Rinaldi, *Piramidi*, 3:38.

35. Isler, "Pyramid Building," *JARCE* 22: 130–31.

36. Hodges, *How the Pyramids Were Built*, 124.

37. Engelbach, *Obelisk*, 89.

38. Petrie, "Building of a Pyramid," *Ancient Egypt* 2:35–36.

39. The fall rains of recent years did considerable damage to the Luxor area, bringing raging floods and water intrusion (Salima Ikram, "Nile-currents," *KMT* 6, no. 1 [1995]: 7).

40. Petrie, *Ancient Egypt*, 36.

41. Arnold, "Pyramidenbaues," *MDAIK* 37: 16–18.

42. Arnold, *Senwosret I*, 100; Arnold, *Building*, 85–86; Arnold, *Senwosret I*, 92.

43. Arnold, *Building*, 85, 90, figs. 3.38–3.42, and personal conversation; Arnold, *Senwosret I*, 93.

44. Dunham, "Building of an Egyptian Pyramid," *Archaeology* 9, no. 3:163–65. Dunham's scale model was not completed to the top of the pyramid and therefore did not address the problems that would be encountered by the ramp.

45. Petrie, *Pyramids and Temples*, 212

46. Dunham, "Building of an Egyptian Pyramid," 165.

47. CEAEM, 86–89.

48. Petrie, *Egyptian Architecture*, 36.

49. Arnold, "Pyramidenbaues," 22–23.

Chapter 10: Gathering Material

1. Vyse, *Operations*, vol. 1, pl. opposite p. 159.

2. Maragioglio and Rinaldi, *Piramidi*, 5:44; CEAEM, fig. 13.

3. CEAEM, 16–17.

4. Gillette, *Rock Excavation*, 4–5.

5. This procedure was shown to me some years ago at the Vermont Marble Company in Rutland, Vermont. The entrance to the covered marble quarry was not on ground level, as in Egypt, but instead from an open shaft one entered an enormous chamber 500 feet beneath the surface. The artificial lighting that reflected off the dust-filled area softened and blended everything into a white fairyland. The water to feed the cutting tools, and the natural dampness of the chamber, made for a cold and very humid environment.

6. CEAEM, 13–14.

7. Arnold, *Building*, 266–67.

8. Casson, *Early Greek Sculpture*, 237–38. Although I have limited experience with hard stones, those occasional trials indicated that igneous rock or even hard variegated marble could not be cut with iron tools. It was found, however, that the vertical stroke of an iron bullpoint chisel would stun the surface, permitting the stone to be reduced with a carving stroke and a flat chisel.

9. Gillette, *Rock Excavation*, 184–85.

10. Winkler, *Stone*, 58.

11. Burchfield, et al., *Physical Geology*, 100.

12. Engelbach, *Obelisk*, 48–49.

13. CEAEM, 203–4, figs. 246, 248.

14. Petrie, *Pyramids and Temples*, 173–77; CEAEM, 203–4, fig. 247.

15. Stocks, "Sticks and Stones," *Popular Archaeology* 7:26, fig. on p. 28.

16. Trial at Aswan, 1994, under the auspices of Nova/WGBH television program, "Obelisk."

17. Petrie, *Pyramids and Temples*, 177.

18. Brooklyn Museum, 48.110, granite sarcophagus from the reign of Chephren.

19. Gorelick and Gwinnett, "Stone Drilling," *Expedition*, 41–47.

20. CEAEM, 31, figs. 32–33.

21. Hawass and Lehner, "The Sphinx," *Archeology* 47, no. 5:35, 37.

22. CEAEM, 27.

23. Gorringe, *Obelisks*, 147.

24. Isler, "Monolithic Carving," *MDIAK* 48: 55.

25. Barker et al., *Science and Technology* 11:631.

26. Krynine and Judd, *Geology and Geotechnics*, 303, 341.

27. *I.C.S. Reference Library*, 159: 10.

28. Shadmon, *Stone*, 14–15.

29. Blackman, *Fellahin*, 307, fig. 178.

30. Saleh and Sourouzian, *Catalogue*, no. 119.

31. Mannoni and Mannoni, *Marble*, figs. 134–37.

32. Cotterell and Kamminga, *Mechanics*, 206.

33. Barber, *Mechanical Triumphs*, 37.

34. Cole, "Land Transport," *HT*, 1:705.

35. Fitchen, *Building Construction*, 172.

36. *New York Times*, 19 July 1994, A8.

37. Arnold, *Building*, 57–58, fig. 3.2.

38. Fitchen, *Building Construction*, 172–73.

39. Andrew Yarrow, "Joy and Challange Mix in Dancing of the Giglio," *New York Times*, 9 July 1990, B3.

40. Childe, "Rotary Motion," *HT*, 1:206.

41. Cole, "Land Transcript," 710–11.

42. CEAEM, 89, fig. 85.

43. Shaw, "Kafra's Quarries," *Egyptian Archaeology*, 16:28–30.

44. Turning grooves in the bases of the colossi of Memnon suggest that they were transported to their destination on their backs and erected on site, as were obelisks.

45. Arnold, *Building*, 63.

46. Isler, "Luxor Obeleisks," *JEA* 73:141.

47. Arnold, *Building*, 62. For a list of heavy monuments transported in Egypt see Arnold, *Building*, 60, table 3.1.

48. *New York Times Magazine*, 20 December 1998, 27.

49. Arnold, *Building*, 278, fig. 6.39.

50. Newberry, *El-Bersheh*, 15.

51. Saleh and Sourouzian, *Catalogue*, fig. 142a.

52. Mohen, *World of Megaliths*, 176–78.

53. Arthur H. Bagnold, "Colossal Statues," *Biblical Archaeology* 10:455–59.

54. Davison, "Transporting," *Technology and Culture*, 1961, 12.

55. Fitchen, *Building Construction*, 177–78.

56. Chevrier, "Technique," *RdE*, 22:20.

57. Arnold, *Building*, 63.

58. Cotterell and Kamminga, *Mechanics*, 222.

59. Engelbach, *Obelisk*, 94–95.

60. Petrie, *Tools and Weapons*, 49:38–39; CEAEM, 90–91; Arnold, *Building*, 273–74, fig. 6.31; BM, Exhibit No. 43229.

61. Petrie, *Arts and Crafts*, 75–76.

62. CEAEM, 102–3.

Chapter 11: Building the Nucleus

1. Dickinson, *Wonders*, 263.

2. Maragioglio and Rinaldi, *Piramidi*, 5:50.

3. Arnold, *Senwosret I*, 3:93.

4. Isler, "Pyramid Building," *JARCE* 22:137, 140, figs. 14–16.

5. The limestone block had dimensions of 2.5 × 3.6 × 3 feet. Limestone, according to its grade, weighs from 144 to 165 pounds per cubic foot. Assuming the lowest value, the block weighed 3,888 pounds.

6. Julian Keable, an English architect and editor of Peter Hodges' *How the Pyramids Were Built*, claims to have raised a 2.5-ton block the height of a pyramid step in under four minutes (*KMT* 4, no. 1 [1993]: 3–4).

7. O'Brian, *Machines*, 19,

8. Pliny, *Natural History*, 10:71.

9. Adkins, *Moving*, 38–39.

10. Arnold, *Building*, 269.

11. Lucas, *Materials and Industries*, 134–36; Gilbert, "Rope-Making," *HT* 1:451–54, figs. 284–85.

12. Donald P. Ryan, "Old Rope," *KMT* 4, no. 2 (1993): 72–75.

13. Severn, *Rope and Knots*, 5.

14. Lucas, *Materials and Industries*, 135.

15. Ibid., 135.

16. Arnold, *Building*, 269.

17. Dibner, *Moving the Obelisks*, 29–30.

18. Isler, "On Pyramid Building," *JARCE* 22:140, figs. 17–19.

19. Petrie, *Egyptian Architecture*, 38–40, fig. 10 (item 61).

20. Adkins, *Moving*, 40.

21. Gorringe, *Obelisks*, 8, pl. 3.

22. As shown by field tests, a stick of wood tied to the block by a single loop of rope is an effective means of tipping over a large block.

23. CEAEM, 92, fig. 86.

24. Arnold, *Building*, 91–93, fig. 3.45. Also see 79–101 for a thorough review of construction roads and ramps.

25. CEAEM, 99–100.

26. Arnold, *Building*, 24–25, figs. 3.21–3.23.

27. A man may exert a force of 110 to 130 pounds in pushing an object or in pulling a suspended load. He may be expected to push or pull a crowbar with a force of about 100 pounds, lift it with about 200 pounds, and push it downward with a force not greater than his own weight (Rossnagel, *Rigging*, 345).

28. CEAEM, 44–45.

29. I have removed boulders too heavy to handle from inaccessible locations by fixing the boulder with 3/4-inch hemp rope, running the rope around a tree, and pulling the boulder out with a truck.

30. Hassan, *Great Pyramid*, 10:51.

31. Isler, "Raising Weights," *JARCE* 13: 36–37, fig. 23.

32. Wheeler, *Geography of Herodotus*, 394.

33. Mannoni and Mannoni, *Marble*, 116–18.

34. Simonds, "Colossal Statues," *Building News* 19, no. 542: 236.

Chapter 12: The Second Stage

1. Edwards, *Pyramids of Egypt*, 277–79.

2. Hogben, *Mathematics*, 150, fig. 45A.

3. Ibid., 154–55, fig. 49.

4. CEAEM, 216–23.

5. Arnold, *Building*, 15.

6. Magdolen, "The Solar Origin," 4.

7. Ibid., 4–6, diagram 1, figs. 1–3.

8. Petrie, *Pyramids and Temples*, 37.

9. Maragioglio and Rinaldi, *Piramidi*, 5:50, pl. 6, fig. 8.

10. Ibid., 6, pl. 4, fig. 2.

11. Petrie, *Pyramids and Temples*, 40–41, 126, fig. 10.

12. Personal conversation with Dieter Arnold.

13. Arnold, *Building*, 165–67.

14. Petrie, *Pyramids and Temples*, 221

15. CEAEM, 128–29.

16. Brinks, "Cheops-Pyramide," *GM* 48: 17–21, fig. 2: Arnold, *Building*, 168, 172, fig. 4.102.

Chapter 13: The Final Building Stage

1. Badawy, "Building a Pyramid," *JEA* 63: 52.

2. Petrie, *Pyramids and Temples*, fig. 10.

3. CEAEM, 100.

4. Ibid., 101.

5. Ibid., 98, fig. 94.

6. Petrie, *Pyramids and Temples*, 44.

7. Petrie, et al., *Meydum and Memphis*, 3:5, pl. 20 (1).

8. Arnold, *Building*, 266, figs. 6.20–21.

9. Petrie, *Egyptian Architecture*, 38, fig. 10 (item 60).

10. Lucas, *Materials and Industries*, 74–79.

11. Ibid., 78.

12. Cotterell and Kamminga, *Mechanics*, 27.

13. Petrie, *Pyramids and Temples*, 44.

14. F. Arnold, *Control Notes*, 14.

15. Arnold, *Building*, 20–21.

16. An observation made during Nova/WGBH television show, "This Old Pyramid."

17. Arnold, *Building*, 122, fig. 4.19.

18. Arnold, *Building*, 122–23, fig. 4.20.

19. CEAEM, 101–2, figs. 107–9.

20. According to a lecture by Karla Kroeper, "The Nile Before the Pharoahs" (MMA, May 1994), a copper saw with teeth has been found in the Delta dating from 3400 BCE.

21. Petrie, *Egyptian Architecture*, 50.

22. Arnold, *Building*, 123, fig. 4.23.

23. Petrie, *Egyptian Architecture*, 30.

24. Maragioglio and Rinaldi, *Piramidi*, 5:50, 100.

25. F. Arnold, *Control Notes*, 31–32.

26. Isler, "On Pyramid Building," *JARCE* 22:134–36, figs. 7–11.

27. Demonstrated by Roger Hopkins on Nova/WGBH television show, "This Old Pyramid."

28. Maragioglio and Rinaldi, *Piramidi*, 5:50.

29. Lehner, *Complete Pyramids*, 222–23.

30. Hawass and Verner, "Discovered Blocks," *MDAIK* 52:181, 182, n. 37. My thanks to Dieter Arnold for bringing this to my attention.

31. Wheeler (trans.), *Herodotus*, 2.125, p. 394.

GLOSSARY

Accretion layers: An architectural construction consisting of inwardly leaning layers of stone.

Alluvium: Any sediment deposited by flowing water, as in a riverbed, floodplain, or delta.

Altitude: The angular distance of a celestial object above the horizon.

Apse: A vaulted extension of a hall semicircular in plan, as at the sanctuary end of a Christian church.

Arcminute: In an angular measurement, the sixtieth part of a degree.

Arcsecond: In an angular measurement, the sixtieth part of an arcminute.

Axis: An imaginary straight line about which parts of an object, such as a building, are arranged.

Azimuth: The horizontal angular distance of an object along the horizon, usually measured in clockwise degrees from a fixed reference point due south.

Ba: Symbolized as a bird with a human head and arms, the ba was originally considered to be only the psychic force of the sun-god, Ra. By the end of the Old Kingdom, it also came to represent the soul or vital principle of all human beings. Possessing the gift of animation if supplied with a corpse or statue, the ba was thought to have the ability to move in and out of the tomb while assuming any shape it wished.

Backing stone: Those stones immediately behind the casing stone.

Batter: A slope, as of the outer side of a wall, that recedes from bottom to top.

Benben: A sacred stone object upon which the sun shines.

Boss: A knob or projection.

Buttress: An additional support, usually of brick or stone, built against a wall for reinforcement.

Capital: The topmost part or head of a column or pillar. In Egypt, it is shown as lotus, palm, or papyriform.

Capstone: The top stone of a structure or wall.

Casing stone: A mantle of smooth, well-fitted stone meant to cover imperfections of the underlying masonry.

Catenary: The sag in a stretched line caused by the weight of the line.

Causeway: A raised road or path.

Celestial pole: An extension of the earth's axis.

Celestial sphere: An imaginary globe of infinite radius surrounding the earth and serving as a screen against which all celestial objects are seen. The axis of the globe is an extension of the earth's axis.

Chamfer: To bevel the edge or corner of something, such as a building block or piece of wood.

Circumpolar stars: Those stars in the latitude of the observer that never go below the horizon.

Column: A freestanding vertical cylindrical support.

Compression: The force in a structure that pushes together and can crush architectural members.

Corbeling: An overlapping arrangement of bricks or stone where each course extends farther out from the wall than the course below.

Cosmology: Speculation on the composition and workings of the universe.

Cross section: A section formed by a plane cutting through an object, usually at right angles to an axis.

Cubit: A unit of linear measurement based on the length of the forearm from the elbow to the tip of the middle finger. The cubit of 20.62 inches (52.5 cm) is divided into seven palms, each of which is divided into four digits.

Cylinder seal: A small cylinder of stone incised with an inscription identifying the owner.

Declination: Angular distance of an object from the celestial equator, measured in degrees, minutes, and seconds; analogous to latitude in geography.

Diopter: An instrument for measuring angles and altitude.

Dolmen: A prehistoric tomb made of large upright stones capped with a horizontal stone.

Early Dynastic period: A chronological phase, often described as the Archaic period, comprising the 1st and 2nd Dynasties (3100–2686 BCE). The 3rd Dynasty (2686–2613 BCE) is placed in the Old Kingdom, which is estimated as the period 2686–2181 BCE. Some consider the Early Dynastic period to include the 3rd Dynasty, which they give different dates (2649–2575 BCE), estimating the Early Dynastic period also as different (2920–2575 BCE); and there are additional views.

Ecliptic: The apparent path of the sun among the stars; the intersection plane of the earth's solar orbit with the celestial sphere.

Elevation: A scale drawing of the side, front, or rear of a given structure.

Equinox: One of two points of intersection between the ecliptic and the celestial equator. When the sun is at either point, which occurs on or about March 21 (vernal equinox) and September 23 (autumnal equinox), the length of day and night are equal everywhere on earth.

Fetish: A symbol associated with a deity, believed to invoke the supernatural power of the deity.

Frieze: Any decorative horizontal band.

Gnomon: An object that projects a shadow, such as a vertical pole, so that the shadow can be used as an indicator.

Headers: Stones with their long dimension placed at right angles to the wall.

Heliacal star: A star that rises or sets with the sun.

Henge: A circle of upright stones or posts.

Iconography: A system of symbols and motifs used in a consistent way to express notions of theology and ideology.

Inclined Plane: For an object resting on the plane, the force of gravity is split into two smaller forces; one perpendicular to the plane and one parallel to the plane.

Inundation: The flooding that annually renewed the fertility of the soil until construction of the Aswan Dam.

Ka: A life force. Born with a person as his or her other self, the ka supposedly continued to reside inside a tomb after the death of the individual, possibly returning the person to life if supplied with sustenance. Although it was known that the ka did not physically eat or drink supplies left near the deceased, it was thought magically to absorb their life-giving qualities.

Lever: A simple machine consisting of a rigid body that pivots on a fulcrum.

Lintel: A horizontal beam or stone that spans an opening.

Masonry: Stonework or brickwork.

Mastaba: A low, generally flat-topped structure with sloping (battered) sides, used as an Egyptian tomb.

Menhir: A prehistoric monument in the form of a single upright stone.

Meridian: In geography, a great circle on the surface of the earth that passes through the north and south poles.

Mortise and tenon: A wood-joining method whereby a projecting tongue (tenon) of one member fits into a hole (mortise) of corresponding shape in another member.

Mosaic: Surface decoration formed by small pieces of glass or stone set in mortar or plaster.

Necropolis: A large ancient burial ground.

Niche: A recess in a wall.

Obelisk: A tall stone shaft, square in cross section and tapering upward to end in a pyramidal tip.

Old Kingdom: A chronological phase comprising a period from the 3rd to the 6th Dynasties (2686–2181 BCE). Some consider the Old Kingdom to comprise a period from the 4th to the 8th Dynasty (2575–2134 BCE), giving the 3rd Dynasty different dates (2649–2575 BCE) and placing it in the Early Dynastic period; and there are other views.

Packing stone: Smaller stone used to bring the tiered nucleus to a more pyramidal shape.

Palace-facade: An architectural facade consisting of alternating panels and recesses.

Passage tomb: A megalithic grave with a long passage leading to a chamber near the center of the covering mound.

Penumbra: A partial shadow between regions of complete shadow and complete illumination.

Pilaster: A rectangular column set into a wall, as a support or ornamental motif.

Pillar: A freestanding vertical support, usually rectangular in cross section.

Plan: A planar surface; a view from above.

Portal: A monumental entranceway to a building or courtyard.

Portcullis block: A sliding stone suspended in a passageway and designed to be lowered to block the entrance.

Post and beam: A method of construction using vertical supports (post) spanned by horizontal beams.

Primeval mound: According to Egyptian theology, the first land to emerge from the primeval waters when the sun-god, Atum, found himself without a place to stand at the moment of creation; supposedly imbued with a mysterious power to aid in resurrecting the dead.

Pulley: A simple machine; basically, a lever that circles around its fulcrum (axle).

Pylon: A monumental gateway in the form of two truncated pyramids serving as the entrance to an ancient Egyptian temple.

Pyramidion: A form of benben used as the capstone of a pyramid or obelisk.

Ra (Re): The sun god, the supreme deity of the ancient Egyptians, represented as a man with the head of a hawk, crowned with a solar disk and uraeus (a serpent-image of kingship placed just above the forehead in most royal crowns and headdresses).

Section: A drawing of a slice through a building at some imagined plane, showing its internal structure.

Serdab: An ancient Egyptian closed chamber holding a statue.

Serekh: A rectangular frame imitative of the mud-brick designs found on mastabas of early Egypt and on temples of the Near East. Surmounted by a falcon in Egypt, the Serekh contains the Horus name of the king.

Solstice: The point of maximum declination of the earth on the ecliptic. In the northern hemisphere, the summer solstice (about June 22) occurs when the sun is farthest north from the equator and the winter solstice (about December 22) when the sun is farthest south.

Spanish windlass: Tightens a rope by twisting it with a lever; a rope loop around two objects which upon being twisted with a lever exerts a force to draw the objects together.

Stela (*plural* stelae): An upright stone or slab with an inscribed or sculptured surface, used as a monument or as a commemorative tablet.

Story-pole: A stick used to establish the height of masonry courses.

Stretcher: Stones with their long dimension placed parallel to the wall.

Stupa: A Buddhist memorial mound that enshrines relics or marks a sacred site.

Style: A gnomon tipped to the celestial pole, making an angle with the horizon equal to the latitude at which it is positioned.

Tafl: A natural claylike desert substance that forms a hard concretion when mixed with water.

Temenos: A Greek term used to describe an area that separates the sacred sector from the secular.

Tension: The force tending to bend, stretch, or pull apart an architectural member.

Terrace: A level embankment top, roof, or raised platform, adjoining a building.

Thrust: Lateral or outward stress on a structure.

Transept: The lateral arms of, for example, a cruciform church.

Vault: An arched structure of stone or brick forming a ceiling or roof.

Wedge: An active inclined plane; a piece of metal or wood tapered for insertion in a narrow crevice and used for splitting, tightening, securing, or levering.

Zenith: The point on the celestial sphere directly overhead.

Ziggurat: A Mesopotamian temple tower in the form of a stepped pyramid.

BIBLIOGRAPHY

Adams, Barbara. *Predynastic Egypt*. Aylesbury, U.K.: Shire Publications, 1988.

———. "Unprecedented Discoveries at Hierakonpolis." *BEES* 15 (1999):29–31.

Adkins, Jan. *Moving Heavy Things*. Boston: Houghton Mifflin, 1980.

Aldred, Cyril. *Egypt to the End of the Old Kingdom*. New York: McGraw-Hill, 1965.

Algaze, Guillermo. *The Uruk World System: The Dynamics of Expansion of Early Mesopotamian Civilization*. Chicago: University of Chicago Press, 1993.

Allen, James P. *Genesis in Egypt: The Philosophy of Ancient Egyptian Creation Accounts*. Ed. William Kelly Simpson. Yale Egyptological Studies 2. New Haven: Yale University Press, 1988.

———. *Middle Egyptian: An Introduction to the Language and Culture of Hieroglyphs*. Cambridge: Cambridge University Press, 2000.

Amiet, Pierre. *La Glyptigne Mésopotamienne Archaique*. 2nd ed. Paris: CNRS, 1980.

Ammarell, Gene. "Sky Calendars of the Indo-Malay Archipelago." In Swarup et al., *HOA*, 241–47.

Armour, Robert A. *Gods and Myths of Ancient Egypt*. With the research assistance of Alison Baker. Cairo: American University in Cairo Press, 1986.

Arnold, Dieter. *Building in Egypt: Pharaonic Stone Masonry*. New York: Oxford University Press, 1991.

———. *The Pyramid Complex of Senwosret I. The South Cemeteries of Lisht*, vol. 3. With contributions by Dorothea Arnold and Felix Arnold and an appendix by Cheryl Haldane. New York: MMA, 1992.

———. "Royal Cult Complexes of the Old and Middle Kingdoms." In *Temples of Ancient Egypt*, ed. Byron E. Shafer. London: I. B. Taurus, 1998.

———. "Überlegungen zum Problem des Pyramidenbaues." *MDAIK* 37 (1981):15–28.

Arnold, Felix. *The Control Notes and Team Marks. The South Cemeteries of Lisht*, vol. 2. In collaboration with Dieter Arnold, I. E. S. Edwards, and Jürgen Osing. Using notes by William C. Hayes. New York: MMA, 1990.

Aveni, Anthony F. *Skywatchers of Ancient Mexico*. Foreword by Owen Gingerich. Austin: University of Texas Press, 1990.

——— (ed.). *World Archaeoastronomy*. Selected papers, 2nd Oxford Conference on Archaeoastronomy, Merida, Yucatan, Mexico, 13–17 January 1986. Cambridge: Cambridge University Press, 1989.

Badawy, Alexander. *Architecture in Ancient Egypt and the Near East*. Cambridge, Mass.: M. I. T. Press, 1966.

———. *Le Dessin Architectural chez les Anciens Egyptiens*. Service des Antiquités de L'Egypte. Le Cäire: Imprimerie National, 1948.

———. "Min, The Cosmic Fertility God of Egypt." *MIO* 7, Heft 2 (1959):163–79.

———. "The Periodic System of Building a Pyramid." *JEA* 63 (1977):52–58.

Bagnold, Arthur H. "Account of the Manner in Which Two Colossal Statues of Rameses II at Memphis Were Raised." In *Proceedings of the Society of Biblical Archaeology*, vol. 10. 18th session, 7th meeting, 5 June 1888. London: Offices of the Society. 452–63.

Baines, John, and Jaromír Málek. *Atlas of Ancient Egypt*. New York: Facts on File, 1985.

Barber, F. M. *The Mechanical Triumphs of the Ancient Egyptians*. London: Kegan Paul, Trench, Trübner, 1900.

Basic Field Manual. 3. Basic Weapons Part One, Rifle Company. Chapter 1, Rifle Marksmanship U. S. Rifle, Caliber .30, M1903. Prepared under direction of the Chief of Infantry. Washington D.C.: U.S. Government Printing Office, 1938.

Bernbaum, Edwin. *Sacred Mountains of the World*. San Francisco: Sierra Club Books, 1990.

Betrò, Maria Carmela. *Hieroglyphics: The Writings of Ancient Egypt*. New York: Abbeville Press, 1995.

Blackman, Winifred S. *The Fellahin of Upper Egypt*. London: George G. Harrap, 1927.

Boorstin, Daniel J. *The Discoverers: A History of Man's Search to Know His World and Himself*. New York: Random House, 1983.

Borchardt, L., J. Drecker, M. Engelmann, J. Frank, F.K. Ginzel, F. Hauser, A. Rehm, K. Schoy, E. Seler, E. Wiedemann, and A. Weidemann. "Die Altagyptische Zeitmessung." In *Die Geschichte der Zeitmessung und der Uhren*. Ed. Ernst von Bassermann-Jordan. Berlin: Walter de Gruyter, 1920.

Breasted, James Henry. *A History of Egypt*. New York: Charles Scribner's Sons, 1905.

Breed, Charles B. *Surveying*. New York: John Wiley, 1942.

Brinks, Jürgen. "Die Stufenhöhen der Cheops-Pyramide: System oder zufall?" *GM* 48 (1981):17–23.

Burchfiel, B. Clarke, Robert J. Foster, Edward A. Keller, Wilton N. Melhorn, Douglas G. Brookings, Leigh W. Mintz, and Harold V. Thurman. *Physical Geology*. Columbus, Ohio: Charles E. Merrill, 1982.

Burl, Aubrey. *Prehistoric Astronomy and Ritual*. Aylesbury, U.K.: Shire Publications, 1983.

Burney, Charles. *The Ancient Near East*. Ithaca, N.Y.: Cornell University Press, 1977.

The Cambridge Encyclopedia of Archaeology. Ed. Andrew Sherratt. New York: Crown Publishers–Cambridge University Press, 1980.

Carrasco, David. "The King, the Capital and the Stars: The Symbolism of Authority in Aztec Religion." In Aveni, *WA*: 45–54.

Casson, Stanley. *The Technique of Early Greek Sculpture*. Oxford: Clarendon Press, 1933.

Chevrier, Henri. "Technique de la Construction dans l'Ancienne Egypte." *RdE* 22 (1970):15–39.

Childe, V. Gordon. "Rotary Motion." In Singer et al., *HT*, 1:187–215.

Clark, R. T. Rundle. *Myth and Symbol in Ancient Egypt*. London: Thames and Hudson, 1959.

Clarke, Somers, and R. Engelbach. *Ancient Egyptian Masonry*. London: Oxford University Press, 1930.

Cole, J. H. *Determination of the Exact Size and Orientation of the Great Pyramid of Giza*. Survey of Egypt Paper no. 39. Cairo: Government Press, 1925.

Cole, S. M. "Land Transport without Wheels, Roads and Bridges." In Singer et al., *HT* 1:704–15.

Cotsworth, Moses B. *The Rational Almanac: Tracing the Evolution of Modern Almanacs from Ancient Ideas of Time and Suggesting Improvements*. . . . York, 1905. Self-published.

Cotterell, Brian, and Johan Kamminga. *Mechanics of Pre-Industrial Technology*. Cambridge: Cambridge University Press, 1990.

Crawford, Harriet. *Sumer and the Sumerians*. Cambridge: Cambridge University Press, 1992.

Davidson, Norman. *Astronomy and the Imagination: A New Approach to Man's Experience of the Stars*. London: Routledge and Kegan Paul, 1985.

Davies, N. de Garis. *Tomb of Ken-Amun*, vol. 1. New York: Metropolitan Museum of Art, 1930.

Davies, Vivian, and Renée Friedman. *Egypt Uncovered*. London: British Museum Press, 1998.

Davison, C. St. C. "Transporting Sixty-Ton Statues in Early Assyria and Egypt." *Technology and Culture* (1961): 11–16.

Dearborn, David S. P., and Katharina J. Schreiber. "Here Comes the Sun: The Cuzco–Machu Picchu Connection." *JCA* 9, nos. 1–4. (January–December 1986): 15–37.

Degani, Meir H. *Astronomy Made Simple: New Revised Edition*. 3rd ed. Garden City, NY: Doubleday, 1976.

Depuydt, Leo. "Gnomons at Meroë and Early Trigonometry." *JEA* 84 (1998):171–80.

———. "On the Consistency of the Wandering Year as the Backbone of Egyptian Chronology." *JARCE* 32 (1995):43–58.

Dibner, Bern. *Moving the Obelisks*. Cambridge, Mass.: Society for the History of Technology and M. I. T. Press, 1950.

Dickinson, Mary B. (ed). *Wonders of the Ancient World*. Washington, D.C.: National Geographic Society Press, 1994.

Dorner, Josef. *Die Absteckung und astronomische Orientierung ägyptischer Pyramiden*. Ph. D. diss., University of Innsbruck, 1981.

Dreyer, Günter, and Nabil Swelim. "Die kleine Stufenpyramide von Abydos-Süd (Sinki)." *MDAIK* 38 (1982):83–93.

Drower, M. S. "Water-Supply, Irrigation, and Agriculture." In Singer, et al., *HT*, 1:520–57.

Dunham, Dows. "Building of an Egyptian Pyramid." *Archaeology* 9, no. 3 (September 1956):159–65.

Edwards, I. E. S. "Do the Pyramid Texts Suggest an Explanation for the Abandonment of the Subterranean Chamber of the Great Pyramid?" *Hommages à Jean Leclant*, vol. 1. *BdE* 106/1 (1994): 159–67.

———. *The Pyramids of Egypt*. Rev. ed. London: Viking, 1985.

Emery, Walter B. *Archaic Egypt*. London: Penguin, 1972.

———. *Great Tombs of the First Dynasty*. 3 vols. Cairo: Cairo Government Press and Quaritch, 1949–58.

Engelbach, R. "A Foundation Scene of the Second Dynasty." *JEA* 20, pts. 3–4 (1934): 184–85, pl. 24.

———. *The Problem of the Obelisk*. New York: George H. Doran, 1923.

Firneis, Maria G., and Christian Köberl. "Further Studies on the Astronomical Orientation of Medieval Churches in Austria." In Aveni, *WA*: 430–35.

Fischer, Henry G. "Notes on Sticks and Staves." *Ancient Egypt in the Metropolitan Museum Journal*, supplement: vols. 12–13 (1977–78). New York: MMA, 1980. 5–32.

———. "The Origin of Egyptian Hieroglyphs." In *The Origins of Writing*, ed. Wayne M. Senner. Lincoln: University of Nebraska Press, 1990. 59–76.

Fitchen, John. *Building Construction before Mechanization*. Cambridge, Mass.: M. I. T. Press, 1986.

Frankfort, H., with chapters by A. De Buck and Battiscombe Gunn. *The Cenotaph of Seti I at Abydos*. 2 vols. London: Thirty-Ninth Memoir of the Egypt Exploration Society, 1933.

Frankfort, Henri. *Ancient Egyptian Religion*. New York: Harper and Row, 1948.

———. *The Art and Architecture of the Ancient Orient*. 4th rev. ed. Harmondsworth, U.K.: Penguin Books, 1985.

———. *The Birth of Civilization in the Near East*. Garden City, N.Y.: Doubleday Anchor, 1956.

———. *Kingship and the Gods*. 2nd ed. Chicago: University of Chicago Press, 1978.

———. "The Origin of Monumental Architecture in Egypt." *American Journal of Semitic Languages and Literature* 58, no. 4 (October 1941): 329–58.

Frazer, James George. *The Golden Bough, Pt. 4: Adonis Attis Osiris*, vol. 1. 3rd ed., rev. and enlarged. New York: Macmillan, 1935.

———. *The Golden Bough, Pt. 5: Spirits of the Corn and of the Wild*, vol. 1, New York: Macmillan, 1935.

Friedman, Renée, with contributions by Amy Maish, Ahmed G. Fahmy, John C. Darnell, and Edward D. Johnson. "Preliminary Report on Field Work at Hierakonpolis: 1996–1998." *JARCE* 36 (1999):1–35.

Gallagher, Patricia (ed.). *Exploring the Ancient World*. Washington, D.C.: St. Remy, 1993.

Gardiner, Alan. *Egyptian Grammar*. 3rd ed. rev. Oxford: Griffith Institute, 1988.

Garrison, Evan. *A History of Engineering and Technology*. Boca Raton, Fla.: CRC Press, 1991.

Gilbert, K. R. "Rope-Making." In Singer et al., *HT* 1:451–55.

Gillette, Halbert Powers. *Rock Excavation*. New York: M. C. Clark, 1904.

Goff, Beatrice Laura. *Symbols of Prehistoric Mesopotamia*. New Haven: Yale University Press, 1963.

Goldsmith-Carter, George. *Sailing Ships and Sailing Craft*. New York: Grosset and Dunlap, 1970.

Gordon, Andrew H., and Calvin W. Schwabe. "The Egyptian *was*-Scepter and Its Modern Analogues: Uses as Symbols of Divine Power or Authority," pt. 1. *Agricultural History* 62, no. 1 (1988): 61–84.

———."The Egyptian *was*-Scepter and Its Modern Analogues: Uses as Symbols of Divine Power or Authority," pt. 2, *JARCE* 32 (1995):185–96.

Gorelick, Leonard, and A. John Gwinnett. "Ancient Egyptian Stone Drilling." *Expedition* (University of Pennsylvania), spring 1983: 40–47.

Gorringe, Henry H. *Egyptian Obelisks*. New York: Published by the author, 1882.

Görsdorf, Jochen, Günter Dreyer, and Ulrich Hartung. "C Dating of the Archaic Royal Necropolis Umm el-Qaab at Abydos." *MDAIK* 54 (1998):169–75.

Grant, Bruce. *Concise Encyclopedia of the American Indian*. Originally published in 1958 as *American Indians Yesterday and Today*. New York: Wings Books, 1989.

Gray, John. *Near Eastern Mythology*. 2nd ed. New York: Peter Bedrick, 1982.

Habachi, Labib. *The Obelisks of Egypt: Skyscrapers of the Past*. Ed. Charles C. Van Siclen III. New York: Charles Scribner's Sons, 1977.

Haddingham, Evan. *Early Man and the Cosmos*. Norman: University of Oklahoma Press, 1984.

Hale, George Ellery. "The Oriental Ancestry of the Telescope." *Scribners Magazine* (April 1925): 392–404.

Hassan, Selim. *Excavations at Giza*, vol. 6, pt. 2: "The Offering-List in the Old Kingdom." Cairo: Government Press, 1948.

———. *The Great Pyramid of Khufu and Its Mortuary Chapel*. Excavations at Giza, season 1938–39, vol. 10. Cairo: Government Press, 1960.

Hawass, Zahi, and Mark Lehner. "The Sphinx: Who Built It, and Why?" *Archeology* 47, no. 5: 30–47.

Hawass, Zahi, and Miroslav Verner. "Newly Discovered Blocks from the Causeway of Sahure." *MDAIK* 52 (1996):177–87.

Hawkes, Jacquetta. *Atlas of Ancient Archaeology*. New York: McGraw-Hill, 1975.

Hayes, William C. *The Scepter of Egypt*, pt. 1. Rev. New York: MMA, 1990.

Heilbron, J. L. *The Sun in the Church: Cathedrals as Solar Observatories*. Cambridge, Mass.: Harvard University Press, 1999.

Hodges, Peter. *How the Pyramids Were Built*. Ed. Julian Keable. Shaftesbury, U.K.: Element Books. 1989.

Hoffman, Michael A. *Egypt Before the Pharaohs*. New York: Dorset Press, 1990.

———. *The First Egyptians*. Exhibition catalogue, McKissick Museum. Columbia: University of South Carolina, 1988.

Hogben, Lancelot. *Mathematics for the Million*. Rev. ed. New York: W. W. Norton, 1946.

I.C.S. Reference Library 159. Scranton, Pa.: International Textbook, 1909.

Ikram, Salima. "Nilecurrents." *KMT* 6, no. 1 (spring 1995): 7–9.

Isler, Martin. "Ancient Egyptian Methods of Raising Weights." *JARCE* 13 (1976): frontispiece, 31–41, pls. 2–3.

———. "An Ancient Method of Finding and Extending Direction." *JARCE* 26 (1989):191–206.

———. "Concerning the Concave Faces on the Great Pyramid." *JARCE* 20 (1983):27–29.

———. "The Curious Luxor Obeleisks." *JEA* 73 (1987):137–47.

———. "The Gnomon in Egyptian Antiquity." *JARCE* 28 (1991):155–85.

———. "The Merkhet." *Varia Aegyptiaca* 7 (1991):53–67.

———. "On Pyramid Building." *JARCE* 22 (1985):129–42.

———. "On Pyramid Building 2." *JARCE* 24 (1987):95–112.

———. "The Technique of Monolithic Carving." *MDAIK* 48 (1992):45–55.

Jenkins, Nancy. *The Boat beneath the Pyramid: King Cheops' Royal Ship*. New York: Holt Rinehart and Winston, 1980.

Jones, Gwyn. *A History of the Vikings*. Oxford: Oxford University Press, 1968.

Kelly, Allyn L. *The Pottery of Ancient Egypt: Dynasty 1 to Roman Times*. Toronto: Royal Ontario Museum, 1976.

Kemp, Barry J. *Ancient Egypt: Anatomy of a Civilization*. London: Routledge, 1988.

Kostof, Spiro. *A History of Architecture, Settings and Rituals*. Oxford: Oxford University Press, 1985.

Kramer, Samuel Noah. *The Sumerians: Their History, Culture, and Character*. Chicago: University of Chicago Press, 1963.

Krupp, E. C. "The Cosmic Temples of Old Beijing." In Aveni, *WA* 65–75.

———. *Echoes of the Ancient Skies: The Astronomy of Lost Civilizations*. New York: Harper and Row, 1983.

———. "Great Pyramid Astronomy." *Griffith Observer* (Los Angeles) 42, no. 3 (1978): 2–22.

———. "Light in the Temples." In *Records in Stone*, ed. C. L. N. Ruggles. Cambridge: Cambridge University Press, 1988. 473–99.

———. "Shadows Cast for the Son of Heaven." *Griffith Observer* (August 1982): 8–18.

Krynine, Dimitri P., and William R. Judd. *Principles of Engineering Geology and Geotechnics*. New York: McGraw-Hill, 1957.

Kuentz, Charles. *La Face Sud du Massif Est du Pylon de Ramses 2 Louxor*. Cairo: IFAO, 1971.

Lacau, P. "L'Erection du Mat devant Amon-Min." *CdE* 28 (1953):13–22.

Lacau, P., and Henri Chevrier. *Une Chapelle de Sesostris* 1, vol. 1. Cairo: IFAO, 1956.

Lange, K., and M. Hirmer. *Egypt: Architecture, Sculpture, Painting in Three Thousand Years*. 3rd ed. London: Phaidon, 1961.

Lapedes, Daniel L., Sybil P. Parker, and Jonathan Weil (eds.). *McGraw-Hill Encyclopedia of Science and Technology*. Vol. II. New York: McGraw-Hill, 1977.

Lauer, Jean-Philippe. *Les Pyramides à Degrés*. 3 vols. Cairo: IFAO, 1936–39.

———. *Les Pyramides de Sakkarah*. Cairo: IFAO, 1977.

Leach, E. R. "Primitive Time-Reckoning." In Singer et al., *HT* 1:110–27.

LeBas, M. A. *L'Obelisque de Luxor*. Paris: Libraires des Corps Royaux des Ponts des Mines, 1839.

Lehner, Mark. *The Complete Pyramids*. London: Thames and Hudson, 1997.

———. "Some Observations on the Layout of Khufu and Khafre Pyramids." *JARCE* 20 (1983):7–25.

Lesko, Leonard H. "Seila 1981." *JARCE* 35 (1988):215–35.

Lloyd, S. *The Archaeology of Mesopotamia*. London: Thames and Hudson, 1978.

———. "Building in Brick and Stone." In Singer, et al., *HT* 1:456–94.

Lloyd, S., and H. W. Müller. *Ancient Architecture*. New York: Rizzoli, 1986.

Lucas, A. *Ancient Egyptian Materials and Industries*. 4th ed., rev. and enlarged by J. R. Harris. London: Edward Arnold, 1962.

Lurker, Manfred. *The Gods and Symbols of Ancient Egypt*. New York: Thames and Hudson, 1988.

Lyons, Henry. "Ancient Surveying Instruments." *Geographical Journal* 69, no. 2 (February 1927): 132–44.

Magdolen, Dušan. The Solar Origin of the "Sacred Triangle" in Ancient Egypt? Ph. D. diss., Czech Institute of Egyptology, 1997. Unpublished

Malville, J. McKim. "The Rise and Fall of the Sun Temple of Konarak: The Temple versus the Solar Orb." In Aveni, *WA* 377–88.

Malville, J. McKim, Fred Wendord, Ali A. Mazar, and Romauld Schild. "Megaliths and Neolithic Astronomy in Southern Egypt." *Nature* 392 (April 1998): 488–90.

Mannoni, Luciana, and Tiziano Mannoni. *Marble: The History of a Culture*. New York: Facts on File, n.d.

Maragioglio, V., and C. Rinaldi. *L'Architecttura della Piramidi Menfete*. 8 vols. Turin and Rapallo: Tipografia Canessa, 1963–77. (English translation throughout.)

Marshack, Alexander. *The Roots of Civilization*. New York: McGraw-Hill, 1972.

McFarlane, Ann. *The God Min to the End of the Old Kingdom*. Sydney: Australian Center for Egyptology, 1995.

McGovern, Patrick E. "Wine for Eternity." *Archaeology* (July–August 1998): 28–34

Mellaart, James. *Earliest Civilizations of the Near East*. New York: McGraw-Hill, 1974.

Mendelssohn, Kurt. *The Riddle of the Pyramids*. New York: Praeger, 1974.

Michalowski, Kazimierz. *Art of Ancient Egypt*. New York: Abrams, 1968.

Mohen, Jean-Pierre. *The World of Megaliths*. New York: Facts on File, 1989.

Moores, Robert G., Jr. "Evidence for Use of a Stone-cutting Drag Saw by the Fourth Dynasty Egyptians." *JARCE* 28 (1991):139–48.

Moorey, P. R. S. *Ancient Mesopotamian Materials and Industries*. Oxford: Clarendon Press, 1994.

Munro, Irmtraut. "Das Zelt-Heiligtum des Min." *Münchner Ägyptologische Studien* (Berlin) 1983: 1–59, pls. 1–8.

Naville, Edouard, and Ludwig Borchardt. *Denkmäler aus Aegypten und Aethiopien*. Vol. 1: *Unteraegypten und Memphis*. Ed. Kurt Sethe. Leipzig: J. C. Hinrichs'sche, 1897.

Needham, Joseph, with research assistance of Wang Ling. *Science and Civilization in China*. 6 vols. Cambridge: Cambridge University Press, 1956–86.

Neugebauer, O. "On the Orientation of Pyramids." *Centaurus* (Copenhagen) 24 (1980):1–3.

Newberry, Percy E. *El-Bersheh*, pt. 1. London: Special Publication of the Egypt Exploration Fund, 1895.

Nissen, Hans J. *The Early History of the Ancient Near East: 9000–2000 B.C.* Chicago: University of Chicago Press, 1988.

Nissen, Hans J., Peter Damerow, and Robert K. Englund. *Archaic Bookkeeping: Writing and Techniques of Economic Administration in the Ancient Near East*. Chicago: University of Chicago Press, 1993.

Nova. "Secrets of Lost Empires: Obelisk." Boston: WGBH Television, 1997.

———. "This Old Pyramid." Boston: WGBH Television, 1992.

Oates, Joan. "The Emergence of Cities in the Near East." In *Cambridge Encyclopedia*, 112–19.

O'Brian, Robert. *Machines*. Life Science Library. New York: Time Inc., 1964.

O'Connor, David. "New Funerary Enclosures (*Talbezirke*) of the Early Dynastic Period." *JARCE* 26 (1989):51–86.

Orlove, Benjamin S., John C. H. Chiang, and Mark A. Cane. "Forecasting Andean Rainfall and Crop Yield from the Influence of El Niño on Pleiades Visibility." *Nature* 403 (6 January 2000): 68–71.

Parker, R. A. "Ancient Egyptian Astronomy." In *The Place of Astronomy in the Ancient World*, ed. F. R. Hodson. Joint symposium of the Royal Society and the British Academy. London: Oxford University Press, 1974.

———. "Egyptian Astronomy, Astrology, and Calendrical Reckoning." *Dictionary of Scientific Biography*, supplement 1. New York: Scribner, 1978. 706–27.

Peet, T. Eric. *The Cemeteries of Abydos*. Pt. 2: 1911–1912. London: Thirty-Fourth Memoir EEF, 1914.

Perrot, Georges, and Charles Chipiez. *History of Ancient Egyptian Art*. 2 vols. Trans. and ed. Walter Armstrong. London: Chapman and Hall, 1883.

Petrie, W. M. Flinders. *The Arts and Crafts of Ancient Egypt*. The World of Art Series. Chicago: A. C. McClurg, 1910.

———. "The Building of a Pyramid." *Ancient Egypt* pt. 2 (June 1930): 33–39.

———. *Ceremonial Slate Palettes*. London: BSAE, 1953.

———. *Egyptian Architecture*. London: BSAE, University College, 1938.

———. *Naqada and Ballas*. 1896. Reprint, Warminster, U.K.: Arris and Phillips, 1974.

———. *The Pyramids and Temples of Gizeh*. London: Field and Teur, 1883.

———. *Tools and Weapons*. BSAE, Egyptian Research Account Twenty-Second Year, 1916. London: BSAE, University College, 1917.

Petrie, W. M. Flinders, with chapter by D. G. Hogarth. *Koptos*. London: Bernard Quaritch, 1896.

Petrie, W. M. Flinders, with chapter by F. Ll. Griffith. *The Royal Tombs of the First Dynasty 1900*. Pt. 1. London: Eighteenth Memoir of the Egyptian Exploration Fund, 1900.

———. *The Royal Tombs of the Earliest Dynasties 1901*. Pt. 2. London: Twenty-First Memoir of the Egyptian Exploration Fund, 1901.

Petrie, W. M. Flinders, with chapters by F. Ll. Griffith, Dr. Gladstone, and Oldfield Thomas. *Dendereh 1898*. London: Seventeenth Memoir of the Egyptian Exploration Fund, 1900.

Petrie, W. M. Flinders, Ernest Mackay, and Gerald Wainwright. *Meydum and Memphis 3*. BSAE, Egyptian Research Account Sixteenth Year, 1910. London: BSAE, University College, 1910.

Petrie, W. M. Flinders, G. A. Wainwright, and A. H. Gardiner, *Tarkhan 1 and Memphis 5*. BSAE, Egyptian Research Account Sixteenth Year, 1912. London: BSAE, University College, 1913.

Phillips-Birt, Douglas. *A History of Seamanship*. New York: Doubleday, 1971.

Pliny. *Pliny: Natural History*. Trans. D. E. Eichholz. 10 vols. Vol. 2, books 36–37. Loeb Classical Library. Cambridge, Mass.: Harvard University Press, 1962.

Plunket, Patricia, and Gabriela Uruñuela. "Appeasing the Volcano Gods." *Archaeology* (July/August 1998): 36–42.

Quibell, J. E. *Hierakonpolis*. Pt. 1. 1902. Reprint, Egyptian Research Account, Fourth Memoir. London: Histories and Mysteries of Man, 1989.

Quibell, J. E., and F. W. Greene. *Hierakonpolis*. Pt. 2. 1902. Reprint, Egyptian Research Account, Fifth Memoir. London: Histories and Mysteries of Man, 1989.

Rackham, H. (trans.). *Pliny: Natural History*, bk. 2. Loeb Classical Library 2. Cambridge, Mass.: Harvard University Press, 1938.

Ramsey, Charles G., and George Harold R. Sleeper. *Architectural Graphic Standards*. 6th ed. Ed. Joseph N. Boaz. New York: John Wiley and Sons, 1970.

Reinhard, Johan. "Sacred Peaks of the Andes." *National Geographic* 181, no. 3 (March 1992): 84–111.

Reisner, George A. *The Development of the Egyptian Tomb down to the Accession of Cheops*. 1936. Reprint, Storrs-Mansfield, Conn.: Maurizio Martino and John William Pye, 1996.

———. *A History of the Giza Necropolis*, vol. 1. 1942. Reprint, Storrs-Mansfield, Conn.: Maurizio Martino and John William Pye, 1996.

———. *Models of Ships and Boats*. Catalogue Général des Antiquités Égyptiennes du Musée du Caire, nos. 4798–4976 and 5034–5200). Cairo: IFAO, 1913.

———. *Mycerinus: The Temples of the Third Pyramid at Giza*. Cambridge, Mass.: Harvard University Press, 1931.

Renshaw, Steve, and Saori Ihara. "The Brush Daub." *Achaeoastronomy & Ethnoastronamy News* 19 (March 1996): 1–4.

Rey, H. A. *The Stars: A New Way to See Them*. Boston: Houghton Mifflin, 1967.

Rice, Michael. *Egypt's Making: The Origins of Ancient Egypt 5000–2000 B.C.* London: Routledge, 1991.

Riley, Carroll L. *The Origins of Civilization*. Carbondale: Southern Illinois University Press, 1969.

Roaf, Michael. *Cultural Atlas of Mesopotamia and the Ancient Near East*. New York: Facts on File, 1990.

Robert, M. A. "Quelques Graffites Grecs." *ASAE* (Cairo), 1902: 77–79.

Röder, Josef. "Zur Steinbruchgeschichte des Rosengranits von Assuan." *Archäologischer Anzeiger* (Jahrbuch des Deutschen Archäologischen Instituts, Berlin) 1965–66: 467–552.

Rohr, René R. J. *Sundials: History, Theory and Practice*. Dover edition of English translation (Toronto: University of Toronto Press, 1970), of original French work *Les Cadrans solaires* (Montrough, France: Gauthier-Villars, 1965). Mineola, N.Y.: Dover Publications, 1996.

Rossi, Corinna. "Notes on the Pyramidion Found at Dahshur." *JEA* 1999: 219–22.

Rossnagel, W. E. *Handbook of Rigging*. New York: McGraw-Hill, 1964.

Rowe, Alan. *Excavations of the Eckley B. Coxe, Jr., Expedition at Meydûm, Egypt, 1929–30*. Philadelphia: University of Philadelphia, University Museum Press, 1931.

Ruggles, C. L. N. "Recent Developments in Megalithic Astronomy." In Aveni, *WA*, 13–26.

———— (ed). *Records in Stone: Papers in Memory of Alexander Thom*. Cambridge: Cambridge University Press, 1988.

Ryan, Donald P. "Old Rope." *KMT* 4, no. 2 (summer 1993): 72–80.

Saggs, H. W. F. *Civilization before Greece and Egypt*. New Haven: Yale University Press, 1989.

Saleh, Mohamed, and Hourig Sourouzian. *Official Catalogue: The Egyptian Museum Cairo*. Mainz: Philipp von Zabern, 1987.

Schele, Linda, and David Freidal. *A Forest of Kings*. New York: William Murrow, 1990.

Schenkel, Wolfgang. "Schrift." *LÄ* 5 (1984):723.

Schmandt-Besserat, Denise. "The Earliest Precursor of Writing." *Scientific American* (June 1978): 50–59.

Seton-Williams, Veronica, and Peter Stocks. *Blue Guide: Egypt*. New York: W. W. Norton, 1983.

Severn, Bill. *The Book of Rope and Knots*. New York: David McKay, 1960.

Shadmon, Asher. *Stone: An Introduction*. London: Intermediate Technology, 1989.

Shaw, Ian. "Kafra's Quarries in the Sahara." *Egyptian Archaeology* (Egyptian Exploration Society, London) no. 16 (spring 2000): 28–30.

Shaw, Ian, and Paul Nicholson, in association with the British Museum. *The Dictionary of Ancient Egypt*. New York: Harry N. Abrams, 1995.

Sherratt, Andrew. "The Beginnings of Agriculture in the Near East and Europe." In *Cambridge Encyclopedia*, 102–11.

Simonds, George. "The Erection of Colossal Statues." *American Architect and Building News* 19, no. 542 (1886):235–38.

Simpson, William Kelly. *The Mastabas of Qar and Idu: G7101 and 7102*. Vol. 2. Boston: Museum of Fine Arts, 1976.

Singer, Charles. "Cartography, Survey and Navigation to 1400." In Singer et al., *HT* 3 (1957):501–12.

Singer, Charles, E. J. Holmyard, and A. R. Hall (eds.). *A History of Technology*. 5 vols. New York: Oxford University Press, 1954–58.

Singh, Prahlad. *Stone Observatories in India Erected by Maharaja Sawai Jai Sing of Jaipur 1685–1743 at Delhi, Jaipur, Ujjain, Varanasi, Mathura*. Research Series 11. Bharata Manisha: J. D. Bhattacharya, 1978.

Smith, E. Baldwin. *Egyptian Architecture*. New York: Appleton-Century, 1938.

Smith, H. S. "The Making of Egypt: A Review of the Influence of Susa and Sumer on Upper Egypt and Lower Nubia in the 4th millennium B.C." In *The Followers of Horus: Studies Dedicated to*

Michael Allen Hoffman, ed. Renée Friedman and Barbara Adams. Egyptian Studies Association Publication no. 2. Oxbow Monograph 20. Oxford: Oxbow Books, 1992. 235–46.

Smith, W. Stevenson. *The Art and Architecture of Ancient Egypt*. Rev. with additions by William Kelly Simpson. Harmondsworth, U.K.: Penguin, 1981.

Snodgrass, Adrian. *The Symbolism of the Stupa*. Ithaca, N.Y.: Cornell University Press, 1991.

Spencer, A. J. *Early Egypt: The Rise of Civilization in the Nile Valley*. London: British Museum Press, 1993.

Stadelmann, Rainer. *Die Ägyptischen Pyramiden: Vom Ziegelbau zum Weltwunder*. Darmstadt: Wissenschaftliche Buchgesellschaft, 1985.

Stocks, Denys. "Sticks and Stones of Egyptian Technology." *Popular Archaeology* 7, no. 3 (1986): 24–28.

Strabo. *The Geography of Strabo*. Trans. H. L. Jones. 8 vols. Loeb Classical Library. Cambridge, Mass.: Harvard University Press, 1932.

Strommenger, Eva. *5000 Years of the Art of Mesopotamia*. Photographs by Max Hirmer. Trans. Christina Haglund. New York: Abrams, 1964.

Swarup, G., A. K. Bag, and K. S. Shulka (eds.). *History of Oriental Astronomy*. Proceedings of International Astronomical Union Colloquium 91. Cambridge: Cambridge University Press, 1987.

Swelim, Nabil M. A. "Additional Views Concerning the Monument Called Sinki." *MDAIK* 38 (1982): 94–95.

———. *Some Problems on the History of the Third Dynasty*. Alexandria: Archaeological Society, 1983.

Temple, Robert. *The Crystal Sun*. London: Century, 2000.

Trigger, B. G., B. J. Kemp, D. O'Conner, and A. B. Lloyd. *Ancient Egypt: A Social History*. Cambridge: Cambridge University Press, 1990.

Van Tilburg, Jo Anne. *Easter Island*. Washington, D.C.: Smithsonian Institution Press, 1994.

Verner, Miroslav. *Forgotten Pharaohs, Lost Pyramids*. Trans. Anna Byson and Jana Klepetárová. Prague: Academia, Publishing House of the Academy of Science of the Czech Republic, 1994.

Vitruvius. *Vitruvius on Architecture*. Trans. F. Granger. 9 vols. Loeb Classical Library. Cambridge, Mass.: Harvard University Press, 1962.

von der Way, Thomas. "Identification of Architecture with Niches at Buto." In *Followers of Horus: Studies Dedicated to Michael Allen Hoffman*, ed. Renée Friedman and Barbara Adams. Egyptian Studies Association Publication no. 2. Oxbow Monograph 20. Oxford: Oxbow Books, 1992. 217–26.

Vyse, Howard. *Operations Carried on at the Pyramids of Gizeh: With an Account of a Voyage into Upper Egypt and an Appendix*. Vol. 1. London: James Frazer, 1840.

Wainwright, G. A. "The Emblem of Min." *JEA* 17 (1931): 185–95.

———. *The Sky Religions in Egypt*. Cambridge: Cambridge University Press, 1938.

———. "Some Celestial Associations of Min." *JEA* 21 (1935):151–70.

Ward, William A. "Relations between Egypt and Mesopotamia from Prehistoric Times to the End of the New Kingdom," pt. 1. *JESHO* (Leiden) 7 (1964):1–45.

Watson, Philip. *Egyptian Pyramids and Mastaba Tombs*. Shire Egyptology. Bucks, U.K.: Shire Publications, 1987.

Waugh, Albert E. *Sundials: Their Theory and Construction*. New York: Dover Publications. 1973.

Weeks, Kent R. *The Lost Tomb*. New York: William Morrow, 1998.

Wenke, Robert J. *Patterns in Prehistory*. 2nd ed. Oxford: Oxford University Press, 1984.

Westwood, Jennifer (ed.). *Atlas of Mysterious Places*. New York: Weidenfeld, 1987.

Wheeler, J. Talboys (trans.). *The Geography of Herodotus*. London: Longman, Brown, Green, and Longmans, 1854.

Wilbur, C. Keith. *Tall Ships of the World: An Illustrated Encyclopedia*. Chester, Conn.: Globe Pequote Press, 1986.

Wilford, John Noble. "Early Pharaoh's Ghostly Fleet." Science Times, *New York Times*, 31 October 2000, F1, F4.

———. "Finds in Egypt Date Alphabet in Earlier Era." *New York Times*, 14 November 1999.

Wilkinson, Richard H. *Reading Egyptian Art*. London: Thames and Hudson, 1992.

Wilkinson, Toby A. H. *Early Dynastic Egypt*. London: Routledge, 1999.

Winkler, E. M. *Stone: Properties, Durability in Man's Environment*. 2nd rev. ed. New York: Springer-Verlag, 1975.

Younger, Joseph D. "Dayton: Crossroads of Indian Culture." *USAir* (November 1992):75–76.

Yuan Shih, *History of China (1260–1368 CE) Yuan Dynasty*.15 vols. Recorded by Lien Sung. Romanized version (Pei-ching: Chung-Hua Shu Chu, 1976).

Žába, Zbyněk. *L' Orientation astronomique dans l'ancienne Égypte, et la précession de l'axe du monde*. Supplement 2. Prague: Academie Tchècoslovaque des Sciences, 1953.

Zaphiropoulou, Photini. *Delos: Monuments and Museum*. Athens: Krene, 1983.

Zeilik, Michael. "Keeping the Sacred and Planting Calendar: Archaeoastronomy in the Pueblo Southwest." In Aveni, *WA*, 43–166.

Zezong, Xi. "The Characteristics of Ancient China's Astronomy." In Swarup et al., *HOA*, 33–40.

ILLUSTRATION SOURCES

All drawings and photographs are by the author unless otherwise noted.

Chapter 1

1.1 After Ammarell, *HOA*, 244, fig. 3. **1.2** Ibid., 245, fig. 4. **1.4** After Rey, *The Stars*, 121, fig. 21 (John Suh). **1.6** After Davidson, *Astronomy and the Imagination*, 53, fig. 5.3 (William Torres). **1.7** John Suh. **1.8** After Krupp, *Echoes of the Ancient Skies*, 250. **1.9** After Krupp, "Light in the Temples," 476, fig. 21.2. **1.11** Gardiner, *Egyptian Grammar*, 489 n. 27. **1.12** After photo, Kramer, *Sumerians*, following 160 (BM). **1.13** (b) After Krupp, "Light in the Temples," 484, fig. 21.7. **1.14** (a, b) After Mohen, *World of Megaliths*, 107, 269. **1.15** After Firneis and Köberl, *WA*, 434, fig. 33.4. **1.16** After photo, Krupp, *Echoes of the Ancient Skies*, 59. **1.17** (a, b) After Habachi, *Obelisks*, 10, figs. 3, 4. (c) Photo, Edward R. Isler. **1.18** After Snodgrass, *Symbolism of the Stupa*, 162. **1.20** After Schmandt-Besserat, "Earliest Precursor of Writing," 56-57. **1.21** After Roaf, *Cultural Atlas of Mesopotamia*, 72. **1.22** (a) After Roaf, *Cultural Atlas of Mesopotamia*, 72–73. (b) After Nissen et al., *Archaic Bookkeeping*, 18, fig. 19 (Oppenländer collection). (c) After Roaf, *Cultural Atlas of Mesopotamia*, 70. **1.23** (a, b) After Kostof, *History of Architecture*, 58, fig. 3.15. **1.24** Lloyd, *Archaeology of Mesopotamia*, 42, fig. 10. **1.25** After Oates, *Encyclopedia*, 114, 16.3 (State Antiquities and Heritage Organization, Baghdad). **1.26** After Lloyd, *Archaeology of Mesopotamia*, 39, fig. 8. **1.27** After Lloyd and Müller, *Ancient Architecture*, 12, fig. 12 (Sinclair). **1.28** After Crawford, *Sumer and the Sumerians*, 59, fig 4.8 (drawing, Edward R. Isler). **1.29** After Lloyd, *HT* 1, 462, fig. 290. **1.30** Photo, Burney, *Ancient Near East*, 60, fig 40. **1.32** After Lloyd, *Archaeology of Mesopotamia*, 152, fig. 104 (Wooley). **1.33** After Strommenger, *Art of Mesopotamia*, 431, fig. 43 (Ghirshmann). **1.34** After Frankfort, *Birth of Civilization*, fig. 19 (Delougaz). **1.35** After Algaze, *Uruk World System*, 15, 39, figs. 3, 17.

Chapter 2

2.2 (a) After scene, Baines and Málek, *Atlas*, 190, from Theban tomb I, Sennedjem. (b, c) Frankfort, *Birth of Civilization* following 64, fig. 1, D, E. **2.3** (a) After photo, Spencer, *Early Egypt*, 23, fig. 9, BM

58648. (b) After *CPECAM*, 3 (8). (c) After photo, Spencer, *Early Egypt*, 31, 15 BM 32142. (d) After *CPECAM*, 9 (37). (e) After *CPECAM*, 4 (14). (f) After *CPECAM*, 4 (16). (g) After *CPECAM*, 81 (1965). (h) After *CPECAM*, 81 (1959). (i) After *CPECAM*, 77 (1900). (j) After *CPECAM*, 77 (1904). (k) After photo, Petrie, *Ceremonial Slate Palettes*, pl. A, 1. (l) After *CPECAM*, 75 (1839). (m) After *CPECAM*, 77 (1888). (n) After *CPECAM*, 77 (1892). (o) After Adams, *Predynastic Egypt*, 62, 43 (University College London 5479). (p) After *CPECAM*, 26 (243). (q) After *CPECAM*, 29 (409). (r) After *CPECAM*, 41 (864). (s) After Petrie, *Naqada and Ballas*, pl. 31 (19). (t) After photograph, Hayes, *Scepter of Egypt* 1:23, fig. 14 (MMA). (u) After *CPECAM*, 60 (1237). (v) After *CPECAM*, 61 (1253). **2.4** (a) After Quibell, *Hierakonpolis*, 1: pl. 26 (B). (b) After Gardiner, *Egyptian Grammar*, 495, O 22. (c) After Petrie, *Royal Tombs*, 1: pl. 27 (68). (d) After Gardiner, *Egyptian Grammar*, 1988, 494, O 18; 495, O 20. (e) After Petrie, *Royal Tombs*, 1: pl. 29 (86). (f) After Petrie, *Royal Tombs*, 2: pl. 10 (2). (g) After Petrie, *Royal Tombs*, 2: pl. 7 (8). (h) After Petrie, *Royal Tombs*, 2: pl. 4 (11). (i) After Petrie, *Royal Tombs*, 2: pl. 3 (4). (j) After Hoffman, *Egypt Before the Pharaohs*, 202, fig. 54. (k) After Munro, "Zelt-Heiligtum des Min," fig. 20. (l) After Hoffman, *Egypt Before the Pharaohs*, 146, fig. 41. (m) After model, BM no. 32612. (n) After photograph, Spencer, *Early Egypt*, 34, fig. 18. (o) After Petrie, *Royal Tombs*, 2: pl. 5 (4). (p) After Smith, *Egyptian Architeture*, p. 2 (7). (q) After Petrie, *Royal Tombs*, 2: pl. 16 (116). **2.5** After Quibell and Greene, *Hierakonpolis*, 2: pl. 75. **2.6** Ibid., pl. 76. **2.7** After Smith, *Followers of Horus*, 236, (a) fig. 1: *AGMA*, pl. 6.117. (b) fig. 3: *AGMA*, pl. 6.119A. (c) fig. 10: *AGMA*, pl. 7.151. (d) fig. 11: *AGMA*, pl. 14.239. **2.8** (a, b) After photograph, Rice, *Egypt's Making*, fig. 56 (Louvre). **2.9** (a, b) After Breasted, *History of Egypt*, fig. 9 (de Morgan). (c) *AGMA*, pl. 14, item E. (d) *AGMA* pl. 4.85. (e) *AGMA*, pl. 4.97. (f) *AGMA* pl. 15.258. (g) *AGMA*, 25.413. (h) Algaze, *Uruk World System*, 40, fig. 18H. **2.10** After Shaw and Nicholson, *Dictionary* 254 (AM). **2.11** (a, b) After Quibell and Greene, *Hierakonpolis*, 2: pl. 72. **2.12** After photograph, Aldred, *Egypt to the End of the Old Kingdom*, 44–45 (EM). **2.13** After Wilkinson, *Reading Egyptian Art*, 18, fig. 3 (footstool of Tutankhamun). **2.14** After photo, Aldred, *Egypt to the End of the Old Kingdom*, 64, fig. 55 (BM). **2.15** After Emery, *Great Tombs*, 2:102, fig. 105, pl. 35. **2.16** After Kemp, *Ancient Egypt*, 81, fig. 28 (photos courtesy Ashmolean Museum); pictographs, Petrie, *Koptos*, fig. 3(2). **2.17** Based on Emery, *Archaic Egypt*, 106, fig. 68. **2.18** (a, b) Ibid., 96, fig. 59. (c) Ibid., 101, fig. 65. **2.19** Ibid., 96, 101, figs. 59, 65. **2.20** After Kemp, *Ancient Egypt*, 28, fig. 6, from Lange and Hirmer, *Egypt: Architecture, Sculpture, Painting*, 86. **2.21** (a) After Wilkinson, *Reading Egyptian Art*, 48, fig 3. (b) After Smith, *Followers of Horus*, 239; *AGMA*: pl. 46.658.

Chapter 3

3.1 (a) After Petrie, *Royal Tombs*, 2: fig. 58. (b) Plan after Emery, *Archaic Egypt*, fig. 31. **3.2** After Petrie, *Royal Tombs*, 1: pl. 67. **3.3** Ibid., pl. 55. **3.4** (a) After Emery, *Great Tombs*, 3: pl. 1. (b) After Emery, *Archaic Egypt*, fig. 30 (J. Suh). (c) After Aldred, *Egypt to the End of the Old Kingdom*, 66, fig. 56. **3.5** (a) After Emery, *Archaic Egypt*, fig. 51. (b) Ibid., fig. 38 (J. Suh). **3.6** After Petrie, *Meydum and Memphis 3*, fig. 18, (item 76). **3.7** (a) After Perrot and Chipiez, *History of Ancient Egyptian Art*, 2:57, fig 34; (b) After photograph, Petrie, *Tarkhan and Memphis 5*, pl. 28. **3.9** After Emery, *Great Tombs*, 2: pl. 4. **3.10** After Lloyd, *Archaeology of Mesopotamia*, 51, fig 20 (Lenzen). **3.11** After Emery, *Great Tombs*, 2: fig. 201. **3.12** After Emery, *Archaic Egypt*, 48, fig. 7 (J. Suh). **3.13** (a) After Emery, *Archaic Egypt*, 48, fig. 7. (b) Ibid., 55, fig. 16. (c) Ibid., 67, fig. 30. (d) Ibid., 78, fig. 39. **3.14** (a) After photo, Emery, *Archaic Egypt*, pl. 8. (b) After Mellaart, *Earliest Civilizations*, 97, fig. 80. **3.15** (a) After Emery, *Great Tombs*, 3: pl. 86. (b) Ibid., pl. 85. **3.16** After photo, Smith, *Art and Architecture*, fig. 22. **3.17** (a, b) After Emery, *Great Tombs*, 1: fig. 48. (c, d) Ibid., fig. 51. (e, f) Ibid., fig. 51. **3.19** After Emery, *Great Tombs*, 3: pl. 7. **3.20** (a) After Petrie, *Egyptian Architecture*, pl. 7 (28A). (b) Ibid., pl. 7 (27). **3.21** After Petrie, *Tarkhan 1 and Memphis 5*, fig. 17 (J. Suh). **3.22** After Reisner, *Development* *of the Egyptian Tomb*, (a) fig. 133, (b) fig. 140, (c) fig. 129, (d) fig. 131, (e) fig. 132, (f) fig. 144. **3.23** After Petrie, *Dendereh*, pl. 28. **3.24** After Naville and Borchardt, *Denkmäler*, 1:6. **3.25** After Smith, *Art and Architecture*, 80, fig. 72. **3.26** After Simpson, *Mastabas of Qar and Idu*, pl. 29b. **3.27** After von der Way, *Followers of Horus*, 218, fig. 2 (items 12, 13).

Chapter 4

4.1 (a) After Lauer, *Pyramides de Sakkarah*, fig. 12. **4.2** (a) Ibid., fig. 20. **4.3** After Edwards, *Pyramids*, 35, fig. 5, from Lauer, *Les Pyramides à Degrés*, 2: pl. 4. **4.4** (a) After Edwards, *Pyramids*, 38, fig. 6, from Lauer, *Les Pyramides à Degrés*, 3: pl. 2. (b) After Arnold, *Building*, fig. 4.88 (1). **4.7** After Edwards, *Pyramids*, 62, fig. 13. **4.8** After Reisner, *Development*, 135, fig. 57. **4.9** After Emery, *Archaic Egypt*, 146, fig. 85 (J. Suh). **4.16** (a, b) After Dreyer and Swelim, *MDAIK*, 1982, figs. 2, 3. **4.20** After Kemp, *Ancient Egypt*, 87, fig. 30. **4.21** After photo, Frankfort, *Kingship and the Gods*, following 212, fig. 33.

Chapter 5

5.3 (a) After *Piramidi*, 3: pl. 2, fig. 2. **5.5.** (b) Ibid., pl. 3, fig. 5. **5.14** After Rowe, *Expedition at Meydûm*, pl. 9. **5.15** After Fakry, *Monuments of Seneferu 1*, frontispiece (Ricke). **5.16** After *Piramidi*, 3: pl. 8, fig. 8. **5.17** After Rowe, *Excavations*, pl. 11. **5.18** After Stadelmann, *KMT* 8, no. 3, 26. **5.19** From Žába, *L' Orientation*, pl. 1 (Brugsch). **5.22** After *Piramidi*, 4: pl. 10, fig. 9. **5.23** After Lehner, *Complete Pyramids*, 129. **5.24** (b) MMA (27.3.12).

Chapter 6

6.1 After photo from MMA in Arnold, *Building*, fig. 6.2. **6.2** From Cotsworth, *Rational Almanac*, "Natural Solution" 15–16. **6.5** (a–c) After Fischer, "Notes on Sticks and Staves," 7, 13, 14, figs. 2c, 16, 17. **6.6** Ibid., 15, fig. 21. **6.7** (a, b) EM, Room 44. **6.10** After Frankfort, *The Cenotaph of Seti I*, 76–80 (de Buck). **6.11** After Borchardt, "Die Altagyptische Zeitmessung," figs. 13, 18. **6.12** After photo, Needham, *Science*, 3: sections 19–35, pl. 30, fig. 111. **6.13** Ibid., fig. 110. **6.14** (a, b, c, d) After Munro, "Das Zelt-Heiligtum des Min," figs. 9, 7, 11, 4. **6.15** After Lacau and Chevrier, *Une Chapelle de Sesostris I*, pl. 31, scene 10. **6.18** After Wainwright, "Emblem of Min," 185–87: (a) 185, (b, c) 186, (d–f) 185, (g) 185, (h) 187, (i–k) 186, (l) 187. **6.19** After Kuentz, *La Face Sud du Massif*, pl. 19. **6.20** After Lacau and Chevrier, *Une Chapelle de Sesostris 1*, pl. 31, scene 8. **6.21** After a model, EM, Room 32, lower case E. **6.23** After Hassan, *Excavations at Giza*, 6: fig. 56.

Chapter 7

7.4 After Neugebauer, "Orientation of Pyramids," fig. 1. **7.5** (c) After Ramsey and Sleeper, *Architectural Graphic Standards*, 70 (J. Suh). **7.7** After photo, HOA 146. **7.8** (a) After photo, Needham, *Science*, 3: fig. 115, pl. 31; (b) After photo, Krupp, "Shadows Cast" 16. **7.10** (a) Photo courtesy Ägyptisches Museum, Berlin. **7.11** Temple of Edfu.

Chapter 8

8.4 After *Piramidi*, 4: pl. 11, fig. 1. **8.5** (a) After Edwards, *Pyramids of Egypt*, 57, fig. 12. **8.6** After Needham, *Science*, 3: 570, fig. 245. **8.7** After Needham, *Science*, 4: 331, fig. 910.

Chapter 9

9.1 After Reisner, *History of the Giza Necropolis*, 1: map 1. **9.3** After *Piramidi*, 6: pl. 11, fig. 2. **9.4** After *Piramidi*, 4: pl. 11, fig. 1; *Piramidi*, 6: pl. 12, fig. 1. **9.8** After Mendelssohn, *Riddle of the Pyramids*, 116, fig. 23. **9.13** After Petrie, *Meydum and Memphis* 3, pl. 12. **9.14** (a) After Petrie, *Egyptian Architecture*, figs. 2, 10. (b) After Arnold, *Building*, fig. 1.8. **9.15** After Mendelssohn, *Riddle of the Pyramids*, 117, fig. 24. **9.18** After Arnold, "Überlegungen zum Problem," 16, fig. 1. **9.19** (a) After Dunham, "Building of an Egyptian Pyramid," 159, fig. 1. **9.25** After Arnold, "Überlegungen zum Problem," 22, fig. 3.

Chapter 10

10.7 (a–c) *Nova*, "Secrets." **10.8** After CEAEM, 203, fig. 246. **10.9** (a–d) *Nova*, "Secrets." **10.11** (a, b) Ibid. **10.12** (a) After Blackman, *Fellahin of Upper Egypt*, 307, fig. 178; (b) After Saleh and Sourouzian, *Catalogue*, no. 119. **10.16** (a) After Reisner, *Models of Ships and Boats*, 89, fig. 326; now at EM. (b) MMA accession no. 24.1.84. **10.18** After CEAEM, fig. 83. **10.19** After Chevrier, "Technique de la Construction," fig. 3, pl. 54. **10.20** From Newberry, *El-Bersheh*, pl. 15. **10.21** After Saleh and Sourouzian, *Catalogue*, fig. 142a. **10.22** Cotterell and Kamminga, *Mechanics*, 219, fig. 8.15. **10.23** *Nova*, "Secrets." **10.26** After photo, Arnold, *Building*, fig 6.29 (MMA accession no. 96.4.9). **10.27** After Petrie, *Arts and Crafts*, 75. **10.28** After CEAEM, 102–3.

Chapter 11

11.5 (a–e) *Nova*, "This Old Pyramid." **11.6** After O'Brian, *Machines*, 19. **11.12** (a) After CEAEM, 92, fig. 86; (b) After Arnold, *Building*, 93, fig. 3.45.

Chapter 12

12.1 (b) After Hogben, *Mathematics for the Million*, 155, fig. 49. **12.3** After Magdolen, "Solar Origin," fig. 2b. **12.5** After *Piramidi*, 5: pl. 6, figs. 2, 8. **12.7** After *Piramidi*, 6: pl. 4, fig. 2. **12.8** After Petrie, *Pyramids*, fig. 10. **12.18** Ibid., fig. 8. **12.19** After Arnold, *Building*, 172, fig. 4.102.

Chapter 13

13.2 After photo, Arnold, *Building*, 266, fig. 6.21.

INDEX